COACHWORK ON
ROLLS-ROYCE
Twenty, 20/25, 25/30 and Wraith

Published in 2021
by Herridge & Sons Ltd
Lower Forda, Shebbear
Beaworthy, Devon EX21 5SY

© Copyright James Taylor 2021

Design by Ray Leaning, MUSE Fine Art & Design

ISBN 978-1-906133-92-4
Printed in China

COACHWORK ON
ROLLS-ROYCE
Twenty, 20/25, 25/30 and Wraith
1922-1939

By James Taylor
Photography by Simon Clay

Herridge & Sons

FOREWORD AND ACKNOWLEDGMENTS

When publisher Charles Herridge asked me to write this book as a companion to my 2017 volume, Coachwork on Derby Bentleys, I always knew it would be an ambitious undertaking. Quite how ambitious I had no real idea until I was deeply embroiled in it – and by then it was too late to say No.

It was a project that proved both enormous fun and occasionally frustrating. I need hardly explain the fun part of it, but the frustration came from the fact that so much information about some of these cars is still not known for certain. There are theories, and there are suppositions, and there are some wonderful sets of records that are tantalisingly not quite complete.

In some cases – and this is so particularly of the Twenty models – the coachbuilder for a chassis is simply not known at all. In other cases, the name of the coachbuilder may be known but there is next to no information about the company itself. So although I hope this book pulls together existing information in a way that allows it to be viewed from an unusual perspective, I am well aware that there is much more work to be done before everything that is knowable can be known. (It should keep a few enthusiasts busy for many more years yet.)

I have deliberately focused here on the bodies that were fitted to the various chassis when they were new, and have in general avoided rebodies except where it seemed appropriate to mention them. My method has been to present separate chapters on British and overseas coachbuilders who worked on these Rolls-Royce models, and within each of those chapters to discuss the coachbuilders and their work in alphabetical order. I also thought it would be helpful to include a pair of introductory chapters, one explaining something about the various chassis that the book covers, and the other giving an overview of coachbuilding in the relevant period.

Many researchers have done a great deal of work over very many years on aspects of the subject covered here, and I can thoroughly recommend a number of books that were very useful to me in putting this one together. In alphabetical order of the author's surname, then, to avoid favouritism, they are:

Serge Bellu . . . . *Encylopédie de la Carrosserie Française*
Tom Clarke . . . . *The Rolls-Royce 20/25hp*
Lawrence Dalton . . . . *Those Elegant Rolls-Royce*
Pedr Davis . . . . *Australians on the Road*
John Fasal . . . . *The Rolls-Royce Twenty*
Ferdinand Hediger . . . . *Schweizer Carrossiers*
Bernard L King . . . . *Rolls-Royce 25/30 and Wraith*
Ian Rimmer . . . . *Rolls-Royce & Bentley Experimental Cars*
Claude Rouxel & Laurent Friry . . . . *Gotha de l'Automobile Française*
Halwart Schrader . . . . *Automobil-Specialkarosserien*
Brian Smith . . . . *Vanden Plas Coachbuilders*
Nick Walker . . . . *A-Z British Coachbuilders*

I should also mention that some valuable information and insight came from the remarkable web site, www.coachbuild.com

Lastly, a book like this depends heavily on the photographs it contains, and I am particularly grateful to my photographer friend Simon Clay and to the Real Car Company (www.realcar.co.uk) for providing so many of the pictures here. Other pictures have come from Magic Car Pics, from Klaus-Josef Rossfeldt, from Rolls-Royce Motor Cars and from the Rolls-Royce Enthusiasts' Club, and some have come from the David Hodges Collection and from my own archives.

James Taylor
Oxfordshire,
March 2021

CONTENTS

Chapter One: THE CHASSIS 6

Chapter Two: THE BODIES 19

Chapter Three: COACHWORK BY BRITISH COACHBUILDERS A-Z 31

Chapter Four: THE OVERSEAS COACHBUILDERS 183

Chapter One

THE CHASSIS

The primary focus of this book is the coachwork that was built for the "junior" Rolls-Royce models in the years between 1922 and 1939, and that coachwork has to be seen against a background of the social and economic changes that affected those two decades. The inter-war years have their own fascination as a time when the motor car

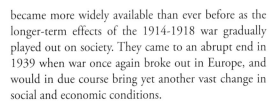

became more widely available than ever before as the longer-term effects of the 1914-1918 war gradually played out on society. They came to an abrupt end in 1939 when war once again broke out in Europe, and would in due course bring yet another vast change in social and economic conditions.

This is not the place to elaborate at length on those social and economic changes, but it is the place to explain the changes that were made to the Rolls-Royce chassis that were, quite literally, the foundation on which that coachwork was built. Social and economic changes also influenced the development of those chassis, which were always the limit of the Rolls-Royce remit. In those days, the company confined itself to building the mechanical elements of the car, and invariably left construction of the bodies to professional coachbuilders.

This chapter therefore provides a brief overview of the four "junior" Rolls-Royce chassis types produced in the inter-war period. It describes their gestation and development, lists their principal characteristics and, above all, it provides lists of chassis numbers. All Rolls-Royce models of this period are identified by their chassis numbers, and those chassis numbers will occur time and time again in later chapters. This chapter provides the reference against which they can be decoded and understood.

Why "junior" Rolls-Royce models? Simply because that is the way their manufacturers saw them. In the wider context, "junior" seems a description that is entirely out of place because these were large and expensive cars. Nevertheless, they were "junior" to the 40/50hp Silver Ghost model that was the only one the company had available in the first few years after the First World War ended.

The Rolls-Royce radiator grille shape was firmly established by the time of the Twenty, and so was the Flying Lady mascot. Early models had the Rolls-Royce motif in red, as on this 1931 20/25. (Simon Clay)

THE TWENTY

That war had made a huge difference to the Rolls-Royce company. For a start, it had brought a greater focus on aero engines as these took centre-stage ahead of the company's passenger car chassis. It had required expansion to deal with the demand for those engines, leaving Rolls-Royce with a large workforce and large factories that now needed to be filled. It had also brought major social changes, among them being a greater demand for motor cars in general.

By spring 1918, the Rolls-Royce Board were agreed that in the aftermath of the war, the company would not be able to survive on the 40/50 alone. Not only was it now quite old-fashioned, but it was also much too expensive to attract buyers in quantity. What was needed was a newly designed and less expensive model that would not eat into the market for the 40/50 but would be as close to it in appeal as was possible. As early as May 1918, Royce proposed to the Board that he should start on the design of such a new second model.

It was then the custom at Rolls-Royce to use the names of birds as code names for new projects under development, and the one chosen for the new small model was Goshawk. The initial G from that name would be seen in the experimental development models for the "junior" range of chassis right through

the 1930s. As for what sort of product it should be, the decision was taken that the new junior Rolls-Royce should be a 20hp model – in other words, its annual taxation would be around half that of the 40/50 Silver Ghost. Although Rolls-Royce expected customers to buy this new Rolls-Royce as an owner-drive model, in practice many would treat it as another chauffeur-driven type and would order appropriate bodies for it. A 20hp car was still a large and expensive car at a time when volume manufacturers like Ford, Austin and Morris were focusing on models of between 7hp and 10hp to attract the middle-class customers who were the major new target of motor manufacturers.

Central to the first Goshawk was a new design of engine, intended from the start as a six-cylinder in order to provide the smoothness that Royce considered essential to a car engine. His earliest design was influenced by the design of the 1913 Grand Prix Peugeot engine with its twin overhead camshafts, but only one experimental example of this first Goshawk had been built before it became abundantly clear that the specification would have to be simplified. Cost, development time and timing gear noise all counted against it – Royce's legendary perfectionism was not infrequently at odds with the realities of production and running a business – and so, probably in late 1920, it was redesigned.

Goshawk II retained the basic concept and shared

After Royce's initial plan for a six-cylinder engine with twin overhead camshafts had been rejected, design settled on the use of pushrod-operated overhead valves. This was the original production engine, a 3127cc size that was introduced for the new Twenty in 1922. (Simon Clay)

SPECIFICATIONS

ROLLS-ROYCE TWENTY

ENGINE
Six-cylinder with pushrod-operated overhead valves
3127cc (3.0in/76.2mm bore x 4.5in/114.3mm stroke)
Compression ratio 4.6:1; later 4.75:1
Seven main bearings
Single Rolls-Royce two-jet carburettor
50bhp unsilenced, 45bhp silenced

GEARBOX
Three-speed with central change (1922-1925)
Ratios 3.17:1, 1.63:1, 1.00:1
Four-speed with right-hand change (1925-1929)
Ratios 3.73:1, 2.33:1, 1.51:1, 1.00:1

AXLE RATIO
4.28:1 (1922-1925)
4.55:1 (1925-1929)
4.4:1   (1925-1929, optional)

STEERING
Rolls-Royce worm and nut type

SUSPENSION
Semi-elliptic leaf springs front and rear
Friction dampers (1922-1926)
Hydraulic front dampers from September 1926
Hydraulic rear dampers from December 1927

BRAKES
Drum type on rear wheels only (1922-1925)
Drum type on all four wheels, with mechanical servo (1925-1929)

DIMENSIONS

Overall length	178in (4520mm) – chassis only
Wheelbase	129in (3277mm)
Track	54in (1372mm), 1922-1925
	56in (1422mm), 1925-1929

He drew up a chassis of riveted construction, with a wheelbase of 129 inches that would make this quite a big car but still considerably smaller than the 40/50, which had another 15 inches between axle centres. He did not yet trust four-wheel braking systems, and so designed the car with rod-operated brakes on the rear wheels only. The radiator would have enamelled horizontal slats and the readily identifiable Rolls-Royce shape. As for the bodies, those would be left to specialist coachbuilders.

The new Rolls-Royce was brought to market in October 1922 as the Twenty model, but all early publicity was through the press, and the first public display of a Twenty was at the Paris Salon in 1923. There were no such displays in Britain until the British Empire Exhibition in April 1924, and the model was two years old by the time of its first Olympia appearance in October that year. Nevertheless, the Twenty was an immediate success, and orders were plentiful. They kept the company afloat until the original 40/50 model could be replaced by a more modern 40/50 called the Phantom in 1925 – and demand would remain strong until the end of the decade.

There were, of course, multiple improvements and refinements to the Twenty, and far more of them than there is either the room or the need to describe here. However, it is worth mentioning the change to four-wheel brakes in July 1925, accompanied by a mechanical servo that was made by Rolls-Royce under licence from Hispano-Suiza. Other changes in 1925 brought lower gearing for better acceleration, and a four-speed gearbox in place of the original three-speed type; at the same time the change lever and handbrake both moved from the centre of the car to the right-hand side. Then in two stages over the next couple of years, the original friction dampers gave way to more modern hydraulic types.

With coachwork of appropriate weight, a Twenty could achieve 60mph. Inevitably, many customers ordered rather grand coachwork that was heavier than Royce considered ideal, and as a result some completed cars fell quite a long way short of that speed. A Twenty with the right coachwork was fairly competitive in the early part of the 1920s – although it has to be remembered that the contemporary Bentley 3-litre with an engine of similar size was capable of over 80mph. The Bentley was of course a sporting car that lacked the refinement of the Rolls-Royce, but the huge discrepancy between the performance of the two cars highlighted the Twenty's conservative nature. It was also undeniable that at that level of cost, some customers were prepared to sacrifice refinement for performance.

the same bore and stroke dimensions, but instead of the twin overhead camshafts it had overhead valves operated by pushrods from a single camshaft. It also incorporated a modern single block casting (the 40/50 engine had two blocks of three cylinders each) and a detachable cylinder head. There would be both coil and magneto ignition systems, as Royce favoured back-ups in case of failure.

Royce arranged for the new engine to transmit its power through a three-speed gearbox and Hotchkiss drive (the 40/50 had a torque tube arrangement).

CHASSIS SEQUENCES

ROLLS-ROYCE TWENTY

Total built: 2940, 1922-1929.

In all series, the number 13 was omitted.

NUMBERS	SERIES	TOTAL	DATES	REMARKS
40G1 to 40G9	A	9	1922	
41G0 to 41G9		10	1922	
42G0 to 42G9		10	1922	
43G0 to 43G9		10	1922	
44G0 to 44G9		10	1922	
45G0 to 45G9		10	1922	
46G0 to 46G9		10	1923	
47G0 to 47G9		10	1923	
48G0 to 48G9		10	1923	
49G0 to 49G9		10	1923	
50G0		1	1923	
50S1 to 50S9		9	1923	
51S0 to 51S9		10	1923	
52S0 to 52S9		10	1923	
53S0 to 53S9		10	1923	
54S0 to 54S9		10	1923	
55S0 to 55S9		10	1923	
56S0 to 56S9		10	1923	
57S0 to 57S9		10	1923	
58S0 to 58S9		10	1923	
59S0 to 59S9		10	1923	
60S0		1	1923	
60H1 to 60H9		9	1923	
61H0 to 61H9		10	1923	
62H0 to 62H9		10	1923	
63H0 to 63H9		10	1923	
64H0 to 64H9		10	1923	
65H0		1	1923	
65H1 to 65 H9	B	9	1923	
66H0 to 66H9		9	1923	One renumbered in GRK series
67H0 to 67H9		10	1923	
68H0 to 68H9		10	1923	
69H0 to 69H9		10	1923	
70H0		1	1923	
70A1 to 70A9		9	1923	
71A0 to 71A9		10	1923	
72A0 to 72A9		10	1923	
73A0 to 73A9		10	1923	
74A0 to 74A9		10	1923	
75A0 to 75A9		10	1923	
76A0 to 76A9		10	1923	
77A0 to 77A9		10	1923	
78A0 to 78A9		10	1923	
79A0 to 79A9		10	1923	
80A0		1	1923	
80K0 to 80K9		10	1923	
81K0 to 81K9		10	1923	
82K0 to 82K9		10	1923	
83K0 to 83K9		10	1923	
84K0 to 84K9		10	1923	
85K0 to 85K9		10	1923	
86K0 to 86K9		10	1923	
87K0 to 87K9		10	1923	
88K0 to 88K9		10	1923	
89K0 to 89K9		10	1923	
90K0		1	1923	
GA1 to GA81	C	78	1923	One renumbered in GLK series and one in GAK series.
GF1 to GF81		77	1923-1924	Two renumbered in GRK series and one in GAK series.
GH1 to GH81		80	1923	
GAK1 to GAK7		7	1923	
GAK8 to GAK81	D	73	1924	
GMK1 to GMK81		80	1924	
GRK1 to GRK84		80	1924	
GDK1 to GDK15		15	1924	
GDK16 to GDK81	E	65	1924-1925	
GLK1 to GLK81		80	1924-1925	
GNK1 to GNK54		54	1925	
GNK55 to GNK94	F	40	1925	
GPK1 to GPK81		80	1925	
GSK1 to GSK80		79	1925-1926	
GSK81	G	1	1925	
GCK1 to GCK81		80	1925-1926	
GOK1 to GOK81		80	1926	
GZK1 to GZK37		36	1926	
GZK38 to GZK81	H	44	1926	
GUK1 to GUK81		80	1926	
GYK1 to GYK92		91	1926	
GMJ1 to GMJ81	J	80	1926-1927	
GHJ1 to GHJ81		80	1927	
GAJ1 to GAJ41		40	1927	
GAK42 to GAJ81	K	40	1927	
GRJ1 to GRJ81		80	1927	
GUJ1 to GUJ81		80	1927	
GXL1 to GXL82	L	81	1927-1928	
GYL1 to GYL82		81	1927-1928	
GWL1 to GWL41		40	1928	
GBM1 to GBM81	M	80	1928	
GKM1 to GKM82		81	1928	
GTM1 to GTM41		39	1928	One renumbered in GFN series
GFN1 to GFN82	N	81	1928-1929	
GLN1 to GLN87		80	1928-1929	Several chassis renumbered within the series
GEN1 to GEN41		40	1929	
GEN42 to GEN82X	O	40	1929	
GVO1 to GVO81		56	1929	24 chassis modified to 20/25 standard and renumbered in GXO series
GXO1 to GXO10		4	1929	6 chassis modified to 20/25 standard and renumbered in GXO series

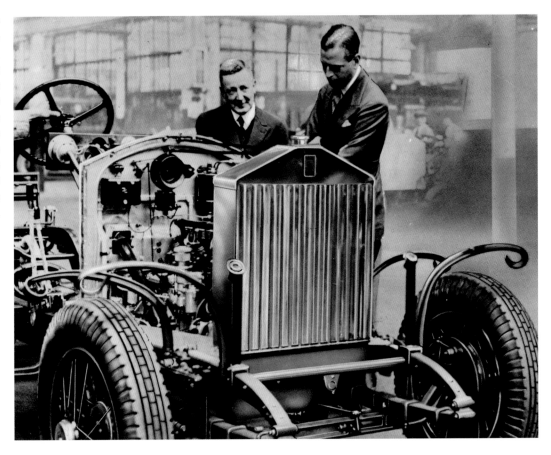

The front suspension depended on a beam axle until 1938, when the Wraith introduced independent front suspension to the junior Rolls-Royce range. Front wheel brakes were not added until 1925. This is the front axle of a 1931 20/25 model. (Simon Clay)

20/25 MODELS

By the late 1920s, it was clear that Rolls-Royce needed to increase the performance of its Twenty, which was beginning to appear slow and pedestrian. Other car makers had caught up fast, and there were now several competitors for the Twenty that were not only faster but considerably cheaper as well. So work began on a heavily revised model that again used the development code name of Goshawk.

The obvious thing to do was to increase the power of the engine by increasing its size. After evaluating several options, some of which were abandoned because they threatened reliability or refinement, the Rolls-Royce engineers chose to increase the bore of the existing engine from 3in to 3.25in; the stroke remained unchanged at 4.5in. As the RAC horsepower formula which governed annual taxation in Britain was dependent on bore size, this increase in the engine's bore inevitably led to an increase in that annual tax. It also lay behind the adoption of a new name for the Twenty's replacement.

The new car was called a Rolls-Royce 20/25, the initial figure perhaps intended to stress its connection with the earlier Twenty, and the second figure

indicating that it was now rated as a 25hp model. In fact, by the RAC method it was rated at 25.4hp. In the rather more technical sphere of swept volume, the new engine had a swept volume of 3675cc – although Rolls-Royce usually quoted it as 3669cc.

In all other respects, the new Goshawk engine was recognisably a development of the Twenty, and indeed the 20/25 as a whole was very much an updated continuation of the Twenty at first. It was nevertheless distinguished by a new and slightly taller radiator with vertical shutters instead of the Twenty's horizontal type. Rolls-Royce introduced the 20/25 at the Olympia Show in October 1929, expecting to sell it to the same group of wealthy owner-drivers who had been the target market for the Twenty. And, just as before, the car would go on to appeal to many buyers who wanted to have it driven for them by a chauffeur.

Over the next seven years, the 20/25 would go on to sell no fewer than 3824 examples (the total built was inflated by a few experimental chassis not sold to the public). This gave average sales of 546 a year, a figure considerably in excess of the Twenty's annual average of 420, and in fact the 20/25 was by far the best-selling Rolls-Royce model of the inter-war years. It sold more than twice as many overall as its larger

and more expensive Phantom II contemporary, and its success helped move the Phantom into a more rarefied area of the market. Nevertheless, without periodic improvements, it could not have sold so well.

Rolls-Royce kept abreast of developments from rival manufacturers by increasing the 20/25's performance in small increments. Thus in 1930 the engine's compression ratio went up to 5.25:1 from its original 4.75:1, and then again in 1932 to 5.75:1, when the change was accompanied by a new high-lift camshaft.

The 20/25 was powered by a 3675cc derivative of the original six-cylinder engine, the increase in swept volume coming from enlarged cylinder bores. Here it is in a 1933 chassis, GEX28. The company always took great care over the appearance of its engines. (Simon Clay)

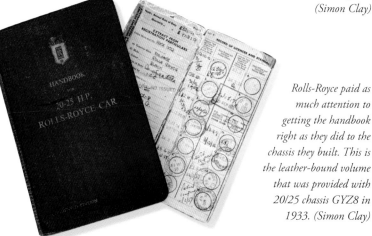

Rolls-Royce paid as much attention to getting the handbook right as they did to the chassis they built. This is the leather-bound volume that was provided with 20/25 chassis GYZ8 in 1933. (Simon Clay)

The radiator badge changed from red to black lettering during 1933, although not, as is commonly believed, in mourning for Royce's death that year. (Simon Clay)

Meanwhile, almost unnoticed, the wheelbase had been extended in March 1930 by three inches (from 129in to 132in) in order to meet demand for more roomy coachwork. The effects of such changes tended to cancel one another out, and for most of the car's production life a typical 20/25 was capable of a top speed in the region of 75mph.

Other important improvements in 1932 were a larger fuel tank and the addition of a Bijur "one-shot" lubrication system that simplified chassis maintenance. That same year brought thermostatically controlled radiator shutters and synchromesh on third and fourth gears; a further gearbox improvement brought a "silent" second gear in 1933. In 1934 came carburettor improvements and a standard DWS built-in jacking system, and in 1936 there were changes to a hypoid rear axle and to Marles cam-and-roller steering. By this time, Rolls-Royce considered that a further major change was necessary, and the 20/25 gave way in the autumn to the new 25/30 model.

Less relevant to the present book but by no means to be ignored is the fact that the 20/25's engine allowed Rolls-Royce to create a new Bentley model after their purchase of the bankrupt company in 1931. The Bentley name was too widely respected for Rolls-Royce to discontinue it altogether, and instead the company broadened its product offerings by developing the new 3½-litre model that was released in 1933. With a tuned version of the 20/25's engine (incorporating a crossflow cylinder head and twin carburettors), the Bentley's chassis was developed from the lightweight one designed for the Rolls-Royce Peregrine that was drawn up as an economy variant of the 20/25 but did not enter production.

Despite continued export sales, the majority of 20/25 chassis were sold in Britain, and the proportion has been calculated as 93%. A persistent story associated with the 20/25 (and its larger companion model, the

Rolls-Royce supplied the appropriate instruments with its chassis, but it was up to the coachbuilder to decide how to incorporate them into the dashboard. This was the arrangement adopted by Gurney Nutting for its Owen Sedanca Coupé bodies. (Simon Clay)

Phantom II) is that the RR letters on the grille badge were changed from their original red to black as a mark of mourning after Royce died in April 1933. The change certainly was made progressively at about this time, although it appears that the decision to make it had been taken before 1933 and that the reason was more associated with black being a more neutral colour that would not clash with certain paintwork colours.

Engines, of course, had their own numbers, but Rolls-Royce did not indulge in a "matching numbers" system. Here is the engine number on a 1934 20/25 model. (Simon Clay)

Some Twenty chassis were supplied with artillery-type spoked wheels, but most of the cars covered in this book had wire-spoked wheels. These could be, and often were, covered by protective discs that were much easier to clean. They also tended to give the cars a sleeker and more modern appearance. (Simon Clay)

SPECIFICATIONS

ROLLS-ROYCE 20/25

ENGINE
Six-cylinder with pushrod-operated overhead valves 3675cc
(3.25in/82.6mm bore x 4.5in/114.3mm stroke)
Compression ratio 4.75:1 (1929); 5.25:1 (1930); 5.75:1 (1932)
Seven main bearings
Single Rolls-Royce two-jet carburettor (1929-1933);
Rolls-Royce single-jet carburettor of SU design (1933-1936)
57bhp unsilenced, 50bhp silenced

GEARBOX
Four-speed; from 1932 with synchromesh on
3rd and Top gears
Ratios 3.73:1, 2.33:1, 1.53:1, 1.00:1;
later 3.30:1, 2.07:1, 1,37:1, 1.00:1

AXLE RATIO
4.55:1

STEERING
Rolls-Royce worm and nut type (1929-1936)
Marles cam-and-roller type (1936)

SUSPENSION
Semi-elliptic leaf springs front and rear
Hydraulic dampers front and rear; with speed-variable feature and
manual over-ride from 1934

BRAKES
Drum type on all four wheels, with mechanical servo

DIMENSIONS
Overall length	180in (4572mm) – chassis only, 1929-1930	
	183in (4648mm) – chassis only, 1930-1936	
Wheelbase	129in (3277mm), 1929-1930	
	132in (3353mm), 1930-1936	
Track	56in (1422mm)	

CHASSIS SEQUENCES

ROLLS-ROYCE 20/25

Total built: 3830, 1929-1936
(this includes eight experimental chassis,
of which two were renumbered as production types).
In all series, the number 13 was omitted.

NUMBERS	SERIES	TOTAL	DATES	REMARKS
12-G-IV to 14-G-IV		2	1928	Experimental
16-G-IV to 17-G-IV		2	1929	Experimental
18-G-IV		1	1930	Experimental
19-G-IV to 20-G-IV		2	1931	Experimental
21-G-IV		1	1934	Experimental
GXO11 to GXO111	O	100	1929	Some were renumbered Twenty chassis
GGP1 to GGP81	P	80	1929	
GDP1 to GDP81		80	1929	
GWP1 to GWP41		40	1930	
GLR1 to GLR82X	R	81	1930	GLR82X was originally 14-G-IV
GSR1 to GSR81		80	1930	
GTR1 to GTR41		40	1930	
GNS1 to GNS81	S	80	1930	
GOS1 to GOS81		80	1931	
GPS1 to GPS41		40	1931	
GFT1 to GFT81	TA	80	1931	
GBT1 to GBT21		20	1931	
GBT22 to GBT82	TB	61	1932	GBT82 was originally 16-G-IV
GKT1 to GKT41		40	1932	
GAU1 to GAU81	U	80	1932	
GMU1 to GMU21		20	1932	
GMU22 to GMU81	V	60	1932	
GZU1 to GZU41		40	1932	
GHW1 to GHW81	W	80	1932	
GRW1 to GRW81		80	1932	
GAW1 to GAW41		40	1932	
GEX1 to GEX81	X	80	1933	
GWX1 to GWX81		80	1933	
GDX1 to GDX41		40	1933	
GSY1 to GSY101	Y	100	1933	
GLZ1 to GLX81	Z	80	1933	
GTZ1 to GTZ81		80	1933	
GYZ1 to GYZ41		40	1933	
GBA1 to GBA81	A2	80	1933	
GGA1 to GGA81		80	1933	
GHA1 to GHA41		40	1933	
GXB1 to GXB81	B2	80	1933	
GUB1 to GUB81		80	1934	
GLB1 to GLB41		40	1934	
GNC1 to GNC81	C2	80	1934	
GRC1 to GRC81		80	1934	
GKC1 to GKC41		40	1934	
GED1 to GED81	D2	80	1934	
GMD1 to GMD81		67	1934	13 chassis renumbered in GYD series
GYD1 to GYD69		62	1934	4 chassis renumbered within the series
GAE1 to GAE81	E2	80	1934	
GWE1 to GWE83		82	1934	
GFE1 to GFE41		40	1934	
GAF1 to GAF81	F2	80	1934	
GSF1 to GSF81		80	1934	
GRF1 to GRF41		40	1935	
GLG1 to GLG81	G2	80	1935	
GPG1 to GPG81		80	1935	
GHG1 to GHG41		40	1935	
GYH1 to GYH81	H2	80	1935	
GOH1 to GOH81		80	1935	
GEH1 to GEH41		40	1935	
GBJ1 to GBJ81	J2	80	1935	
GLJ1 to GLJ81		80	1935	
GCJ1 to GCJ41		40	1935	
GXK1 to GXK81	K2	80	1935	
GBK1 to GBK81		80	1936	
GTK1 to GTK63		62	1936	

25/30 MODELS

The need to keep up with the Sunbeams, the Alvises, the Lagondas and the American imports did not diminish as the 1930s wore on. Once again, Rolls-Royce realised that their junior model was going to need more power if it was going to remain competitive, and initial thoughts focussed on eight-cylinder and even twelve-cylinder engines as favoured by many rivals from overseas. Not that such an engine was ever a realistic proposition for Rolls-Royce at that time, because the engineering department was heavily committed to work on several new projects, including aero engines and a new Bentley.

So there was little progress on the requirement until July 1935, by which time examples of a further redesigned six-cylinder engine were on test. It was the same old OHV six-cylinder, still with a 4.5in stroke but now overbored once again to 3.5in. With a higher compression ratio, a new cylinder head with the so-called "turbulent" design, and the carburettor relocated from the right-hand to the left-hand side, the new engine delivered as much extra performance as Rolls-

Royce considered necessary. A further change was to a Stromberg carburettor instead of the Rolls-Royce-built SU type of the 20/25, while the earlier combination of magneto and coil ignition now gave way to a pure coil type – with, of course, a second coil as standby.

The new engine displaced 4257cc, and of course its larger bore gave it a higher horsepower rating under the RAC system: it would be a 29.4hp model, which qualified for taxation as a 30hp. So for public consumption, this third iteration of the original Goshawk design became a 25/30 – 25 reminding people of its predecessor and 30 being the actual taxation figure. The extra annual tax did not cause Rolls-Royce any concerns this time around, because the British government had recently reduced the annual car tax from £1 per horsepower to 15 shillings (75p) per horsepower: the higher rating would therefore have less impact on sales than it might have done earlier. In different tune, the 4257cc engine was also adopted for the new Bentley 4¼-litre model.

The chassis remained much as before, retaining its 132in wheelbase and riveted construction, and now featured hydraulic dampers all round. Otherwise, the

The final increase in engine size was to 4257cc for the 25/30 models in 1936, and the same capacity was retained for the later Wraith, which also incorporated various improvements. Here is that engine, now sporting a large cylindrical air cleaner and silencer, in a 1937 25/30 chassis, number GMP73. (Simon Clay)

SPECIFICATIONS

ROLLS-ROYCE 25/30

ENGINE
Six-cylinder with pushrod-operated overhead valves
4257cc (3.5in/88.9mm bore x 4.5in/114.3mm
stroke)
Compression ratio 6.2:1
Seven main bearings
Single Stromberg carburettor
85bhp-103bhp

GEARBOX
Four-speed, with synchromesh on 3rd and Top gears
Ratios 3.30:1, 2.099:1, 1,37:1, 1.00:1

AXLE RATIO
4.55:1

STEERING
Marles cam-and-roller type

SUSPENSION
Semi-elliptic leaf springs front and rear
Hydraulic dampers front and rear, with speed-variable
feature and manual over-ride

BRAKES
Drum type on all four wheels, with mechanical servo

DIMENSIONS

Overall length	191in (4850mm) – chassis only
Wheelbase	132in (3353mm)
Track	56.3in (1430mm)

CHASSIS SEQUENCES

ROLLS-ROYCE 25/30

Total built: 1203, 1936-1939
(this includes one experimental chassis, 22-G-V).
In all series, the number 13 was omitted.

NUMBERS	SERIES	TOTAL	DATES	REMARKS
22-G-V		1	1936	Prototype chassis
GUL1 to GUL83	L2	82	1936	
GTL1 to GTL81		80	1936	
GHL1 to GHL41		40	1936	
GRM1 to GRM81	M2	80	1936-1937	
GGM1 to GGM41		40	1936-1937	
GAN1 to GAN81	N2	80	1937	
GWN1 to GWN81		80	1937	
GUN1 to GUN41		40	1937-1938	
GRO1 to GRO81	O2	80	1937-1938	
GHO1 to GHO81		80	1937-1938	
GMO1 to GMO41		40	1937-1938	
GRP1 to GRP81	P2	80	1937-1938	
GMP1 to GMP81		80	1937-1938	
GLP1 to GLP41		40	1937-1938	
GAR1 to GAR81	R2	80	1938	
GGR1 to GGR81		80	1938-1939	
GZR1 to GZR41		40	1938-1938	

transition from the last of the 20/25s to the first of the new 25/30s in April 1936 was smooth and simple; the new models incorporated a number of incremental changes that had been made on the final 20/25s, and indeed a number of the last 20/25 chassis were actually renumbered as 25/30 types and fitted with the new engine. Six months after the start of availability, the new 25/30 made a more public bow at the Olympia Motor Show.

More far-reaching changes were in the pipeline, but for the moment the new 25/30 held the fort extremely capably. With a top speed of around 80mph, it was well up with its rivals, and in fact sold faster than either of its predecessors. Sales of 1201 in just two years gave an average of 600 cars a year – a useful increase over annual sales of the 20/25 which indicated that the apparently minimal changes approved by Rolls-Royce had hit their mark.

WRAITH

The model that became the Rolls-Royce Wraith in 1938 developed from those early ideas that were interrupted by the decision to minimise changes between the 20/25 and 25/30. From late 1935, there had been proposals for a model with the big-bore 25/30 engine that would also have independent front suspension. Eight-cylinder and twelve-cylinder engine proposals fell by the wayside and in the end the car that replaced the 25/30 had an uprated version of the same engine – but it did have the proposed independent front suspension, which was a major change for the Goshawk series of cars.

The independent front suspension was similar to that designed for the V12-engined Rolls-Royce Phantom III that had appeared in 1936, and was based on a General Motors design. With it came front dampers that were controlled by a governor and varied the stiffness of the dampers to suit the speed of the car; there was a manual over-ride system as well. But the new suspension was far from the only new feature, and in fact the whole chassis had been redesigned for the new Wraith.

First of all, the Wraith chassis was physically larger than that of its direct predecessor, with an extra four inches in the wheelbase. This extra size had become necessary to provide adequate room in some of the grander bodies that were now being requested on the junior Rolls-Royce chassis, as this increasingly appealed to a proportion of buyers who might in earlier times have ordered a Phantom; the Phantom III, meanwhile, had moved up a notch and was now out of reach of some of its former clientele.

The Wraith's chassis was also welded rather than riveted together, and it incorporated substantial cross-bracing and box-section side frames. It had a very different front cross-member to suit the new independent suspension, and it had axles with wider tracks. Another new chassis feature was a built-in DWS hydraulic jacking system, which was operated by a lever under the front passenger seat. The wheels now had a 17in diameter rather than the 18in size of the 25/30, and although still wire-spoked were normally fitted with removable discs. To offset the lower gearing that their small size would give, a taller axle ratio was specified. While the gearbox remained substantially as before, synchromesh was now added to second gear.

As for the engine, the 4257cc six-cylinder of the 25/30 had again been redesigned. This time, it was fitted with a new cross-flow cylinder head (as pioneered on the Bentley engines from 1933), and the carburettor moved back to the right-hand side. There were bigger valves to improve the breathing, a stronger crankshaft with bigger bearings and webs, and the engine mounting arrangement was changed as well. The extra power from this latest version gave the Wraith a top speed of about 85mph – depending,

of course, on the body fitted – which was a useful improvement over the 80mph or so that the 25/30 typically gave. Yet it did not keep the model ahead of its opposition for long, and cheaper rivals from the likes of Daimler and Lagonda could deliver 90mph and a little more.

The Wraith was first seen in public at the Paris Salon in October 1938, where French coachbuilder Vanvooren (a Rolls-Royce favourite of the time) had a Touring Saloon ready in time for the show. In Britain, its first public outing came a week later at the Earls Court Motor Show, although the relatively late introduction of the new chassis had prevented more than a handful of the most favoured coachbuilders from having coachwork ready in time to display it there. The name of Wraith, incidentally, is supposed to have come from the affectionate name bestowed on a 40/50 Silver Ghost by its owner, and Rolls-Royce had probably chosen to use a name because the car's horsepower ratings were no different from those of the 25/30 it replaced. One unexpected result of that was that some members of the motor trade referred to the car as a "25/30 Wraith", which was not a name that Rolls-Royce ever gave it.

Rolls-Royce supplied a comprehensive kit of hand tools with each chassis, to enable owners (or their chauffeurs) to carry out minor maintenance tasks. It was up to the individual coachbuilder where these were carried, but this position within the boot lid was a popular choice. The body is a Drophead Coupé by HJ Mulliner, built in 1934. (Simon Clay)

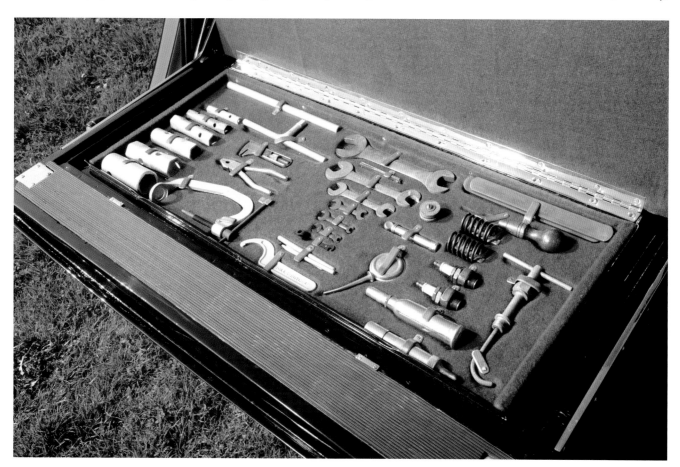

This tribute to the engineer behind the Rolls-Royce marque was erected by the Rolls-Royce Enthusiasts' Club at his former home in West Wittering, near Chichester in Sussex. (Simon Clay)

By the time of the 1938 Motor Show, Europe was more or less resigned to war with Germany, and Prime Minister Neville Chamberlain's September 1938 "peace for our time" pact with Hitler in Germany could do no more than buy a little time. Rolls-Royce car production was halted in 1939 as the company was instructed to focus on aero engine work, and in all only 491 examples of the Wraith would ever be built. Some of these were completed during 1940 and were sold or registered during the war years; 16 chassis were not bodied until 1946, when they were taken into government use (mainly in the Diplomatic Service), and the final Wraith was not delivered until 1947.

CHASSIS SEQUENCES

ROLLS-ROYCE WRAITH

Total built: 492, 1938-1939
(All six experimental chassis were renumbered as production types in the WXA series.) In all series, the number 13 was omitted.

NUMBERS	SERIES	TOTAL	DATES	REMARKS
24-G-VI to 29-G-VI		6	1937-1938	Experimental or prototype chassis
WXA1 to WXA109	A	108	1938	
WRB1 to WRB81	B	80	1938-1939	
WMB1 to WMB81		80	1938-1939	
WLB1 to WLB41		80	1938-1939	
WHC1 to WHC81	C	80	1939	
WEC1 to WEC81		80	1939	
WKC1 to WKC25		24	1939	

SPECIFICATIONS

ROLLS-ROYCE WRAITH

ENGINE
Six-cylinder with pushrod-operated overhead valves
4257cc
(3.5in/88.9mm bore x 4.5in/114.3mm stroke)
Compression ratio 6:1
Seven main bearings
Single Solex downdraught carburettor
105bhp

GEARBOX
Four-speed, with synchromesh on 2nd, 3rd and Top gears
Ratios 3.10:1, 2.00:1, 1,35:1, 1.00:1

AXLE RATIO
4.25:1

STEERING
Marles cam-and-roller type

SUSPENSION
Independent front suspension with coil springs
Semi-elliptic rear leaf springs
Hydraulic dampers front and rear, with speed-variable feature and manual over-ride

BRAKES
Drum type on all four wheels, with mechanical servo

DIMENSIONS
Overall length   191in (4850mm) – chassis only
Wheelbase   136in (3454mm)
Track   58.5in (1486mm) front
                   59.5in (1511mm) rear

Chapter Two

THE BODIES

Coachwork evolved to follow the social norms of those who could afford it. This 1931 20/25 chassis has a grand Sedanca de Ville body by Barker, where the owners sat in comfort in the enclosed rear section and the chauffeur was exposed to the elements in an open front compartment. If the weather turned really nasty, he could always deploy a fabric roof section to keep the worst off. (Simon Clay)

Rolls-Royce never forgot that their customers were at liberty to order whatever style of body they wanted from whichever coachbuilder they chose, and in the 1920s there were very many coachbuilders they could choose from; the choice was still wide in the following decade.

Some coachbuilders had achieved national and even international renown, while others catered for a regional clientele and were little known elsewhere. Some of the larger firms specialised in particular types of body, although the smaller ones could only survive by remaining versatile. Probably all achieved a high degree of competence in construction (if not always in design), and admiration of the skills of the craftsmen who built these bodies is a major factor in enthusiasm for coachwork today.

Even so, Rolls-Royce did stipulate maximum weights for coachwork on their small-horsepower chassis of the inter-war years, and retained the right to refuse the issue of a guarantee if they considered a body exceeded this weight limit. Many bodies were much heavier than was ideal, with a consequent impact on performance and even (though Rolls-Royce buyers seldom cared) fuel consumption.

For the modern reader with an interest in the different coachwork styles that were built for these cars, it is important to remember that the cars were not thought of as indivisible and immutable wholes in the way that has since become the norm. Body and chassis had come from separate makers and could be separated again. It was not uncommon for a well-liked body to be transferred to an owner's new chassis, the

This is how they turn up today, and this quite well-preserved Park Ward Tourer body is sadly no longer on its original chassis; doubtless an enthusiast made one good car out of two Twenties back in the day – and as chassis and body were separate elements, this was a feasible option. The Tourer body has four doors and a folding fabric roof, but the detachable sidescreens had to be erected separately. (Simon Clay)

Coachwork could be used to express grandeur, like this supremely elegant Gurney Nutting Sedanca Coupé that was delivered new to Prince Aly Khan in 1933. It had the exclusive "Owen" design sold only through the London dealer HR Owen, but widely imitated. (Simon Clay)

old one perhaps then being sold to a specialist dealer and eventually ending up on a completely different type of chassis. Sometimes, an accident-damaged body had to be replaced. Equally, owners sometimes tired of the body they had originally bought for their Rolls-Royce chassis and had it modified or changed for a new one. Modifications could and did range from more fashionable wing shapes to more radical transformations, such as from drophead coupé to fixed-head coupé.

Ultimately, bodies tended not to last as well as the chassis on which they were mounted. As a result, by the late 1930s it was already becoming common for older models to be rebodied for a new lease of life, and

these bodies would typically have newer styles that (in their owners' eyes) rejuvenated the car and retained its prestige value. These bodies are beyond the scope of this book, but they are a fascinating subject in their own right.

THE COACHBUILDERS

Although the body styles of the 1920s are more of a matter of taste, there is a general consensus among car enthusiasts that the 1930s produced some of the most attractive car bodies ever designed, and that a good number of those were erected on Rolls-Royce chassis. But even though a look through the diversity of styles and ideas illustrated in this book might

suggest that coachbuilding was a thriving industry, the reality was rather different. Business was gradually drying up, partly thanks to social changes which reduced demand for certain types of older chauffeur-drive bodies, and partly because of cost pressures that were forcing more and more manufacturers towards adopting mass-produced types. Cheaper to make than traditional hand-built bodies, they were also becoming increasingly attractive.

As demand fell away, the number of coachbuilders who remained in business gradually shrank. Some had started out with high hopes immediately after the First World War, and never really attained a firm business footing. Others were unable to survive the Depression. Some turned to commercial bodybuilding as a more reliable source of business. Mergers and company purchases accounted for more, particularly in the later 1930s. In 1937, London dealer Jack Barclay made a personal purchase of the coachbuilder James Young. In 1938 Hooper absorbed its rival Barker, and in the first six months of that year Park Ward recorded a loss; a year later, it was bought by Rolls-Royce, which had bought a share of the business in 1933, when the coachbuilder's finances had looked rocky. Cockshoot and Arthur Mulliner were two more coachbuilders that shut up shop in 1939.

This attrition among British coachbuilders during the 1930s is quite dramatically reflected in the numbers of coachbuilders who worked on each of the small-horsepower Rolls-Royce chassis. No fewer than 168 British companies are known to have built coachwork for the Twenty between 1922 and 1929. For the 20/25 that succeeded it and was in production between 1929 and 1936, the figure was 78 – and there were far more 20/25s sold than Twenties. Just 37 British coachbuilders worked on the 25/30 between 1936 and 1938, and the figure was down to 27 for the Wraith of 1938-1939. These figures should not, of course, be taken as definitive because of such things as misattributions and some gaps in the record, but they do give a very clear idea of what was happening to the British coachbuilding industry.

It is very easy to think of coachbuilders as producing only bespoke coachwork, but that is far from the reality. In practice, genuinely bespoke bodies were few and far between even before the decline of the coachbuilding industry during the 1930s. Many coachbuilders relied on a few basic designs that were more or less standard; for example, six-light saloons from any one coachbuilder did not vary greatly during the 1920s, and in fact it is not always easy to distinguish a six-light saloon of that era from its counterparts constructed by other coachbuilders.

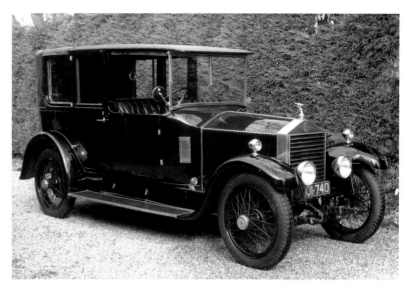

In the 1930s, some of the larger coachbuilders turned to the practice of batch-building to streamline production and reduce costs. If a new body design looked as if it might sell well (and customer interest at the autumn motor shows each year was a good indicator), a coachbuilder might choose to build six or as many as ten to hold in stock against future orders. As those orders came in, individual variations could be accommodated so that the customer could feel he or she was buying a bespoke body. Occasionally, sales would not match expectations, and in those cases the spare bodies might be sold to one of the specialist companies that would buy up such redundant bodies and adapt them to fit whatever chassis their customers brought along. Among these, perhaps the best known was Cooper of Putney.

Rolls-Royce themselves had actually encouraged this process, and in the early 1930s recruited a number of coachbuilders to build bodies to standardised designs. Maythorn was one; Park Ward was another. For a variety of reasons, the scheme did not quite work out as planned, but it did indicate how things would go later in the decade.

This is another clear reflection of social norms in the 1920s. The body is a Hooper Landaulette, and although the chauffeur has a roof, he has no side protection. By contrast, the owners in the rear could choose between an enclosed compartment and an open one in fine weather: the rear of the roof folded down when required. That would have been another job for the chauffeur, of course. (Simon Clay)

WHO BUILT THE MOST?
The five coachbuilders who built the largest number of bodies on the small-horsepower Rolls-Royce chassis were (in descending order of quantity):

	Twenty	20/25	25/30	Wraith	TOTAL
Hooper	447	676	209	75	1407
Park Ward	332	620	162	170	1284
Barker	444	372	125	NIL	941
Thrupp & Maberly	83	474	206	42	805
HJ Mulliner	150	303	96	62	611

Tricks of the trade: although the body style sometimes dictated where the spare wheel or wheels had to be carried, coachbuilders could vary the appearance of a body considerably by their choice of position. On this formal Sedanca de Ville, it was mounted alongside the scuttle. (Simon Clay)

CHANGING FASHIONS, CHANGING STYLES

Twenty bodies

Just like Bentley, whose founder repeatedly railed against heavy coachwork on the 3-litre chassis that he had designed as a sporting type, Rolls-Royce had misunderstood their target audience. Although many early Twenties received the Tourer bodies for which the chassis had been designed, there were also many that were bodied as Landaulettes or Limousines, and the extra weight of such luxury coachwork inevitably hurt performance, especially when it was increased by the sort of internal furnishings that were the pride of the best coachbuilders.

The arrival of Weymann bodies with fabric panels reduced weight quite dramatically, although their typically matt finish did not meet with Rolls-Royce approval, and a famous memo from the Sales Department in 1926 reminded salesmen that "the appearance of a Weymann body is not what one usually associates with a Rolls-Royce chassis. Therefore every effort should be made to order coachbuilt bodies in preference to Weymanns."

As lighter bodies became available, so the popularity of closed saloons increased (although questions of weatherproofing and comfort also had an influence). Provision for luggage to be carried – particularly in the form of a drop-down luggage grid at the rear – was also made to meet demand, and by the end of the Twenty's production run the earliest bodies with an integral luggage boot had made their appearance. During 1928, the introduction of a wider scuttle on the Twenty chassis also had an important effect, as it allowed the width of the body to be increased without an awkward transition just behind the engine compartment.

20/25 bodies

Although several early 20/25 chassis were ordered with Weymann coachwork, the fashion for fabric panelling soon died out, and the half-metal, half-fabric "semi-Weymann" type that followed it did not last long either. Composite construction with metal (or fabric) panels on a wooden frame was almost universal at the start of the 1930s, but some coachbuilders began to experiment with metal frame elements. Park Ward, for example, was one of the first to introduce metal centre pillars within an otherwise wooden frame in order to increase body rigidity. Valuable coachwork innovations also arrived from the European continent, especially France, and Silentbloc construction (with rubber mountings to insulate body from chassis) was a French invention that was welcomed by several coachbuilders in the mid-1930s.

Buyers of the Rolls-Royce 20/25 chassis tended to be quite conservative in outlook, and as a result there were relatively few examples that reflected the fashion trends of the early 1930s – Art Deco swoops and colour contrasts, and streamlining. On the other hand, many buyers did embrace the tidier appearance (and easier cleaning) that was provided by solid wheel covers over the wire wheels that were still standard. Similarly, some later bodies reflected the continental European trend to cover the rear wheels with spats, which were sometimes stylishly cut away or adorned with chromed motifs.

It was during the currency of the 20/25 that the traditional folding luggage grid gradually gave way to the enclosed luggage boot. Sometimes this was not well integrated into the lines of the body and unbalanced the design, but on other bodies it very much enhanced the appearance. A notable style that was adopted by several coachbuilders in the early 1930s was the so-called Continental Saloon, which had been pioneered by Park Ward in 1931. This was a four-light (and therefore sporting) saloon with a neat built-in boot capable of carrying the luggage needed on a trip to the

European continent; its appeal lay not only in its well-balanced lines but also in the aspirations it suggested. The Continental name, of course, also deliberately recalled the glamorous Rolls-Royce Phantom II Continental models at the top of the chassis maker's range.

25/30 bodies

Some years before the time of the 25/30 in 1936, closed bodies had become the norm. Tourers and All-weathers had become rare, and open bodies tended to be rather grander and more elegant types such as Drophead Coupés. Sports Saloons with four-light designs were particularly popular, relegating the six-light Saloon to a more formal role, and Divisions almost always had a disappearing or folding upper section. For the chauffeur-drive market, the Limousine predominated over the Landaulette, although that style was still far from extinct.

The all-steel body also became more common. Park Ward had introduced the type on a Bentley chassis in 1936, and from 1937 made it available for Rolls-Royce models as well; an advantage that other coachbuilders could not ignore was that the body pillars could now be made thinner. Razor-edge styling, introduced by Freestone & Webb on Bentley Sports Saloons some years earlier, was now becoming fashionable and made the transition to Rolls-Royce models; it would remain fashionable, latterly softened a little, well into the 1950s.

Carrying the spare wheel at the rear quite literally made the car longer, and removing it from the side position also tended to add to the overall visual length. (Simon Clay)

Contemporary fashions had their own effect on coachwork. The influence of the Art Deco movement is very obvious in the way coachbuilder Gurney Nutting created a scalloped side moulding as a boundary for the two colours of this delightful Coupé on a 20/25 chassis. (Simon Clay)

Another stylist's trick was to let louvres into the sides of the scuttle to match those in the sides of the bonnet. This tended to make the nose of the car look longer, which not only helped the proportions but suggested a bigger and more powerful engine. (Simon Clay)

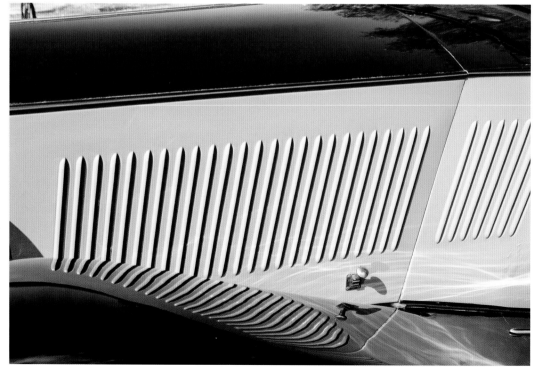

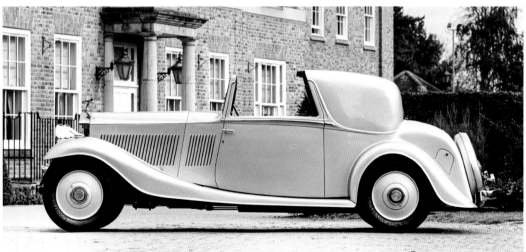

Imitation was also the sincerest form of flattery. It would be hard not to see where some of the inspiration for this Sedanca de Ville body by Offord came from. (Simon Clay)

Gurney Nutting produced some of the most attractive bodies of all, and this Sedanca de Ville is deliciously elegant. Ideas had moved on considerably by the time of this body, which can be compared with the Barker Sedanca de Ville illustrated earlier and built only three years before this one. The rear compartment is quite different in concept, and the chauffeur is no longer separated by a glass division. The plain rear panels allow the owners to ride in luxury, unseen by prying eyes, and the De Ville front portion of the roof is no longer simply a form of class demarcation; its removal also brings extra light and air into the rear compartment. (Simon Clay)

WEYMANN BODIES

In the late 1920s and early 1930s, many coachbuilt bodies depended on the Weymann construction principles. These were the work of two French aviators, Charles Weymann and Maurice Tabuteau, and borrowed ideas from aircraft construction. In 1922, Weymann established a factory in Paris to exploit this new system of building car bodywork.

Weymann construction addressed a problem caused by the weak chassis frames of the time. As they flexed over bumps and potholes, so their movement was transmitted directly to the bodywork that was rigidly mounted to them. This quite literally led to the bodies falling apart, as well as to unwelcome rattles and squeaks. The Weymann system used metal joints that allowed the wooden body framework to flex, while an aircraft-style fabric rather than metal covering reduced weight. Attaching seats directly to the chassis rather than to the bodywork further reduced stresses on the body structure.

Weymann soon started licensing the system to other coachbuilders in Europe and the USA, and to chassis makers who had their own body building departments. So popular did the Weymann system become that by 1925, its inventor decided to establish his own coachworks in Britain as well, and bought the old Cunard workshops at Putney in London for the purpose.

Weymann's success in Britain prompted a move to larger premises in 1928, when the company moved to Addlestone in Surrey. However, not everybody liked the Weymann system. The fabric skin panels had poor durability, and their finish was almost invariably duller than that of a cellulose-painted metal panel (although a gloss finish could be achieved by a long and expensive process). By the time of the 1929 Paris Salon, Weymann was looking at alternative construction methods, and had attempted to deal with the durability problem by using metal panels for the lower body and fabric above the waist.

This brought only a temporary stay of execution, however, and in Britain, the Weymann company refocused its activities on bus bodywork from 1931. The market for car coachwork using the Weymann patents collapsed in the early 1930s – although some buyers swore by them and a few coachbuilders were still building them to special order as late as 1937.

Another Gurney Nutting Sedanca de Ville helps to illustrate how styling progressed during the 1930s. The rounder, more voluminous wings and the rear wheel spats were by no means universal but were having an influence by the time of this 1937 body. (Simon Clay)

Wraith bodies

The introduction of the Wraith chassis in 1938 presented several new challenges to the coachbuilders then still in business. It came with a wheelbase that was four inches longer than that of the 25/30 (and later 20/25), it had smaller-diameter wheels, and its radiator grille was set further forward than before. All of these were visual changes that meant the earlier body designs could not be carried over without change; they had to be adapted or else replaced altogether.

As for bodywork types, the predominant ones were now Saloons and Limousines. Open bodies were rare, and most were probably Drophead Coupés, which allowed for displays of style and good taste far better than the Tourers of the 1920s and early 1930s. Landaulettes were not quite extinct but were rare, although Hooper would oblige when asked. Interestingly, Thrupp & Maberly planned to display one at the 1939 Earls Court Motor Show (which was of course cancelled because of the war), but this was almost certainly intended to show off their skills rather than to carry any realistic hope of attracting further Landaulette orders.

BUILDING THE BODIES

Many buyers were quite happy to buy a car displayed in their local Rolls-Royce showroom, or to ask for a similar one to be built for them. However, if a customer wanted a bespoke design, there would be a more involved process where the selected coachbuilder might draw up sketches of possibilities from which the customer would make a choice. There might then follow a process of to-ing and fro-ing as these drawings were amended to reach a satisfactory compromise between what the customer wanted and what was actually possible. Eventually, the customer would approve a coloured rendering of the completed vehicle, and then work would begin on the actual construction of the body.

Whether to bespoke or standardised designs, the actual construction of coachwork was a labour-intensive and quite laborious process that was carried out by highly skilled men. Although a certain amount of jig-building was possible when several bodies were built in batches to a common design, a great deal still depended on the eye and experience of the coachbuilder's craftsmen. Work on a body might not begin immediately after a contract had been agreed; there might be a delay until the coachbuilder could fit the body into his schedule.

Working from the agreed drawings, these craftsmen would begin by creating the framework or skeleton of the body, usually (in Britain at least) from seasoned ash wood. There would be carpentry joints between sections of the frame, which would be glued and bolted together, and the joints might be reinforced with metal gussets. Some coachbuilders used one of the various patented systems which were intended to reduce movement at these joints or at least to prevent the squeaks and other unwelcome noises that resulted from the wooden sections fretting against one another when the car was in motion. Some tried to circumvent the patents (and the cost of a licence) by developing their own systems. The best known of the patented systems was the Weymann type, which is explained in the sidebar on p.28. It gave way in the early 1930s to the Silentbloc system, in which unwelcome movement between body and chassis was damped out by the use of rubber mounting blocks.

Once the framework was in place and had been checked for compliance with the design drawings, the next stage was to make and attach the panels. Mostly, these would be of metal – although fabric outer panels were used on Weymann and Weymann-type bodies. Typically, the metal used was aluminium alloy because this was easy for the skilled panel-beaters to work by hand, was light in weight, and was also durable.

Panels would be attached to the wooden frame by coachbuilder's nails, although different processes were used later in the 1930s as steel-framed bodies gradually entered the picture.

With the panels all attached, there would obviously be a further inspection, and any blemishes or unsatisfactory fits would be dealt with. The body was then ready for painting, and that was a much longer and more skilled process than was typically used on mass-produced car bodies of the time. The paint used was cellulose, which had been introduced in the mid-1920s and was sprayed onto the panels, and the whole process might take six days or more at a top-quality coachbuilder. Each coat of paint had to be left to dry naturally; the drying ovens used in manufacture today were not available to coachbuilders in the 1930s.

On the first day, primer would be applied. On the second day, the finish would be inspected and stopper applied as necessary. The third day would be devoted to rubbing down – by hand, of course – to achieve a perfectly smooth finish. The fourth day would typically see the undercoat or surface sealer applied. The top coats, of which there could be several, would not be put on until the fifth day. Fine lining might follow, and of course would be hand-applied by another skilled craftsman. Any rectification at this stage could delay the process further, but in an ideal world the body would be polished on the sixth day. It would then have to be mounted to the chassis, and then a Rolls-Royce representative would inspect the car before it could be signed off. The inspection would

Many coachbuilders signed their work, with a cast or printed plate screwed to one of the body sills. This one from Gurney Nutting is typical; some coachbuilders, such as Freestone & Webb, added the body number to the plate as well. (Simon Clay)

Sometimes, the supplying dealer wanted to get in on the act, too. This sill plate is on the Park Ward Tourer body for a Twenty that is illustrated on p.22.

Some dealers, such as Jack Barclay in London, added their own plates alongside the coachbuilder's plates as a matter of course. (Simon Clay)

Naggingly familiar, and yet not quite familiar enough? Many overseas buyers of a small-horsepower Rolls-Royce had its coachwork constructed in their own country, and this 1937 example from Erdmann & Rossi in Berlin has all the heaviness and self-confidence characteristic of German coachbuilding at the time. The chassis is a Rolls-Royce 25/30.

include a road test, designed to detect squeaks and rattles, and might be followed by some rectification work.

Delivery to the supplying dealer (or in some cases direct to the customer) would follow only once everything had been completed to the satisfaction of both chassis maker and coachbuilder, and the whole process in some cases could take as long as six months from the date the order was placed to the date when the car was delivered.

THE TABLES

This book looks at the coachwork mounted on the small-horsepower or junior Rolls-Royce chassis when the cars were still in production. There were of course many later rebodies, which are not considered here. The coachbuilders themselves are divided into British companies (Chapter 3) and Overseas companies (Chapter 4). Each entry for a coachbuilder begins with a brief overview of the company and of the coachwork it constructed for each type of chassis. That coachwork is then broken down by type, and the types are listed alphabetically within each entry.

Inevitably, the description chosen may not meet every reader's expectations, and it is only necessary to take a look through the Coachwork Descriptions section below to see that some bodies could have been described in several different ways, each accurate on its own terms. Some coachbuilders also invented new descriptive terms to make their products sound more exotic.

The tables typically contain sections devoted to each major body type produced by a coachbuilder; in some cases, single examples of different types are grouped together for convenience. There is then a list of the chassis for which these bodies were originally constructed. Each entry is accompanied by a date, which is deliberately shown only as a calendar year; actual dates of completion are notoriously difficult to determine.

This was the style known as a Salamanca – a term used only by Rolls-Royce. The body pictured was on a 1925 Twenty chassis and was built for a customer in the USA by the French coachbuilder Kellner. The flimsy fabric roof over the chauffeur's compartment is just visible here, and the whole of the rear roof section could be folded down in fine weather. The Salamanca style later gave way to such confections as the Cabriolet de Ville. (Simon Clay)

COACHWORK DESCRIPTIONS

ALL-WEATHER

Essentially an open car, usually with four doors. It has a canvas hood that can be erected as protection against the elements. The difference between an All-weather and a four-door Tourer is that the All-weather has fixed (or folding) side windows, while the Tourer depends on removable sidescreens.

BROUGHAM

This style of body was named after the Scottish jurist who popularised it in the 19th century. It is a formal style with an open, de ville or enclosed driving compartment for the chauffeur, and a rear body fronted by a fixed division. More obviously, key characteristics are a sharp-edged profile, a rear panel with long curved sides, and a door that (usually) curves forwards at the toe. The Brougham Saloon design from Freestone & Webb in the mid-1930s borrowed these key characteristics but was not a Brougham in the traditional sense.

CABRIOLET

The meaning of this description evolved over the years. It typically refers to a four-door body with a canvas hood that is permanently attached to the coachwork, and is therefore not easy to distinguish from an All-weather. On the European continent, it often meant the same as a Drophead Coupé, and some coachbuilders imported the term to make their creations sound more exotic.

CABRIOLET DE VILLE

This is a Cabriolet with a "de ville" head: that is, the section of the roof above the driving compartment can be removed separately. The term gradually went out of use and was replaced by Three-position Drophead Coupé, although the intention of the two types was different. The Cabriolet de Ville was typically driven by a chauffeur, while the Three-position Drophead Coupé was an owner-driver car.

COUPÉ

A Coupé is a closed body, typically with two doors and only two windows, although some were built as "three-quarter" types with two side windows. The distinction between a three-quarter Coupé and a Saloon Coupé then becomes rather blurred, although the Coupé typically has more sporting lines. The word "coupé" means "cut" in French, and suggests a body that has been shortened in some way.

D-BACK

On bodies with a D-back style, the name indicates that the rear panel of the body has the profile of a (usually somewhat elongated) letter D. D-back designs generally disappeared as coachbuilders began to incorporate luggage boots, although in later years they were sometimes used for Limousines where no external boot was required.

DE VILLE

The words are French and mean "in town". A "de ville" head on any kind of body means that the front portion of the roof above the driving compartment can be removed to highlight the fact that the car is being driven by a chauffeur, while the owners ride in comfort in the rather more weatherproof rear section of the body.

DICKEY SEAT

A Dickey Seat was an occasional seat that folded out from the boot area. It provided exposed accommodation, typically for two passengers.

DIVISION

The Division would be a feature of a formal body, and was usually a partition between the passenger compartment in the rear and the driving compartment in the front, present to give the rear-seat occupants greater privacy. The top section was usually glass. It was more or less standard on Limousine coachwork (which typically but not always had folding "occasional" seats in the rear as well), and was sometimes incorporated into the more spacious Saloon bodies too. In later years, some Touring Limousines had Divisions where the upper section could be folded away or dropped into the base of the partition, so turning the car into an owner-driver type.

DROPHEAD COUPÉ

Like a Coupé, this is typically a two-door type with side windows only in the doors. The "head" (roof) is arranged to "drop" (to open the car to the elements), and to that end the roof is made of fabric so that it can be folded away at the back of the body. A Three-position Drophead Coupé is arranged so that the front or "de ville" section of the folding roof can be furled separately, so exposing the front seat occupants to the elements but leaving the rear enclosed.

FAUX CABRIOLET

This description came from French coachbuilding, and indicated a body with a fixed roof that was covered in fabric to make it look like a Cabriolet. Some examples even had dummy hood-irons. The word "faux" is French for "false".

FIXED-HEAD COUPÉ

It would be nice to think that a Fixed-head Coupé was a car designed to look like a Drophead Coupé that actually had a fixed roof. However, although some coachbuilders did use the term this way, others (and the motor trade) tended to use it as an alternative to Coupé, probably because it sounded more grand.

LANDAULETTE

The word is also spelled Landaulet, and different coachbuilders chose one or the other; for consistency the form Landaulette is used here. On a Landaulette, the rear section of the roof can be folded down to expose the rear seat passengers, the original point being to enable the hoi polloi to admire the wealthy occupants as they were driven past. Landaulettes began to fall out of favour as social attitudes changed.

COACHWORK DESCRIPTIONS

LIMOUSINE

A Limousine body is normally an enclosed type with a large amount of legroom in the rear and a division to separate the passengers from the chauffeur. There may be folding "occasional" seats in the rear compartment to provide additional passenger capacity when necessary. A Limousine de Ville of course has a removable front roof section, and some early bodies in this period were built as open-drive types, where the front compartment for the chauffeur has neither roof nor side windows.

OPEN DRIVE

Open Drive indicates that the driving compartment is not enclosed. This arrangement was found on some Limousine bodies in the earlier years of the 1920s, where the chauffeur was provided with an open space on each side of his compartment instead of a glazed window. There might or might not be a fixed roof section.

PILLARLESS

In a pillarless saloon body, the central pillars are eliminated and the front and rear doors shut against each other. When open, they offer unimpeded access to the interior, which was a key attraction of the design. The French coachbuilder Vanvooren was the acknowledged leader but not the inventor of pillarless construction, which was already available in Britain by 1933. Another attraction of pillarless construction was weight saving, although that was sometimes countered by the additional body reinforcement needed to maintain rigidity.

SALAMANCA

The Salamanca designation was only (correctly) ever used for bodies on Rolls-Royce chassis. It was essentially a Cabriolet de Ville with a four-light design and, usually, a degree of luxury in its execution. It came from a design by the Count de Salamanca, who was the Rolls-Royce agent in Madrid.

SALOON

A Saloon body was fully enclosed, usually had four doors and typically (but not invariably) had a six-light design. Four-light types were often described as Sports Saloons and were typically more sporting in appearance, but there were inevitably some more upright four-light Saloons and some more sporting six-light Sports Saloons.

SALOON COUPÉ

A Saloon Coupé had a fixed roof, two doors, and a four-light design. The latter characteristic made it different from a Fixed-head Coupé, which normally had a two-light design, but the terms were not always used consistently.

SEDANCA DE VILLE

Theoretically, the Sedanca name was enough on its own to describe a body with an enclosed rear compartment and an exposed driving position for the chauffeur. However, many coachbuilders favoured the Sedanca de Ville name, and this eventually became more common.

SEDANCALETTE

The Sedancalette was a hybrid of Sedanca and Landaulette designs. It combined a De Ville head with a closed rear body that incorporated a Landaulette-style folding rear section.

STREAMLINE

The short-lived vogue for streamlining lasted roughly from 1934 to 1936. It drew on some of the theories of aerodynamics that were coming out of the aviation industry, but never employed these to full effect. In practice, most streamline bodies were not streamlined at all, but simply had a sloping tail panel to give the impression that they were.

SWEPT-TAIL

A swept-tail design was typically a fastback or sloping-tail saloon in which the bottom edge of the rear panel was swept outwards for stylistic effect.

THREE-POSITION

This term was used of Drophead Coupé coachwork and of some De Ville types. It indicated that the folding roof could be used in three positions: open, closed, or with the rear section raised and the roof above the driving position furled to give a De Ville configuration.

THREE-QUARTER

The term "three-quarter" was largely confined to the 1920s and was added to the main description of a body to indicate that there was a rear quarter window on each side. What was known as a three-quarter Coupé was later generally described as a four-light type.

TOURER

A Tourer body invariably had a folding hood, and typically had four or five seats (although there were two-seat and three-seat types as well). A key distinguishing characteristic was that it had removable sidescreens, typically made of canvas, instead of windows.

TWO-SEATER

The description Two-seater indicates clearly enough the key characteristic of such a body, but it was normally used of an open car. The term has sometimes been used to mean the same thing as Drophead Coupé or two-seat Tourer.

Chapter Three

COACHWORK BY BRITISH COACHBUILDERS A-Z

By far the greater proportion of coachwork on post-war Rolls-Royce chassis came from British coachbuilders. This chapter lists them in alphabetical order, and for the larger companies breaks down each coachbuilder's output into appropriate categories to aid understanding.

ABBOTT

Farnham – 20/25, 25/30

ED Abbott had been the London sales representative of Page & Hunt (qv), and when that company failed in 1929 he took over its premises and assets at Wrecclesham near Farnham, and formed a new company under his own name.

Like its predecessor, Abbott's built some bus bodies, but from the mid-1930s the company focussed on its mainstream car work, and on its retail business. It constructed nine bodies on Rolls-Royce 20/25 chassis between 1930 and 1935, and a single body on the 25/30 chassis in 1936. On the larger Rolls-Royce chassis, there were also a single body on the Phantom II chassis and three on the Phantom III.

The Abbott tally on the small-horsepower Rolls-Royce chassis was one body in 1930, four in 1932, two in 1933, and one each in 1934, 1935 and 1936. The company also replaced one of its 1932 bodies with a new one in 1937.

20/25 COACHWORK

Four of the Abbott bodies on 20/25 chassis were Saloons, but all were probably individual designs. The earliest was on chassis GNS26 in November 1930. Two were built in 1933, one on GWX3 and one later in the year on GGA3, the latter a four-light design with the shapely boot characteristic of the time and twin side mounts to help make room for luggage. The last of the saloons was a six-light design on chassis GCJ4, delivered in November 1935.

Three 20/25 chassis received Limousine coachwork, and all were delivered within a period of four months in mid-1932. The earliest of them was on chassis

This 1932 20/25 chassis, GHW17, was originally bodied by Abbott as a Landaulette. In 1937, it was returned to the Abbott works to be fitted with this attractive Drophead Coupé body.(Real Car Company)

20/25 GAU79 was another 1932 chassis, this time bodied by Abbott as a Limousine. Despite the formal lines, the body has a quite rakish air about it.

GKT27 that was delivered to the writer Rudyard Kipling in May that year. Just two months later, the familiar six-light Limousine shape was given an appealingly rakish look in the body for GAU79, and then the final Abbott limousine on 20/25 chassis was delivered a further two months after that, on chassis GZU15.

Abbott built just one Landaulette body on the 20/25, which was for chassis GHW17 in October 1932. Its owner clearly had a change of heart, however, because the car returned to Abbott's in 1937 to be rebodied as a Drophead Coupé. Meanwhile, there had also been a Drophead Coupé for GNC77, which was new in April 1934.

25/30 COACHWORK

Testifying perhaps to Abbott's success with Limousine coachwork on the 20/25 chassis, a Limousine body was ordered for 25/30 chassis GWN33 that was delivered in December 1936. However, this was the last Abbott coachwork on the small-horsepower Rolls-Royce chassis.

ABERDEEN MOTORS
Location unknown – Twenty
Aberdeen Motors is recorded as the builder of a single Saloon body for the Rolls-Royce Twenty chassis, which was mounted on chassis number GA64 in 1923. There is no indication whether Aberdeen Motors was based in Aberdeen itself or not.

ADAMS
Newcastle-on-Tyne – 20/25
Horace Adams (Newcastle) Ltd was a small Newcastle-on-Tyne coachbuilder that was incorporated in 1924 and was active perhaps until the end of the following decade. It is known to have bodied a Bentley in 1925 and a Morris Bullnose some time in the 1920s, and

also built a single body on a Rolls-Royce chassis. This was for 20/25 number GNS20, and was a Saloon completed in 1930. The company is thought to have had some connection to the Newcastle car dealership Adams & Gibbon.

ALBANY
London – Twenty
The Albany Carriage Company built only one known body on the small horsepower Rolls-Royce chassis, and that was a Saloon delivered in 1928 on Twenty number GFN38. The Albany workshops were at that time in the west London district of Hanwell, but by the time of this body the company was entering a period of decline. It had built up a strong reputation for Weymann coachwork, with a contract for the Alvis 12/50 chassis, among others. The cancellation of the Alvis contract at the start of 1928 followed hard on the heels of the death of Albany's managing director, and by 1930 the company had folded.

ALBERT BRIDGE GARAGE
London – Twenty
The Albert Bridge Garage that built two Saloon bodies on Rolls-Royce Twenty chassis in 1924 was very probably the establishment of the same name based in London's Chelsea district that was responsible for a car called the Alberford. This was built between 1922 and 1924 and was based on a modified Ford Model T chassis with the garage's own three-seater body.

The two Twenties known to have had coachwork by this company were GRK14 and GDK54. No pictures are known.

ALL-WEATHER
London – 20/25
All-Weather Motor Bodies Ltd was based at Kilburn in the Paddington area of north-west London and was a subsidiary of TH Gill & Son (qv) that was formed in 1931. The company was sometimes known as Gill All-Weather bodies and remained in business long beyond the 1935 closure of the parent company. It built bodies on the larger Rolls-Royce chassis of the 1930s, as well as three examples for the 20/25.

Despite its name, All-Weather did not only make bodies that conformed to that description. The rather elegant "Empire" All-weather coachwork on Rolls-Royce 20/25 chassis GAU34 in 1932 nevertheless did conform to type. The later two bodies, both built in 1934, did not. The earlier one, on chassis GWE4, was a six-light Landaulette, and the later one, on GSF9, was a Limousine.

ARTHUR MULLINER

Northampton – Twenty, 20/25, 25/30

This coachbuilder was founded as a carriage-maker in Northampton in 1760, and had family links to the other Mulliner companies in Britain. Under Colonel Arthur Felton Mulliner, who took over the business in 1887, it moved from carriage work into motor car body work, and expanded greatly in the first decade of the 20th century. In the 1920s it was particularly associated with Armstrong Siddeley and Vauxhall, and in 1926 won the first ever IBCAM award at Olympia for its Limousine body on a Rolls-Royce 40/50 chassis.

Although the company did not turn away customers who asked for open coachwork, the overwhelming majority of its bodies on the small-horsepower Rolls-Royce chassis were closed types. Limousines predominated. Arthur Mulliner was always known for a high-quality product and for its clean and well-balanced designs, although it was quite capable of flamboyance when working for Indian potentates. Like others, it found business harder to come by in the 1930s, and in 1939 sold out to motor dealers Henleys, who closed down the coachbuilding work.

The company built a total of 229 known bodies for new small-horsepower Rolls-Royce chassis. These can be broken down into 76 bodies for the Rolls-Royce Twenty, 104 for the 20/25, and 49 for the 25/30. Arthur Mulliner did not construct any bodies for the Wraith chassis.

TWENTY COACHWORK

Arthur Mulliner is known to have built the bodies for 76 Rolls-Royce Twenty chassis between 1922 and 1929. There was just one in 1922; 18 followed in 1923, and 11 more in 1924. The following year was less busy, and just five more bodies for the Twenty were delivered. In 1926 there were nine; in 1927 the figure was up to 14; in 1928 there were 10 and in 1929 just eight. By far the largest number of bodies were Limousines of which there were 30 plus a further three Weymann types, followed by Saloons with a total of 22 plus two Weymann types.

Cabriolets

There were just five Cabriolets on Twenty chassis between 1922 and 1928, and these were as follows:

42G3	1922	GUK6	1926	GKM53	1928
78A4	1923	GXL63	1928		

Coupés

Coupé bodies were also a rarity from Arthur Mulliner, and there were just three for the Twenty chassis. These

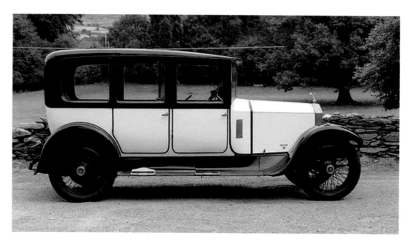

were for GH42 in 1923 and GLK24 in 1924; the third was a Three-quarter Coupé for GNK17 in 1925.

Drophead coupés

Four Drophead Coupé bodies were built in the early years of the Twenty. Three of these (on chassis 72A9, 74A9 and GA41) were of 1923 vintage, and the fourth was for chassis GLK22 in 1924.

Landaulette

There was a single Landaulette body, which was for chassis 73A6 in 1923.

Limousines

Arthur Mulliner built 33 Limousine bodies for the Rolls-Royce Twenty between 1923 and 1929, of which three (all in 1929) were Weymann types. These three were for chassis numbers GLN54, GLN66, and GEN69. The full list of 33 is as follows:

51S3	1923	GYK24	1926	GBM74	1928
61H0	1923	GYK83	1926	GKM3	1928
GA10	1923	GHJ62	1927	GKM51	1928
GA23	1923	GHJ80	1927	GKM59	1928
GH44	1923	GAJ64	1927	GFN5	1928
GMK31	1924	GAJ65	1927	GLN54	1929
GMK81	1924	GRJ33	1927	GLN66	1929
GLK43	1924	GUJ21	1927	GLN87	1929
GSK17	1925	GXL28	1927	GEN69	1929
GSK69	1925	GYL31	1928	GEN71	1929
GUK43	1926	GYL70	1928	GVO1	1929

Saloons

The Saloon bodies for Rolls-Royce Twenty chassis numbered 25 in all, of which one was a two-door type (for GA31 in 1923) and two were Weymann types (for GOK67 and GYK58, both in 1926). It is interesting that there seems to have been a three-year gap in which

Limousine body styles did not change very much for many years, and this one by Arthur Mulliner dates from 1924 and was for Twenty chassis GMK31. (Real Car Company)

Many coachbuilders offered Continental Saloon designs in the early 1930s, and this was the Arthur Mulliner option. Chassis GLZ41 is a 20/25 that dates from 1933. Note the louvred scuttle to make the bonnet look longer, and the moulding on the scuttle – a cross between Art Deco and a Brougham-style door leading edge!
(Real Car Company)

no more Weymann bodies were built for the Twenty until the three Limousines (see above) in 1929; perhaps the company was not happy with the results. The 25 Saloon bodies of all types are listed below, with their dates of construction:

68H7	1923	GRK54	1924	GMJ27	1927
85K7	1923	GPK23	1925	GMJ40	1927
GA31	1923	GPK78	1925	GMJ78	1927
GA47	1923	GOK67	1926	GAJ66	1927
GF56	1923	GZK64	1926	GUJ69	1927
GH57	1923	GUK47	1926	GXL36	1927
GMK26	1924	GYK30	1926	GXL59	1928
GRK32	1924	GYK58	1926	GLN21	1929
GRK40	1924				

Sedanca

Just one Sedanca body was constructed for a Twenty chassis, which was GLN49 in 1929.

Tourers

Arthur Mulliner clearly preferred building closed bodies, and there were few open models such as Tourers on the Twenty chassis. Nevertheless, three examples were built in the early years of the Twenty, when such bodies were more in fashion. These were for chassis GH1 in 1923, and for GMK20 and GMK74 in 1924.

Two-seater

There was a single Two-seater body, which was for chassis GRJ23 in 1927.

20/25 COACHWORK

Arthur Mulliner built 104 bodies for the Rolls-Royce 20/25 chassis between 1929 and 1936. The best years

were 1934 with 26 bodies and 1935 with 29. There were five in 1929, 12 in 1930, four in 1931, 11 in 1932, 13 in 1933, and four in 1936. Half of the 104 bodies were Limousine types, and once again the company showed an obvious preference for building closed bodies.

Tom Clarke (*The Rolls-Royce 20/25hp*) adds three rebodies, of which two were done in the 1950s by the same taxi firm in Stockport, using older Limousine bodies. These were on chassis GHW15 and GWE77. The third was on GFT20.

All-weather

Open coachwork was unusual from Arthur Mulliner, and there was only one example for a Rolls-Royce 2/25. This was an All-weather Tourer for chassis GEX53 in 1933.

Landaulettes

There were four Landaulette bodies. These were for chassis GXO58 in 1929, and for GLG21, GOH29 and GOH45 in 1935.

Limousines

Limousines were an Arthur Mulliner forte, and the company built 52 such bodies for the 20/25 chassis between 1929 and 1936. These are listed, with dates, below. GXO40 may have been the optional 132-inch "long" chassis that was available before that wheelbase became standard: it is recorded as GXO40L. One (GBK39) was used by the coachbuilder's Managing Director, and one was built with a fabric body – a most unusual commission as late as 1935 when such bodies had been out of fashion for several years.

GXO40	1929	GAW15	1933	GAE1	1934
GGP31	1929	GDX18	1933	GFE22	1934
GDP45	1930	GLZ29	1933	GAF37	1934
GLR15	1930	GTZ71	1933	GAF67	1934
GSR15	1930	GGA56	1933	GPG76	1935
GSR72	1930	GHA35	1933	GYH80	1935
GNS48	1930	GXB24	1934	GBJ4	1935
GOS48	1931	GXB64	1934	GBJ42	1935
GFT42	1931	GUB8	1934	GLJ48	1935
GFT56	1931	GUB51	1934	GLJ67	1935
GFT73	1931	GUB78	1934	GCJ6	1935
GBT41	1932	GNC2	1934	GXK9	1935
GBT70	1932	GNC30	1934	GXK21	1935
GAU26	1932	GNC49	1934	GXK55	1935
GAU72	1932	GRC42	1934	GXK62	1935
GMU22	1932	GMD42	1934	GBK39	1936
GMU64	1932	GYD48	1934	GBK51	1936
GRW66	1932				

Saloons

Saloons were the second most numerous type of body that Arthur Mulliner built for the 20/25 chassis, and there were 43 in all. The best years were 1934, when 10 were built, and 1935, when 12 were built. There were none in 1931. Totals for the other years were two in 1929 and seven in 1930; four in 1932 and six in 1933; and two in 1936.

There were both six-light and four-light designs, and between 1932 and 1936 these included 18 Continental Saloons, a four-light design that was fashionable at the time. Park Ward (who had pioneered the style) and Freestone & Webb were among other companies who offered similar designs called Continental types.

The Continental Saloon was in fact the most numerous of the four-light designs, and the 18 examples were built for the chassis listed below. The body on GHG18 had a Division.

GMU71	1932	GUB10	1934	GAF53	1934
GMU78	1932	GRC19	1934	GLG73	1935
GLZ41	1933	GRC62	1934	GHG18	1935
GYZ11	1933	GED59	1934	GOH23	1935
GGA10	1933	GFE37	1934	GEH19	1935
GGA76	1933	GAF33	1934	GBK45	1936

Eleven more four-light Saloon bodies were built for the 20/25, and three (GSY43, GRF10 and GHG39) had Divisions. Some shared a common design (such as GXO79 and GDP22), and there was just one that was described as a Sportsman's Saloon. This was on chassis GBK18 in 1935, and it came with a fashionable swept-tail design and attractive Art Deco mouldings on the doors that allowed a two-tone finish. The 11 four-light Saloons were on the following chassis:

GXO79	1929	GSY43	1933	GYH55	1935
GDP22	1930	GFE3	1934	GBK18	1935
GSR74	1930	GRF10	1935	GTK26	1936
GAU17	1932	GHG39	1935		

The 14 remaining Saloons were six-light designs, and one of them (for chassis GAF4) may have had a Division. The list is as follows:

GGP49	1929	GTR2	1930	GPG16	1935
GDP38	1930	GAU5	1932	GEH31	1935
GDP39	1930	GWX4	1933	GLJ39	1935
GDP53	1930	GUB20	1934	GXK43	1935
GWP17	1930	GAF4	1934		

Saloon Coupés

Arthur Mulliner built either one or two Saloon Coupé bodies for the 20/25 chassis. Such bodies were certainly fitted to two chassis from new, but it may be that there was actually only one that was transferred from GMD25 (built in 1934) to GRF34 (built in 1935).

Sedanca de Ville

The Sedanca de Ville was not a common Arthur Mulliner style, and only one example was built for a 20/25 chassis. This was GLJ21, which was new in 1935.

Tourer

Tourers were also not normally an Arthur Mulliner style, but the company responded to an order for one, which was a four-door type that was built for chassis GCJ35 in 1935.

25/30 COACHWORK

Of the 49 bodies commissioned from Arthur Mulliner for new 25/30 chassis, 24 were completed in 1936, 22 in 1937, and just three in 1938. The coachbuilder's reputation for Limousine bodies remained intact, and these accounted for more than half (27) of its bodies for the 25/30. Saloons of various types were the next most commonly ordered variety, and there were De Ville types and Landaulettes in penny numbers, plus a single Fixed-head Coupé.

De Ville types

Arthur Mulliner built four De Ville bodies for the 25/30 chassis. Two were Limousine de Ville types, built in 1936 on chassis GTL60 and GWN48. The other two were Sedanca de Ville bodies, both built in 1937 on chassis GRP12 and GAR24.

Fixed-head Coupé

The single Fixed-head Coupé was both neat and discreet, as could be expected of Arthur Mulliner. It was for chassis GUL40 in 1936.

This six-light Saloon body was built in 1936 on a late 20/25 chassis, GXK43. The shape of the rear side window gives the body some welcome character. (Real Car Company)

Arthur Mulliner's only Coupé body for the 25/30 chassis was this one in 1936, on GUL40. The contrasting colour for wings and upper panels adds a lighter touch to an otherwise solid-looking body.

Landaulettes
Both Landaulette bodies were built in 1936, and were for chassis GRM10 and GWN26.

Limousines
Of the 26 Limousine bodies on the 25/30 chassis, 13 dated from 1936, 12 from 1937, and just one from 1938. In addition, there was a single Touring Limousine, a four-light type built in 1937 on chassis GLP19. The full list of 27 is as follows:

Limousine bodies were an Arthur Mulliner speciality, and this one for 25/30 chassis GRO56 dates from 1937. The colours seen here probably reflect a more modern taste than the one current when the car was new. (Real Car Company)

GTL12	1936	GAN39	1936	GHO21	1937
GHL22	1936	GAN57	1936	GHO54	1937
GHL38	1936	GAN72	1936	GRP11	1937
GRM45	1936	GWN66	1936	GRP30	1937
GRM63	1936	GUN14	1937	GRP46	1937
GRM78	1936	GUN30	1937	GMP71	1937
GXM50	1936	GRO7	1937	GLP3	1937
GGM11	1936	GRO56	1937	GLP19	1937
GGM40	1936	GRO71	1937	GZR11	1938

Saloons
Of the 15 Saloon bodies for the 25/30 chassis, six were built in 1936, seven in 1937, and two in 1938. Most were six-light (or otherwise unspecified) types, of which three had Divisions, and there were six Sports Saloons. They are listed in more detail below; the first table shows the six-light types, and the three with Divisions are marked with an asterisk (*).

GUL51	1936	GGM30	1936	GLP36	1937
GXM21*	1936	GAN27	1936	GAR8	1937
GXM37	1936	GMP43*	1937	GGR19*	1938

The six Sports Saloons were:

GTL46	1936	GMP31	1937	GAR59	1937
GHO59	1937	GAR21	1937	GZR41	1938

ATCHERLEY
Birmingham – Twenty, 20/25, 25/30
WC & RC Atcherley was a small Birmingham coachbuilder that was established in 1920 by two brothers. Clive Atcherley had previously worked at Mulliners of Birmingham. Nick Walker speculates that their coachwork activity may have been accompanied by some commercial vehicle bodybuilding.

Brother Clifford left the company in 1930, but Clive continued in business and in 1935 picked up the contract to build bodies for the Brough Superior. The company remained active when war broke out in 1939 but was absorbed by the Birmingham Ford dealership Bristol Street Motors Ltd in 1946.

Four Rolls-Royce Twenty chassis are known to have received Atcherley coachwork between 1923 and 1928. There was just one body for the 20/25 chassis, in 1934, and one more on the 25/30 in 1936. After that the only known bodies on Rolls-Royce were two Limousines on Phantom III chassis (one of which was rebodied after the war by Freestone & Webb as the flamboyant "Copper Kettle" Sedanca for John Gaul).

TWENTY COACHWORK
Atcherley's bodied one Twenty chassis in 1923, two in 1927 and one in 1928. All were Saloons except the 1923 body, and it is likely that all were bespoke designs.

The exception in 1923 was a Cabriolet, on chassis 86 K0. The two 1927 Saloons were on GAJ10 and GUJ6, the latter body being described (by John Fasal) as a Weymann type. The third Saloon body was on chassis GYL74 in 1928.

20/25 COACHWORK

The only Atcherley body on the 20/25 model was on chassis GMD75 and was delivered in July 1934. It was a two-door Sports Saloon with a rather pert rear end design.

25/30 COACHWORK

The last coachwork by Atcherley's on a small horsepower Rolls-Royce was a Saloon on 25/30 chassis GAN19 that was delivered in November 1936.

BAMBER
Southport – Twenty

The Bambers recorded as the builder of the Saloon coachwork for Twenty chassis GDK50 in 1924 was probably the same R Bamber who bodied two Bentley 3-litre chassis at around the same time. The company later became a major car dealership in northern England.

BARKER
London – Twenty, 20/25, 25/30

Barker began coachbuilding for the small-horsepower Rolls-Royce models in 1922 with a distinct advantage: in 1905, CS Rolls & Co had declared the company their preferred supplier of coachwork. It certainly had an impressive pedigree, and could trace its origins back to 1710 when it was established in London by a former Guards officer. Royal commissions followed.

By the start of the 1920s, Barker had become the leading coachbuilder for Rolls-Royce chassis, although of course the company also built on other quality makes. In the 1930s Barker advertisements included the description, "acknowledged the world's best". Barker coachwork was expensive and prestigious, and although the company turned its hand to many different types over the years, its reputation was for the rather grand and formal coachwork that it did best. The company was also skilled at making maximum use of a relatively small number of designs, using minor variations to make essentially similar bodies look quite different from one another at first sight.

Barker also patented a double-dipping headlamp system that was used on some of its bodies (and was sold for others to build under licence), and developed its own wheel discs to cover wire wheels and ease cleaning; these were distinguished by a hinged flap that gave access to the tyre valve.

However, despite its enviable reputation, Barker was not in the best of financial health during the 1930s. By 1938 things came to a head, and the receiver was called in. The company was bought by Hooper, and a small number of the final "Barker" bodies were actually built at the new Hooper works in Park Royal, west London.

Barker was one of the most prolific coachbuilders on the small-horsepower Rolls-Royce chassis, for which the company built well over 900 bodies. There were 444 on Twenty chassis, 372 on the 20/25, and 125 on the 25/30, the declining quantities being symptomatic of the coachbuilder's own decline during the interwar period. Barker did not build any coachwork for the Wraith chassis.

TWENTY COACHWORK

Barker's best year for Twenty coachwork was 1923, when the chassis was still new and fashionable, and in that year the company delivered 121 bodies. Orders settled down after that, but were strong throughout the decade. The lowest annual totals were in 1922 (12 bodies) and 1929 (19 bodies), which were both partial years for sales of the Twenty. For other years, the figures were: 1924 (75), 1925 (44), 1926 (61), 1927 (57) and 1928 (54).

All-weather

There was only ever one All-weather body from Barker on the Rolls-Royce Twenty chassis, and that was built in 1923 for chassis GA43.

Broughams

Brougham coachwork was not particularly in demand, but Barker completed a total of six examples between 1923 and 1928. These were on the following chassis:

| 51S0 | 1923 | GDK14 | 1924 | GYL82 | 1928 |
| GMK47 | 1924 | GHJ24 | 1927 | GBM55 | 1928 |

Cabriolets

Cabriolet coachwork was a popular choice, and Barker supplied no fewer than 98 bodies of this type on Rolls-Royce Twenty chassis, making it their most numerous type. There were three in 1922, 24 in 1923,

The most popular type of coachwork from Barker on the Twenty chassis was the Cabriolet. This example is on chassis GHJ79, and is one of 14 delivered in 1927. It went to an American owner, and the whitewall tyres seen here reflect the way it probably looked when new. (Real Car Company)

20 in 1924, 12 in 1925, 16 in 1926, 14 in 1927, and nine in 1928. One of the 1925 bodies was for a development car, 10-G-III, and was later transferred to another development car, 17-G-IV (which is not listed separately here). The full list of chassis, with dates, was as follows:

44G4	1922	GMK22	1924	GUK49	1926
44G5	1922	GMK33	1924	GUK61	1926
45G2	1922	GMK51	1924	GUK64	1926
50S2	1923	GMK60	1924	GUK69	1926
56S5	1923	GMK73	1924	GYK3	1926
57S6	1923	GRK8	1924	GYK35	1926
62H5	1923	GRK11	1924	GYK85	1926
65H4	1923	GRK15	1924	GMJ21	1926
65H6	1923	GRK46	1924	GMJ62	1926
65H9	1923	GRK47	1924	GHJ34	1927
68H6	1923	GRK81	1924	GHJ39	1927
71A5	1923	GRK82	1924	GHJ74	1927
71A6	1923	GDK34	1924	GHJ79	1927
75A7	1923	GLK64	1924	GAJ34	1927
78A2	1923	10-G-III	1925	GAJ56	1927
78A7	1923	GNK52	1925	GAJ72	1927
79A9	1923	GPK27	1925	GRJ26	1927
82K6	1923	GPK32	1925	GRJ68	1927
85K5	1923	GSK3	1925	GRJ73	1927
87K8	1923	GSK29	1925	GUJ39	1927
GA14	1923	GSK50	1925	GXL31	1927
GA71	1923	GSK64	1925	GXL40	1927
GF31	1923	GCK37	1925	GXL62	1927
GF53	1923	GCK39	1925	GYL10	1928
GF71	1923	GCK72	1925	GWL15	1928
GH21	1923	GCK74	1925	GWL30	1928
GH38	1923	GOK20	1926	GBM23	1928
GAK27	1924	GOK41	1926	GBM39	1928
GAK43	1924	GZK29	1926	GBM53	1928
GAK59	1924	GZK35	1926	GKM22	1928
GAK74	1924	GZK36	1926	GFN35	1928
GMK11	1924	GZK53	1926	GFN59	1928
GMK14	1924	GUK12	1926		

Drophead Coupés were quite numerous on the Twenty chassis. This one, also described as a Doctor's Coupé, was for chassis GLK9 in 1924 and incorporated a dickey seat. (Real Car Company)

Coupés

The Coupé was another relatively uncommon body style from Barker on the Twenty chassis. There were 11 examples in all, of which just one (for GCK41 in 1925) was a three-quarters type. The list was:

51S8	1923	GDK47	1924	GAJ2	1927
GH47	1923	GNK58	1925	GKM8	1928
GMK32	1924	GCK1	1925	GEN33	1929
GRK69	1924	GCK41	1925		

Drophead Coupés

Drophead Coupé bodies attracted nearly three times as many customers as fixed-head types, with a total of 32. Several of these were three-quarters types, and these are marked with an asterisk (*) in the table below.

80K4	1923	GDK20	1924	GHJ22	1927
89K1*	1923	GLK9	1924	GHJ36	1927
GA33*	1923	GLK23	1924	GRJ69*	1927
GAK15	1924	GSK33	1925	GUJ8	1927
GAK52	1924	GSK56	1925	GUJ53	1927
GAK58	1924	GOK14	1926	GXL2	1927
GMK10	1924	GZK39*	1926	GXL10*	1927
GMK25	1924	GUK33	1926	GXL14	1927
GMK48*	1924	GUK77	1926	GTM40	1928
GMK76	1924	GYK11	1926	GEN80	1929
GDK9	1924	GMJ68	1926		

Landaulettes

Barker did brisk business in Landaulette bodies for the Twenty, although their popularity did decline a little as time went on. Eighty chassis had such coachwork, although there were actually only 79 bodies because the one on development car 11-G-III in 1925 was transferred from 1923 chassis GF68. Just one body, for 43G3 in 1922, was described as an open-drive type. The full list, with dates, was as follows:

41G3	1922	70H0	1923	GF35	1923
43G1	1922	71A1	1923	GF40	1923
43G3	1922	74A4	1923	GF68	1923
47G4	1923	75A4	1923	GH24	1923
48G3	1923	76A4	1923	GH73	1923
53S0	1923	83K0	1923	GAK42	1924
53S6	1923	83K9	1923	GMK19	1924
55S7	1923	84K0	1923	GMK34	1924
55S9	1923	84K6	1923	GMK80	1924
58S9	1923	86K4	1923	GRK1	1924
60H4	1923	89K9	1923	GRK56	1924
64H3	1923	GA9	1923	GRK80	1924
66H0	1923	GF18	1923	GDK4	1924
67H5	1923	GF20	1923	GDK18	1924

GDK26	1924	GZK14	1926	GYL52	1928
GDK35	1924	GZK31	1926	GYL57	1928
11-G-III	1925	GZK57	1926	GWL29	1928
GNK19	1925	GUK51	1926	GWL41	1928
GNK39	1925	GUK54	1926	GBM36	1928
GPK77	1925	GMJ4	1926	GBM40	1928
GSK12	1925	GHJ14	1927	GKM27	1928
GSK35	1925	GHJ65	1927	GKM38	1928
GCK47	1925	GAJ41	1927	GFN33	1928
GCK52	1925	GAJ79	1927	GFN36	1928
GCK80	1925	GRJ32	1927	GEN1	1929
GOK48	1926	GUJ1	1927	GEN48	1929
GZK3	1926	GUJ11	1927		

Limousines

No fewer than 87 customers came to Barker to order Limousine coachwork for a Twenty chassis, and demand was fairly consistent in each year between 1922 and 1929. The full list of 87 chassis, with dates, is as follows:

40G3	1922	GLK28	1924	GXL65	1927
40G7	1922	GLK44	1924	GXL71	1927
47G1	1923	GLK76	1924	GXL77	1927
48G7	1923	GNK48	1925	GXL81	1927
53S4	1923	GPK36	1925	GYL29	1928
61H2	1923	GPK47	1925	GWL10	1928
62H9	1923	GPK68	1925	GWL12	1928
67H7	1923	GOK61	1925	GWL26	1928
71A7	1923	GOK80	1926	GWL27	1928
84K7	1923	GZK2	1926	GBM9	1928
88K6	1923	GZK30	1926	GBM24	1928
GA78	1923	GUK14	1926	GBM47	1928
GF16	1923	GYK17	1926	GBM62	1928
GF58	1923	GYK29	1926	GKM26	1928
GH12	1923	GYK79	1926	GKM33	1928
GH25	1923	GMJ16	1926	GKM41	1928
GH29	1923	GMJ48	1926	GKM60	1928
GH31	1923	GMJ60	1926	GKM81	1928
GH33	1923	GAJ21	1927	GTM8	1928
GAK5	1923	GAJ38	1927	GTM36	1928
GAK57	1924	GAJ53	1927	GFN2	1928
GAK77	1924	GAJ58	1927	GFN48	1928
GMK71	1924	GRJ63	1927	GFN70	1928
GMK79	1924	GRJ67	1927	GEN52	1929
GRK21	1924	GUJ65	1927	GEN63	1929
GRK29	1924	GXL3	1927	GVO30	1929
GRK33	1924	GXL9	1927	GVO43	1929
GDK36	1924	GXL35	1927	GVO57	1929
GDK69	1924	GXL45	1927	GVO74	1929

Salamancas

The Salamanca was a fairly rare style from Barker, and only five examples were built between 1924 and 1929.

Only one (on GEN3) was for a British customer; GMK36 was for a customer in the USA, and the other three all went to Argentina. The full list, with dates, was:

GMK36	1924	GCK4	1925	GEN3	1929
GNK80	1925	GUK57	1926		

Saloons

Barker Saloon coachwork became more popular for the Twenty chassis as the years went by, but there were only 19 examples in all. The chassis and dates were as follows:

81K4	1923	GYK21	1926	GUJ20	1927
88K7	1923	GYK27	1926	GYL4	1928
GA45	1923	GYK52	1926	GYL41	1928
GRK28	1924	GYK82	1926	GBM44	1928
GNK38	1925	GMJ35	1926	GKM62	1928
GCK81	1925	GHJ56	1927	GLN6	1929
GOK76	1925				

Sedancas

Sedanca coachwork was quite rare, but became more popular later in the decade. Barker built 16 examples in all:

GSK46	1925	GYL7	1928	GLN9	1929
GZK17	1926	GBM17	1928	GEN28	1929
GYK7	1926	GFN3	1928	GEN64	1929
GYK49	1926	GFN78	1928	GVO41	1929
GMJ75	1926	GLN3	1929	GVO80	1929
GAJ7	1927				

Tourers

Tourer coachwork was consistently popular, although orders slowed down as the type became less fashionable generally. Barker built 87 examples for the Twenty chassis between 1922 and 1929. They were:

40G9	1922	72A6	1923	GNK72	1925
41G6	1922	77A1	1923	GPK1	1925
42G0	1922	77A9	1923	GPK6	1925
42G2	1922	81K2	1923	GPK20	1925
46G9	1923	82K1	1923	GPK71	1925
47G6	1923	85K0	1923	GSK80	1925
47G8	1923	85K3	1923	GCK46	1925
48G2	1923	86K1	1923	GOK2	1926
49G4	1923	GA8	1923	GOK27	1926
49G5	1923	GF22	1923	GOK37	1926
49G8	1923	GF48	1923	GZK10	1926
52S8	1923	GH10	1923	GZK12	1926
54S1	1923	GH68	1923	GUK67	1926
54S4	1923	GH70	1923	GUK74	1926
54S9	1923	GAK39	1924	GYK64	1926
55S5	1923	GAK40	1924	GMJ77	1926
58S5	1923	GAK60	1924	GHJ15	1927
58S7	1923	GMK5	1924	GHJ81	1927
59S7	1923	GMK52	1924	GAJ8	1927
61H4	1923	GMK53	1924	GAJ19	1927
62H7	1923	GMK65	1924	GAJ52	1927
63H0	1923	GRK19	1924	GRJ1	1927
64H9	1923	GDK21	1924	GUJ45	1927
65H0	1923	GDK46	1924	GXL57	1927
65H5	1923	GDK78	1924	GYL5	1928
66H3	1923	GLK1	1924	GYL55	1928
66H9	1923	GLK21	1924	GWL2	1928
68H2	1923	GLK56	1924	GBM25	1928
72A2	1923	GNK71	1925	GEN16	1929

Two-seaters

Two-seater bodies were somehow too frivolous for a company like Barker, but the company obviously responded when two customers placed orders. The bodies were built for chassis GPK8 in 1925 and for GOK3 in 1926.

20/25 COACHWORK

Barker coachwork was mounted on 372 examples of the 20/25 chassis, including two of the experimental prototypes in 1928-1929. One of these (16-G-IV) was later renumbered as a production chassis. The earlier one (12-G-IV) was the only one to be fitted with a Barker body in 1928.

There were then 15 in 1929, 41 in 1930, but just 21 in 1931, which was the worst year for most coachbuilders. Numbers rose again to 31 in 1932 (including the renumbered prototype), 61 in 1933, and 96 in 1934. There were subsequently 86 in 1935, 20 in 1936 and one late delivery in 1937.

Just two Saloon Coupé bodies came from Barker for the 20/25 chassis, this one on GYH35 in 1935. The superb proportions once again show Barker's mastery of line, while the scallop behind the door is typical of mid-1930s designs. (Real Car Company)

Cabriolets

Coachwork described as a Cabriolet type was built for only three 20/25 chassis, and the Drophead Coupé took over as the popular style after 1930. The three Cabriolet bodies, all built in 1930, were for GWP27 (which was described as a Torpedo Cabriolet), for GSR36, and for GTR28, which had a four-light design.

Coupés

There were 16 Coupés of various sorts on the 20/25 chassis, some described as Fixed-head Coupés. Two of the bodies listed here (for GLG25 and GYH35 in 1935) were strictly Saloon Coupé types. The body on experimental prototype 12-G-V in 1928 was a two-light design that incorporated the Weymann construction principles.

12-G-V	1928	GDX31	1933	GMD30	1934
GDP51	1930	GLZ63	1933	GAF18	1934
GSR5	1930	GBA36	1933	GSF20	1934
GSR9	1930	GBA81	1933	GLG25	1935
GAU70	1932	GXB17	1933	GYH35	1935
GRW72	1933				

De Ville types

De Ville types were popular right through the production life of the 20/25 chassis, and Barker built exactly 100 in all. There were three of these in 1929, 11 in 1930, and nine in 1931. The calendar years 1932 and 1933 brought 16 De Ville bodies each, and totals bounced back to 25 for 1934. Thereafter numbers declined, to 16 in 1935 and four in 1936.

Barker used a variety of descriptions for some of these bodies, but the lists and tables below group them into similar types for convenience. By far the most popular style was the Sedanca de Ville.

a) All-weather de Ville

Just one body was built as an All-weather de Ville, a rather interesting description for a body that had something of the four-door Tourer about it. This was built in 1932 for chassis GBT57.

b) Cabriolets de Ville

Barker put their name to four Cabriolet de Ville bodies for the 20/25 chassis. These were for GWP28 and GLR48 in 1930, GKT16 in 1932, and GOH64 in 1935. As Tom Clarke has pointed out, the general lines of the body on GOH64 were similar to those of the All-weather de Ville for GBT57 (see above).

c) Coupés de Ville

Grouped together here under the generic title of Coupés de Ville are nine bodies that Barker variously described as Fixed-head Sedanca Coupés, Three-position Sedanca Coupés, and Faux Cabriolets de Ville. They were:

GTZ48	1933	GLB11	1934	GAF21	1934
GXB4	1933	GNC65	1934	GHG27	1935
GUB28	1934	GYD35	1934	GLJ9	1935

d) Limousines de Ville

Eight bodies were described as Limousine de Ville types, and of these, two came with the additional description of Pullman; these were for GMD14 and GFE10 in 1934. The seven were as follows:

GGP72	1929	GMD14	1934	GOH7	1935
GLR32	1930	GYD57	1934	GTK8	1936
GYZ35	1933	GFE10	1934		

e) Saloon de Ville

Just one Saloon de Ville body was built, for chassis GRW73 in 1932.

f) Sedancas de Ville

The most popular of the Barker de Ville types was the Sedanca de Ville. There were 77 bodies that carried this description or that of Sedancalette – of which there were just three. Even these were not all the same: GDX7 in 1933 had a simple Sedancalette body, but later that year GHA9 was specifically described as a four-light type, and GNC26 in 1934 had a six-light body.

Barker produced some most elegant Sedanca de Ville designs, and this one is seen on a 1931 20/25, GNS60. The deep rear quarters allowed the occupants to retain their privacy when travelling in town. (Simon Clay)

GNS60 has spent some time in the USA, and in this picture retains a US registration plate as well as its British original. The overall proportions here help to show why Barker coachwork was so highly regarded. (Simon Clay)

The front window of the closed compartment could be lowered to provide cooling air when weather conditions were right. (Simon Clay)

The chauffeur's compartment was neatly finished, although not particularly spacious. Hard-wearing leather was used for the upholstery. (Simon Clay)

Winding windows for the chauffeur's compartment included this split one in the driver's door that allowed hand signalling. (Simon Clay)

In this case, the rear compartment was fitted with folding occasional seats – which still left plenty of legroom for the rear-seat occupants when deployed. The upholstery was in soft cloth. (Simon Clay)

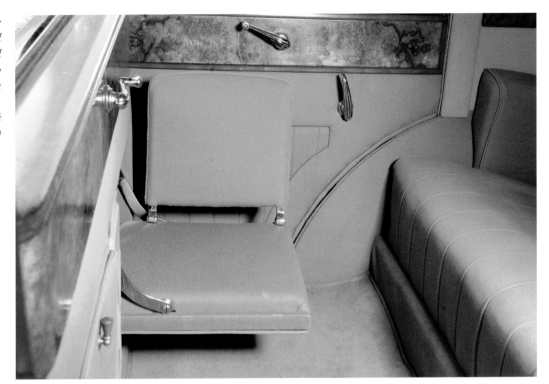

With the occasional seats folded away, the space in the back was generous. Note also the hanging strap to aid entry and exit, and the neat companion set into the rear quarter-panel. (Simon Clay)

The Barker sill plate was both neat and discreet. (Simon Clay)

Top-quality woodwork and the fittings for an opening windscreen are clear on the Sedanca de Ville coachwork for GNS60. (Simon Clay)

Barker developed their own headlamp dipping mechanism, and an example was fitted to GNS60. (Simon Clay)

Drophead Coupés

Barker constructed five bodies described as Drophead Coupés for the Rolls-Royce 20/25 chassis. The earliest of these was built in 1929 on experimental prototype chassis 16-G-IV, which was used by Royce himself for a time and was then renumbered in the production series as GBT82 and sold on. For that reason, there are six entries in the table below. Three bodies (for GWP8, GNS32 and GBT66) had dickey seats.

GGP18	1929	GMU12	1932	GNC63	1934
GGP40	1929	GMU17	1932	GRC37	1934
GDP72	1930	GMU33	1932	GKC17	1934
GWP11	1930	GMU72	1932	GKC37	1934
GLR35	1930	GHW66	1932	GMD63	1934
GSR37	1930	GAW1	1932	GAE70	1934
GSR40	1930	GWX42	1933	GWE9	1934
GSR78	1930	GWX56	1933	GFE23	1934
GTR15	1930	GDX7	1933	GSF15	1934
GNS28	1930	GSY21	1933	GSF38	1934
GNS30	1931	GSY75	1933	GSF67	1935
GNS60	1931	GLZ5	1933	GRF15	1935
GNS67	1931	GLZ17	1933	GLG71	1935
GNS72	1931	GTZ37	1933	GHG12	1935
GOS6	1931	GYZ16	1933	GHG41	1935
GPS4	1931	GBA2	1933	GOH37	1935
GPS17	1931	GBA76	1933	GOH71	1935
GFT7	1931	GGA63	1933	GBJ80	1935
GFT58	1931	GHA9	1933	GLJ22	1935
GBT31	1932	GXB62	1934	GLJ75	1935
GBT43	1932	GXB77	1934	GXK7	1935
GBT61	1932	GUB54	1934	GXK34	1935
GBT81	1932	GUB81	1934	GXK70	1936
GKT15	1932	GLB14	1934	GBK36	1936
GAU18	1932	GLB22	1934	GTK42	1936
GMU6	1932	GNC26	1934		

16-G-IV	1929	GLR25	1930	GBT66	1932
GWP8	1930	GNS32	1930	GBT82	1932

Landaulettes

Barker met orders for 29 Landaulette bodies on the 20/25 chassis, the best year being 1934 when seven were built. Some of these bodies were described as Pullman types, which presumably indicated a higher level of interior luxury than was used for the standard types. The bodies were mounted on the following chassis:

GXO51	1929	GZU11	1932	GKC40	1934
GXO90	1929	GWX24	1933	GED48	1934
GDP79	1930	GDX16	1933	GAF41	1934
GLR17	1930	GLZ78	1933	GSF70	1935
GLR36	1930	GYZ12	1933	GRF14	1935
GLR75	1930	GGA27	1933	GPG3	1935
GSR77	1930	GUB69	1934	GPG74	1935
GNS45	1931	GUB71	1934	GLJ1	1935
GOS3	1931	GNC4	1934	GTK11	1936
GFT17	1931	GRC80	1934		

Limousines

Barker was very much favoured as a builder of Limousine bodies for the Rolls-Royce 20/25 chassis, and the company put its name to no fewer than 113 examples. Two examples from 1929 had fabric panelling (GGP71, and GDP7, the latter having the company's own Barkerlite construction), but all the others appear to have been conventionally coachbuilt. One body (for GBJ68 in 1935) was a Brougham Limousine, and several were described as Pullman types, presumably to indicate an especially high level of interior luxury. The full list is as follows:

GXO18	1929	GBA55	1933	GAE76	1934
GXO30	1929	GBA62	1933	GWE5	1934
GXO44	1929	GBA63	1933	GWE41	1934
GXO74	1929	GBA80	1933	GWE48	1934
GXO103	1930	GGA12	1933	GWE55	1934
GGP9	1929	GGA49	1933	GWE57	1934
GGP71	1929	GGA53	1933	GWE68	1934
GDP7	1929	GXB22	1934	GAF8	1934
GDP15	1930	GUB11	1934	GAF14	1934
GDP50	1930	GLB12	1934	GAF22	1934
GDP76	1930	GLB38	1934	GAF63	1934
GLR70	1930	GNC8	1934	GSF10	1934
GSR55	1930	GNC10	1934	GSF55	1935
GNS34	1930	GNC26	1934	GRF41	1935
GOS33	1931	GNC45	1934	GLG39	1935
GPS19	1931	GNC53	1934	GLG55	1935
GPS25	1931	GRC54	1934	GLG79	1935
GPS32	1931	GRC58	1934	GPG5	1935
GFT12	1931	GRC70	1934	GPG21	1935
GBT6	1931	GRC78	1934	GPG36	1935
GBT20	1932	GKC12	1934	GPG51	1935
GBT42	1932	GKC25	1934	GYH69	1935
GKT32	1932	GED3	1934	GOH20	1935
GAU43	1932	GED42	1934	GBJ43	1935
GZU22	1932	GED53	1934	GBJ68	1935
GHW3	1932	GED61	1934	GLJ34	1935
GAW17	1933	GMD1	1934	GLJ43	1935
GAW32	1933	GMD70	1934	GLJ53	1935
GWX65	1933	GYD7	1934	GLJ56	935
GSY89	1933	GYD18	1934	GLJ69	1935
GSY97	1933	GYD25	1934	GCJ2	1935
GLZ25	1933	GYD27	1934	GXK46	1935
GLZ37	1933	GYD46	1934	GBK23	1936
GLZ48	1933	GYD64	1934	GBK48	1936
GTZ76	1933	GAE14	1934	GBK70	1936
GYZ28	1933	GAE25	1934	GTK36	1936
GBA41	1933	GAE35	1934	GTK60	1937
GBA48	1933	GAE51	1934		

Saloons

Barker Saloon bodies were strong sellers on the 20/25 chassis, and the company built 101, of several different types. There were both four-light and six-light designs, and 32 (just under a third) are known or thought to have been fitted with a Division when new. These are distinguished in the table below by an asterisk (*).

Some of these bodies deserve comment. There was just one fabric-panelled type built to the Barkerlite patents in 1930, on chassis GXO99. There was also a single swept-tail Saloon, for GFT2 in 1931, responding to a short-lived fashion. Two bodies incorporated Tickford-patent folding heads in 1930, and these were for GLR29 and GLR31. There were also eight Barker Sunshine Saloons, which had a very large opening panel in the roof. These were on GNS78 and GNS80 in 1931, GSY50 in 1933, GSF63 in 1934, GLJ2, GCJ22 and GCJ25 in 1935, and GBK72 in 1936.

GXO99*	1930	GRC21*	1934	GEH33	1935
GDP14	1930	GRC53*	1934	GBJ10	1935
GLR29	1930	GED22	1934	GBJ17	1935
GLR31	1930	GED 29*	1934	GBJ34	1935
GSR6	1930	GED32*	1934	GBJ65	1935
GSR27	1930	GED39*	1934	GLJ2	1935
GSR44*	1930	GED49	1934	GLJ6	1935
GTR9	1930	GMD77*	1934	GLJ15*	1935
GNS78	1931	GYD67	1934	GLJ24*	1935
GNS80	1931	GAE67	1934	GLJ32	1935
GFT2	1931	GAE81*	1934	GLJ44	1935
GBT68	1932	GFE40*	1934	GLJ60	1935
GMU45*	1932	GAF63	1934	GLJ70*	1935
GMU52*	1932	GSF22	1934	GLJ71	1935
GMU80	1932	GSF29	1934	GCJ12	1935
GEX29	1933	GRF2*?	1935	GCJ17*	1935
GEX41	1933	GRF30	1935	GCJ22	1935
GEX42	1933	GLG75*?	1935	GCJ25	1935
GEX56*	1933	GPG4*	1935	GCJ31*	1935
GEX72	1933	GPG8*	1935	GCJ34*	1935
GDX34*	1933	GPG49	1935	GXK15	1935
GSY50	1933	GPG65	1935	GXK31	1935
GLZ74*	1933	GPG66	1935	GXK58*	1936
GTZ26*	1933	GPG71	1935	GXK67*	1936
GGA4	1933	GHG16	1935	GBK61	1936
GGA44	1933	GYH12	1935	GBK66	1936
GGA75	1933	GYH18	1935	GBK67	1936
GHA20	1933	GYH27	1935	GBK72	1936
GXB7	1933	GYH36	1935	GTK5*	1936
GXB25*	1933	GYH52	1935	GTK10	1936
GUB38	1934	GOH1	1935	GTK17	1936
GUB48	1934	GOH27	1935	GTK24	1936
GLB26	1934	GOH32	1935	GTK33*	1936
GRC6*	1934	GOH54	1935		

Tourers

Tourers were rapidly going out of fashion by the time of the 20/25 chassis, and Barker built only five examples for it. Most of these were in the early years of the model. There were Tourer bodies for GXO35 and GXO87 in 1929, and for GSR17 in 1930. The two later bodies were an All-weather Tourer for GBT46 in 1932 and a Torpedo Tourer for GSF75 in 1935, the latter name suggesting that the body drew on French designs.

25/30 COACHWORK

Barker built 125 bodies for the Rolls-Royce 25/30 chassis. There were 62 in 1936, 50 in 1937, and 13 in 1938, which was the company's last year as an independent coachbuilder.

Cabriolet

Cabriolet bodies were rare by the time of the 25/30 models, and just one was ordered from Barker. This was for chassis GMP46 and was delivered in 1937.

De Ville types

De Ville bodies were gradually going out of fashion, but Barker built no fewer than 17 of various types for the 25/30 chassis. Of these, 10 were Sedancas de Ville; three were described as Sedanca Coupés; three were Limousines de Ville; and there was a solitary Brougham de Ville.

The Brougham de Ville was for chassis GTL23 in 1936, and although originally ordered by an Englishman was delivered to a South American diplomat in Paris. The three Limousines de Ville were for chassis GRM54 in 1936 and for GLP32 and GAR27 in 1937. The Sedancas de Ville are shown in the table below; the three described as Sedanca Coupés are marked with an asterisk (*).

GUL41	1936	GRM75	1936	GRO43	1937
GUL43*	1936	GGM8	1936	GHO14	1937
GUL70	1936	GWN2*	1936	GMP30	1937
GTL7	1936	GWN25*	1936	GLP24	1937
GHL11	1936				

Landaulettes

Landaulettes were another of the formal styles that were gradually falling from popularity, and Barker built only five of them on the 25/30 chassis. One, on chassis GTL24 in 1936, was described as a Saloon Landaulette. The others were for chassis GXM15 and GAN60 in 1936, and for GUN16 and GHO77 in 1937.

Limousines

Limousine bodies were popular for the 25/30, and Barker built them for no fewer than 40 chassis. Of these, the one for GAN25 in 1935 was described as a Pullman Limousine, implying that it had a particularly luxurious interior. The full list of 40 Limousines is as follows:

GUL15	1936	GGM26	1936	GRO42	1937
GUL20	1936	GAN16	1936	GRO80	1937
GUL29	1936	GAN21	1936	GHO37	1937
GUL56	1936	GAN25	1936	GHO55	1937
GUL75	1936	GAN70	1936	GMO5	1937
GTL43	1936	GAN81	1936	GRP3	1937
GHL25	1936	GWN39	1936	GRP20	1937
GHL37	1936	GWN52	1937	GMP79	1937
GRM41	1936	GWN78	1937	GMP81	1937
GRM71	1936	GUN7	1937	GAR18	1937
GXM3	1936	GUN27	1937	GAR65	1938
GXM60	1936	GRO2	1937	GAR66	1938
GGM3	1936	GRO29	1937	GGR47	1938
GGM9	1936				

Saloons and Sports Saloons

This was a period when many Saloons were being ordered with Divisions, while the less formal-looking Sports Saloon was gaining in popularity. Barker built 62 Saloons of all types for the 25/30 chassis, of which 35 were Saloons pure and simple, 15 were Saloons with Division, and 12 were Sports Saloons.

The Saloons are listed below. Those marked with an asterisk (*) were the ones delivered with a Division.

GUL7*	1936	GTL72*	1936	GXM63	1936
GUL26*	1936	GRM3	1936	GXM75	1936
GUL38	1936	GRM14	1936	GGM18	1936
GUL50*	1936	GRM15	1936	GGM36*	1936
GUL67	1936	GRM33	1936	GAN2	1936
GUL82	1936	GRM79	1936	GAN74	1936
GTL32	1936	GXM32*	1936	GUN20	1937
GTL56	1936	GXM43*	1936	GRO6	1937

The shape of the rear body on this Saloon for 25/30 chassis GRP1 is typical Barker, with its deep rear quarters and swept tail. The body was new in 1937. (Frank Dale & Stepsons)

GRO28	1937	GRP63	1937	GGR8	1938
GRO54	1937	GRP70	1937	GGR18*	1938
GRO65	1937	GMP25	1937	GGR46	1938
GMO26	1937	GMP39	1937	GGR51	1938
GMO34*	1937	GLP16*	1937	GGR66	1938
GMO35	1937	GAR39	1937	GZR9	1938
GRP1*	1937	GAR40*	1937	GZR15*	1938
GRP17	1937	GAR75	1937	GZR18	1938
GRP52*	1937	GGR7*	1938		

The lines of this 1936 Sedanca de Ville body for 25/30 GUL41 are worth comparing with those of the 1931 body for 20/25 GNS60. This body is elegant and formal, yet not forbiddingly so. (Real Car Company)

Complete with fashionable falling waistline, this was Barker's idea of a Sports Saloon for the 25/30 chassis in 1936. The bright trim moulding was typical of the time. This body was for chassis GAN8. (Real Car Company)

The 12 Barker Sports Saloons were on the following chassis:

GTL27	1936	GWN62	1936	GHO69	1937
GTL67	1936	GRO70	1937	GMO3	1937
GAN8	1936	GHO18	1937	GMP68	1937
GAN47	1936	GHO47	1937	GGR12	1938

BASSET MOTORS
Location unknown – Twenty

A single Coupé body by Basset Motors is recorded as built on Rolls-Royce Twenty chassis 68H9 in 1923. Nothing more is known about the coachwork, and there are no hard facts about the coachbuilder either.

BEADLE
Dartford – Twenty, 20/25

John C Beadle founded his carriage works at Dartford in Kent in 1894, and had moved into building bodies for motor cars by 1899. In the years just prior to the Great War, the company bodied some 40/50 Ghost chassis. From quite early on, Beadle appears also to have built commercial bodywork for motor vehicles, and during the 1920s regularly exhibited bus and coach bodies at the Commercial Motor Show. Car bodies gradually became a sideline and in the early 1930s Beadle abandoned that line of work to focus on the much healthier bus and coach market.

Just two Beadle bodies are known on small-horsepower Rolls-Royce chassis. The earlier of these is recorded as by "Beadles" but it seems reasonable to assume that it was built by the Dartford firm. It was a Limousine body, built in 1924 on Twenty chassis GMK64. The later one was not built until 1935, and was a substantial-looking four-light Saloon with division that was delivered in March that year on 20/25 chassis GPG61.

BELL & TOWNSEND
Location unknown – Twenty

A company called Bell & Townsend is recorded as the maker of a Limousine body on Rolls-Royce Twenty chassis 64H8 from 1923. Nothing further is known about this body or about the coachbuilder responsible for it.

BERTELLI
Feltham – 20/25

Gus (Augustus) Bertelli was on the Aston Martin Board for a time and drafted in his brother Harry (Enrico) to run the company's body-building workshops and design the bodies. In 1929, Harry set up his own coachwork business in the Aston

Martin works at Feltham, and in 1930 formalised it as E Bertelli Ltd. Over the next eight years, he built sporting coachwork for a variety of chassis, closing the business after his brother left Aston Martin. Perhaps an odd choice as the coachbuilder for a Rolls-Royce 20/25, Bertelli nevertheless supplied a Drophead Coupé with dickey seat on GYH45 in 1935.

BOWDEN & SONS
Wallingford – Twenty, 20/25
There is no hard information about Bowden & Sons of Wallingford, who built two bodies on small-horsepower Rolls-Royce chassis for the same local resident. Wallingford was then in Berkshire but since 1974 has been in Oxfordshire. The earlier of these bodies was a Tourer on Twenty chassis GAK55 from 1924. The later one was a Saloon, completed in 1931 on 20/25 chassis GPS8.

BRADBURN & WEDGE
Wolverhampton – Twenty, 20/25
Bradburn & Wedge was primarily a motor dealer, with headquarters in Wolverhampton. It became one of the first Morris dealers in 1912, and subsequently expanded to take on several other franchises, including one for Rolls-Royce. It put its name to several car bodies in the 1920s, although these may have been constructed by Forder & Co, a local company that had once specialised in building hansom cabs. There was at least one body for a Sunbeam chassis; 10 are known for the Rolls-Royce Twenty, and one for the 20/25. Although the coachwork activities ceased in the early 1930s, the company remained an important car dealership. It still survives, as Jonathan Bradburn Historic Cars, now based in the Isle of Man.

TWENTY COACHWORK
All of the 10 Bradburn & Wedge bodies for the Twenty chassis were completed between 1922 and 1926. There was just one in 1922; four were built in 1923 and three in 1924; and the last two were completed in 1926.

Three of these bodies were Cabriolets, for 43G6 in 1922 and for GLK46 and GNK41 in 1924. Four were Saloons, which were for 81K1 and GH50 in 1923, GPK45 in 1924, and GUK37 in 1926. The body described as a Coupé for 55S4 in 1923 in practice seems to have been a four-door Tourer, but there was a genuine three-quarters Coupé the same year for chassis 66H2. The complement of 10 was made up by a single Limousine body, for GOK30 in 1926.

20/25 COACHWORK
The original Saloon coachwork on chassis GBT15, new in early 1932, is attributed to Bradburn & Wedge but is also thought to have been made by Forder's.

BRADSHAW
Hemel Hempstead – 20/25
Tom Clarke has identified Dennis R Bradshaw, of Bridge Motor Body Works in Hemel Hempstead, as the builder of the Faux Cabriolet de Ville body for 20/25 chassis GDP6 in 1930. There is no further reliable information about this coachbuilder.

BRAINSBY
Peterborough – Twenty
Brainsby was a Peterborough coachbuilder with a showroom at Long Acre in London's West End. The company was active before the Great War, and among other bodies built a large landaulette on Mercedes chassis for an Indian Maharaja. However, by the 1920s it was typically turning out competent, workmanlike designs on a variety of mid-priced chassis. From 1929, the company became Brainsby-Woollard, which had links with other coachbuilders, such as Lancefield.

The company also built seven bodies on the Twenty chassis between 1923 and 1928. Two of these were Tourers, in 1923 and 1924, and two more were Saloons, in 1926 and 1928. The remaining bodies were a Three-quarter Coupé in 1924 and a Three-quarter Drophead Coupé in 1925. The list is below.

Chassis no	Date	Type
82 K9	1923	Tourer
87 K2	1923	DHC
GRK64	1924	¾ Coupé
GDK56	1924	Tourer
GNK49	1925	¾ DHC
GUK48	1926	Saloon
GWL8	1928	Saloon

BRIDGE & SON
Location unknown – Twenty
A company recorded as J Bridge & Son built the Cabriolet body for Twenty chassis 51S5 in 1923. Unfortunately, no further details have been found to identify this company more precisely.

BRIDGES
Cirencester – Twenty
Bridges Garage was a Cirencester company that operated a coachbuilding department alongside its dealer franchises. The main one in the first half of the 1920s was for Sunbeam, but after 1926 the company

ran down its coachbuilding work and refocused on retail and repair work. The single body that it built for a Rolls-Royce Twenty was a Limousine on GOK10 in 1926; it may have been one of the last bodies to come from this coachbuilder.

BRIDGEWATER MOTOR CO

Bridgewater – Twenty

A 1914 advertisement for the Bridgewater Motor Company adds the name of West of England Carriage Works and notes that the company was based at Eastover in the Somerset town of Bridgewater. This was clearly a car dealer with its own body making shop and must have been the company that built the Saloon body on a single Rolls-Royce Twenty in 1927. The body was on chassis number GRJ41 and the car acquired a Somerset registration number. There are no known pictures of it.

BUCHANAN

Glasgow – Twenty, 20/25

John Buchanan & Co (Coachbuilders) Ltd were based at North Street in Glasgow and probably entered the business in 1921 when they showed their work at the Scottish Motor Show.

The company is known to have built four bodies on Rolls-Royce chassis, the earliest on a 40/50. There were two on the Twenty chassis, one a Coupé for GZK22 in 1926 and the other a Tourer for GTM9 in 1928.

The company was responsible for a single body on the 20/25 chassis in late 1929, which was a four-door Tourer on chassis GGP44.

BUCKINGHAM

Birmingham – Twenty

Buckingham Motor Bodies was the trading name of

John Buckingham Ltd, established in 1878 and based in Birmingham. The company's main business was in bus and hearse bodies, but it also built at least two bodies on Rolls-Royce Twenty chassis. By 1931 the company was in financial trouble, and it closed down in August 1934.

The two known bodies are both Saloons. The earlier one was built for chassis GRK45 in 1924, and the later one for GLK40 the following year.

CADOGAN

London – Twenty

Cadogan Motors Ltd was initially based in the Chelsea district of London, and became known for building formal closed bodies on expensive chassis. The company was probably at its height in the mid-1920s, by which time it was also building more stylish sporting coachwork for chassis that included Bentley, Invicta and OM. After a financial reconstruction in 1927, it moved to new premises in nearby Fulham, but was no longer in business after 1930.

The company had taken out a licence to build Weymann-patent bodies, and its sole contribution to the story of the small-horsepower Rolls-Royce was a Weymann Saloon on Twenty chassis GYK54. This was completed in 1926.

CAFFYNS

Eastbourne – Twenty, 20/25

Caffyns Ltd had been founded in Eastbourne in Sussex in 1865 as a household supplies shop, but in 1903 it entered the motor business as a car dealer. Its first coachwork catalogue appeared in 1912, showing both car and commercial types, and it would continue in that vein until the start of war in 1939. (There was subsequently a single rebody on a Rolls-Royce 25/30 in 1949.) The company bodied a variety of chassis, but always declined to add dealership franchises for imported cars to a growing portfolio that, after 1927, included a Rolls-Royce franchise. During the 1930s Caffyns became one of the largest dealer groups in Britain, with premises all over the south-east, and it remains so today.

Caffyns bodied a total of 16 Rolls-Royce Twenty chassis and three 20/25 chassis.

TWENTY COACHWORK

The earliest of the Caffyns bodies for Rolls-Royce Twenty chassis was completed in 1924. There were then six in 1925, one in 1926, four in 1927, one in 1929, and three in 1929. The types were a typical mix of those provided by most provincial coachbuilders of the time, but with Saloons and Landaulettes making up the majority.

Buckingham was a provincial coachbuilder whose main business was not car bodies, but the company built this wholly creditable six-light Saloon in the idiom of the day for Twenty chassis GLK40.

Coupés

Caffyyns bodied two Twenty chassis as Coupés. The earlier one, strictly a three-quarters Coupé, was for GNK62 in 1925, and the later one was for GHJ20 in 1927.

Landaulettes

There were five Landaulette bodies between 1925 and 1929. These were for chassis GSK28 (in 1925), GYK88 (1926), GRJ64 and GXL52 (both 1927) and GLN23 (in 1929).

Limousines

Three Twenty chassis received Limousine bodies by Caffyns in the middle of the decade. These were GCK60 (in 1925), GHJ72 (in 1927) and GBM59 (in 1928).

Saloons

There were six Saloon bodies altogether, of which the first four were built in 1924-1925 and the last two both in 1929. The body on GEN73, one of the 1929 cars, was described as a Weymann Saloon. Caffyns did not hold a Weymann licence by 1928 and it is unlikely that they would have obtained one as late as 1929, when Weymann bodies were starting to go out of fashion. It therefore seems likely that the coachwork for GEN 73 was actually built elsewhere; the nearest coachbuilder with a Weymann licence was Harringtons, in Hove. The six chassis bodied as Saloons were as follows:

GRK79	1924	GNK42	1925	GEN73	1929
GLK77	1925	GPK11	1925	GVO38	1929

20/25 COACHWORK

All three of the Caffyns bodies for 20/25 chassis were Limousines. These were on chassis GGP61 in 1929, GLR22 in 1930, and GSY90 in 1933.

CARBODIES

Coventry – Twenty, 20/25

Carbodies was founded in 1919 in Coventry when Bobby Jones bought out the timber merchants' business of his employers and renamed it. Jones had earlier been works manager for Charlesworth and general manager of Hollick & Pratt, both Coventry firms. From the start, the new company focussed on contract bodywork rather than on bespoke work, and that helped it to survive the Depression when others went to the wall.

Carbodies kept busy right through the 1950s and 1960s with conversion work for manufacturers like

Austin and Ford, and moved into taxi production in 1958. Rebranded as London Taxis International in 1992, it was eventually bought out by the Chinese Geely company and rebranded as the London EV Company in 2017.

TWENTY COACHWORK

There were probably five bodies for the Rolls-Royce Twenty, and a further ten for the 20/25 chassis. The four Twenty bodies that can definitely be attributed to Carbodies were a Landaulette for GYK70 in 1926, Saloons in 1928 (GKM23) and 1929 (GLN32), and a Limousine in 1929 (GEN50). The fifth body, recorded as by Car Bodies (no coachbuilder of that name is known), was a Landaulette on GUK19 in 1926.

20/25 COACHWORK

Orders for bodies on the 20/25 chassis were somewhat sporadic. There were two in each of the years 1930 and 1931, five in 1932, and one in 1934. There is also some confusion over what appears to have been a body transfer rather than a rebody in the strictest sense.

The earliest Carbodies coachwork on a 20/25 was a high-sided four-door Tourer for chassis GDP81. This was delivered in March 1930, and was followed in August that year by a six-light Saloon on GSR57. This body appears to have had Carbodies' rather grand "Pacific" design that had originally been developed for a large Sunbeam chassis.

There was a four-light Saloon with division on GOS12 in February 1931, and then a six-light Limousine on GOS25 a month later. The 1932 deliveries began with a four-light Fixed-head Coupé on GKT7 in April 1932, which was followed by two Saloons with removable Divisions. These were for

Caffyns built three Limousine bodies for the 20/25 chassis, and this 1933 example was the last of them. It was for chassis GSY90. (Copyright unknown)

*Sleek and stylish were epithets commonly used of Carlton, who built this Coupé body for 20/25 chassis GEX32 in 1933. The hatch ahead of the rear wheel was probably designed to take a set of golf clubs.
Mattporta/WikiMedia Commons*

chassis GKT33 and GAU80, and were delivered in May and July respectively.

The 1932 complement was completed by a Limousine for GZU28 in September, and a Coupé for GHW57 in November. There was then a gap until the last Carbodies 20/25 was delivered with a Saloon body in July 1934. This was on chassis GMD66.

These appear to have been the only bodies that Carbodies constructed for the 20/25 chassis, but it is possible that the Limousine body from GOS25 was later transferred to GSR55, or perhaps to GSR57.

CARLTON
London – Twenty, 20/25, 25/30
The Carlton Carriage Co was established in Willesden, north London, in 1925 after a brief period under the Kelvin name. It built catalogued bodies in quantity for the likes of Humber and Talbot, and worked with importers on various American chassis as well. It also took on sub-contract work for other London coachbuilders such as Offord.

However, Carlton was most noted for its bespoke work on chassis that included Rolls-Royce of all sizes and Bentley models as well. Customers went to Carlton for a sleek, stylish and well-proportioned body – although of course there were some more conventional designs as well. The company's best work was seen in its Coupé, Coupé de Ville and Drophead Coupé styles. Its last car bodies were made in 1939, apart from a single prototype for Jowett in 1949, but the company survived until 1965.

There were three bodies for the Rolls-Royce Twenty, 27 for the 20/25, and three for the 25/30.

TWENTY COACHWORK
Disappointingly, none of the three bodies for new Twenty chassis between 1927 and 1929 displayed Carlton's talents to the full, although the company

did show what might have been when it rebodied two Twenty chassis (GMJ61 and GFN67) as Drophead Coupés in the 1930s. The three bodies for new chassis were all Saloons, and were on GXL25 and GYL73 in 1927, and on GLN22 in 1929. Carlton held a Weymann licence and built the body on this last example as a Weymann type.

20/25 COACHWORK
Carlton attracted considerably more 20/25 customers than it had done of those who bought a Twenty. It put its name to just one body in 1929, to five more in 1930, and then dropped back to two in 1931. Unusually, 1932 was a boom year, when 10 bodies were built for the 20/25 chassis at a time when many other coachbuilders were suffering or had already gone to the wall; perhaps Carlton offered a price incentive! There were then five bodies in 1933 and four in 1934.

Coupés
Two of the Carlton bodies for the 20/25 chassis were Coupés. These were on GDP41 in 1930 and on GEX32 in 1933.

Drophead Coupés
Carlton fielded seven orders for Drophead Coupé bodies, a style that was one of its specialities. The last three examples, built in 1933 and 1934, all had dickey seats. The seven chassis, with dates, were as follows:

GFT78	1931	GAU52	1932	GGA29	1933
GBT71	1931	GBA72	1933	GUB7	1934
GBT80	1932				

Limousine
There was a single Limousine body, which was built for chassis GLB31 in 1934.

Saloons

Carlton built 14 Saloon bodies for the 20/25 chassis between 1929 and 1934. The first three, in 1929-1930, were all Weymann types, and there was a single two-door Saloon for GAU71 in 1932. GLZ12 was described as a Continental Saloon, and GED23 was a particularly successful Sports Saloon design for a London surgeon. GBA23 was built on behalf of Offord and carried that coachbuilder's plates, and GHW21 may also have been for Offord. Carlton is generally thought to have built the Sports Saloon body on GWE59 that carried Connaught plates.

The full list of Saloon-bodied 20/25 chassis, with dates, is below.

GGP66	1929	GAU71	1932	GHW61	1932
GGP79	1930	GMU1	1932	GLZ12	1933
GDP16	1930	GMU7	1932	GBA23	1933
GSR75	1930	GMU30	1932	GED23	1934
GAU22	1932	GHW6	1932		

Sedanca de Ville

There was just one Sedanca de Ville body, for chassis GED44 in 1934. Of interest is that the body on GYZ8 in 1932, variously described as a Sedanca Coupé and a Coupé de Ville, was probably built for Offord by Carlton.

Tourers

Carlton built two Tourer bodies for the 20/25 chassis, one a conventional Tourer for GDP74 in 1930 and the other an All-weather Tourer for GHW65 in 1932.

25/30 COACHWORK

The number of customers for Carlton bodies on the small horse-power Rolls-Royce chassis thinned out dramatically in the mid-1930s. No bodies were built in 1935, and there was just one in 1936. This was a Saloon on chassis GAN65. The following year there were two Drophead Coupé bodies, for chassis GMO21 and GRP59, both a little heavier looking than earlier examples of the type from this coachbuilder. There were then no more.

CASTLE MOTOR CO
Probably Kidderminster – Twenty

The Castle Motor Co that built two bodies on Rolls-Royce Twenty chassis was probably the company of that name that operated from Kidderminster in Worcestershire. It started out as a car repair business but between 1919 and 1922 built its own three-wheeler cyclecar. Little is known of its coachbuilding activities and one report suggests that it closed in 1922 – although

one of the bodies for the Twenty was on a 1926 chassis.

The two bodies were a Limousine built in 1922 for chassis 44G2, and a Saloon built in 1926 for GMJ42.

CHARLESWORTH
Coventry – Twenty, 20/25, 25/30

The Coventry coachbuilder Charlesworth opened for business in 1907 and quickly became a leading exponent of the art. After a pause during the Great War it returned to business and by the mid-1920s was focusing on bespoke coachwork. The general decline in demand for coachbuilt bodies around 1930 led to a brief absence but the company was restructured in November 1931 as Charlesworth Bodies (1931) Ltd. It picked up contract work during the 1930s, most notably for Alvis and Daimler, but continued to produce bespoke coachwork as well.

Charlesworth built a variety of coachwork styles for the small-horsepower Rolls-Royce chassis between 1923 and 1936. There were six bodies on Twenty chassis between 1923 and 1927, three on the 20/25 between 1929 and 1931, and a further two on the 25/30 chassis in 1936. In addition, the company rebodied a pair of Twenties and one 20/25.

TWENTY COACHWORK

Charlesworth built six bodies on new Twenty chassis between 1923 and 1927, and also rebodied a seventh chassis. The company produced a variety of styles.

Three Twenties were bodied in 1923, 51S2 becoming a Coupé, and 68H4 and GF72 both receiving Tourer coachwork. There were then a Cabriolet for GMK49 in 1924, a smart Doctor's Coupé for GUK29 in 1926, and a Saloon for GHJ63 in 1927. The rebody was on a 1924 chassis, GDK27, which had a Park Ward Saloon body when new and gained a straight-backed six-light Saloon body by Charlesworth.

20/25 COACHWORK

There were just three bodies on Rolls-Royce 20/25 chassis, the first one delivered in the time of the

Charlesworth incorporated a fashionable swept tail into this Saloon design for 20/25 chassis GMD51 in 1934.

The typical All-weather body could look rather stodgy, but Charlesworth made a good job of this one for 25/30 GWN17 in 1936.

original Charlesworth company and the other two by Charlesworth Bodies (1931) Ltd. That first body was a Limousine, delivered in 1929 on chassis GGP63.

The other two bodies were for GMD51, a well-proportioned swept-tail six-light Saloon delivered in 1934, and for GPG68 in April 1935. This later car had four-light coachwork with a rather pert tail treatment incorporating an enclosed luggage boot.

Charlesworth also rebodied GWE24, a 1934 chassis, as an estate car in 1938. A second 1934 chassis, GMD56, survives with a Charlesworth Saloon body that was probably fitted to it in the 1940s or early 1950s.

25/30 COACHWORK

The two bodies on 25/30 chassis were both delivered in 1936. The earlier one was a Limousine for GRM11 in August, and the later an unusually sleek All-weather Tourer on GWN7 that was delivered in December.

CIRENCESTER CARRIAGE WORKS
Cirencester – Twenty

The identity of the Cirencester Carriage Works is far from clear, although the company may possibly be associated with local carriage maker FW Constable. There was of course also a railway carriage works in the town for a time, which could perhaps have sub-let some premises.

The company name was applied to a single Tourer body that was built on a Rolls-Royce Twenty chassis, number 85K4, in 1923. Nothing further is known about this car.

CLARK (CHARLES)
Wolverhampton – Twenty

Charles Clark & Sons was a Wolverhampton coachbuilder active in the 1920s. It is known to have bodied some Sunbeam chassis and is best known for a magnificent Brougham de Ville with highly ornate interior on a Rolls-Royce Phantom in 1927.

The company was also responsible for the coachwork

on three Twenty chassis. These were a Landaulette for GUK24 in 1926, a Weymann Saloon in 1927 for GHJ10 in 1927, and an otherwise unidentified Saloon on GUJ43 later the same year.

CLARK (JC)
London – Twenty, 20/25

JC Clark was active as a builder of vehicle bodies in Shepherds Bush from 1921, its main business being hearse and bus bodywork. Nevertheless, it did build the bodies for two small-horsepower Rolls-Royce chassis, some 11 years apart. The earlier one was a Cabriolet on a 1923 Twenty, 88K9. The later one was a Saloon, delivered in December 1934, on a 20/25 chassis GSF31.

CLYDE
Glasgow – Twenty

Based in Glasgow, the Clyde Automobile Company were Rolls-Royce agents for south, south-west and central Scotland. Their name is recorded as builders of the coachwork for 18 Rolls-Royce Twenty chassis, but there is a strong chance that all these bodies were in fact constructed for them by John Robertson & Co of Glasgow. The Robertson company was founded in 1857 as a carriage-builder and earned itself an excellent reputation, and in the years before the First World War constructed the bodies for many grand chassis, including the Rolls-Royce Silver Ghost. Its close link with the Clyde company is clear from the fact that it exhibited on their stand at the Scottish Motor Show between 1923 and 1925.

Clyde bodies were at their most popular for the Twenty in 1923, when 12 were built. There were two in 1924, and one each year in 1922, 1925, 1926 and 1927. The company's forte was clearly Landaulette and Tourer bodies, of which eight and seven respectively were built. The other three bodies for Twenty chassis were two Cabriolets (on 55S2 and 60H1, both in 1923) and a single Saloon (on 63H5, also in 1923).

The eight Landaulette bodies, with dates, were as follows:

50S4	1923	GH69	1923	GPK24	1925
70A5	1923	GMK30	1924	GAJ3	1927
GH35	1923	GLK75	1924		

The seven Tourers were:

42G5	1922	61H3	1923	GH55	1923
57S8	1923	73A9	1923	GOK12	1926
60H5	1923				

COACHCRAFT
London – 20/25, 25/30, Wraith

Coachcraft took over part of the old Arrow Coachworks premises in Hanwell, west London, during 1934. The company focused on low-volume series building for chassis makers such as Railton and Delage, and from 1938 was one of the coachbuilders that worked for Southern Motor Bodies to produce modern "replica" bodywork on older Rolls-Royce chassis. After the war, it was purchased by University Motors and was renamed University Coachwork.

The company built just three bodies between 1936 and 1938 for "new" small-horsepower Rolls-Royce chassis, one each on the 20/25, 25/30 and Wraith. The multiple "replicas" built for the Southern Motor Co are not considered here because all were rebodies of earlier chassis. There is more information about them in John Dyson's book, *Coachcraft, 1930s Coachbuilding Style*.

20/25 COACHWORK

The Coachcraft body on a 20/25 chassis was a two-door Saloon for Captain Butler, who had provided the start-up finance for the company. This was an elegant design that reflected the influence of the French coachbuilder Chapron, and was delivered on chassis GBK8 in 1936.

25/30 COACHWORK

Coachcraft were wont to describe their "replica" bodies as "special saloons", and used the same description for the four-light Saloon they constructed on chassis GHO71 in 1937.

WRAITH COACHWORK

The six-light Saloon for Wraith chassis WXA46 in 1938 was a neat but undistinguished body that, inevitably perhaps, incorporated some elements of Coachcraft's "replica" style for Southern Motor Bodies. When completed, this car was actually supplied to Southern Motor Bodies, too.

COCKSHOOT
Manchester – Twenty, 20/25, 25/30 and Wraith

Manchester coachbuilder Joseph Cockshoot & Co Ltd enjoyed considerable prestige as one of the leading coachbuilders in the north-west. Established in 1844, it built its first body in 1903 and became a Rolls-Royce agent in 1907. Unsurprisingly, it supplied many of the bodies on the Rolls-Royce chassis it sold until its coachbuilding activities ceased in 1939, and was a regular exhibitor at Olympia. Demand was high in the early interwar years, but as customers for coachbuilt bodies became harder to find in the 1930s, the company focused more on its car dealership activities. When it re-opened after the war, its activities were confined to car sales, repairs and servicing.

Cockshoot designs tended to be conservative, with a heaviness and dignity about them. There were some neat Sports Saloons in the mid-1930s, but other designs in that decade sometimes suffered from awkwardly shaped luggage boots. As a leading provincial coachbuilder, the company did not specialise in any one type but remained versatile to meet customer demand. Cockshoot was a prolific builder of coachwork for the small-horsepower Rolls-Royce models, and delivered 68 bodies for the Twenty, 41 for the 20/25, 13 for the 25/30 and four for the Wraith, those declining numbers reflecting at least in part the gradual decline of coachbuilding in the period.

TWENTY COACHWORK

In the early 1920s, Tourers and Landaulettes predominated among the orders placed with Cockshoot for coachwork on the Twenty chassis. The quantity of bodies built gradually declined over the decade, as demand switched to closed coachwork. Cockshoot fulfilled orders for a single body in 1922, then a total of 20 made 1923 its best year. There were 14 in 1924, 12 in 1925, seven in 1926, five in 1927, and six in 1928. The figure of three bodies for Twenty chassis in 1929 was low but is partially explained by the changeover to the 20/25 model that autumn.

Cabriolets

Cabriolet coachwork was popular in 1923-1924, and Cockshoot delivered five in the first year and two in the second; there were none at all after that. The company built different designs to order, some having two doors and others four (such as GMK9 in 1924). The full list, with dates, was as follows:

53S2	1923	GA26	1923	GMK9	1924
61H6	1923	GF6	1923	GRK7	1924
63H1	1923				

Coupés

Cockshoot delivered just two Coupé bodies on Twenty chassis, both being "three-quarters" (ie four-window) types. They were for GLK69 in 1925 and GUJ58 in 1927.

Drophead Coupés

The three Cockshoot Drophead Coupé bodies on

Cockshoot built three Drophead Coupé bodies for the Twenty chassis, and this one is probably on GSK6, which had a dickey seat.

Drophead Coupé or Two-seater? The terms were not mutually exclusive and this body was made by Cockshoot for Twenty chassis GF38 in 1923.

The lines of this six-light Saloon by Cockshoot in 1926 are fairly typical of the period, although there is a certain severity to them that was not seen in similar bodies from other coachbuilders. The chassis is a Twenty, GOK49. (Real Car Company)

The Cockshoot body for Twenty GLK69 in 1925 was a three-quarter Coupé with the protuberant tail that was fashionable for a time.

Twenty chassis were spread out across the decade. The earliest was for 71A9 in 1923, which had a "three-quarters" configuration. Next came a Drophead Coupé with dickey seat in 1925 on GSK6. The last one was then for GLN15 in 1929.

Landaulettes

Demand for Cockshoot Landaulettes was confined to the years 1923-1925, and there were no later examples on Twenty chassis. Four were delivered in 1923 (on 48G0, 63H2, GA7 and GF25), one in 1924 (on GRK57) and the last two of a total of seven in 1925 (on GSK19 and GSK43).

Limousines

Formal Limousines were the most numerous Cockshoot bodies on the Twenty chassis. There were 22 of them between 1923 and 1929, many exhibiting a degree of haughtiness that their customers no doubt requested. There were several different designs, and at least one was an open-drive type (on 72A1 in 1923). The full list, together with dates, is as follows:

70A7	1923	GNK47	1925	GYK89	1926
72A1	1923	GPK39	1925	GXL17	1927
GH43	1923	GPK56	1925	GWL11	1929
GAK16	1924	GSK67	1925	GFN25	1929
GRK36	1924	GCK77	1925	GFN41	1929
GDK49	1924	GZK16	1926	GEN42	1929
GLK5	1924	GZK66	1926		
GLK38	1924	GUK9	1926		

Saloons

There were 17 Saloon bodies for the Twenty between 1923 and 1928, and of course these embraced a variety of styles. Most were unexceptional; some had the briefly fashionable vee windscreen (such as GRJ52 in 1927). At an unknown date, Cockshoot also built a folding-head Saloon to replace the original Barker Tourer on 1928 chassis GYL55.

69H9	1923	GPK21	1925	GRJ52	1927
GAK11	1924	GOK47	1926	GBM34	1928
GLK11	1924	GOK49	1926	GKM18	1928
GLK20	1924	GOK78	1926	GTM24	1928
GLK79	1925	GHJ3	1927	GTM35	1928
GNK53	1925	GHJ6	1927		

Tourers

Cockshoot built nine Tourer bodies for early Twenty chassis, all of them in 1922-1924. The last one, GRK53, was a special two-door design for an Indian Maharaja.

45G6	1922	76A0	1923	GAK14	1924
56S1	1923	85K9	1923	GMK2	1924
71A3	1923	GH71	1923	GRK53	1924

Two-seater

Just one body was described as a Two-seater. This was built in 1923 on chassis GF38 and had what appears to have been a folding roof. Some might therefore describe it as a Drophead Coupé.

20/25 COACHWORK

Cockshoot built a total of 39 bodies on new 20/25 chassis between 1929 and 1937. There were three for the "short" year of 1929 and 10 in 1930 before the effects of the Depression reduced the annual totals to three for 1931 and just one for 1932. Business began to pick up again with three bodies in 1933, nine in 1934, nine in 1935 and finally one in the 20/25's last year of 1936. Most Cockshoot bodies on the 20/25 chassis were Saloons, with Limousines coming second in terms of volume, and there was only one other body, a Drophead Coupé built in 1933.

Cockshoot clearly worked with other coachbuilders in the 1930s. There are indications that some of its bodies were actually constructed by fellow Manchester coachbuilder William Arnold, and that Cockshoot returned the compliment. One Cockshoot body may have been constructed by Weymann Motor Bodies, and in 1936 the company certainly built a Saloon Landaulette on GBK 60 for Knibbs & Parkyn, who put their plates on it. At an unknown date, Cockshoot also rebodied GED68, new in 1934 with a Park Ward Saloon body, as an estate car.

Drophead Coupé

The single Drophead Coupé body was built in 1933 for 20/25 chassis GWX17.

Limousines

There were nine Limousines between 1929 and 1935, some early examples having the vee-windscreen design. At least two of these were shown at Olympia (GSR33 in 1930 and GFT8 in 1931), and one (GLR11 in 1930) was probably built for Cockshoots by William Arnold. The Limousine body for GPS14 was transferred to new chassis GWE36 in 1934. The list is as follows:

GXO64	1929	GSR33	1930	GFT8	1931
GLR11	1930	GSR67	1930	GEH5	1935
GLR32	1930	GPS14	1931	GLJ26	1935

Saloons

Cockshoots put their name to 29 Saloon bodies of various types for the 20/25 chassis between 1929 and 1936. Two were built in 1929, six in 1930, but just one each in the difficult years 1931 and 1932. There were two in 1933, nine in 1934, seven in 1935 and one in 1936.

Some were six-light types and some were attractive four-light Sports Saloons. At least one (GMU21 in 1932) had a Tickford-type folding head, and there were three Weymann types, on GGP77 in 1929, and GLR26 and GSR62 in 1930. Of these three, the one for GGP77 may have been built by Weymann themselves, and the one for GSR62 was transferred onto new chassis GLZ15 in 1933.

The Saloon body for GWP23 had occasional seats and may have been built by William Arnold; meanwhile, GXB11 may have been built for that company, as it had the same design as the body on GGA6 that was built by William Arnold themselves.

GXO86	1929	GTZ51	1933	GFE15	1934
GGP77	1929	GBA30	1933	GRF25	1935
GDP31	1930	GXB11	1934	GLG48	1935
GDP75	1930	GUB21	1934	GPG25	1935
GWP23	1930	GLB17	1934	GBJ31	1935
GWP29	1930	GNC12	1934	GBJ73	1935
GLR26	1930	GRC41	1934	GLJ79	1935
GSR62	1930	GAE9	1934	GCJ40	1935
GFT44	1931	GWE23	1934	GTK14	1936
GMU21	1932	GWE69	1934		

25/30 COACHWORK

Cockshoot built a total of 13 bodies for the Rolls-Royce 25/30 chassis between 1936 and 1938. There were four in the first year, six in 1937 (the only full 12-month year for the model), and three in 1938. The majority were Saloons; Limousines again followed in terms of quantity; and there was a single All-weather type.

All-weather

The only All-weather body that Cockshoot built for a small-horsepower Rolls-Royce was for GRP31 in 1937. It was for a customer who was a regular customer of the coachbuilder.

Limousines

Three of the 13 bodies for 25/30 chassis were Limousines. These were for GUL27 and GRM30 in 1936, and for GWN67 in 1937.

Saloons

Most of the nine Saloon bodies for 25/30 chassis were described as Sports Saloons, but they also included one six-light Saloon (for GMP8 in 1937) and one Saloon with Division (for GZR24 in 1938).

GHL6	1936	GMP8	1937	GGR31	1938
GAN59	1936	GMP21	1937	GZR24	1938
GRP69	1937	GLP29	1937	GZR25	1938

WRAITH COACHWORK

Cockshoot was not at its best when working with the Rolls-Royce Wraith chassis, and the bodies built in 1938-1939 exhibited a heaviness and even a certain awkwardness. There were four of them: two were Limousines (WXA21 and WRB5 in 1938) and the other two were Saloons (WHC14 and WEC52 in 1939).

COLE

London – Twenty

William Cole & Sons was a "motor body builder" that could trace its origins back to the start of the nineteenth century. Based in Kensington in the early 1900s, it claimed by 1909 to be a coachbuilder to the Royal Family. By 1913 it had a second address in Hammersmith and by 1920 had moved there completely. Re-established soon after as Wm Cole & Sons (1923) Ltd, it seems to have remained in business right through to 1939.

The company was responsible for just one known body on a small-horsepower Rolls-Royce chassis, and that was a three-quarter Coupé on Twenty GNK77 in 1925. No further details of the car are known.

CONNAUGHT

London – Twenty, 20/25, 25/30

The Connaught Motor & Carriage Company was founded in London in 1770, and made the transition from carriage building to car coachwork early in the 20th century. The company always worked with the grander and more prestigious chassis, and had

bodied several Rolls-Royce Silver Ghost types before the First World War began. In the mid-1920s, the company had premises in Willesden, north-west London, as well as offices in London's West End, and it remained busy, building no fewer than 37 bodies on the New Phantom chassis as well as 56 on the Twenty.

Most experts believe that Connaught later changed from being a coachbuilder to a design house that sub-contracted body construction to others, including both Carlton and Palmer of Dover (qqv). Connaught had a fallow period in 1931-1932 and the most likely date of this change is 1933. From 1934 it changed its name to Connaught Coachwork Ltd and by 1935 was advertising special coachwork for the bigger Vauxhall chassis as Howard Godfrey & Connaught Coachwork Ltd.

Nevertheless, Connaught put its name to 28 bodies for the Rolls-Royce 20/25 chassis, but there was just one for a 25/30. The company probably closed down during 1937, when owner Howard Godfrey took a post elsewhere in the motor trade.

TWENTY COACHWORK

In fairness to Connaught, it must be said that there was nothing striking or unusual about their coachwork for the Twenty. The known designs were all highly competent but conventional. Customers went to Connaught mainly for Landaulette coachwork before 1926, and shortly after that the company appears to have acquired a Weymann licence, although such bodies seem to have remained secondary within its output. An increase in demand for Tourer and closed coachwork also followed from the middle of the decade, perhaps reflecting changing customer tastes rather than any deliberate change of policy by Connaught.

The company's best year with the Twenty was 1926, when it built the coachwork for 12 chassis. There were 10 in 1923, eight in 1927, and six in 1929; 1922, 1924, 1925 and 1928 saw five bodies each.

Brougham

A unique order in 1927 called for a Brougham design on chassis GXL73, which was built as a rather old-fashioned open-drive body with enclosed passenger compartment and not even a De Ville head for the driver's comfort.

Cabriolets

Connaught put its name to three Cabriolets on early Twenty chassis. These were for 69H1 and GA22 in 1923, and for GRK51 in 1924.

Connaught stuck to a tried and tested shape for this spacious six-light Saloon body on Twenty GYK34 in 1926. (Real Car Company)

Coupés

The company built two Coupés on Twenty chassis. The earlier was a "three-quarters" type, for chassis GPK72 in 1925, and the later one was for GEN4 in 1929.

Landaulettes

Connaught dealt with a strong demand for Landaulette bodywork between 1922 and 1926, but only delivered two thereafter; perhaps the companies to which it sub-contracted work were not able to produce such bodies satisfactorily. There were 18 Landaulette bodies in all:

43G4	1922	GF60	1923	GCK49	1925
44G9	1922	GH23	1923	GOK11	1926
74A7	1923	GAK48	1924	GZK52	1926
80K8	1923	GAK68	1924	GUK79	1926
81K3	1923	GNK33	1925	GLN41	1929
GF7	1923	GCK45	1925	GEN14	1929

Limousine

There was little demand for Limousine bodies in the early years of the Twenty, but 1926-1927 saw a marked increase. Of the 13 examples that Connaught built (or put its name to), only two were built using the Weymann patents; these were for chassis GFN57 in 1928 and GVO48 in 1929. The full list of the Limousine bodies is below.

49G3	1922	GMJ28	1926	GKM6	1928
GA15	1923	GHJ38	1927	GFN57	1928
GLK32	1924	GUJ19	1927	GLN79	1929
GYK 34	1926	GUJ28	1927	GVO48	1929
GYK76	1926				

Saloons

Only one of the 11 Saloon bodies for the Twenty was built as a Weymann type, and this was for GUJ41 in 1927. The full list is below.

52S4	1922	GYK61	1926	GBM14	1928
52S6	1922	GMJ51	1926	GBM27	1928
GMK37	1924	GUJ41	1927	GXO6	1929
GYK34	1926	GUJ51	1927		

Sedanca

A single open-drive four-door Sedanca body was built, for chassis GFN65 in 1928.

The overall lines of this open-drive Sedanca body were fairly conventional, too, although this was the only one of its type that Connaught built on the Twenty chassis. It was on GFN65 in 1928.

Tourers

There were seven Tourer bodies between 1923 and 1927, their popularity increasing markedly in mid-decade. They were:

GA20	1923	GZK69	1926	GAJ62	1927
GNK31	1925	GZK71	1926	GRJ77	1927
GZK20	1926				

20/25 COACHWORK

Business remained good for Connaught in the first two years of 20/25 production, and the company built eight bodies for the model in 1929 and a further eight in 1930. Orders then collapsed, and there were no bodies in 1931 or 1932. A recovery began slowly, with just two bodies in 1933, but the numbers were back up to six in 1934. There were then four more in 1935, making for a grand total of 28.

Connaught continued to focus on the grander coachwork styles such as Landaulettes and Limousines for the 20/25 chassis, but there were also healthy numbers of Saloons. Weymann bodies made only an occasional appearance. From about 1933, some bodies – perhaps all of them – were built for Connaught by other coachbuilders.

Coupé

Unique in the Connaught repertoire was a Weymann Coupé, a neat but unadventurous two-seater for chassis GXO73 in 1929.

Drophead Coupés

There was, strictly, just one Drophead Coupé body, and that was for chassis GKC4 in 1935. However, for convenience, the three-position Sedanca Coupé body for GYH9 in 1935 is also listed in this category.

Landaulettes

There was a brief resurgence of Landaulette orders in the early days of the 20/25, and Connaught produced three of them. There were two in 1929, for chassis GXO16 and GXO89, and the third was for GSR42 in 1930.

Limousines

Limousine bodies made up the greatest number of orders for Connaught on the 20/25 chassis. There were at least 13 of them, and to this total can be added one or perhaps two Limousine bodies built by Palmer of Dover in 1933. These were for chassis GEX74 (which probably wore Connaught plates) and GBA66 (which definitely did). Just one of the 13 bodies that Connaught built themselves is believed to have been a Weymann type; this was for chassis GSR32 and was displayed on the Connaught stand – the company's last – at Olympia in 1930. The 13 Limousine bodies are listed below, with dates.

GXO22	1929	GLR80	1930	GNS36	1930
GXO36	1929	GSR1	1930	GNC39	1934
GXO85	1929	GSR32	1930	GAE54	1934
GGP10	1929	GTR12	1930	GEH9	1935
GGP46	1930				

Saloons

Connaught put its name to nine Saloon bodies of various types on the 20/25 chassis. The first two, in 1929 and 1930, were six-light types but all subsequent bodies were four-light designs. The two built in 1933 were described as Continental types, and reflected the latest fashion for a neat four-door Saloon with an integral boot large enough to accommodate luggage for touring on the European continent; other coachbuilders used the same description. GAE41 in 1934 was described as a Special Saloon, and the last two bodies dating from 1935 both incorporated a division. The body with sporting lines for GWE59 in 1934 was probably built by Carlton. The nine Saloons were:

GXO61	1929	GSY77	1933	GWE59	1934
GWP34	1930	GRC10	1934	GLG40	1935
GDX41	1933	GAE41	1934	GOH48	1935

25/30 COACHWORK

The only coachwork on a 25/30 chassis claimed for Connaught is a Limousine on GAN9. It was actually built by Palmer of Dover and was completed late in 1936.

COOPER

London – 20/25

Cooper Motor Bodies were not coachbuilders in the traditional sense. They were body dealers, who bought surplus bodies from both the major volume manufacturers and from the independent coachbuilders. Bodies from the latter source would become available if, for example, an order was cancelled at a late stage, or if a batch of popular bodies built in advance had failed to sell through. Coopers would then supply and fit these bodies, either to new chassis or to older ones whose owners wanted a new style, making such dimensional adjustments as might be necessary. Their activities resulted in some unusual combinations.

Coopers were based in the Shepherds Bush area of London in the 1920s, but by the start of the 1930s had moved to Putney. They certainly rebodied several Rolls-Royce Twenty chassis with newer coachwork, but during the era of the 20/25 they also mounted

Cooper's skill was in adapting bodies to suit chassis for which they had not originally been intended. This is 20/25 chassis GLR2 from 1930, wearing a Weymann Saloon body that was probably built for a big Austin chassis. The combination actually worked rather well.

Corsica coachwork was usually readily recognisable, and this Sports Saloon on 20/25 chassis GFT43 was quite futuristic for 1931.

In this case, the body that Cooper fitted may well have originally been intended for a 20/25 chassis like GHW72, on which it was pictured here. The lines suggest Freestone & Webb, who were one of the coachbuilders that disposed of surplus bodies through Coopers.

five bodies onto brand-new chassis. There were two in 1930, one in 1932, and two more in 1934.

The earliest of these was for chassis GLR2, which received a six-light Weymann saloon that was most probably originally intended for an Austin 20hp. Also in 1930, chassis GLR63 received a six-light Saloon body with Division, the origin of which remains unidentified.

In 1932, chassis GHW72 was bodied with a neat four-light Saloon body that may well have originated with Freestone & Webb. The origins of the two 1934 bodies, however, remain uncertain. One was a six-light Saloon on chassis GRC20, and the second was another Saloon on chassis GYD12.

Coopers also rebodied three other 20/25 chassis. GPS14 gained an estate car body, probably in the late 1940s or early 1950s. GYH18 seems to have had a body built by Barker but carrying Cooper coachplates from 1935, and GYH19 gained a Park Ward Saloon body that was fitted by Coopers.

CORSICA
London – 20/25, Wraith

Corsica was a small London coachbuilder founded in the Islington area of London in 1920 and later based in Cricklewood. It was well known for creating low-cost coachwork based on ideas provided by its customers, and that endeared it to the sporting fraternity. Some of those bodies were quite exotic, and that tradition continued through the 1930s, but the company did not survive into the post-war era.

Corsica was not a popular choice as a coachbuilder on small-horsepower Rolls-Royce chassis; perhaps there was a dissociation in customers' minds between the high cost of the chassis and the low cost of Corsica coachwork. Nevertheless, the company did built the bodies for four new chassis in the 1930s, of which three were 20/25 types and one was a Wraith.

20/25 COACHWORK

The first of the three Corsica bodies for 20/25 chassis was perhaps the most individual, and was a sloping-tailed four-door Sports Saloon on GFT43 in 1931. The second body was also unusually proportioned, and was a six-light Saloon with no running-boards and helmet-type wings. This was built in 1932 on GRW34. The third body was rather more ordinary by comparison, and was a Limousine built in 1936 on GTK40.

Two other Corsica bodies are known on 20/25 chassis, but both were later rebodies.

WRAITH COACHWORK

The last Corsica body mounted to a new small-horsepower Rolls-Royce chassis was for Wraith WMB16 in late 1938. As a rather heavy-looking six-light razor-edge Saloon, it was perhaps uncharacteristic of Corsica's output, but it maintained the company's tradition of building highly individual bodies. This body was also the last one that Corsica mounted on any new Derby-built chassis.

CROALL
Edinurgh – Twenty, 20/25

John Croall & Sons of Edinburgh was the leading Scottish coachbuilder in the inter-war years. Its relationship to a lesser known Edinburgh coachbuilder, Croall & Croall, is acknowledged but unclear. The company was very successful in the early years of the 20th century and in 1908 bought out HJ Mulliner, which certainly helped its relationship with Rolls-Royce.

Built for Wraith chassis WMB16 in 1938, this Corsica Saloon was as conventional as this small London coachbuilder got.

From 1927 Croall pandered to the growing popularity of Weymann bodies and that year claimed to be the only Scottish builder of the genuine article. Nevertheless, a year later it introduced its own derivative called Croallight, which was later rendered as Krolite. This was short-lived, and it appears that Croall ceased its coachwork activities at the end of 1929. The name survived, however, perhaps partly as a way of retaining loyal customers. Coachwork with Croall plates continued until 1934, but it was actually built by HJ Mulliner.

TWENTY COACHWORK

John Croall & Sons built 39 known bodies for the Rolls-Royce Twenty chassis between 1922 and 1929. Annual volumes fluctuated quite noticeably. From just one in 1922, the total went up to 14 in 1923 and then down to eight in 1924. There was just one in 1925, and the total rose to four in 1926. There were five in 1927, four in 1928, and just two in the "short" year (for the Twenty) of 1929.

The largest number of any one body type was the Saloon, of which there were a round dozen, the last few using Weymann construction. Next most numerous were the Landaulettes, of which there were eight in 1923-1924. There were also eight Tourers between 1922 and 1925.

Cabriolets

All three Cabriolets by Croall on the Twenty chassis were delivered in 1923. They were for chassis numbers 89K7, GA57 and GF59.

Coupé

The only example of this body style from Croall was a neat Doctor's Coupé that was delivered in 1929 on chassis GVO52.

Drophead coupé

There were two Drophead Coupés, the earlier one built in 1923 for chassis GA51, and the later one a rather heavy-looking design for GHJ21 in 1927.

Landaulettes

Of the 10 Landaulette bodies built between 1923 and 1928, two were described as Three-quarter Landaulettes, indicating that they had an additional window behind each rear door. These two were on GAK23 and GRK73, both dating from 1924. The 10 bodies and their dates were as follows:

82K4	1923	GAK23	1924	GZK46	1926
89K2	1923	GRK73	1924	GUJ14	1927
GA3	1923	GLK42	1924	GTM23	1928
GA24	1923				

Limousines

The two Limousine bodies were both on early chassis, which were GH19 in 1923 and GDK70 in 1924.

Saloons

Croall built 12 Saloon bodies on the Twenty chassis between 1924 and 1929. The last four, in 1928-1929, were Weymann types. The full list is below.

GMK16	1924	GZK59	1926	GYL24	1928
GRK55	1924	GHJ31	1927	GBM1	1928
GDK3	1924	GRJ65	1927	GKM63	1928
GOK18	1926	GUJ12	1927	GLN53	1929

Tourers

The eight Tourer bodies were all on early chassis, and there were none after 1925. One (GH18) was a two-door type. The eight were:

43G8	1922	GF55	1923	GDK79	1924
57S0	1923	GF69	1923	GPK31	1925
64H0	1923	GH18	1923		

Two-seater

There was a single Two-seater body, which was built in 1926 for chassis GDK33.

20/25 COACHWORK

John Croall & Sons put their name to a dozen bodies for the 20/25 chassis between 1929 and 1934, but

Edinburgh coachbuilder Croall built this solid-looking Drophead Coupé for Twenty chassis GHJ21 in 1927.

Tom Clarke (*The Rolls-Royce 20/25hp*) believes that every one of them was actually built by HJ Mulliner. These dozen bodies necessarily affect the total from each coachbuilder according to whether they are counted for Croall or for HJ Mulliner. There was just one in 1929; three followed in 1930; three more in 1932; there were four in 1933; and the last one was completed in 1934. As had been the case with the Twenty chassis, most demand was for Saloon bodies, and Landaulettes came second in terms of numbers.

Landaulettes

There were three Landaulette bodies for the 20/25 chassis. The first two were built in 1930, on GLR47 and GSR59, and the third was on GAU54 in 1932.

Limousine

Just one Limousine was built. This was completed in late 1932 and was on chassis GRW19.

Saloons

There were seven Saloon bodies. The earliest was for GXO37 in 1929, was of Weymann construction, and was displayed at the Scottish Show that year. The second was also of Weymann construction but was metal panelled; this too became a Scottish Show car, this time in 1930. GKT 24 in 1932 appears to have been the company's first body to use the Silentbloc mounting principles. The seven Saloons were as follows:

GXO37	1929	GSY6	1933	GYZ29	1933
GTR33	1930	GTZ66	1933	GUB75	1934
GKT24	1932				

Saloon Coupé

Croall built a single Saloon Coupé body (sometimes described as a Fixed-head Coupé), which was for chassis GDX11 in 1933. In 1936, this body was transferred onto brand-new chassis GTK16.

CROFTS
Croydon – 20/25

Alban Crofts was a small coachbuilder based in Croydon, Surrey that worked on a variety of chassis in the 1920s but was perhaps best known for its work for Trojan. In the 1930s, it focused on commercial bodywork, but not entirely to the exclusion of car bodies: not only did it build the coachwork for all the original HRG 1500 models, but there was also a single Limousine body for a Rolls-Royce 20/25 chassis in 1930. That chassis was number GWP35.

CROSBIE & DUNN
Smethwick – Twenty, 20/25, 25/30

The Smethwick coachbuilder Crosbie & Dunn was formed in 1927 by two former employees of the Birmingham coachbuilder Flewitt. In the period up to 1939 it constructed around 75 bodies on Rolls-Royce chassis, and these formed the bulk of its output. There were bodies on the Phantom chassis of the period as well as on the small-horsepower models.

Crosbie & Dunn built at least ten bodies on the Twenty chassis in 1927 and 1928; there were 23 more for the 20/25 between 1929 and 1936; and there were just two on the 25/30 in 1937. There was also at least one rebody of an earlier Twenty chassis.

TWENTY COACHWORK

Three bodies were delivered on Twenty chassis during 1927, the company's first year of operation, and a further seven followed in 1928. They embraced a fairly typical variety for the period.

Two of the 1927 bodies were Saloons, for chassis GAJ55 and GAJ59. That on GAJ55 was a six-light type, but it is not clear whether both had the same configuration. The third body that year was a Landaulette, for chassis GUJ26.

Among the 1928 bodies, Coupés were in the majority. There was a three-quarters Coupé in March 1928 on GXL75, and then three more Coupé bodies for GYL37, GYL75, and GFN60. Two Saloons were built, for GYL20 and GFN42, and there was a single Drophead Coupé for GWL9.

Crosbie & Dunn also rebodied GEN9, which had been new in 1929 with a Weymann Saloon body. Its new body was a Drophead Coupé with a long tail that probably incorporated a dickey seat.

20/25 COACHWORK

Crosbie & Dunn built 23 bodies for the Rolls-Royce 20/25, beginning with one in 1929 and three in 1930. There were five in 1931 but 1932 was a poor year for most coachbuilders, and just two bodies were made.

A raked centre pillar gives distinction to this 1928 Coupé by Crosbie & Dunn for Twenty chassis GFN60. (Real Car Company)

There were five again in 1933, three each in 1934 and 1935, and just one in 1936. The 23 bodies were made up of just three body types, which were Landaulettes, Limousines, and Saloons. Within those categories, however, there was plenty of variation.

Landaulettes
Three of the 23 bodies on 20/25 chassis were Landaulettes. These were for GFT35 in 1931, GBA5 in 1933, and GOH30 in 1935. GBA5 has been described as a four-light Saloon Landaulette.

Limousine
There were four Limousine bodies, spread evenly over the years of the 20/25's production run. The earliest was completed in 1929 for chassis GGP59, and the next one was for GOS68 in 1931. The third one followed in 1933 for GDX20, and the last was in autumn 1936 for GTK58 – a less successful design that made the chassis look rather overbodied.

Saloons
Saloon bodies were fitted to 16 of the 23 bodies for 20/25 chassis that came from the Crosbie & Dunn workshops. There were nevertheless several sub-types. GSY53, for example, was a swept-tail Sports Saloon, and GRF12 and GOH15 were also four-light Sports Saloons, the latter with a Division for good measure. Other bodies with Divisions were for GSR20, GMU74, and (probably) GED80. The four-light body for GFT50 seems to have been Crosbie & Dunn's version of a Thrupp & Maberly style. The 16 Saloon bodies were built for the following chassis:

GLR5	1930	GMU74	1932	GED18	1934
GLR24	1930	GHW79	1932	GED80	1934
GSR20	1930	GSY53	1933	GYD38	1934
GNS17	1931	GLZ 54	1933	GRF12	1935
GOS23	1931	GLZ55	1933	GOH15	1935
GFT50	1931				

25/30 COACHWORK
The company built just two bodies for the 25/30 chassis in 1937; there were none for the later Wraith chassis. The two bodies were both six-light Saloons, and were for chassis GHO26 and GAR2.

CUBITT
Aylesbury – Twenty
Cubitt built a single body for the small-horsepower Rolls-Royce, and that was a Coupé on a Twenty chassis, GLK12, in 1924. The car was for SF Edge, who at that time was Managing Director of Cubitts

Engineering Co Ltd in Aylesbury and was building up his shareholding in AC Cars while farming at Ditching in Sussex. Nick Walker notes that the main quality of the bodies produced by Cubitt was their cheapness, and that "the quality was at a similarly low level."

CUNARD
London – Twenty, 20/25
Two different incarnations of the Cunard company built coachwork on Rolls-Royce chassis in this period. The earlier one was the Cunard Motor & Carriage Company Ltd, which had been founded in 1911 with premises in Putney, south-west London. This company became a subsidiary of Napier soon after it was established and was generally considered to be that maker's in-house coachbuilder. However, it continued to build for other chassis until being acquired in 1925 by Weymann Motor Bodies Ltd after Napier closed down in 1924. It constructed five bodies on the Rolls-Royce Twenty chassis in 1923-1924.

The second version of the Cunard company was established in August 1930 by Cunard's former Managing Director, RI Musselwhite, who had more recently been with Thrupp & Maberly. He and VE Freestone (formerly of Freestone & Webb and also latterly with Thrupp & Maberly) revived the company in a brand-new factory in the London district of Acton, but the venture ended in 1931 when the business was taken over by Stewart & Ardern, the London Morris agents. During its brief existence, this company put its name to two bodies on 20/25 chassis – although the earlier one was actually sub-contracted to Thrupp & Maberly and the other might have been so, too.

TWENTY COACHWORK
The earliest Twenty with a Cunard body was GA32 in 1923, which was built as a Limousine in 1923. There was a second Limousine on GDK62 the following year. The other three bodies, all built in 1924, were a Cabriolet on GAK30, a Saloon on GDK59, and a Landaulette on GLK10, the latter the last body by this incarnation of Cunard.

20/25 COACHWORK
The earlier of Cunard's two bodies on the 20/25 chassis was delivered in September 1930 and was a six-light Landaulette on GSR63. As noted above, this was actually built by Thrupp & Maberly, who were the former employers of Cunard's two principals. The second body was a Sedanca de Ville for GNS25 that was delivered later in 1930. The construction of this body might also have been sub-contracted to another company.

DALLING
Location unknown – Twenty

The Dalling Motor Co is recorded as the builder of a Tourer body on Rolls-Royce Twenty number 63H8 in 1923. Unfortunately, nothing is known about the coachbuilder itself.

DAVIES
Location unknown – Twenty

A company called Davies is recorded as building the Limousine body for Rolls-Royce Twenty GH8 in 1923. There is no further information to help identify this coachbuilder more precisely.

EASTER
London – Twenty

JH Easter was a small London coachbuilder that operated from a mews just off Baker Street in the Marylebone area. The company was active before the Great War, and built coachwork for some of the DFP chassis that WO Bentley and his brother imported. The connection was retained when WO Bentley set up in business making his own chassis, and JH Easter bodied several early examples up to 1924.

The company also bodied one Rolls-Royce Twenty chassis as a Saloon. This was GYK74, in 1926.

ELKINGTON
London – Twenty

The Elkington Carriage Company worked out of premises in London's smart Chelsea district until 1928, when it moved to Chiswick; its old premises were taken over by Gurney Nutting. The company worked mainly with the more prestigious chassis, and in particular with Minerva and, later, with Talbot. A later alliance was with Frazer Nash, but that company opened its own bodyshop in 1934 and Elkington

These two Twenty Limousines from Elkington illustrate some of the minor differences that made one body different from the next. This one was on chassis GPK41 in 1925 and is a fairly straightforward six-light design with vee windscreen and the embellishment of wheel discs.

This second Limousine, built on GOK59 just a year later, has a more pronounced difference in the colour of the upper panels but has plain wire wheels with no discs. The triangular windows alongside the windscreen are interesting, and would briefly be fashionable about four years later; their purpose was to improve the driver's vision at junctions. This car is also fitted with bumpers front and rear.

seems to have disappeared soon afterwards.

The company built several bodies for the larger Rolls-Royce chassis, and five bodies for the Twenty. There were two in 1923, two in 1925, and one in 1926.

Two of the bodies were Saloons, for chassis 65H1 in 1923 and GNK23 in 1925. Two more were Limousines, both very solid-looking constructions, for GPK41 in 1925 and GOK59 in 1926. There was a single Coupé, built on chassis 89K8 in 1923.

ELLIOTT
Reading – Twenty

Samuel Elliott & Sons of Reading in Berkshire began life as a joinery and moulding company in Newbury in the nineteenth century, and its Reading branch in Caversham became one of the area's largest employers. The two parts of the company separated in 1904, and it was the Reading branch that diversified into coachbuilding in the 1920s, apparently as a sideline.

It held the sole concession for the Belgian branch of Vanden Plas for a couple of years from 1924, and subsequently built what was probably a small number of bodies to its own designs. The company then returned to joinery and developed the shopfitting side of its business. When times were difficult in the years immediately after the Second World War, Elliott's turned to coachbuilding again, building the bodies for the Healey Elliott saloon, but subsequently returned to shopfitting and finally closed in 1999.

Elliott's are known to have built a single Limousine body on a Rolls-Royce Twenty chassis in 1928. The recipient chassis was GBM19 and the car was registered (as YW 7616) in London.

FERGUSON
Belfast – 25/30
JB Ferguson & Co Ltd was a car dealership in Belfast, founded in 1903 by the older brother of tractor manufacturer Harry Ferguson. The company had its own coachbuilding department, and in 1937 built its only body on a Rolls-Royce chassis. This was a Limousine on 25/30 chassis GRO74; some years later, the car was donated to the Ulster Folk Museum.

FLEWITT
Birmingham – Twenty, 20/25
The Flewitt Company was established in Birmingham in 1905, and was building coachwork for Rolls-Royce Silver Ghost chassis by 1912. The company is known to have worked with several other upmarket makes of chassis, and built coachwork for both the Rolls-Royce Twenty and the 20/25 model. However, these activities ceased in the mid-1930s when Flewitt gained a contract from Austin for some of its catalogued bodies. The company subsequently devoted itself to commercial body building.

There were 49 Flewitt bodies on the Twenty chassis and just two on the 20/25. The company displayed the versatile repertoire expected of a provincial coachbuilder at the time. By 1928, it held a Weymann licence, but appears not to have built any Weymann bodies before that year.

TWENTY COACHWORK
Flewitt dealt with a flurry of interest in the new Twenty chassis, building no fewer than 18 bodies for it in 1923. Interest dropped steadily over the next few years, however, and there were nine bodies in 1924, five in 1925, and just three in 1926. Thereafter, business picked up again, and the company provided six bodies in 1927 and seven in 1928, dropping back down again to just one in 1929.

Cabriolet
There was a single Cabriolet body, which was built for chassis 59S4 in 1923.

Coupés
Of the six Coupé bodies that Flewitt built between 1923 and 1925, two were three-quarters types, as shown by an asterisk (*) in the table below. The Coupés were among the more attractive Flewitt creations for the Twenty.

59S8	1923	GRK60	1924	GCK44*	1925
GA68*	1923	GNK57	1925	GCK63	1925

Drophead Coupé
Only one Drophead Coupé came from Flewitt for the Twenty chassis, and that was a three-quarter type for chassis GWL31 in 1928.

Landaulettes
Flewitt fulfilled orders for eight Landaulette bodies, all but one of them in the first two years of Twenty production. They were as follows:

54S8	1923	86K8	1923	GLK34	1924
75A3	1923	GA65	1923	GWL23	1928
81K8	1923	GAK29	1924		

Limousines
There was strong demand for Limousine bodies, too, and Flewitt built nine of them for the Twenty chassis:

59S1	1923	GRK39	1924	GAJ30	1927
83K4	1923	GNK30	1925	GKM56	1928
87K4	1923	GZK45	1926	GKM82	1928

Saloons
The most common Flewitt bodies on the Twenty chassis were Saloons, typically both neat and sturdy in appearance. Weymann types appeared in 1928, and there were three of them among the total of 15, as indicated in the list below by an asterisk (*):

GA34	1923	GUK36	1926	GXL67	1927
GF47	1923	GMJ72	1926	GYL40*	1928
GRK74	1924	GHJ1	1927	GYL71	1928
GDK19	1924	GHJ9	1927	GFN26*	1928
GCK26	1925	GHJ35	1927	GEN5*	1929

Two-seater
There was little demand for two-seater bodies, and Flewitt built only one, which was for chassis 52S0 in 1923. This was its first body on a Twenty chassis.

Tourers
Tourer bodies were in demand between 1923 and 1927, and Flewitt built eight of them, mostly in the first two years of production. They were as follows:

58S2	1923	GF5	1923	GDK11	1924
72A7	1923	GAK18	1924	GXL19	1927
GA61	1923	GAK41	1924		

20/25 COACHWORK
It is noteworthy that there were no bodies from Flewitt for the 20/25 chassis until 1934, when the first of two Saloon types was built for chassis GLB36. The later

one was a four-light design for GPG44 in 1935.

In addition, Flewitt rebodied a 1930 chassis, GNS36, as a hearse.

FOUNTAIN

Horsham – Twenty, 20/25

Fountain's Auto Carriage Works was established at Horsham in Sussex in 1913, and exhibited at Olympia every year between 1921 and 1930. The company then disappeared from view. The company's early work was largely with imported chassis, but in later years it also built drophead bodies on Hillman chassis.

Fountain's built two known bodies on the small-horsepower Rolls-Royce chassis, and both were Tourers. The earlier one was on Twenty chassis GUJ2 in 1927, a car that was registered locally in East Sussex. The later one was delivered in May 1931 on 20/25 chassis GOS58 and acquired a London registration. This second body may well have been one of the last that Fountain's ever built. The company also built a small number of bodies for larger Rolls-Royce models.

FREESTONE & WEBB

London – Twenty, 20/25, 25/30, Wraith

Newly established in 1923, Freestone & Webb was a London coachbuilder located close to the Bentley factory. They picked up a good deal of Bentley work but quickly spread to other makes as well, particularly imported ones. The company took out a Weymann patent and most of their 1920s bodies depended on Weymann principles, but before the end of the decade they were working with metal panels that allowed wider scope for their designs. The 1930s saw batch-building and some highly successful designs, the best known being the razor-edged Brougham Saloon that was originally designed for Bentley chassis but was adapted to several others.

Freestone & Webb built eight bodies on the Rolls-Royce Twenty chassis (plus one rebody in 1929). On the 20/25 there were at least 86 bodies, although the company's practice of building for stock seems to have led to a surplus of bodies suitable for the 20/25, and these extra bodies may have been sold off to companies such as Coopers, who would have adapted them to suit other chassis. There were then 26 bodies for the 25/30 – plus as many as four "spares" that may have ended up on other makes – and just nine for the Wraith, with a tenth body built but not allocated to a chassis.

TWENTY COACHWORK

Freestone & Webb were heavily committed to Weymann coachwork when the Twenty was in production, and probably all their bodies for that

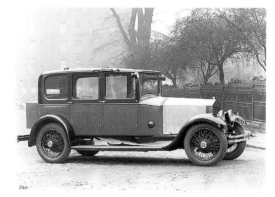

The fabric panelling of the Freestone & Webb Saloon body on Twenty chassis GMJ7 is very apparent in this picture. Although the overall shape of the body was to a familiar design, there were several special features on this 1927 example.

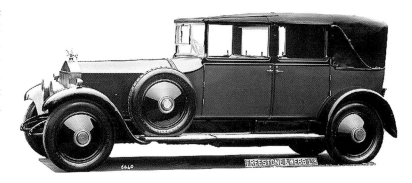

Weymann construction is again apparent in this four-light Saloon from late 1927, on Twenty chassis GUJ25. The front of the roof appears to have had a folding section, and possibly removable cantrails as well.

chassis had the characteristic fabric panels. The earliest was delivered in 1924; there were then two in 1925, three in 1927, and two in 1929 (three if the rebody is included).

Cabriolets and Coupés

No pictures are known of the Cabriolet built in 1925 on GYK18, but the 1927 Coupé on GUJ60 was a nicely proportioned "three-quarter" (four-light) type. There were then two interesting Coupés to essentially the same design in 1929, one on new chassis GEN75 and the other a rebody on 1926 chassis GYK82. Both had dummy landau irons on the rear panel with a neat triangular window below them, an arrangement that allowed rear-seat passengers to see out while retaining a degree of privacy. It would be repeated on other Freestone & Webb bodies, notably the Grafton Coupé for the Bentley six-cylinder chassis.

Saloons

Five of these bodies were Saloons, although they were not all to the same design. No pictures are known of the bodies on GDK61 from 1924 or GYK56 from 1925, but both are likely to have had the coachbuilder's standard six-light design. The same basic design was built for GMJ7 in 1927, but with several special features, including a front roof section that both contained a sliding sunroof and could be

This Coupé for 20/25 chassis GKT29 in 1932 was a bespoke design. By this stage, the lower panels appear to have been metal, but the roof was certainly covered in fabric to give a Drophead Coupé effect. Extra louvres in the scuttle sides give a "long-bonnet" effect.

In the early 1930s, Freestone & Webb actively developed designs they could build in small volumes, and this was their very neat Saloon for the 1935 season, with design number 1403. This was the first of four, for chassis GHA11. Two-tone paintwork adds to the pleasing effect.

folded back onto the main roof. The almost formal body for GUJ25 in 1927 was a four-light design with dummy landau irons and probably also a removable or folding roof section, but the 1929 four-light body on GEN74 could hardly have been more different, with clear sporting overtones.

20/25 COACHWORK

All the Freestone & Webb bodies on 20/25 bodies were closed types, with the single exception of a Cabriolet de Ville for chassis GFT29 in 1932. The vast majority were four-light Saloons, although there was a handful of six-light types as well, some being described as Limousines. Next most common were Fixed-head Coupés and Saloon Coupés, and finally there was also a clutch of Sedanca Coupés.

Coupés

There was a certain blurring of the boundaries between the Fixed-head Coupé and the Saloon Coupé as designs evolved in the first half of the 1930s. The

earliest Freestone & Webb design, in 1932, was a bespoke body for chassis GKT29 and certainly was a Fixed-head Coupé, with dummy landau irons on blind rear quarters and a fabric roof covering. However, the "volume" design 1281 introduced in 1933 made no pretence to a fabric roof and the two examples for GEX44 and GLZ7 simply had blind rear quarters. This design evolved: the two examples of design 1281/A for chassis GED81 and GXB58 in 1933-1934 were four-light variants, but when 1281/B arrived in 1934 it reverted to the original blind rear quarters for three chassis: GED17, GYD44 and GYD56.

Jack Barclay's order for four Coupés to a special design numbered 1569 in 1935 was for four-light bodies, now with a prominent Art Deco scallop on each side and side-mounted spare wheels instead of the rear-mounted ones on earlier designs. These bodies were built as a batch and were mounted on chassis GLG53, GYH44, GOH8 and GOH72. Meanwhile, individual requests were still welcomed, and there were three one-off bodies in 1935, to designs 1592 (chassis GLG18), 1624 (GBJ15) and 1377/A (GWE80).

Saloons

The early Saloon design was neat, with a rather pert rear end that did not allow much room for luggage in the built-in boot. This appeared in 1932, and there was a single example in 1933 of a derivative design (number 1272 on chassis GHW4) with a swept tail that had even less boot space. However, by 1933 the design had matured into what Freestone & Webb called their Continental Saloon, no doubt inspired by Park Ward and now featuring a boot that was both decently sized and attractively shaped. Just two were built to the original design 1275; there were then six more to 1275/A and at least seven to the further-evolved 1275/B in 1933-1934. By the end of 1933, the final 1275/C design had appeared, with an enlarged boot, and at least six of these were built. The 21 chassis for which design 1275 and its variants were built are listed below. Note, though, that the Freestone & Webb order book lists one additional example of 1275/B and one additional 1275/C as well; in both cases, the identity of the destination chassis is disputed. Dates shown are those for delivery of completed cars.

GHW47	1933	GDX2	1933	GXB23	1934
GRW54	1933	GSY65	1933	GUB27	1934
GAW34	1933	GSY94	1933	GKC9	1934
GAW35	1933	GLZ18	1933	GKC18	1934
GWX29	1933	GLZ27	1933	GYD20	1934
GWX57	1933	GBA51	1933	GYD42	1934
GWX80	1933	GBA53	1933	GWE25	1934

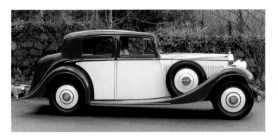

The second "volume" Saloon design was 1567, an evolution of the earlier 1403 with a neat body side moulding that allowed this style of two-colour paintwork. This one is on 1935 20/25 chassis number GLG69. (Real Car Co)

A new "volume" design numbered 1403 first appeared in 1934, but only four were built in this year and 1935; these were for chassis GHA11, GRC61, GYH46, and GOH58. This design evolved into design 1567, with an Art Deco scallop on the rear doors that lent itself to two-colour paint schemes. London dealer Jack Barclay took a batch of eight of these in 1935, some with Divisions, and two further examples were built that year to individual order. The full list of ten chassis for which these bodies were built was:

GSF54   GLG69   GHG30   GYH58   GEH24
GLJ5   GRF24   GPG26   GYH20   GEH3

Design 1567 developed into design 1628/A during 1936, but only two were built on the 20/25 chassis. These were for chassis GLJ54 and GLJ73, and the design remained available for the 25/30. There was also a 20/25 version of Freestone & Webb's famous razor-edged Brougham Saloon, which had been a major success on Bentley chassis since its introduction in 1935. This had design number 1632/A, and two examples were built: GCJ39 in 1935 and GBK63 in 1936 were the only ones on the 20/25 chassis, but this was another design that remained available into the 25/30 era.

There were of course some bespoke four-light Saloon designs between 1933 and 1936 on the 20/25 chassis. During 1933 there were one each of designs 1296 (for GRW62) and 1307 (for GAW40). In 1934 came single examples of designs 1381 (for GUB3), 1462 with division (for GNC75), and 1478 (for GNC6). During 1935 the company built one example of design 1536 with a Division (for GFE31), and in 1936 the singletons had designs 1562 (on GTK46) and 1643 (on GCJ41).

A six-light Saloon with Division design appeared in 1933 as number 1283, and at least two examples were built for the 20/25 chassis that year, on GRW26 and GSY12; without a Division and with revised wings, the design became 1283/C for GBK12 in 1936. Other six-light types were described as Limousines, but there were only two: design 1286 was for chassis GRW60 in 1933 and design 1528 for GWE39 in 1934.

Sedanca Coupés

The first Sedanca Coupé was a most elegant design, number 1324, with a gently curving waistline and a distinctly sporting air to it. It made its debut in late 1933 on chassis GLZ42, but only one other example was built, for GBA64 early the following year. There was then a single example of design 1568 for chassis GPG2 in 1935, this time with a straight waistline and a fabric-covered roof.

25/30 COACHWORK

Very noticeable among the bodies for the 25/30 chassis is that there were no closed two-door types, whether Fixed-head Coupés or Saloon Coupés. Otherwise, the mix of body types was very much as it had been for the 20/25. Most numerous were four-light Saloons, supplemented by a handful of six-light types and Limousines. Also in penny numbers were de Ville bodies, and there was a single Drophead Coupé, built on chassis GRO1 in 1937 and apparently deliberately similar to a John Charles body that the customer owned.

De Ville types

De Ville bodies were never numerous, and Freestone & Webb built just five on the 25/30 chassis, all to different designs. Three of them were Sedanca de Ville types. Design 1741 for GRM20 in 1936 was suitably formal, in marked contrast to design 1761, built later that year for the band-leader Geraldo on GTL66 and incorporating rear-wheel spats. Design 1806 for GRO19 in 1937 was actually described as a Brougham de Ville and incorporated the curved rear quarters of the company's Brougham Saloons in an otherwise quite severe design. There was then a Coupé de Ville in 1938 to design 1937 for GZR7, but perhaps the most attractive was a two-light Sedanca Coupé to design 1851 on GRP45 in 1937, incorporating the Brougham curved rear quarters again.

Saloons

The first "volume" Saloon style was number 1628/A, which was carried over from the 20/25. Five were built in 1936, for chassis GUL68, GRM24, GTL52, GRM57 and GWN1. The last two each had a

Freestone & Webb hit the jackpot with their razor-edge Brougham Saloon design in 1935, originally designed for Bentley chassis and always more numerous there than on the contemporary Rolls-Royce. This one is a 1936 example, on 25/30 chassis GUL39.

Division, and GUL68 may have done, too. Then for 1937, the popular style was design 1827, of which Jack Barclay took a batch of three (all with Divisions); one more was built for a customer and four more were listed as built for stock and were probably later sold off. The four that were definitely allocated to chassis went onto GHO73, GRP75, GGR48, and GAR5.

Just one razor-edged Brougham Saloon to design 1632/A found a home (on GUL39 in 1936), and there were four more individual designs: 1562 on GWN74 in 1937, 1705 on GTL51 in 1936, 1805 on GGM33 in 1936, and 1809 on GRO55 in 1937, the latter two both having Divisions.

Six-light Saloons were very much in a minority, with one described as a Sports Saloon to design 1743 on GXM29 in 1936, and one to design 1821 on GMO11 in 1937. Of the four bodies described as Limousines, one had a gently curving waistline and stylish side scallops to design 1615 and was on GHO12 in 1937; the other three had design 1867, which was similar but with a straight waistline and no scallops, and were on GMP42 and GGR42 in 1937, and GZR20 in 1938.

WRAITH COACHWORK

The range of Freestone & Webb bodies on the Rolls-Royce Wraith chassis was much more limited than on earlier small-horsepower models. There were Saloons with both four and six lights, Touring Saloons (with larger luggage boots), and Touring Limousines (with six lights and large boots) – but that was all. Just nine bodies were delivered on Wraith chassis, all during 1939, and a tenth was built for stock but apparently not fitted to a chassis by Freestone & Webb.

Design 2027 was the only four-light Saloon that the coachbuilder drew up; it had a Division and just the one was built, for chassis WGC4. Design 1996 was described in the order book as along the lines of an Arthur Mulliner job, and there was just the one of these, too, on WRB58. The single six-light Saloon was to design 2033 on chassis WLB34.

Design 1993 was a four-light Touring Saloon with Division, of which just the one was built, for WHC54. There were then four Touring Saloons to design 1998, which had cutaway rear-wheel spats most uncharacteristic of Freestone & Webb and was in fact based on a 1938 HJ Mulliner Show design. Three were mounted on WMB26, WMB39 (both with Divisions), and WHC55, but the fourth was built for stock and its fate remains unknown. Lastly, there were two Touring Limousines, six-light bodies to design 2034 that were mounted on WHC50 and WEC29.

Completed just a few months before the outbreak of war in 1939, this elegant Touring Saloon for Wraith WMB39 was based on an HJ Mulliner design. It was one of two with this design that were equipped with a Division.

The essential elements of the razor-edge design were carried over to this unique Sedanca Coupé for 25/30 chassis GRP45 in 1937. The curvature of the rear upper panels that gave this design the Brougham name is very apparent here.

GAISFORD & WORBOYS
London – Twenty
This short-lived London coachbuilder was founded in 1922, apparently from the original Lancefield Motor Body Works. It took over that company's premises in Lancefield Street in West Kilburn. George Worboys left the business in 1927, and it was probably at about the same time that the company moved to larger premises locally and was renamed the Lancefield Coachworks (qv).

Gaisford & Worboys probably survived largely as a sub-contractor to other coachbuilders in its early days, but by the time it was renamed Lancefield the company was certainly building complete bodies under its own name. Only one is known on a small-horsepower Rolls-Royce, and that was a rather unexciting saloon on Twenty chassis GMJ70 in 1927. That the car was registered in Cambridge suggests the company's catchment area was not confined to London.

GARNER
London – Twenty
The H Garner who built two bodies for Rolls-Royce Twenty chassis in the mid-1920s was probably Garner Motors Ltd whose premises were at North Acton Road in London NW10. The company had been founded by Henry Garner and originated from Birmingham. It also built single-deck bus bodies and was probably acquired in 1926 by Hawson's of Sunbury-on-Thames to become Hawson-Garner Ltd.

The company built a Tourer body for GSK68 in 1925 and a three-quarters Coupé for GZK33 the following year.

GELLITT
London – 20/25
The records show the name of Gellitt as the builder of a Limousine body for 20/25 chassis number GNS46 in 1930. The coachbuilder is known to have been located in north-west London, but there is no further clear information.

GILL
London – Twenty, 20/25
TH Gill & Son Ltd was established in 1891 as a London carriage maker, and from 1912 moved into coachwork for motor cars. During the 1920s, the company gained a reputation for specialising in All-weather bodies, and in 1931 formed a subsidiary called Gill All-weather Bodies Ltd. The original Gill company closed in 1935, but the subsidiary company, renamed All-weather Bodies in 1932,

carried on building specialised coachwork until 1939 and did not finally close until 1955. (For the bodies by the subsidiary company, please see the separate entry for All-weather Bodies.)

TH Gill & Son built a total of 25 bodies for the small-horsepower Rolls-Royce models, 16 of them for the Twenty and nine for the 20/25.

TWENTY COACHWORK
In the 16 bodies that Gill constructed for Rolls-Royce Twenty chassis, there was no advance warning of the company's later specialisation in All-weather types. The most numerous were Cabriolets, Limousines and Saloons. The company held a Weymann licence by 1928, but again there is little evidence that this was used on bodies for the Twenty.

Cabriolets
Five of the Gill bodies for the Twenty were Cabriolets. These were on chassis GUK16, GUK45, GMJ34 and GMJ57 in 1926, and on GUJ74 in 1927.

Coupé
There was a single Coupé body, which was for chassis GVO12 in 1929.

Landaulette
There was also just one Landaulette body, in this case for chassis GAJ23 in 1927.

Limousines
Four customers ordered Limousine coachwork from Gill for the Twenty, and the four bodies were delivered on chassis 56S9 and 82K2 in 1923, and on GSK27 and GSK61 in 1925.

Saloons
Of the four Saloon bodies that Gill built, just one employed the Weymann patents. This was for chassis GKM58 in 1928. The other three Saloons were for GPK76 in 1925, and for GVO47 and GVO67 in 1929.

Tourer
Gill also built a single Tourer body, in this case in 1926 for chassis GMJ54.

20/25 COACHWORK
Of the nine bodies that Gill built for the 20/25 chassis between 1930 and 1933, only one was an All-weather type. Interestingly, this one was attributed to the parent company, while a later one to the same design on the 20/25 chassis was claimed by All-weather Bodies.

All-weather

The single All-weather body had the "Empire" design that undoubtedly helped to make the company's reputation. It was for chassis GFT25 in 1931.

Landaulettes

Gill built three Landaulette bodies on early 20/25 chassis. These were for GLR16 and GSR34 in 1930, and for GAU9 in 1932.

Limousine

There was just one Limousine body, which was for chassis GSR7 in 1930.

Saloons

Three of the nine bodies for the 20/25 were Saloons. The first two were six-light types that were built in 1930. They were for chassis GXO92 and GDP19, the latter being a Weymann type. The third had a four-light design and a Division, and was built for chassis GGA40 in 1933.

Sedanca de Ville

Gill's only Sedanca de Ville body for a small-horsepower Rolls-Royce chassis was built in 1930, for 20/25 number GTR1.

GILL ALL-WEATHER

See **All-Weather Bodies Ltd.**

GLASSBROOK

London – 20/25

FW Glassbrook founded the Mascot Motor Body Works in the Ladbrooke Grove area of west London in 1922. His company specialised in servicing Rolls-Royce models, and also built some coachwork for them under the Glassbrook name. It specialised in formal coachwork, and in more recent years also built hearses.

The company constructed just one body for a new 20/25 chassis, which was a D-back Limousine for GYD14 in 1934. There has been some suspicion that this was actually a rebody, but this seems unlikely.

Glassbrook did of course rebody several other 20/25 chassis, perhaps all under the Mascot brand name. Tom Clarke lists seven with hearse bodies (GRW63, GAW11, GSY14, GSY63, GGA80, GGA81 and GKC28) and one (GHW23) with an All-weather body. There was also at least one hearse rebody on a Wraith, WXA93.

GREYSMITH

Location unknown – Twenty

Nothing is known for certain about the coachbuilder called Greysmith, who built a single Tourer body

on Twenty chassis GOK53 in 1926. However, the Cheshire registration number shown for the car in John Fasal's lists may give some clue about the company's location.

GRIFFINS

Location unknown – Twenty

An otherwise unidentified company called Griffins was responsible for a single Landaulette body on a 1923 Rolls-Royce Twenty chassis, number 69H2. The company may have been local to Tunbridge Wells, where the car's owner lived in 1928, but this is not proven. He replaced it with another Twenty that had Cabriolet de Ville coachwork by Barker.

GRIMSHAW, LEATHER

Sunderland – Twenty

Local records show that Chas Grimshaw & Sons were car body builders in Sunderland's Union Street by 1911, and from 1919 the company appears to have taken on another partner and become Grimshaw, Leather & Co at the same address. Under that name, the body building activities were continued for a few more years, although the business refocused its activities on car sales and during the 1920s became agents for several makes, including Austin, Alvis and Rolls-Royce. An advertisement at the time of the 1926 Olympia Show makes no mention of any coachbuilding activities.

All the bodies for small-horsepower Rolls-Royce models from Grimshaw, Leather & Co were on Rolls-Royce Twenty chassis. There were nine of these, all delivered between 1922 and 1924, and the variety recorded suggests that Grimshaw, Leather may have treated each body as a bespoke order.

The first body for a Twenty chassis was a Tourer for 42G4 in 1922. There were then five bodies in 1923, three being Tourers and the other two a Limousine and a Cabriolet. The Tourers were on chassis 71A2, 87K1 and GF70. The Limousine was on chassis 70A6, and the Cabriolet was on chassis number 80K5.

There were then three more bodies in 1924, of which two were Saloons (on GAK73 and GLK37) and the third a Drophead Coupé on GAK28.

GROSVENOR

London – Twenty

The Grosvenor Carriage Company was founded at Kilburn in north-west London around 1910, and had established itself as a builder of coachwork for Rolls-Royce chassis before the start of the First World War in 1914. After the war's end, the company

The earliest Grosvenor body for a Twenty was this 1924 Saloon with vee windscreen for GF80.

cultivated close connections with Vauxhall, and was at some point bought out by London dealer Stewart & Ardern. It nevertheless continued to build bespoke coachwork for a variety of chassis, including Rolls-Royce, Daimler and Lanchester. After 1932, however, the company's output was entirely for Vauxhall.

Grosvenor built three bodies for the Rolls-Royce Twenty chassis. The earliest was a Saloon for GF80 in 1924. The other two were solid-looking Limousines, both built in 1926. They were for chassis GZK37 and GYK92.

GURNEY NUTTING
London – Twenty, 20/25, 25/30, Wraith

J Gurney Nutting established his coachworks at Croydon in Surrey in 1919, and delivered his first body for a small-horsepower Rolls-Royce chassis in 1923. That year, the Croydon works was destroyed by fire, but the company took the opportunity to move to the fashionable London district of Chelsea, closer to potential customers. Success prompted a move to larger premises in the same district during 1929, and an arrangement with the dealer HR Owen allowed Gurney Nutting to display its wares at that company's

Grosvenor succeeded in making the Twenty look larger than it really was with this Limousine body for GZK37 in 1926. (Real Car Company)

Gurney Nutting built the Owen Sedanca Coupé specifically for the HR Owen dealership. (Simon Clay)

This early example for 20/25 chassis GEX28 in 1933 shows the characteristic lines, with fabric roof and separate trunk-like boot. (Simon Clay)

showrooms in Berkeley Street, Mayfair.

Gurney Nutting produced some of the most inspired and beautifully proportioned bodies of all British coachbuilders in the interwar years. Between 1925 and 1937, these were invariably the work of its talented chief designer, AF McNeil, whose designs were central to the company's success. When he moved to James Young in 1937, Gurney Nutting design remained in good hands as his assistant John Blatchley took over. Blatchley would go on to become the chief body designer at Rolls-Royce when that company began to oversee its own coachwork after the Second World War.

Although Gurney Nutting focused primarily on Bentley and Rolls-Royce work in the 1930s (and many designs were shared between the two marques), the company also worked on other high-quality chassis, such as Delage and Talbot. Between 1931 and 1935, its coachwork on larger Rolls-Royce chassis earned it a prestigious Royal Warrant from the then Prince of Wales (later King Edward VIII).

Records show that there were 11 bodies on the Twenty chassis, 90 on the 20/25, 39 on the 25/30 and a further 11 on the Wraith. The grand total of 151 made Gurney Nutting one of the more prolific coachbuilders on the interwar junior Rolls-Royce chassis.

TWENTY COACHWORK

Gurney Nutting was not particularly well patronised by buyers of Rolls-Royce Twenty chassis, perhaps because its staple Weymann Saloon bodies did not offer anything very obvious that was not available elsewhere. Nevertheless, both these and the Drophead Coupés that came from the company's workshops were neat and satisfying designs. There was just one body on the Twenty in each of the years 1923, 1926 and 1929; 1925 saw two completed and the best years were 1927 and 1928 with three bodies each.

Coupé

Just one example of a Coupé body was built for the Twenty chassis, and this was a Weymann type for GXO 8 in 1929.

Drophead Coupés

The two Drophead Coupés were for chassis GH56 in 1923 and GUJ72 in 1927. It is not clear whether the two were built to the same design, but the body on GUJ72 was particularly handsome.

Saloons

At least seven of the eight Gurney Nutting Saloon bodies for Twenty chassis were Weymann types. The eighth, for GCK51 in 1925, may also have had Weymann construction. The eight bodies with their dates of construction were as follows:

GCK11	1925	GAJ4	1927	GWL17	1928
GCK51	1925	GXL11	1927	GBM77	1928
GYK38	1926	GYL77	1928		

20/25 COACHWORK

Orders for coachwork on the new 20/25 chassis seem to have been quite slow to reach Gurney Nutting. The company completed just three bodies for it in 1930 and only one the following year. However, 1932 saw an upturn in the business with the completion of ten bodies; 1933 was better again with a total of 19, and then there were 30 in 1934 and 27 in 1935.

The Gurney Nutting dependence on Weymann coachwork gradually decreased, and one of the last (on chassis GBT34) was built for Sir Malcolm Campbell, whose Bluebird record car body was also built by Gurney Nutting in 1931. Sedanca Coupé styles became a major success from late 1932, and the "Owen" design (built for dealers HR Owen) was a stand-out that was also offered for the contemporary Bentley chassis. There were some related designs, some under different descriptions that were perhaps designed to preserve the exclusivity of the Owen design.

Coupés

There were several different Coupé designs among the 10 bodies of that type for the 20/25 by Gurney Nutting, and all are grouped together here for convenience.

The very earliest, for chassis GTR40 in 1931, was a Weymann type with a side-mounted spare that allowed for a stylish treatment of the running-board and front wing. Most had four windows, but two were two-light designs. These were on GAU64 in 1932 and GTZ28 in 1933. One body, for GPG47, had an individual specification and was described as a Faux Cabriolet with Division.

Four of the Coupé bodies were "pillarless" types, with no pillar between the door window and the side window so that there appeared to be an unbroken expanse of glass on each side. McNeil's finely judged proportions allowed for a slight fall in the waistline under the rear window, and this design was also seen on contemporary Bentley chassis. The pillarless bodies were on chassis GLZ22, GRF18, GYH29 and GBJ53. GYH29 had the additional feature of rear-wheel spats.

The full list of the Gurney Nutting Coupés on the 20/25 chassis is as follows:

GTR40	1930	GTZ28	1933	GYH29	1935
GAU 64	1932	GRF18	1935	GOH73	1935
GSY79	1933	GPG47	1935	GBJ53	1935
GLZ22	1933				

De Ville types

For convenience again, all the De Ville types by Gurney Nutting are grouped together here, although there were several sub-types. The De Ville bodies all had a removable roof section above the front seats, although other elements of their lines were shared with some three-position Drophead Coupé styles. Similar designs were also built for the larger Rolls-Royce chassis of the time.

The Owen design was always known as a Sedanca Coupé and was to all intents and purposes a three-position Drophead Coupé, with a folding rear roof and a separate De Ville roof section. A key detail of the Owen design was its separate luggage boot, deliberately designed to resemble a trunk; other De Ville types from Gurney Nutting had a boot more conventionally blended into the lines of body.

There were 24 examples of the Owen Sedanca Coupé between 1932 and 1935, as follows:

GHW45	1932	GLZ75	1933	GNC79	1934
GRW11	1932	GTZ9	1933	GKC26	1934
GEX28	1933	GTZ40	1933	GMD16	1934
GEX65	1933	GYZ7	1933	GYD26	1934
GWX28	1933	GBA27	1933	GYD69	1934
GDX19	1933	GXB15	1934	GAE47	1934
GLZ39	1933	GLB33	1934	GAE71	1934
GLZ61	1933	GNC36	1934	GLG31	1935

There were also 22 other De Ville types. Some were broadly similar to the Owen cars (such as GRW16, which was a Jack Barclay version of the same body design). Others had quite different four-door designs that were more Saloon-like in their overall shape; these included GRW39, GLB3, GPG24 and GBJ70. Various names have been given to these designs, including Sedanca Coupé and Sedanca de Ville.

GRW16	1932	GWE22	1934	GYH26	1935
GRW39	1932	GFE1	1934	GOH39	1935
GAW2	1932	GAF29	1934	GEH2	1935
GSY20	1933	GRF20	1935	GEH27	1935
GSY84	1933	GRF27	1935	GBJ55	1935
GLB3	1934	GPG24	1935	GBJ70	1935
GYD55	1934	GYH14	1935	GLJ74	1935
GYD63	1934				

Drophead Coupé

Just two Drophead Coupé bodies were built on the 20/25 chassis. These were on GNC42 in 1934 and GXK6 in 1935.

Limousines

Gurney Nutting was not particularly well known for Limousine coachwork, but the company provided two

Despite minor differences between individual cars, the Owen Sedanca Coupé was a batch-built design. This example, on GEX65 and again built in 1933, was built for Prince Aly Khan, the socialite son of the Aga Khan. It is seen here with the De Ville roof open.
(Simon Clay)

The Owen Sedanca Coupé was a registered design, although that did not prevent other coachbuilders making some very close copies of it.
(Simon Clay)

The welcoming driving compartment of GEX65 shows the rope pulls fitted to the doors. (Simon Clay)

Despite its name, the Owen Sedanca Coupé was really a three-position Drophead Coupé. With the fabric top folded, rear-seat passengers could enjoy the good weather. (Simon Clay)

Also dating from 1933 is this pillarless Coupé for 20/25 chassis GLZ33. The absolute mastery of line achieved by Gurney Nutting is interesting to compare with the De Ville body by Offord that attempts much the same thing. (Simon Clay)

The coachbuilder's plate is a permanent reminder of the company responsible for the body on GLZ33. (Simon Clay)

Exquisite figured wood is a feature of the Coupé body for GLZ22. (Simon Clay)

Even though the Coupé body style is essentially close-coupled, there is no lack of luxury for the rear-seat passengers. (Simon Clay)

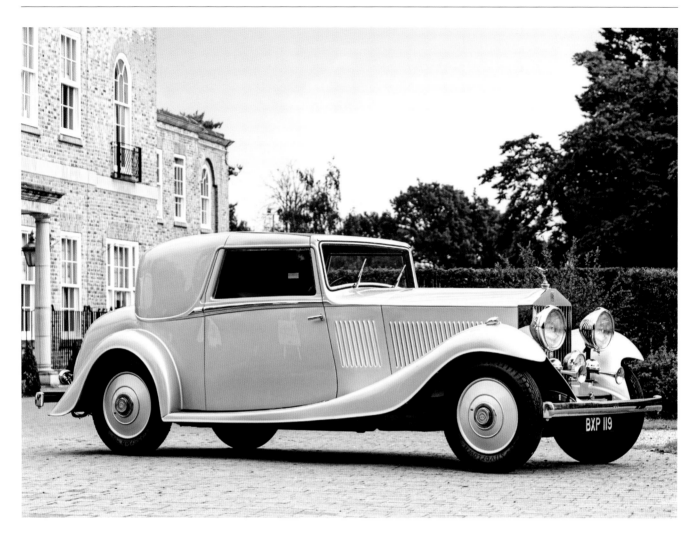

Superb proportions from Gurney Nutting again, this time for a Sedanca de Ville on 1934 chassis GYD55. (Simon Clay)

*Despite the space afforded
by the chassis, rear legroom
was not great in this design,
which made some sacrifices
to achieve pleasing lines.
(Simon Clay)*

on the 20/25 chassis. The earlier one was a Weymann type in 1930 on chassis GLR34; the later one was a metal-panelled body for GAF49 in 1934.

Saloons

Saloon bodies formed a large part of the Gurney Nutting output for the 20/25, although the first one was not completed until 1931 and it was not until 1934 that the company built them in quantity. There were 28 in all, and of course these included several different designs. Four-light Sports Saloons predominated, although one listed here (GYD3) was a four-light Saloon Coupé with two doors. The first two were Weymann types, although GFT75 in 1931 actually had metal body panels while the second (GBT34) was a traditional fabric-bodied type for Sir Malcolm Campbell.

Fabric roof coverings on some bodies gave a more sporting appearance, such as on GHW43. Three Saloons had Divisions, and these were for GLZ4, GNC54, and GOH31. GMU8 was a Silentbloc type with a trunk-shaped boot like that on the Owen Sedanca Coupés. Three of the 1935 bodies were Damita types, named after film actress and singer Lili Damita, and these were on chassis GOH11, GOH31 and GCJ15. Sadly, there was no connection at all to the lady herself: the HR Owen dealership merely used the name to add a little glamour to the design.

The full list of 28 bodies, with dates, was as follows:

GFT75	1931	GNC54	1934	GLG62	1935
GBT34	1932	GRC25	1934	GHG3	1935
GMU8	1932	GRC44	1934	GHG14	1935
GHW8	1932	GKC20	1934	GYH4	1935
GHW43	1932	GED11	1934	GYH 57	1935
GLZ4	1933	GYD3	1934	GOH11	1935
GLZ14	1933	GAE18	1934	GOH31	1935
GUB29	1934	GFE27	1934	GOH77	1935
GUB61	1934	GSF80	1934	GCJ15	1935
GLB 41	1934				

Tourers

Tourers were not a Gurney Nutting speciality, and the company built only two for the 20/25 chassis. The first was for GSR8 in 1930, and the second was strictly an All-weather Tourer, built for GLZ8 in 1933.

25/30 COACHWORK

Demand for Gurney Nutting coachwork on the smaller Rolls-Royce held up fairly well when the 25/30 chassis came on-stream, and 39 bodies were completed for the type in 1936-1938. Of these, 23 bodies were built in 1936, 14 in 1937, and the last two in 1938.

Several of the bodies on the 25/30 chassis were distinguished by a curved triangular fairing above the external spare wheel on the tail, and some had rear-wheel spats. These typically carried a "comet" motif (of which there were different versions) that was favoured by designer John Blatchley.

All-weather

The description of All-weather does no justice to the two cars that were built to a common design (number 132) for Indian potentates. Designed primarily to be used in open form as parade cars, they were not intended to be seen with the acres of flapping canvas commonly associated with All-weather designs, and were four-door models with sleek lines that were accentuated by rear-wheel spats. A third body, about which less is known, was completed for another Indian customer and is said to have dispensed with the occasional seats fitted to the first two.

All three examples were built in 1937. The ones to design number 132 were on chassis GRO48 and GRO59, and the third was on chassis GMP28.

Coupés

There were two Coupé bodies with the falling-waistline pillarless design carried over from the 20/25 chassis. These were for chassis GUL80 in 1936 and for GHO6 in 1937. A third Coupé body, built in 1938 for chassis GGR1, was essentially a version of the Owen Sedanca Coupé with a solid instead of De Ville roof.

Drophead Coupés

Gurney Nutting built two Drophead Coupé bodies for the 25/30 chassis. Both were three-position types but it is not clear if they shared the same design. The earlier was for chassis GWN29 in 1936 and the later for GRO8 in 1937.

Limousine

Limousine bodies were not a common Gurney Nutting product and the company built just one for the 25/30 chassis. This was for GRM51 in 1936.

Saloons

There were seven Saloon bodies. Two 1936 examples had Divisions, on chassis GUL52 and GRM62. The other five were all Sports Saloons. With dates, the seven were:

GUL52	1936	GXM56	1936	GHO28	1937
GTL47	1936	GGM17	1936	GMP59	1937
GRM62	1936				

The overall style of the body for 25/30 GMP73 in 1937 has evolved considerably, and now incorporates more voluminous front wings and spats over the rear wheels. (Simon Clay)

Sedanca Coupés

The popularity of Gurney Nutting as a builder of Sedanca Coupé coachwork continued unabated into the 25/30 era. There were some to the Owen design as late as 1937 (such as the one for GUN31, delivered to Prince Birabongse, the racing driver "B Bira") but others interpreted the theme differently. The design for GRP56 was unique, and so was that for GZR21, which featured faux cane side panelling. The eight Sedanca Coupés were as follows:

GRM7	1936	GAN73	1936	GRP56	1937
GRM18	1936	GUN31	1937	GZR21	1938
GXM11	1936	GRO81	1937		

Sedancas de Ville

Customers also continued to patronise Gurney Nutting for Sedanca de Ville designs, and few other coachbuilders could equal the rightness of line that this one so effortlessly achieved. Some of these four-door designs depended on shapes similar to those for the company's Sports Saloons, but there were also

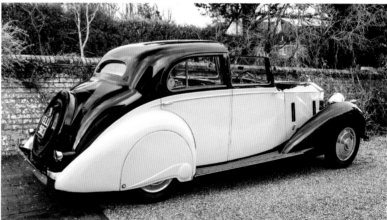

interesting variations such as the fascinating treatment of the meeting between running-board and front wing seen on chassis GHL10 and GMP73. Some designs used rear-wheel spats to achieve a sleeker look. There were 15 Sedanca de Ville bodies in all for the 25/30 chassis, as follows:

Clear in this picture is the way Gurney Nutting used a fairing to blend the spare wheel cover into the rear of the bodywork. (Simon Clay)

GUL9	1936	GHL35	1936	GAN43	1936
GUL79	1936	GRM47	1936	GHO5	1937
GTL14	1936	GRM56	1936	GRP18	1937
GHL10	1936	GXM25	1936	GMP73	1937
GHL34	1936	GGM6	1936	GLP17	1937

The 1937 body has a more traditional Sedanca de Ville style, with what is in effect a Division between the front and rear compartments. The glass section, of course, could be dropped to provide a flow of air into the rear compartment. (Simon Clay)

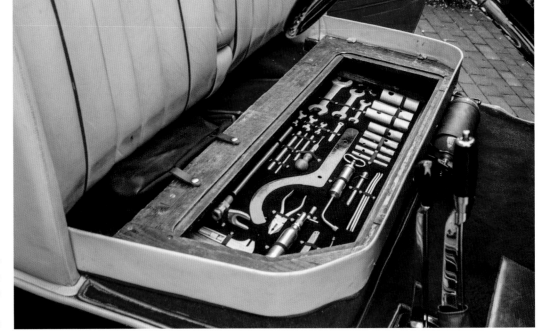

The tools, often mounted in the boot on closed bodies, were here carried under the front seat to save space in the boot and provide easy access for the chauffeur. (Simon Clay)

WRAITH COACHWORK

Gurney Nutting built just 11 bodies for the Wraith chassis in 1938-1939, five in 1938 and six the following year. Sedanca styles accounted for eight of those bodies.

All-weather Tourer

A single All-weather Tourer with a six-light design was built for chassis WMB56 in 1939. This was a rather heavy-looking body, not helped by its large boot.

Saloons

There were only two Saloon bodies for the 25/30 chassis, and both were built in 1939. Of these, the more interesting was perhaps the coachwork for WHC19, which came from the drawing-board of Alec Hale. It was a version of a strikingly successful design that Gurney Nutting had provided to the Carlton Carriage Company for a pair of bodies on Bentley 4¼-litre chassis, with a vee-shaped rear window line and rear spats. However, with the long angular bonnet of the Wraith chassis and less curvaceous front wings,

it did not work as well. The second Saloon was on chassis WHC53.

Sedanca Coupé

Three of the four Sedanca Coupés on Wraith chassis shared design number 289, which has been described as having a Brougham style. It was a most attractive shape, with an angled leading edge to the rear roof section. The first example, for chassis WRB2, was for the entertainer George Formby in 1938. The

The chauffeur's compartment was upholstered to the same standard as the rear, although there was rather less room. (Simon Clay)

All-weather Tourers were uncommon by the time Gurney Nutting built this one for Wraith chassis WMB56 in 1938. The inherent heaviness of the style is relieved by a dose of the coachbuilder's characteristic flair. (Real Car Company)

other two were both delivered in 1939, and were for chassis WMB19 and WHC49. The fourth of the Sedanca Coupé bodies was a three-position type, also completed in 1939 and for chassis WHC33. This one also featured cutaway rear-wheel spats and was converted to fixed-head condition in the 1950s, with a teardrop-like rear side window; it has since been rebuilt in its original form.

Sedancas de Ville

There were four rather grand Sedanca de Ville four-door bodies from Gurney Nutting on Wraith chassis. These were for chassis WXA75, WRB45 and WRB75 in 1938, and for WEC6 in 1939.

HALL LEWIS
London – Twenty

Hall, Lewis & Co Ltd was founded in Cardiff in 1889 to manufacture, repair and lease railway vehicles. It subsequently opened several subsidiary operations around the country and during 1920 diversified into building bodies for prestige cars as well. In 1924, the company moved its headquarters to Abbey Road in Park Royal, London NW10, where it had been

Hall Lewis bodied only two Twenty chassis, the earlier being GRJ75, which was given this very upright-looking Landaulette coachwork in 1927.

The second Hall Lewis body for a Twenty was this good-looking Coupé for GKM75 in 1928.

using a former munitions factory for railway wagon repair work. By the middle of the decade it claimed to specialise in coachwork for Daimler, Lanchester, Minerva and Rolls-Royce chassis, and had a London showroom in Pall Mall.

Hall, Lewis also diversified into building charabanc and bus bodies, but by the end of the decade a decline in the railway business and increasing competition from other coachbuilders forced the company into liquidation. Its assets formed the basis of Park Royal Coachworks in April 1930, which went on to become a major player in the bus and coach body business.

Most Hall, Lewis coachwork on Rolls-Royce chassis was for the Phantom and New Phantom chassis, and there were just two bodies for the Twenty. The earlier of these was a Landaulette delivered in 1927 on chassis GRJ75. This was a square-rigged, six-light design in the idiom of the day. The second body was a stylish Coupé with a pert tail and dummy landau irons, which was delivered on chassis GKM75 in 1928.

HAMILTON
Aberdeen – Twenty

Claud Hamilton was a major coachbuilder in Aberdeen, but the company appears to have been little known outside Scotland and never attempted to attract business by taking a stand at the Olympia show in London. Hamilton was certainly active before the First World War, when it bodied at least two Rolls-Royce Silver Ghost chassis. During the 1920s, it worked on several makes of high-grade chassis, but does not appear to have survived into the 1930s.

Hamilton built the coachwork for 15 Rolls-Royce Twenty chassis between 1923 and 1929. Its best years were 1923 and 1925, with four bodies in each year. There were two in each of the years 1926 and 1927, and a single example in each of the years 1924, 1928 and 1929.

Most of the Hamilton bodies on the Twenty were Saloons, of which there were eight in all. Otherwise, the company provided the sort of variety that was required of a provincial coachbuilder. There was just one Landaulette (for GPK30 in 1925), but there were two Cabriolets (for GNK79 and GNK92, both in 1925), two Coupés (for GAJ44 in 1927 and GYL30 in 1928), and a pair of Two-seaters (for GRK41 in 1924 and GRJ60 in 1927). The Saloons, with dates, are listed below. There is no indication that they were anything other than fairly conventional designs.

68H3	1923	GH52	1923	GYK72	1926
88K2	1923	GPK28	1925	GEN49	1929
GA76	1923	GOK44	1926		

HAMSHAW

Leicester – Twenty

The part played in Rolls-Royce history by the Leicester coachbuilder Hamshaw has often been underestimated, and the company built at least 20 bodies on the Twenty chassis rather than the half-dozen with which it is sometimes credited.

HA Hamshaw was probably established in the 1880s as a coach and carriage builder, and was originally Hamshaw & Parr. The company was building car bodies by 1905 and after the Great War focussed on quality chassis such as Humber, Sunbeam, Vauxhall and Wolseley. Hamshaw exhibited regularly at Olympia between 1919 and 1928, but its coachbuilding activities appear to have been discontinued after that as it focussed on its Morris dealership.

The known Hamshaw bodies had an air of grandeur and solidity about them. The 20 examples known on the Twenty chassis consisted of eight Saloons (1923-1925), six Landaulettes (1923-1928), five Tourers (1922-1925) and a single Coupé (1923). The earliest of the Landaulette bodies was actually transferred from an earlier chassis and is not therefore representative of the company's output in the period covered by this book.

Coupé

The sole Coupé was delivered in 1923 on chassis GA53.

Landaulettes

The earliest Twenty chassis to have a Hamshaw Landaulette body was 58S1 in 1923, which belonged to Lord Lonsdale and was given the body from his 1910 Napier; it was painted bright yellow from the outset. The first of the new-build Landaulette bodies was on GOK24 in 1926, and there was a second example that year on GZK27. Just one Landaulette was built in 1927, on GAJ74, and the final two were built in 1928 on GWL20 and GKM24.

Saloons

The first of the eight Saloons was on chassis 60H7 in 1923. The four in 1924 were on GMK40, GDK43, GDK52, and GDK81. The remaining three delivered in 1925 were on GNK16, GSK5, and GSK77.

Tourers

The five Tourer bodies were on 46G2 (in 1922), 58S4, 83K1 and GA66 (all 1923) and GNK75 (in 1925).

HARRINGTON

Brighton – Twenty, 20/25

Thomas Harrington & Sons Ltd began life in 1897 in Brighton, constructing horse-drawn carriages; the company later began bodying motor cars and before the Great War had begun to specialise in commercial vehicles, buses and coaches. After 1919, the focus was on luxury coaches, with a few single-deck bus bodies and other general coachbuilding work, but the company also built small numbers of bespoke car bodies. These included two on Rolls-Royce Twenty chassis and three on the 20/25; the company had supposedly built its first body on a Rolls-Royce chassis as early as 1906, and certainly built the coachwork for some Phantom I models.

Fitted with more modern rear lighting arrangements by the time of this picture, 1924 Twenty GDK52 carries a Hamshaw Saloon body that was typical of its era.

One of five Tourer bodies from Hamshaw for the Twenty chassis, this one was built in 1923 for 83K1. In the "open" picture, the second windscreen for the rear-seat passengers is clear.

TWENTY COACHWORK

The two bodies on Twenty chassis were a Saloon for GDK75 in 1924 and a Tourer for GHJ25 in 1927.

20/25 COACHWORK

All the bodies for 20/25 chassis were built in 1930, and they embraced a variety of types. The earliest of the three was a rather heavy-looking Drophead Coupé known as a "Vitesse" on chassis GDP59, delivered in February. In March came a four-door Weymann Saloon on GWP5, and there was then a further Saloon on GNS38 in December.

HARRISON
Dewsbury – Twenty

From the ashes of another company, Alfred Harrison established his coachworks at Dewsbury in Yorkshire in 1906. By the 1920s, the company was being run by his two sons and was focusing on coachwork for prestige chassis that included Rolls-Royce. From around 1923 it also built some single-deck bus bodies. Sadly, both brothers died in 1927, and after that the company refocused its activities on commercial bodywork. The company built 15 bodies for Rolls-Royce Twenty chassis to a variety of designs, mostly in 1923 and 1924.

The most common body type that Harrison built for the Twenty was the Saloon, and there were seven of these. The first five were built in 1923 and were for chassis 53S3, 54S5, 89K3, GA39 and GH64. The body on 54S5 may have had fabric panels. The last two Saloons were built in 1924 for chassis GAK12 and GMK24.

Next most numerous were Landaulettes, of which there were four in 1924-1925. The 1924 group were bodies for GAK67, GMK38 and GLK25, and the last Harrison Landaulette for a Twenty was on GSK8 in 1925. There were then four individual bodies: a Cabriolet for 51S7 in 1923, a Coupé for GH16 the same year, a Limousine for GUJ80 in 1927, and a Two-seater for GA67 in 1923.

HARRISON
London – Twenty

Coachbuilder R Harrison was best known for its association with Bentley, for whom the company built more than 200 bodies in the 1920s. Established in the Camden area of London in 1883, the company was focusing on coachwork for prestige makes by the 1920s, Rolls-Royce and Hispano-Suiza among them. However, from 1924, a second factory was opened to build bodies "for the trade", which were presumably cheaper and probably more standardised in design.

Harrison's interpretation of the Cabriolet style for Twenty GPK40 in 1925 involved retaining the full frames around the side windows.

This Drophead Coupé by Harrison was built for Twenty chassis GEN56 in 1929.

Harrison did not survive the Depression and the collapse of Bentley, and closed in 1931. Some of its elements may have survived in Wood Reeves & Co, the company that described itself as Harrison's successors and which took over its north London premises.

Harrison built nine bodies for the Rolls-Royce Twenty chassis between 1925 and 1929, its best year being 1926 when four bodies were supplied. The most numerous type was the Landaulette, of which there were four. The first three (for GOK55, GZK49 and GYK87) were built in 1926, and the fourth for GKM76 in 1928. There were two Drophead Coupés, which were for GRJ47 in 1927 and GEN56 in 1929. The three other bodies were a Cabriolet in 1925 for GPK40, a three-quarter Coupé the same year for GCK76, and a Saloon for GOK23 in 1926.

HARRODS
London – Twenty

Just one body on a small-horsepower Rolls-Royce chassis is recorded as coming from Harrods Ltd, the famous and prestigious department store in London's Knightsbridge district. Presumably the lady buyer took literally the store's motto ("Omnia Omnibus Ubique", which means "all things for all people, everywhere") and ordered her new car there.

It seems likely that Harrods actually sub-contracted construction of the Saloon body for Twenty chassis GA27 to one of the many small local coachbuilders. It was delivered in 1923.

HAYWARD
Wolverhampton – Twenty

CW Hayward & Co of Wolverhampton was primarily a builder of motorcycle sidecars, but also took on contract work to build car bodies for Morris and Rootes in the 1920s. The company is known to have built at least one body for a Rolls-Royce Phantom (in 1923), and one for a Twenty in 1925. This latter was a Tourer for chassis GCK66. Hayward's later sold out to the AJS motorcycle firm, probably in 1926.

HAYWOOD
Location unknown – Twenty

A company called EG Haywood is recorded as building the Cabriolet body for Rolls-Royce Twenty 88K3 in 1923. There is no further information to help identify this coachbuilder more accurately.

HILL & BOLL
Yeovil – Twenty

By the 1920s, Hill & Boll were highly regarded car dealers and coachbuilders based at Yeovil in Somerset. Hill's Carriage Works had been founded around 1838, and by 1889 had become Hill & Boll when Hill's son-in-law became a partner. Towards the end of the century, the company experimented with Petter engines in their own carriagework to create early motor cars, by 1908 they were selling several makes of car, and in 1924 they amalgamated with a local garage business. They appear not to have survived beyond 1930.

A Hill & Boll advertisement of the early 1920s describes their coachwork as being "highest quality work at provincial prices". They had a special connection with Delage, and were highly regarded locally. Hill & Boll constructed the coachwork on four Rolls-Royce Twenty chassis between 1923 and 1928.

The first three bodies were all built in 1923. The earliest was a Cabriolet for chassis number 49G9. This was followed by a Landaulette for chassis number 62H1, and a few months later by a Limousine for 76A6. The last of the company's known Twenty bodies was not built until 1928, and was a Saloon for chassis GFN52.

HIRD
Location unknown – Twenty

A single Rolls-Royce Twenty chassis was bodied in 1928 by a company recorded as A Hird. The chassis was GFN74 and the body was a Limousine, but unfortunately nothing is known about the coachbuilder.

HISKIN
Location unknown – Twenty

An otherwise unidentified company called Hiskin Bros constructed two bodies on Rolls-Royce Twenty chassis. Both appear to have been for the same customer. The earlier one was a Tourer, and was completed in 1923 for chassis GA18. The later one was a Two-seater on GOK72 in 1926.

HJ MULLINER
London – Twenty, 20/25, 25/30, Wraith

The London coachbuilder HJ Mulliner was considered to be one of Britain's top exponents of the art by the start of the 1920s. It had been founded in 1900 by a distant relative of the Mulliner family of Northampton, but there were no business links with any of the other Mulliner coachbuilding companies of the time. HJ Mulliner himself had retired in 1908, and the business was taken over by John Croall & Sons of Edinburgh.

The first HJ Mulliner coachwork on Rolls-Royce chassis was not built until 1928, by which time the company had already developed strong connections with Bentley. There were more than 600 HJ Mulliner bodies on the small-horsepower Rolls-Royce models, many of them on the Twenty and early 20/25 using the Weymann patents. During the 1930s, the company built on few chassis other than Rolls-Royce and Bentley, and those others it did clothe were from top-quality makers.

Generally, customers made their way to HJ Mulliner for a body that was beautifully proportioned,

Neat and accomplished Tourer coachwork from HJ Mulliner on a 1926 Twenty chassis, GMJ52.

HJ Mulliner used the Weymann patents for a time, and the fabric panels are clear on this 1928 Saloon body for Twenty GFN8. (Magic Car Pics)

That large folding roof section on the body for GFN8 allowed an airy feel to the interior when it was opened. (Magic Car Pics)

somewhat conventional, and ultimately discreet. The company's two attempts to offer more consciously modern alternatives, on Bentley chassis in 1934 and 1935, both failed to excite any orders.

The company built 150 bodies on new Twenty chassis, 303 for new 20/25 chassis, 96 for new 25/30 chassis, and 62 for new Wraith chassis.

TWENTY COACHWORK

HJ Mulliner was one of the more prolific coachbuilders to work with the Twenty chassis, and built a total of 150 bodies for it, including three for experimental prototype cars. The company received healthy numbers of orders in the first few years (one in 1922, 15 in 1923, 13 in 1924 and 10 in 1925), but those numbers shot up after it introduced Weymann fabric Saloons in late 1925. The annual numbers thereafter were 24 in 1926, 33 in 1927, 29 in 1928, and 22 in 1929.

Despite the undoubted excellence of HJ Mulliner's work, Weymann bodies were not much liked at Rolls-Royce. John Fasal quotes an August 1926 memorandum from the Sales Department: "in the opinion of the Company the appearance of a Weymann body is not what one usually associates with a Rolls-Royce chassis." Nevertheless, if the customer insisted on having a Weymann body, he should be directed to HJ Mulliner. This was not because of the superiority of the company's product, but "because this firm buy chassis from us and are in consequence reasonably entitled to look for a share of our business."

All-weather

Just three of the bodies for Twenty chassis from HJ Mulliner were All-weather types, and the first of those was on experimental chassis 5-G-II. The other two were on GAK25 in 1924 and GXK47 in 1926.

Cabriolets

Cabriolet bodies were in demand in the early days of the Twenty, and the majority of the 14 from HJ Mulliner were built before 1925. Those 14 bodies were for the following chassis:

45G1	1922	GA4	1923	GPK18	1925
56S2	1923	GAK24	1924	GZK11	1926
77A7	1923	GAK80	1924	GLN7	1929
81K5	1923	GMK55	1924	GLN37	1929
87K6	1923	GRK44	1924		

Coupés

HJ Mulliner built four Coupé bodies for Twenty chassis, and two of them were Weymann types. The two metal-panelled Coupés were for GNK26 (1925) and GTM19 (1928), and the two Weymann types were for GHJ37 (1927) and GYL18 (1928).

Coupé de Ville

Only one customer asked HJ Mulliner for a Coupé de Ville body on a Twenty chassis, and that was completed in 1924 on chassis GMK75.

Drophead Coupés

Drophead Coupé bodies from this coachbuilder were few and far between on the Twenty chassis, and there were just four of them. The earliest, on 66H5 in 1923, was a "three-quarters" or four-light type. The other three were on GUJ15 in 1927, and on GLN77 and GEN47 in 1929.

Landaulettes

Three Landaulette bodies were supplied. The first was in 1923 on chassis 60H9; the second in 1924 on GLK31; and the third in 1929 on GLN27.

Limousines

HJ Mulliner built six Limousine bodies for the Twenty chassis. Weymann construction came late to these bodies, and only the last three of them, all built in 1929, were Weymann types.

GPK51	1925	GFN54	1928	GEN77	1929
GYK57	1926	GLN61	1929	GVO37	1929

Saloons, non-Weymann

Saloons were the most numerous body type on the Twenty chassis, and HJ Mulliner provided Saloon bodies for no fewer than 104 examples. However, only 19 were traditional metal-panelled types, and orders for these more or less dried up altogether after 1925 as demand for Weymann types took over. It seems most

helpful to separate the two types here. The 19 non-Weymann Saloon bodies were as follows:

64H2	1923	GAK65	1924	GOK50	1926
66H7	1923	GMK41	1924	GOK79	1926
72A5	1923	GDK2	1924	GWL19	1928
80K7	1923	GNK73	1925	GBM79	1928
GA48	1923	GSK54	1925	GLN2	1929
GH5	1923	GSK76	1925		
GH20	1923	GOK19	1926		

Saloons, Weymann

HJ Mulliner built its first Weymann Saloon in 1925, and GSK38 was the first of no fewer than 85 examples. Demand was such that very few conventional Saloons for the Twenty chassis left the company's premises in the second half of the 1920s. The full list is below.

GSK38	1925	GRJ21	1927	GKM16	1928
GSK39	1925	GRJ25	1927	GKM28	1928
GOK20	1926	GRJ29	1927	GKM36	1928
GOK73	1926	GRJ40	1927	GTM5	1928
GZK55	1926	GRJ53	1927	GTM15	1928
GZK78	1926	GRJ61	1927	GTM16	1928
GZK80	1926	GRJ66	1927	GTM18	1928
GUK26	1926	GUJ3	1927	GTM38	1928
GUK66	1926	GUJ7	1927	GFN8	1928
GUK75	1926	GUJ35	1927	GFN24	1928
GYK6	1926	GUJ64	1927	GFN46	1928
GYK55	1926	GUJ67	1927	GFN49	1928
GYK67	1926	GXL1	1927	GFN53	1928
GMJ25	1926	GXL18	1927	GFN71	1928
GMJ56	1926	GXL50	1927	GLN26	1929
GMJ65	1926	GXL56	1927	GLN40	1929
GMJ79	1926	GXL70	1927	GLN58	1929
GMJ80	1926	GXK74	1927	GEN2	1929
GHJ12	1927	GXL80	1927	GEN15	1929
GHJ28	1927	GYL61	1928	GEN60	1929
GHJ68	1927	GWL5	1928	GEN65	1929
GHJ71	1927	GWL35	1928	GVO7	1929
GHJ75	1927	GBM7	1928	GVO10	1929
GAJ18	1927	GBM12	1928	GVO36	1929
GAJ47	1927	GBM16	1928	GVO58	1929
GRJ7	1927	GBM29	1928	GVO60	1929
GRJ14	1927	GBM37	1928	GVO73	1929
GRJ18	1927	GBM51	1928		
GRJ19	1927	GBM75	1928		

Tourers

Rolls-Royce doubtless anticipated demand for Tourer coachwork when they ordered examples from HJ Mulliner on two of the prototype Twenty chassis, 2GII and 6GII. However, demand for Tourer bodies dwindled after the middle of the decade, and in fact this coachbuilder constructed its last for a Twenty in 1926. There were eight in all for production chassis, the full list of 10 bodies being as follows:

2GII	1921	GDK12	1924	GCK21	1925
6GII	1922	GDK45	1924	GYK68	1926
70A1	1923	GSK75	1925	GMJ52	1926
GAK61	1924				

Two-seater

Just one customer ordered a Two-seater body from HJ Mulliner for a Twenty, and that was constructed in 1927 on GHJ55.

20/25 COACHWORK

HJ Mulliner built 303 bodies for new Rolls-Royce 20/25 chassis, and this was a period in which the company's coachwork went through an important transition. Bodies for the earliest 20/25s – mostly Saloons – had Weymann construction with fabric panels, but from 1930 the coachbuilder changed over to the later Weymann type with metal panels. By 1932, Silentbloc body mountings were in use, and by the end of that year bodies were traditionally coachbuilt – although a few customers were still insisting on fabric-panelled Weymann bodies as late as 1935.

The most numerous body type was the Saloon,

and after that (although a poor second) came De Ville types, when all the different varieties were added together. Least common were Drophead Coupés and Landaulettes. Some bodies for Scottish customers were fitted with body plates for the Edinburgh coachbuilder Croall (see above), which owned HJ Mulliner but ceased its own coachbuilding activities in 1929.

Coupés

Coupés for the 20/25 were not particularly common in the HJ Mulliner repertoire, and the company built just one or two every year from 1930: a total of 12. Early Coupés with Weymann construction were probably all metal-panelled, and by late 1932 it appears that traditional coachbuilt construction had taken over. The body for GOS43 was ordered as a copy of the Freestone & Webb Grafton type (with distinctive triangular rear quarter-windows), and was transferred to GRW63 in 1932. The Coupé on GFT40 was built in 1931 for aviation pioneer Tommy Sopwith, who had it transferred to his new chassis GAW18 in 1933. The 20/25 chassis that attracted HJ Mulliner Coupé bodies when new were as follows:

GDP10	1930	GRW63	1932	GKC34	1934
GOS43	1931	GRW67	1932	GPG12	1935
GPS2	1931	GAW18	1933	GBK30	1936
GFT40	1931	GLZ59	1933	GTK16	1936

Coupés were not common from HJ Mulliner, but the lines of this 1935 body for 20/25 GPG12 were certainly assured.

De Ville types

The earliest of the 46 De Ville bodies appeared in 1930. Demand increased as time went on. The most numerous were the Sedanca de Ville and Sedanca Coupé types, the latter from 1934, and there were single examples of a Brougham de Ville and a Limousine de Ville.

The Brougham de Ville was for chassis GSR66 in 1930, and the Limousine de Ville was for GBJ76 in 1935. The Sedanca Coupé types were as follows:

GUB49	1934	GFE34	1934	GPG41	1934
GYD37	1934	GSF53	1934	GHG26	1934
GWE8	1934	GRF28	1934	GOH40	1934
GWE56	1934				

Sedanca de Ville bodies were built for the following chassis:

GSR79	1930	GXB6	1933	GLG63	1935
GTR4	1930	GUB68	1934	GYH3	1935
GFT26	1931	GRC15	1934	GOH26	1935
GFT27	1931	GKC29	1934	GEH16	1935
GBT18	1932	GMD28	1934	GEH25	1935
GMU79	1932	GFE24	1934	GBJ2	1935
GSY3	1933	GAF43	1934	GLJ17	1935
GSY14	1933	GRF36	1935	GLJ50	1935
GTZ72	1933	GLG14	1935	GXK60	1936
GYZ9	1933	GLG16	1935	GXK66	1936
GGA81	1933	GLG27	1935	GBK34	1936
GHA37	1933				

Drophead Coupés

The Drophead Coupé was another uncommon style from HJ Mulliner on the 20/25 chassis. Some of the seven examples were built with a Dickey seat, and these are marked with an asterisk (*) in the table below.

GGP35*	1929	GNS39*	1931	GXB45	1933
GWP4	1930	GTZ81*	1933	GWE67	1934
GWP20	1930				

The front section of the hood folded into its own neat compartment. (Simon Clay)

HJ Mulliner's three-position Drophead Coupé body for 20/25 GWE67 in 1934 looks like a Sedanca de Ville type on first sight. Here, the front of the hood has been furled to give the fashionable De Ville look. (Simon Clay)

From this angle, the falling waistline is apparent, along with the neat luggage boot. (Simon Clay)

A trimmed luggage boot was always a sign of quality coachwork, and HJ Mulliner did not disappoint. (Simon Clay)

Figured wood with contrasting edging made for a most attractive dashboard in the body for GWE67....
(Simon Clay)

..... and of course the rear-seat passengers were catered for very comfortably.
(Simon Clay)

Landaulettes

A relatively small quantity of Landaulette bodies was built for the 20/25 chassis, some of which wore Croall coachbuilder's plates. The seven examples were:

GLR47	1930	GWX16	1933	GAE40	1934
GSR59	1930	GMD55	1934	GBK65	1936
GAU54	1932				

Limousines

Limousines were the second most commonly ordered body type after Saloons. Early examples had Weymann construction with fabric panels, but from 1930 Weymann metal-panelled types became more common, and from 1932 the bodies all appear to have been conventionally coachbuilt. The list of 28 Limousines is as follows:

GGP67	1929	GDX23	1933	GAF80	1934
GGP68	1929	GLZ34	1934	GPG53	1935
GDP30	1930	GYZ26	1934	GHG24	1935
GWP9	1930	GBA54	1934	GYH56	1935
GLR77	1930	GNC5	1934	GEH40	1935
GOS41	1931	GKC8	1934	GLJ18	1935
GOS46	1931	GMD81	1934	GLJ47	1935
GFT9	1931	GAE31	1934	GBK16	1936
GRW19	1932	GFE5	1934	GTK29	1936
GWX15	1933				

Saloons

The large majority of HJ Mulliner Saloon bodies for the 20/25 chassis were four-light types. Early ones had Weymann fabric construction, Weymann metal-panelled bodies followed from 1930, and then from 1932 the company began to use Silentbloc body mountings. Nevertheless, a few customers insisted on fabric-panelled Weymann bodies as late as 1935.

Like several other coachbuilders, HJ Mulliner had their version of the Continental Saloon, but it did not arrive until 1934 and only three were built (for chassis GNC41, GNC81 and GKC31). The Burlington Saloon was greeted with a similar lack of enthusiasm in 1935, and only two were built (for GPG63 and GTK20). Two-door bodies were rare, and were limited to a Saloon Coupé for GDX11 and a two-door Saloon for GMG10; this latter body had not been on its original chassis long before it was transferred to a 1936 25/30, GXM6. The body for GRC60 was a four-light Sun Saloon, and GXO26 and GMU23 deserve comment as being displayed at Olympia. GXO37 was built to a design by the dealer Paddon Bros, wore Croall builder's plates and was displayed at the 1929 Scottish Show.

Several bodies were of course built with a Division,

and these are indicated with an asterisk (*) in the tables below. These tables list all 203 chassis that carried Saloon bodies from new, but are divided into smaller groups by calendar-years for easier reference.

1929-1930

GXO11	1929	GDP35	1930	GSR14	1930
GXO20	1929	GDP37	1930	GSR24	1930
GXO25	1929	GDP40	1930	GSR38	1930
GXO26	1929	GDP44	1930	GSR47	1930
GXO37	1929	GDP55	1930	GSR53*	1930
GXO38	1929	GDP60	1930	GSR69	1930
GXO45	1929	GDP80	1930	GTR3	1930
GXO66	1929	GWP10	1930	GTR6	1930
GXO76	1929	GWP30	1930	GTR8	1930
GXO78	1929	GWP33	1930	GTR11	1930
GXO82	1929	GWP38	1930	GTR14*	1930
GXO84	1929	GLR7	1930	GTR23	1930
GGP20	1929	GLR10	1930	GTR27*	1930
GGP39	1929	GLR14	1930	GTR33	1930
GGP64	1929	GLR20	1930	GTR34*	1930
GGP74	1930	GLR37	1930	GTR41	1930
GDP8	1930	GLR50	1930	GNS4	1930
GDP20	1930	GLR52	1930	GNS21*	1930
GDP25	1930	GLR64*	1930	GNS22	1930

1931-1932

GNS59	1931	GBT26	1932	GMU23	1932
GNS63*	1931	GBT37	1932	GMU28	1932
GOS2	1931	GBT40	1932	GMU65	1932
GOS9	1931	GBT56*	1932	GZU6*	1932
GOS11	1931	GKT2	1932	GZU31	1932
GOS18	1931	GAU41	1932	GHW37	1932
GOS19	1931	GAU42	1932	GHW38*	1932
GOS38	1931	GAU68*	1932	GHW80	1932
GPS18	1931	GAU75	1932	GRW4*	1932
GFT57	1931	GMU4	1932	GRW45	1932
GBT23	1932				

1933-1934

GEX12*	1933	GLZ72	1933	GGA70	1933
GEX30	1933	GTZ43	1933	GHA24	1933
GEX57*	1933	GTZ63*	1933	GHA31	1933
GWX46	1933	GTZ66	1933	GXB21	1933
GWX52	1933	GYZ15	1933	GXB52*	1934
GWX81	1933	GYZ29	1933	GXB75*	1934
GDX3	1933	GYZ41*	1933	GUB14	1934
GDX11	1933	GBA18	1933	GUB75	1934
GDX27	1933	GBA20	1933	GUB80*	1934
GDX36	1933	GBA37	1933	GLB24*	1934
GSY6	1933	GBA43	1933	GLB35	1934
GSY57	1933	GGA30	1933	GNC16*	1934
GSY86	1933	GGA55(*)	1933	GNC41	1934

GNC46*	1934	GKC31	1934	GWE35	1934
GNC81	1934	GED62	1934	GWE45	1934
GRC7	1934	GED72	1934	GFE7	1934
GRC16	1934	GMD4	1934	GFE16	1934
GWE44	1934	GYD33	1934	GAF19	1934
GRC33	1934	GYD53	1934	GAF42	1934
GRC36	1934	GAE50	1934	GAF62	1934
GRC55	1934	GAE66	1934	GSF41	1934
GRC60	1934	GAE69(*)	1934		

1935-1936

GSF79	1935	GOH46	1935	GXK20	1935
GRF9	1935	GOH74	1935	GXK32	1935
GLG19*	1935	GOH75	1935	GXK38*	1935
GLG34	1935	GBJ7*	1935	GXK45	1935
GLG37	1935	GBJ9	1935	GXK57	1935
GLG78*	1935	GBJ33	1935	GBK14*	1936
GPG20*	1935	GBJ41*	1935	GBK26	1936
GPG55	1935	GBJ74	1935	GBK40	1936
GPG63*	1935	GBJ77*	1935	GBK44	1936
GPG73	1935	GLJ19	1935	GBK52	1936
GPG75	1935	GLJ28	1935	GBK53	1936
GHG10	1935	GLJ52*	1935	GBK58	1936
GHG19	1935	GLJ57	1935	GBK76	1936
GHG22	1935	GLJ58	1935	GTK6*	1936
GHG36*	1935	GCJ18*	1935	GTK20	1936
GOH28	1935	GXK5	1935	GTK38	1936
GOH42*	1935	GXK19*	1935		

25/30 COACHWORK

HJ Mulliner built 96 new bodies for 25/30 chassis, but 97 chassis were mounted with the company's bodies from new, because an earlier Saloon Coupé was transferred to a new 25/30 chassis in 1936. There were 45 new bodies in 1936 (but 46 25/30 chassis with HJ Mulliner bodies from new!), 42 in 1937, and nine in 1938.

The most numerous body type was the Saloon, of which there were 30. Sports Saloons and Sedancas de Ville were the next most popular, with 20 of each, and there were 18 Limousines. Interestingly, two bodies were ordered with anachronistic fabric panels in 1937, one a Saloon and the other a Limousine.

Drophead Coupé

HJ Mulliner was commissioned to body just one 25/30 chassis as a Drophead Coupé, and that was GAR78 in 1938.

Landaulettes

All four Landaulette bodies for the 25/30 chassis were built in 1936. They were mounted on chassis numbers GTL9, GTL48, GTL63 and GTL64.

This 1933 D-back Saloon body on 20/25 chassis GSY6 was delivered new in Edinburgh and carried coachbuilder's plates for Croall, the local coachbuider that had owned HJ Mulliner since 1908.

Limousines

There were 18 Limousine bodies, of which one (GMO37 in 1937) was ordered with fabric panels. The full list, with dates, is below:

GUL19	1936	GAN75	1936	GHO34	1937
GUL32	1936	GUN35	1937	GMO37	1937
GUL58	1936	GUN39	1937	GRP22	1937
GTL59	1936	GRO41	1937	GRP51	1937
GXM66	1936	GRO57	1937	GAR77	1937
GGM15	1936	GHO33	1937	GGR69	1938

Limousine de Ville

HJ Mulliner met orders for three Limousine de Ville bodies on the 25/30 chassis. These were for GRP44 and GLP25 in 1937, and for GZR4 in 1938.

Saloon Coupé

The single Saloon Coupé body on the 25/30 chassis was a four-light design that HJ Mulliner had built in 1935 for a 20/25 chassis, GHG10. In 1936, the owner had it transferred to his newer chassis, GXM6.

Saloons

Of the 30 Saloon bodies for 25/30 chassis, just one was ordered with fabric panels; this was mounted on chassis GRP19 in 1937. Several bodies were ordered with Divisions, and these are marked with an asterisk(*) in the table below.

GUL5*	1936	GGM31	1936	GMP33	1937
GUL57	1936	GWN5	1936	GMP80*	1937
GTL16*	1936	GWN58*	1936	GLP38*	1937
GHL1	1936	GRO26*	1937	GAR3	1937
GRM6	1936	GRO61	1937	GAR23	1937
GRM72	1936	GHO7*	1937	GAR46*	1937
GXM1	1936	GMO14*	1937	GZR1*	1938
GXM7*	1936	GMO36*	1937	GZR5	1938
GXM18	1936	GRP19	1937	GZR8	1938
GGM10	1936	GRP27	1937	GZR28	1938

This neat body for a 1936 25/30 chassis, GTL68, was typical of HJ Mulliner Sports Saloon designs at the time....
(Real Car Company)

... but this somewhat heavier-looking design for GMP9 in 1937 also qualified as a Sports Saloon.
(Real Car Company)

Sedancas de Ville

Of the 20 Sedanca de Ville bodies, some had Limousine-like rear panels with only a luggage grid, while others had built-in luggage boots. The full list, with dates, was as follows:

GUL11	1936	GAN30	1936	GMO28	1937
GUL81	1936	GWN42	1936	GRP54	1937
GTL53	1936	GWN50	1937	GMP38	1937
GTL71	1936	GUN25	1937	GLP20	1937
GTL76	1936	GRO37	1937	GAR60	1937
GHL15	1936	GHO32	1937	GGR78	1938
GRM43	1936	GHO72	1937		

Sports Saloons

Only the four-light configuration really qualified the 20 HJ Mulliner Sports Saloons for that description: otherwise, they were typically neat and satisfying designs with nothing particularly sporting about them. The list, with dates, was:

GUL17	1936	GXM70	1936	GRO79	1937
GUL77	1936	GXM80	1936	GRP36	1937
GTL42	1936	GAN42	1936	GMP9	1937
GTL68	1936	GAN45	1936	GMP78	1937
GHL2	1936	GAN50	1936	GAR26	1937
GHL24	1936	GWN70	1937	GZR38	1938
GHL31	1936	GRO53	1937		

WRAITH COACHWORK

There were 62 HJ Mulliner bodies for the Wraith, 26 of them in 1938 and 36 in 1939 (although some were delivered later than that). There was a clear family resemblance among Saloons, Limousines and De Ville types. The most commonly requested bodies were Saloons, and the company built 20 of various types, plus a dozen Touring Saloons. Some of these Saloons, and some Touring Limousines too, had the innovative High Vision feature introduced for the 1938 season, which consisted of transparent panels at the front of the roof. These were intended to allow the front seat occupants to see such things as overhead traffic signs and Alpine views more easily, and could be obscured by a blind when required.

All-weather

All-weather coachwork had never been an HJ Mulliner speciality, but when the company came to build such

The lines are typical late-1930s HJ Mulliner, but this All-weather Tourer for Wraith chassis WEC43 in 1939 was a one-off. The method of mounting the second windscreen for rear-seat passengers was noteworthy.

a body it made a characteristically sleek job of it. In closed form, the body for WEC43 in 1939 looked more like a Cabriolet; in open form, the folded hood was concealed beneath a metal panel and a second windscreen for the rear passengers could be deployed. This body was built for the 1939 Earls Court Motor Show that was cancelled after war broke out.

Drophead Coupés

Drophead Coupé coachwork was not common from HJ Mulliner, either, and there was just one example on a Wraith chassis. This was for WHC23 in 1939.

Landaulettes

Landaulette coachwork had been gradually dropping out of favour during the 1930s, and the company was possibly quite surprised to receive an order for such a body as late as 1938. It was built with a six-light design for chassis WRB56.

Limousines

Customer interest in Limousine bodies remained fairly constant, and HJ Mulliner delivered nine examples on Wraith chassis. These were as follows:

WXA38	1938	WMB48	1939	WEC48	1939
WXA100	1938	WHC26	1939	WEC64	1939
WXA102	1938	WHC52	1939	WEC67	1939

Limousines de Ville

The HJ Mulliner Limousine de Ville design was distinguished by what appeared to be a very long window for the enclosed rear section. The illusion was achieved by a pillarless design above the waist, the drop-glass in the door actually overlapping the fixed rear pane. Five of these attractive bodies were built on Wraith chassis; WMB60 was not delivered until 1944:

WXA31	1938	WRB21	1938	WMB73	1939
WXA45	1938	WMB60	1939		

Saloons

Saloon bodies for the Wraith could feature both razor-edge styling and rear-wheel spats, and there were examples with both four lights and six lights. Some had the High Vision feature, and those marked with an asterisk (*) in the table below had a Division. One (WXA93 in 1938) even had fabric panels. There were 20 Saloon bodies in all.

WXA22	1938	WXA87	1938	WXA105*	1938
WXA68*	1938	WXA93	1938	WRB4	1938

WRB25	1938	WRB72	1938	WLB38	1939
WRB27	1938	WMB20*	1938	WHC40	1939
WRB29	1938	WMB64*	1939	WEC26	1939
WRB53	1938	WLB7	1939	WEC47	1939
WRB71*	1938	WLB22	1939		

Sedancas

Sedanca bodies remained in demand, and there were five Sedanca de Ville types and a single Fixed-Head Sedanca Coupé (for WEC76 in 1939). The six chassis were:

WRB41	1938	WLB4	1939	WHC72	1939
WMB14	1938	WLB41	1939	WEC76	1939

Touring Limousines

Touring Limousines, distinguished by a usefully sized luggage boot, came in both four-light and six-light forms. Two of the 1939 examples (WLB14 and WEC33) had the High Vision feature. The seven bodies were on the following chassis:

WRB42	1938	WLB14	1939	WLB37	1939
WMB69	1939	WLB28	1939	WEC33	1939
WMB76	1939				

Touring Saloons

A dozen bodies were described as Touring Saloons, some with razor-edge lines and some with more rounded contours. Several of them had a Division, and these are marked with an asterisk (*) in the table below.

WXA50	1938	WLB8	1939	WEC63*	1939
WRB11*	1938	WLB10	1939	WEC71	1939
WMB2*	1938	WLB33*	1939	WKC4	1939
WLB3	1939	WHC17*	1939	WKC5	1939

HODGSON

Location unknown – Twenty

J Hodgson was another of the many obscure makers of coachwork for the early Rolls-Royce Twenty, and there are no identifying details for the company. It was responsible for just one body, a Tourer delivered on chassis 58S6 in 1923.

HOLLINGDRAKE

Stockport – Twenty

The Hollingdrake Automobile Co was primarily a motor dealer, but from 1904 added a coachbuilding department to its premises in Stockport. It built the coachwork for a number of Rolls-Royce chassis, and also worked on Daimler and Standard models, but seems to have ceased its coachbuilding activities around 1927.

The company built 15 bodies for Rolls-Royce Twenty chassis between 1923 and 1927. There were four in 1923, six in 1924, four in 1925, and a final example in 1927. The variety was typical for a provincial coachbuilder at the time.

Cabriolets

There were two Cabriolet bodies, which were for chassis GA73 in 1923 and GNK88 in 1925.

Coupé

Hollingdrake met two orders for Coupé coachwork on the Twenty chassis. The earlier one, in 1923 for chassis 62H0, was its first body for a Twenty, and the second one was for GNK60 in 1925.

Landaulette

There was a single Landaulette body, which was built for chassis 62H6 in 1923.

Saloons

All three Saloon bodies for the Twenty were built in 1924. They were for chassis numbers GAK36, GRK49 and GDK73.

Tourers

The most popular body type from this coachbuilder was the Tourer, and Hollingdrake built five examples between 1923 and 1927. These were for chassis 71A8 (in 1923), GLK71 and GLK80 (in 1924), GCK70 (in 1925) and GRJ6 (in 1927).

Two-seaters

Hollingdrake built two Two-seater bodies for the Twenty. These were for chassis GLK35 in 1924 and GSK79 in 1925.

HOODS & BODIES
London – Twenty

Hoods & Bodies Ltd seems to have been primarily a builder of commercial bodywork, but in 1917 advertised its willingness to construct "motor bodies of all descriptions". Based at that time in the Canonbury district of north London, it also had premises in Willesden by 1919.

The company built two bodies for early Rolls-Royce Twenty chassis. These were a Coupé for 45G4 in 1922, and a Cabriolet for 52S1 in 1923.

HOOPER
London – Twenty, 20/25, 25/30, Wraith

Hooper had been founded in London in 1805 as a carriage builder with the name of Adams & Hooper, and in 1830 earned the Royal Warrant. As a leading coachbuilder it was among the first British companies to build a motor car body, in 1896.

By the 1920s, the Hooper company was highly regarded for its top quality coachwork and was known particularly for its dignified formal designs. The company built very large numbers of bodies on Rolls-Royce and Daimler chassis, and in 1933 was obliged to open a second factory to keep up with orders. Further expansion followed in 1937, when Hooper joined the shadow factory scheme and opened its third coachbuilding workshops. A year later it bought the Barker company, and the last few Barker bodies were actually completed at this third factory in Park Royal.

Hooper retained the Royal Warrant throughout the 1930s and beyond, and in that period its bodywork was considered to be the best of the best. It was also commensurately expensive. The company was the most prolific coachbuilder for the junior Rolls-Royce models, and built the bodies for just over 1400 chassis: there were 447 for the Twenty, 675 for the 20/25, 209 for the 25/30 and 74 for the Wraith.

TWENTY COACHWORK

Hooper built at least 447 bodies for the Twenty chassis, which put it just ahead of Barker as the most prolific coachbuilder on the new junior Rolls-Royce model. The year-by-year figures show a huge swell of customer interest in 1923, which gradually tailed off as the urge to be one of the first to own the latest Rolls-Royce model subsided. The actual figures for Hooper coachwork on the Twenty were as follows:

1922	14	1924	73	1926	62	1928	46
1923	119	1925	61	1927	40	1929	32

This rather striking Brougham represented Hooper's skills at the 1926 Madrid Show and was sold to a Spanish noblewoman. It was on twenty chassis GCK17.

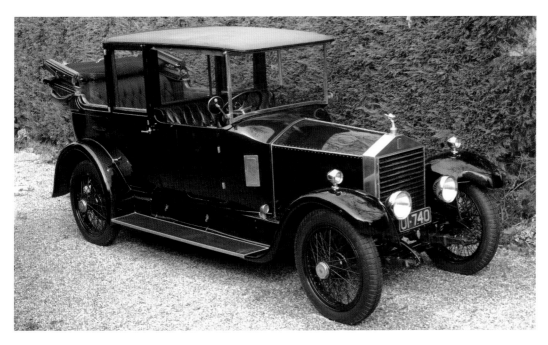

Landaulettes were very much in demand from Hooper for the Rolls-Royce Twenty chassis, and this magnificent 1923 example on 81K6 was typical. (Simon Clay)

The earliest bodies were all Tourers and Landaulettes, but Cabriolets, Broughams and Limousines soon followed. Two-seaters and Saloons followed later. By the middle of the decade, demand for Tourer bodies was falling away, but a new arrival in 1927 was the Sedanca, which retained its popularity into 1929. A late arrival was Weymann construction – despite the disapproval of such bodies expressed by the Rolls-Royce Sales Department – but only two such bodies were built in 1928-1929.

Broughams
There were 13 Brougham bodies for the Twenty between 1923 and 1928, the majority being built before the end of 1925.

52S3	1923	GH15	1923	GCK17	1925
73A3	1923	GLK15	1924	GRJ45	1927
81K0	1923	GNK68	1925	GUJ57	1927
GF28	1923	GSK47	1925	GYL19	1928
GF37	1923				

Cabriolets
Cabriolet bodies were never particularly popular, but the total of 30 built between 1923 and 1929 gives an average of five each year. Twenty chassis GEN82X was renumbered from experimental car 10-G-III in 1929 and had carried its Hooper Cabriolet body since 1925.

49G6	1923	66H6	1923	74A1	1923
56S0	1923	67H9	1923	78A8	1923

GA56	1923	GSK59	1925	GUJ54	1927
GF61	1923	GCK22	1925	GXL32	1927
GMK69	1924	GUK20	1926	GKM49	1928
GDK48	1924	GUK31	1926	GTM29	1928
GLK41	1924	GYK44	1926	GLN44	1929
GNK5	1925	GRJ17	1927	GEN22	1929
GPK54	1925	GRJ51	1927	GEN72	1929
GSK51	1925	GRJ78	1927	GEN82X	1929

Hooper could make even a Coupé look formal – aided in this picture by the stiff-backed chauffeur, of course. This body dated from 1929 and was for Twenty chassis GLN28.

Coupés
Coupé bodies were never numerous from Hooper, and just eight were built on the Twenty chassis. All except one were built in 1927-1929.

88K8	1923	GBM65	1928	GEN30	1929
GAJ70	1927	GLN28	1929	GEN39	1929
GRJ22	1927	GEN6	1929		

There was room for a pair of occasional seats in this Landaulette because the rear seats were mounted right at the rear of the body. (Simon Clay)

Drophead Coupés

Hooper built a total of 16 Drophead Coupé bodies for the Twenty between 1923 and 1928.

The rear-seat passengers benefited from fabric upholstery that was less affected than leather by changes in temperature. (Simon Clay)

65H7	1923	GH4	1923	GMJ30	1926
73A5	1923	GDK22	1924	GUJ61	1927
78A0	1923	GNK22	1925	GKM54	1928
GA11	1923	GYK20	1926	GFN39	1928
GA60	1923	GYK86	1926	GFN72	1928
GA80	1923				

Landaulette

Landaulette bodies were in strong demand from Hooper throughout the production life of the Twenty, and the first of 111 examples was mounted on the second production chassis in 1922.

40G2	1922	52S7	1923	69H7	1923
40G8	1922	54S7	1923	70A3	1923
41G1	1922	56S4	1923	70A8	1923
44G3	1922	57S7	1923	77A6	1923
45G9	1922	60S0	1923	79A5	1923
48G1	1923	64H4	1923	80K6	1923
48G9	1923	67H1	1923	81K6	1923
49G7	1923	67H4	1923	81K9	1923
50S1	1923	68H0	1923	82K0	1923
52S2	1923	68H1	1923	82K7	1923
52S5	1923	69H0	1923	84K9	1923

86K3	1923	GLK60	1924	GZK67	1926	GLN47	1929	GLN65	1929	GEN79	1929
90K0	1923	GLK74	1924	GZK79	1926	GLN63	1929	GEN18	1929	GVO26	1929
GA63	1923	GNK44	1925	GUK44	1926						
GF43	1923	GNK55	1925	GUK63	1926						
GF73	1923	GNK67	1925	GYK28	1926						
GF81	1923	GNK83	1925	GYK33	1926						
GH6	1923	GNK91	1925	GYK43	1926						
GH11	1923	GPK7	1925	GYK46	1926						
GH79	1923	GPK10	1925	GHJ7	1927						
GAK2	1924	GPK34	1925	GHJ73	1927						
GAK33	1924	GPK58	1925	GRJ59	1927						
GAK34	1924	GPK79	1925	GRJ76	1927						
GMK18	1924	GSK2	1925	GXL12	1927						
GMK43	1924	GSK16	1925	GXL41	1927						
GMK46	1924	GSK24	1925	GYL42	1928						
GMK57	1924	GSK62	1925	GBM8	1928						
GRK4	1924	GSK72	1925	GBM33	1928						
GRK18	1924	GCK24	1925	GKM35	1928						
GDK7	1924	GOK15	1926	GKM64	1928						
GDK55	1924	GOK40	1926	GKM66	1928						
GDK58	1924	GOK57	1926	GKM80	1928						
GDK64	1924	GOK75	1926	GTM30	1928						
GLK15	1924	GZK26	1926	GFN81	1928						
GLK36	1924	GZK62	1926	GLN31	1929						

Limousine

The most numerous body type from Hooper for the Twenty chassis was the Limousine, and 137 examples were built between 1923 and 1929.

51S1	1923	70A4	1923	87K5	1923
55S6	1923	70A9	1923	GA44	1923
64H7	1923	76A2	1923	GF21	1923
65H8	1923	78A5	1923	GF34	1923

Even the chauffeur's compartment was exquisitely appointed, although upholstery was in hard-wearing leather. (Simon Clay)

Hooper proudly listed its royal connections on the coachbuilder's plate of 81K6. (Simon Clay)

GF45	1923	GLK51	1924	GYK78	1926
GF65	1923	GLK52	1924	GYK90	1926
GF67	1923	GLK70	1924	GMJ10	1926
GF75	1923	GNK24	1925	GMJ59	1926
GF77	1923	GNK43	1925	GMJ69	1926
GF79	1923	GNK46	1925	GHJ46	1927
GH17	1923	GPK5	1925	GHJ66	1927
GH28	1923	GPL37	1925	GAJ25	1927
GH34	1923	GPK49	1925	GUJ5	1927
GH40	1923	GPK55	1925	GUJ9	1927
GH59	1923	GPK69	1925	GUJ44	1927
GH81	1923	GPK70	1925	GXL16	1927
GAK17	1924	GPK73	1925	GXL46	1927
GAL44	1924	GPK81	1925	GXL78	1927
GAK51	1924	GSK4	1925	GYL15	1928
GAK62	1924	GSK9	1925	GYL28	1928
GAK64	1924	GSK23	1925	GYL32	1928
GAK76	1924	GSK45	1925	GWL34	1928
GMK1	1924	GSK63	1925	GBM22	1928
GMK21	1924	GSK71	1925	GBM49	1928
GMK35	1924	GCK16	1925	GBM80	1928
GMK54	1924	GCK42	1925	GKM17	1928
GMK61	1924	GOK17	1926	GKM20	1928
GRK10	1924	GOK22	1926	GTM2	1928
GRK16	1924	GOK69	1926	GTM3	1928
GRK52	1924	GXK7	1926	GTM25	1928
GRK62	1924	GZK24	1926	GTM32	1928
GRK72	1924	GZK25	1926	GFN12	1928
GDK1	1924	GZK41	1926	GFN15	1928
GDK5	1924	GZK61	1926	GFN23	1928
GDK15	1924	GUK55	1926	GFN56	1928
GDK16	1924	GUK59	1926	GFN58	1928
GDK29	1924	GUK68	1926	GFN68	1928
GDK33	1924	GYK1	1926	GLN48	1929
GDK60	1924	GYK2	1926	GLN67	1929
GDK66	1924	GYK8	1926	GLN76	1929
GDK68	1924	GYK10	1926	GEN37	1929
GDK76	1924	GYK16	1926	GEN61	1929
GLK2	1924	GYK22	1926	GVO5	1929
GLK18	1924	GYK25	1926	GVO31	1929
GLK26	1924	GYK65	1926	GVO56	1929
GLK27	1924	GYK69	1926		

Salamanca

Hooper built just one Salamanca body for the Twenty chassis, and this was for GUK46 in 1926.

Saloons

The 49 Saloon bodies built between 1923 and 1929 average out at seven examples each year. Two late ones, for chassis GFN40 in 1928 and GEN43 in 1929, were built using the Weymann construction principles.

GA16	1923	GSK21	1925	GHJ42	1927
GA55	1923	GCK29	1925	GHJ45	1927
GH60	1923	GCK40	1925	GHJ53	1927
GAK50	1924	GCK68	1925	GAJ28	1927
GMK70	1924	GCK78	1925	GUJ10	1927
GRK42	1924	GOK28	1926	GUJ59	1927
GRK71	1924	GOK56	1926	GYL23	1928
GRK75	1924	GOK66	1926	GYL80	1928
GDK24	1924	GZK50	1926	GBM20	1928
GLK3	1924	GZK73	1926	GBM69	1928
GLK65	1924	GUK34	1926	GFN9	1928
GNK2	1925	GYK32	1926	GFN40	1928
GNK45	1925	GYK59	1926	GLN17	1929
GPK14	1925	GYK77	1926	GLN29	1929
GPK38	1925	GMJ22	1926	GLN52	1929
GPK44	1925	GMJ71	1926	GEN43	1929
GPK63	1925				

Sedanca

Beginning in 1927, Hooper built a total of 10 Sedanca bodies for the Twenty chassis.

GUJ56	1927	GLN12	1929	GEN10	1929
GYL58	1928	GLN50	1929	GVO6	1929
GBM68	1928	GLN72	1929	GVO66	1929
GKM11	1928				

Tourer

The Tourer was a popular body style in the early days of the Twenty, but orders dropped off markedly after 1924. Hooper built a total of 67 such bodies, the last of them in 1928.

40G5	1922	48G5	1922	63H3	1922
41G8	1922	50G0	1922	63H7	1922
41G9	1922	50S8	1922	63H9	1922
42G6	1922	51S4	1922	64H1	1923
44G7	1922	52S9	1922	65H2	1923
44G8	1922	54S2	1922	68H5	1923
45G7	1922	54S3	1922	74A6	1923
46G6	1922	55S3	1922	77A0	1923
47G2	1922	57S1	1922	79A2	1923
48G4	1923	57S5	1922	83K6	1923

Two-seaters were not commonly supplied by Hooper, but the proportions of this one show how well the coachbuilder could rise to the challenge. The body was built in 1923 for Twenty chassis GH58.

88K5	1923	GAK45	1924	GMJ58	1926
GA52	1923	GAK49	1924	GHJ8	1927
GA70	1923	GAK54	1924	GHJ43	1927
GF50	1923	GRK9	1924	GHJ58	1927
GF54	1923	GDK30	1924	GAJ42	1927
GF63	1923	GLK54	1924	GAJ48	1927
GF76	1923	GLK67	1924	GAJ81	1927
GH2	1923	GNK35	1925	GRJ72	1927
GH14	1923	GCK32	1925	GXL54	1927
GH75	1923	GCK61	1925	GBM67	1928
GAK1	1924	GOK68	1926	GTM21	1928
GAK7	1924	GZK76	1926		
GAK37	1924	GMJ9	1926		

Two-seaters

Hooper always seemed somehow too grand to be asked for a Two-seater body, but the coachbuilder nevertheless delivered six known examples on the Twenty chassis between 1923 and 1926.

85K6	1923	GNK11	1925	GCK35	1925
GH58	1923	GPK35	1925	GZK44	1926

20/25 COACHWORK

Hooper were far and away the most prolific coachbuilder for the 20/25 chassis, with a grand total of 676 bodies. The year-on-year totals were as follows:

1928	1	1931	22	1934	167
1929	20	1932	93	1935	133
1930	49	1933	161	1936	31

(These totals actually give an overall figure of 677. This is because the 1928 body on an experimental chassis is shown twice; the car was renumbered in the production series during 1930.)

Tom Clarke also records three definite Hooper rebodies (on GKT3, GYZ41, and GTK54), and two further possibles (on GED41 and GMD76).

All-weathers

All-weather coachwork from Hooper was rare, but there were three examples on the 20/25 chassis. These were for GKT41 in 1932, GSY68 in 1933, and GPG70 in 1935; each one was an individual design.

Cabriolets

Just one Hooper body for a 20/25 was described as a Cabriolet, and this was for chassis GLR53 in 1930.

Coupés

Five early chassis were bodied as fixed-head Coupés. These were GXO27, GXO93 and GDP3 in 1929, and GSR60 and GTR29 in 1930.

De Ville types

Hooper provided De Ville type bodies for a total of 41 Rolls-Royce 20/25 chassis, and these bodies were divided among six major types.

Four bodies were Brougham de Ville types, and these were for chassis GNS53 in 1930, GNS61 in 1931, GEX22 in 1933, and GSF45 in 1935. There was a single Cabriolet de Ville, built in 1930 for chassis GWP36. More numerous were the Limousine de Ville bodies, of which there were six:

GLR79	1930	GDX38	1933	GUB17	1934
GZU10	1932	GHA27	1933	GLG52	1935

The most numerous of the six De Ville types was the Sedanca de Ville, of which Hooper built 25 examples on the 20/25 chassis. Note that GLR82X was renumbered from experimental chassis 14-G-IV in 1930, but that both body and chassis dated from 1928. The body for GHG17 in 1935 was uniquely

The All-weather body for 20/25 chassis GKT41 was a special commission from the Rajah of Mandi in India. It was a highly unusual design that nevertheless worked well in both open and closed forms.

The moulding on the scuttle sides allowed Hooper to describe this body as a Brougham de Ville, although the leading edge of the front door is actually straight. The body was built for 20/25 chassis GSF45 in 1935.

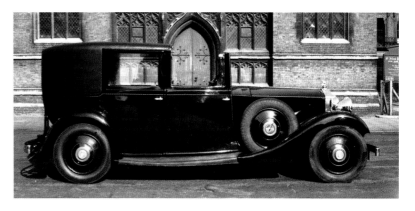

described as a Sports Sedanca de Ville and was delivered to a customer in Spain. The full list of these bodies is below.

GXO43	1929	GAW33	1933	GAE61	1934
GWP18	1930	GEX62	1933	GWE46	1934
GLR82X	1930	GWX53	1933	GPG28	1935
GNS23	1930	GGA38	1933	GPG78	1935
GFT16	1931	GXB71	1934	GHG17	1935
GBT17	1931	GNC62	1934	GOH53	1935
GKT30	1932	GNC70	1934	GBJ38	1935
GAU37	1932	GRC12	1934	GLJ31	1935
GRW9	1932				

There were two Sedanca Coupés, which were for chassis GMD41 in 1934 and GPG40 in 1935. The last of the six De Ville types from Hooper was the Sedancalette, of which three were built. These were for GGP3 in 1929 and for GAW6 and GBA61 in 1933.

Drophead Coupés

There were five Drophead Coupés built to a variety of designs. Two of them had dickey seats, and these were for chassis GDP28 in 1930 and GPS6 in 1931. The other three bodies were for GNS8 in 1930, and for GTZ18 and GHA32 in 1933.

Landaulettes

Hooper Landaulette bodies were consistently in demand, and the company built 49 to a variety of different designs on the 20/25 chassis. The full list was as follows:

GXO29	1929	GNS41	1930	GAW8	1932
GDP70	1930	GOS69	1931	GEX20	1933
GDP73	1930	GBT10	1931	GEX70	1933
GLR44	1930	GBT22	1931	GWX12	1933
GLR45	1930	GBT72	1932	GWX26	1933
GLR81	1930	GHW27	1932	GSY56	1933
GSR43	1930	GHW39	1932	GLZ16	1933
GTR22	1930	GHW40	1932	GLZ81	1933
GNS1	1930	GRW47	1932	GTZ17	1933

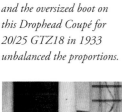

Even Hooper could slip up when the customer insisted, and the oversized boot on this Drophead Coupé for 20/25 GTZ18 in 1933 unbalanced the proportions.

GBA15	1933	GNC64	1934	GLG30	1935
GBA22	1933	GRC77	1934	GPH69	1935
GGA48	1933	GKC28	1934	GBJ50	1935
GGA72	1933	GWE20	1934	GLJ45	1935
GHA17	1933	GWE34	1934	GXK71	1936
GXB43	1934	GAF51	1934	GTK57	1936
GUB33	1934	GAF73	1934		
GUB53	1934	GRF32	1935		

Limousines

Limousine bodies were far and away the most numerous of the various types that Hooper provided for the 20/25 chassis, and there were 314 in all. Hooper relied on several "standard" designs for most of this period but also built a good number of bespoke Limousine bodies. Among the "standard" designs were numbers 4944 (1931-1932), 5104 (1932-1933) and 5430, which was the company's first D-back style in 1933. Others followed. The body on GAU 39 in 1932 was uniquely described as a Pullman type.

For ease of use, the tables of Limousine bodies are broken up into smaller segments of one or two years.

1929-1930

GXO23	1929	GDP77	1930	GSR39	1930
GXO39	1929	GWP22	1930	GSR64	1930
GXO102	1929	GLR18	1930	GSR73	1930
GXO108	1929	GLR30	1930	GSR76	1930
GGP36	1929	GLR33	1930	GNS31	1930
GGP38	1929	GLR41	1930	GNS35	1930
GGP65	1929	GLR58	1930	GNS37	1930
GDP12	1929	GLR59	1930	GNS50	1930
GDP42	1930	GLR62	1930	GNS52	1930
GDP57	1930				

1931-1932

GNS47	1931	GKT34	1932	GZU29	1932
GNS57	1931	GKT39	1932	GZU37	1932
GOS22	1931	GAU32	1932	GHW14	1932
GOS26	1931	GAU39	1932	GHW19	1932
GOS34	1931	GAU40	1932	GHW22	1932
GPS12	1931	GAU44	1932	GHW24	1932
GFT39	1931	GAU49	1932	GHW29	1932
GFT66	1931	GAU66	1932	GHW32	1932
GBT2	1931	GMU5	1932	GHW35	1932
GBT60	1932	GMU14	1932	GHW36	1932
GBT64	1932	GMU39	1932	GHW44	1932
GBT67	1932	GMU42	1932	GHW50	1932
GBT78	1932	GMU44	1932	GHW52	1932
GKT1	1932	GMU49	1932	GHW62	1932
GKT4	1932	GMU54	1932	GHW63	1932
GKT26	1932	GMU62	1932	GHW70	1932

Hooper built more Limousines than any other type of body for the 20/25 chassis, and this 1933 D-back example clearly illustrates their eye for an appropriately dignified shape. It was on chassis GSY10.

GHW71	1932	GRW12	1932	GRW41	1932
GHW77	1932	GRW25	1932	GRW42	1932
GHW81	1932	GRW38	1932	GRW53	1932

1933

GRW80	GWX8	GSY29	GTZ8	GBA1
GBA78	GAW19	GWX11	GSY30	GTZ10
GBA3	GGA7	GAW20	GWX21	GSY45
GTZ11	GBA12	GGA11	GAW21	GWX23
GSY48	GTZ32	GBA16	GGA17	GAW23
GWX39	GSY64	GTZ56	GBA21	GGA20
GAW26	GWX40	GSY66	GTZ62	GBA28
GGA21	GAW30	GWX44	GSY87	GTZ67
GBA35	GGA22	GAW41	GWX47	GSY99
GTZ70	GBA40	GGA51	GEX14	GWX54
GLZ26	GTZ75	GBA45	GHA5	GEX21
GWX62	GLZ32	GTZ77	GBA49	GHA21
GEX40	GWX66	GLZ46	GTZ80	GBA56
GHA41	GEX47	GDX26	GLZ52	GYZ5
GBA58	GXB8	GEX48	GSY8	GLZ53
GYZ19	GBA70	GXB16	GEX64	GSY10
GLZ56	GYZ22	GBA71	GXB20	GEX77
GSY16	GTZ1	GYZ24	GBA74	GXB29
GEX78	GSY19	GTZ2	GYZ36	

1934

GXB53	GLB20	GRC51	GED27	GAE77
GFE21	GXB63	GLB21	GRC64	GED50
GWE1	GFE35	GXB65	GLB29	GRC65
GMD6	GWE15	GFE36	GXB74	GLB40
GRC69	GYD1	GWE21	GAF3	GXB78
GNC22	GRC73	GYD32	GWE31	GAF23
GUB12	GNC50	GKC2	GYD39	GWE37
GAF25	GUB19	GNC51	GKC7	GYD58
GWE47	GAF40	GUB46	GNC59	GKC16
GAE22	GWE73	GAF44	GUB50	GRC1
GKC32	GAE43	GWE83	GSF23	GUB64
GRC27	GKC41	GAE48	GFE2	GSF32
GUB79	GRC38	GED15	GAE72	GFE4

1935-1936

GSF56	1935	GYH59	1935	GBJ61	1935
GSF60	1935	GYH60	1935	GBJ75	1935
GRF7	1935	GYH64	1935	GLJ7	1935
GRF8	1935	GYH66	1935	GLJ12	1935
GRF29	1935	GYH76	1935	GLJ46	1935
GRF38	1935	GYH79	1935	GLJ55	1935
GLG1	1935	GOH10	1935	GLJ68	1935
GLG57	1935	GOH36	1935	GCJ16	1935
GLG81	1935	GOH68	1935	GCJ26	1935
GPG30	1935	GEH1	1935	GCJ37	1935
GPG43	1935	GEH7	1935	GXK3	1935
GHG8	1935	GEH32	1935	GXK8	1935
GHG15	1935	GBJ1	1935	GXK23	1935
GHG28	1935	GBJ3	1935	GXK27	1935
GHG33	1935	GBJ14	1935	GXK29	1935
GHG38	1935	GBJ23	1935	GXK42	1935
GYH30	1935	GBJ46	1935	GXK44	1935
GYH51	1935	GBJ57	1935	GBK1	1936

Despite the many similarities with the body for GSY10, this example for GBA58, also dating from 1933, shows how minor differences could affect the appearance. In this case, there are no wheel discs, no spare wheel alongside the bonnet, and a more sombre colour has been used.

Another variation on the Limousine theme was this four-light body that was delivered new to South Africa in 1935. It was on 20/25 chassis GEH1. (WikiMedia Commons)

Hooper described this body for 20/25 chassis GOS44 as a Saloon Cabriolet. It was a very solid-looking construction that was new in 1931.
(Real Car Company)

GBK3	1936	GBK59	1936	GBK77	1936
GBK4	1936	GBK62	1936	GBK79	1936
GBK15	1936	GBK68	1936	GTK21	1936
GBK17	1936	GBK69	1936	GTK39	1936
GBK28	1936	GBK73	1936		
GBK55	1936	GBK75	1936		

Saloons

In terms of quantities built, Saloons came a worthy second to Limousines, with 251 examples on the 20/25 chassis. There was of course a wider variety of types, and the tables below also include Saloon Cabriolets (17-G-IV and GOS44), Saloon Limousines (GSR26, GBT65 and GSY5), Tickford Saloons (GWE12 and GEH37), and a Saloon Sports Coupé (GEX34).

There were both four-light and six-light designs, although the six-light types became less common after 1933, when almost every body was described as a (four-light) Sports Saloon. From 1932, Hooper

answered Park Ward's successful Continental Saloon with its own Continental Saloon with Division (design 5068), which proved popular, and from 1935 design 6129 was called a Continental Sports Saloon. Several bodies were also built using the Silentbloc patents from 1932. Inevitably, many of these bodies – including some of the later Sports Saloons – were ordered with a Division, and bodies so equipped are marked with an asterisk (*) in the tables. The proportion was very high in some years; in 1932, for example, almost every Saloon body ordered had a Division. Once again, the tables below are broken up into smaller segments of one or two years for ease of use.

1929-1931

17-G-IV	1929	GSR41*	1930	GOS44	1931
GXO105*	1929	GNS33*	1930	GOS50*	1931
GGP80*	1929	GNS51	1930	GFT3	1931
GDP46*	1930	GOS4*	1931	GFT36*	1931
GSR26	1930				

1932

GBT29*	GAU7*	GAU81*	GMU68*
GZU36*	GHW56*	GBT58*	GAU15*
GMU2*	GMU75*	GZU41*	GRW20*
GBT65	GAU16*	GMU9*	GMU81*
GHW21*	GRW32	GBT75*	GAU21*
GMU26*	GZU2*	GHW26	GRW61
GKT9*	GAU59*	GMU34*	GZU4*
GHW46*	GRW69	GKT25*	GAU63*
GMU35*	GZU21*		

1933

GAW25	GWX2	GSY9	GLZ20*
GTZ24	GGA37*	GEX25*	GWX25*
GSY24	GLZ30	GYZ39	GGA45
GEX33*	GWX48	GSY51	GLZ60
GBA6	GGA59*	GEX34	GWX55
GSY54	GLZ65	GBA29	GGA71*
GEX54*	GDX12*	GSY72	GLZ67
GBA34	GHA2*	GEX63*	GDX17
GSY76	GLZ68	GBA47	GXB1*
GEX79*	GSY5	GSY88*	GTZ16
GGA28			

Despite its reputation for formal coachwork, Hooper was not beyond experimenting with new fashions. This sloping-tail Sports Saloon with its hinged spare wheel cover was an experimental design for 20/25 GMU75 that was taken on by one of the Hooper Directors when new in 1932. Not clear from this picture is that the body incorporated a Division.

1934

21-G-IV	GLB28	GRC72	GYD52
GAE60	GAF7	GXB27*	GLB30
GKC35	GYD68	GAE73	GAF12
GXB39	GNC7	GED12	GAE5
GAE75*	GAF30	GXB40	GNC14
GED34	GAE15	GAE78	GAF39
GXB54	GNC19	GED45	GAE17
GWE7	GAF46	GXB59	GNC20
GMD17	GAE21	GWE12	GAF65
GXB70	GNC35*	GMD20	GAE29
GWE16	GAF66	GXB73	GNC44*
GMD32	GAE33	GWE18	GAF75*
GUB2	GNC69	GMD35*	GAE36
GWE53*	GAF78	GUB32*	GNC76
GMD49*	GAE37	GWE63	GSF1
GUB43	GRC14	GMD50	GAE45
GWE81*	GSF4	GUB45*	GRC40
GMD61	GAE46	GWE82	GSF16
GUB60	GRC57	GYD24*	GAE52
GFE18	GSF19	GUB74	GRC66
GYD31	GAE59	GFE26	GSF34
GLB9	GRC68		

1935-1936

GSF57	1935	GHG4	1935	GBJ64	1935
GSF61*	1935	GYH11	1935	GLJ4	1935
GSF64	1935	GYH16	1935	GLJ11	1935
GSF65	1935	GYH17*	1935	GLJ29*	1935
GSF73	1935	GYH25	1935	GLJ41	1935
GSF77	1935	GYH28*	1935	GLJ42*	1935
GSF78*	1935	GYH34*	1935	GLJ78*	1935
GRF1	1935	GYH47*	1935	GCJ30	1935
GRF22	1935	GYH72	1935	GXK14*	1935
GRF23	1935	GOH17	1935	GXK36	1935
GRF26	1935	GOH24*	1935	GXK40*	1935
GLG24*	1935	GOH35	1935	GXK56*	1935
GLG26*	1935	GOH43*	1935	GXK63	1935
GLG33	1935	GOH52*	1935	GXK78	1936
GLG38*	1935	GOH79	1935	GBK10	1936
GLG54*	1935	GEH14	1935	GBK19	1936
GLG67*	1935	GEH17	1935	GBK22*	1936
GPG22*	1935	GEH18	1935	GBK31	1936
GPG23	1935	GEH21*	1935	GBK41	1936
GPG42	1935	GEH37	1935	GBK71	1936
GPG45	1935	GBJ12*	1935	GBK81*	1936
GPG57	1935	GBJ16	1935	GTK4*	1936
GPG58	1935	GBJ28	1935	GTK15*	1936
GPG60	1935	GBJ35	1935	GTK35	1936
GPG81	1935	GBJ44	1935	GTK44*	1936
GHG2	1935	GBJ51	1935		

Special bodies

The Maharaja of Jammu and Kashmir called for two special bodies on the 20/25 chassis that were completed in 1930. They were companions to his Saloon Limousine on chassis GSR26 that had been displayed at the Paris Salon in 1930.

The body on chassis GSR29 was a Shooting Brake, and that on GSR35 was a Luggage Van.

Tourers

The fashion for Tourers died out during the early 1930s, and Hooper built just six such bodies for the 20/25 chassis between 1929 and 1931. They were as follows:

GXO19	1929	GDP2	1929	GNS11	1930
GGP11	1929	GWP31	1930	GOS16	1931

25/30 COACHWORK

Hooper built 209 bodies for new Rolls-Royce 25/30 chassis, and once again the largest numbers were Limousines (111) and Saloons (74). Eleven De Ville types and 10 Landaulettes were built, plus a handful of other types.

Cabriolets

Just one Cabriolet body was built for the 25/30, and that was in 1936 for chassis GWN46. The body was built to design number 6814.

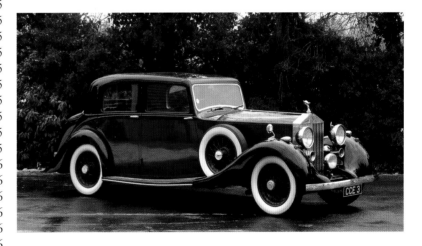

Built on a later 25/30 chassis in 1938, this Sports Saloon had design 6974. (Magic Car Pics)

Coupés

Two Fixed-head Coupé bodies were ordered, each different from the other. The earlier one was built to design 6753 for chassis GWN9 in 1936. The later one was a Pillarless fixed-head Coupé (meaning it had no B-pillar above the waistline) for chassis GGR20 in 1938. This had design number 7268.

De Ville types

Hooper built 11 De Ville bodies of three different major types for the 25/30 chassis.

There were three Brougham de Ville bodies to two different designs. Chassis GXM33 in 1936 had body design 6673, but GMP62 in 1937 and GZR27 in 1938 both had design 7103. Two bodies were built to the same Limousine de Ville design, number 7061. One was for GLP31 in 1937 and the other for GZR26 in 1938.

The remaining six bodies were all Sedanca de Ville types. There were two to design 5951, and these were for chassis GGM38 in 1936 and GHO35 in 1937. The other four were all individual designs built in 1937, and were for chassis GWN79, GRO67, GAR56 and GGR3.

Landaulettes

There were ten Landaulette bodies for the 25/30 chassis. Design 6311 was introduced in 1936 and attracted five orders. These were built on chassis GXM41 in 1936, and on GWN80, GUN29, GRO5 and GRP80 in 1937. There were two examples of design 7125, for GMP69 in 1937 and GGR63 in 1938. The other three were all individual designs, and were for chassis GRM16 in 1936, GGR16 in 1937, and GZR32 in 1938.

Limousines

The 111 Limousine bodies were built to several different designs. Just under half were completed in 1936, when Hooper built 55 Limousines; there were then 49 in 1937 and seven in 1938. The full list is as follows:

GUL18	1936	GHL26	1936	GXM39	1936
GUL21	1936	GHL32	1936	GXM40	1936
GUL23	1936	GRM36	1936	GXM47	1936
GUL35	1936	GRM37	1936	GXM53	1936
GUL44	1936	GRM53	1936	GXM67	1936
GUL47	1936	GRM59	1936	GXM74	1936
GTL1	1936	GRM60	1936	GXM78	1936
GTL8	1936	GRM64	1936	GGM21	1936
GTL18	1936	GRM65	1936	GGM22	1936
GTL37	1936	GRM76	1936	GGM28	1936
GTL38	1936	GXM10	1936	GAN15	1936
GTL74	1936	GXM12	1936	GAN17	1936
GHL12	1936	GXM16	1936	GAN22	1936
GHL16	1936	GXM31	1936	GAN36	1936
GAN40	1936	GRO22	1937	GMP36	1937
GAN41	1936	GRO33	1937	GMP47	1937
GAN48	1936	GRO36	1937	GMP50	1937
GAN56	1936	GRO60	1937	GMP55	1937
GAN63	1936	GHO68	1937	GMP60	1937
GAN64	1936	GHO70	1937	GMP63	1937
GAN71	1936	GMO2	1937	GLP23	1937
GAN78	1936	GMO24	1937	GLP35	1937
GWN14	1936	GMO30	1937	GLP39	1937
GWN27	1936	GMO33	1937	GAR7	1937
GWN34	1936	GMO38	1937	GAR17	1937
GWN35	1936	GRP10	1937	GAR31	1937
GWN47	1936	GRP25	1937	GAR44	1937
GWN53	1937	GRP35	1937	GAR45	1937
GWN54	1937	GRP40	1937	GAR50	1937
GUN9	1937	GRP57	1937	GAR51	1937
GUN17	1937	GRP61	1937	GAR70	1938
GUN18	1937	GRP64	1937	GAR76	1938
GUN26	1937	GRP77	1937	GGR32	1938
GUN36	1937	GMP2	1937	GGR41	1938
GRO4	1937	GMP5	1937	GGR49	1938
GRO10	1937	GMP14	1937	GGR59	1938
GRO18	1937	GMP15	1937	GZR34	1938

Saloons

Among the 74 Hooper Saloon bodies for the 25/30 were both bespoke and "standard" designs. The latter included Sports Saloons, which started as 6245 in 1936, moved on to 6684 for the 1937 season, and then to 7099 for the 1938 season. In the 1938 season, design 7133 seems to have been the "standard" Saloon with Division. There were several six-light bodies, but the four-light types were more numerous, and all seem to have been described as Sports Saloons. The full list, with dates, is below; an asterisk (*) indicates a body with a Division.

GUL1	1936	GXM24	1936	GHO1	1937
GUL6*	1936	GXM48	1936	GHO3	1937
GUL34	1936	GXM58	1936	GHO44	1937
GUL62	1936	GXM65	1936	GHO46*	1937
GTL15	1936	GGM4	1936	GHO51	1937
GTL26*	1936	GGM20	1936	GHO74	1937
GTL31	1936	GGM39	1936	GMO1	1937
GTL39	1936	GAN3	1936	GMO19	1937
GTL49	1936	GAN37	1936	GMO31	1937
GTL79	1936	GAN79	1936	GRP38	1937
GTL81	1936	GAN80	1936	GRP55*	1937
GHL8	1936	GWN8	1936	GRP72*	1937
GHL36	1936	GWN10	1936	GMP26	1937
GRM31	1936	GWN24*	1936	GMP40	1937
GRM38	1936	GUN33	1937	GMP57	1937
GXM4*	1936	GRO75	1937	GMP64	1937

GMP70	1937	GAR33	1937	GGR36	1937
GMP75	1937	GAR37*	1937	GGR37	1938
GMP76*	1937	GAR53*	1937	GGR44	1938
GLP4	1937	GAR61	1937	GGR53	1938
GLP6	1937	GAR67	1937	GGR62	1938
GLP8*	1937	GAR69	1937	GGR68	1938
GLP18*	1937	GAR73	1937	GGR73*	1938
GLP26	1937	GAR79*	1937	GZR10*	1938
GAR22	1937	GGR2	1938		

WRAITH COACHWORK

Hooper built 74 bodies for the Rolls-Royce Wraith chassis.

Overwhelmingly, the customers who visited Hooper to order a coachbuilt body for the Wraith chassis wanted Limousines and Saloons. By this stage, many were ordered as Touring Limousines or Touring Saloons.

De Ville types

There was the usual smattering of orders for De Ville bodies on the Wraith, and Hooper built seven of them. There was one Limousine de Ville (for chassis WMB6 in 1938), and there was also a single Sedanca Coupé with a three-position head for WLB1 in 1939.

Four bodies were Sedanca de Ville types, each one to a different design. These were for chassis WXA80 in 1938, and for WMB29, and WEC17 in 1939. By this stage, of course, Hooper had taken control of Barker and the last Sedanca de Ville for a Wraith, on chassis WHC29, actually had a Barker design. It was not delivered until 1941.

Drophead Coupés

Two Drophead Coupé bodies were built in 1938. The earlier one, for chassis WXA78, was to design and incorporated a dickey seat. The second one had design 7482 and was for chassis WRB30.

Landaulettes

Hooper built just three Landaulette bodies for Wraith chassis, all in 1939 and all to different designs. The first two were for chassis WHC1 and WHC2. The third body, for chassis WEC10, used a Barker design.

Limousines

A total of 44 bodies were described as Limousines, and these included Touring Limousine types with both four- and six-light designs. The largest number had design 7377, and the last two bodies were completed after the war in 1946 as Touring Limousines to design 7676; the one on chassis WKC16 was delivered to the Ministry of Supply for use at the British Embassy in Cairo.

This well-proportioned Hooper Sports Saloon was built for 25/30 chassis GXM24 in 1936 to "standard" design 6245.

WXA23	1938	WMB4	1938	WHC12	1939
WXA30	1938	WMB5	1938	WHC34	1939
WXA32	1938	WMB17	1938	WHC36	1939
WXA35	1938	WMB22	1938	WHC38	1939
WXA47	1938	WMB30	1939	WHC56	1939
WXA66	1938	WMB31	1939	WHC70	1939
WXA76	1938	WMB34	1939	WEC5	1939
WXA95	1938	WMB65	1939	WEC32	1939
WXA101	1938	WMB74	1939	WEC46	1939
WRB1	1938	WMB75	1939	WEC53	1939
WRB18	1938	WLB6	1939	WEC69	1939
WRB37	1938	WLB16	1939	WEC77	1939
WRB39	1938	WLB23	1939	WEC80	1946
WRB43	1938	WLB24	1939	WKC16	1946
WRB48	1938	WLB26	1939		

Saloons

Of the 19 Saloon bodies for Wraith chassis, many were described as Touring Saloons. Not one was a Sports Saloon – perhaps Hooper customers saw the Wraith as too grand for such frivolity. Several bodies had a Division – marked here with a * – and included in the table for convenience is the single Saloon Coupé built to design 7748 for chassis WEC57 in 1939. This was a most unusual two-light body with dummy landau irons, a vee windscreen, chromed wire wheels and cutaway rear-wheel spats. Note that the body on

Elegant and formal as ever, this was a 1938 Hooper Limousine design for the Wraith, complete with a swept tail feature.

WMB52 in 1939 had design 7377 (a Limousine) but was described as a six-light Saloon.

WXA34*	1938	WMB35	1939	WLB12*	1939
WXA65	1938	WMB49	1939	WHC79*	1939
WRB26	1938	WMB52	1939	WEC28*	1939
WRB31*	1938	WMB61	1939	WEC42	1939
WRB60	1938	WMB72	1939	WEC57	1939
WMB7*	1939	WLB2	1939	WEC70	1939
WMB18	1938				

HOWARTH
Probably Manchester – Twenty

The Howarth & Co recorded as building coachwork for two Rolls-Royce Twenty chassis is likely to have been James Howarth, a little-known Manchester coachbuilder. The two bodies were built for the same customer in 1926, and were Landaulettes for chassis GOK42 and GMJ55.

HOWELL
Location unknown – Twenty

A company called J Howell is recorded as building the Saloon body on a 1923 Rolls-Royce Twenty, with chassis number GA2. Unfortunately, nothing is known about the company.

HOWES & SONS
Norwich – Twenty

Based in Norwich, Howes & Sons had been founded in the eighteenth century as a carriage maker, and during the following century supplied carriages to the British Royal Family and to members of the German aristocracy. It built its first car bodies early in the twentieth century. Always closely associated with Wolseley, the company usually worked with the more expensive quality makes of the day, but refocused its activities on commercial body building after 1929.

Howes & Sons provided the coachwork for two Rolls-Royce Twenty chassis, in both cases during 1927. The earlier one was a Doctor's Coupé for GAJ31 and the later a Weymann Saloon for GUJ32.

HOYAL
Weybridge – Twenty

The Hoyal Body Corporation began to use that name in 1926, although it had been formed as Chalmer & Hoyer in 1921. Based at Hamworthy near Poole in Dorset, it expanded into a second factory at Weybridge in 1924. The name Hoyal came from the surnames of Hoyer and the other principal figure in the company, HW Allingham.

Chalmer & Hoyer was the first British company to take out a Weymann licence, and much of its early work was for makers such as Austin and Morris. It also built bus bodies at the Weybridge factory. Bespoke coachwork always came second to contract work, but the company did construct five bodies for Rolls-Royce Twenty chassis. When the business environment became more challenging, Hoyal went into voluntary liquidation in August 1931.

Four of those five bodies for Twenty chassis were completed in 1926. Two of them were Coupés, on chassis GOK51 and GZK74, and the other three were all Saloons. The earliest of those, on GYK40, was for HW Allingham himself. The second was on GYK53. The fifth body for a Twenty chassis was not delivered until 1929, and was another Saloon; it was on GEN25.

JACKSON BROS
Probably Blackpool – Twenty

The Jackson Bros who bodied Rolls-Royce Twenty 59S2 as a Landaulette in 1923 may have been the same company as the Jackson responsible for a Cabriolet on GF46 the same year. The company is likely to have been the Jackson Bros who were garage proprietors and car dealers in Blackpool, Lancashire.

JAMES YOUNG
Bromley – Twenty, 20/25, 25/30, Wraith

James Young had a good reputation as a carriage maker before it moved into car bodywork in 1908. The company was based at Bromley in Kent and was building coachwork for Rolls-Royce chassis by 1923, although was relatively little known until the mid-1920s, when it began exhibiting at Olympia. It balanced the books through a series of alliances with car makers and importers under which it built standard designs in quantity for their chassis, but also specialised in bespoke coachwork on the more expensive chassis. The company was bought by London Rolls-Royce dealer Jack Barclay in 1937, and at about the same time AF McNeil moved from Gurney Nutting to become its chief designer.

The company built a large number of bodies for the small-horsepower Rolls-Royce models. There were 27 for the Twenty between 1923 and 1929. After these came 88 for the 20/25, 45 for the 25/30, and 30 for the Wraith to make a grand total of 190 bodies.

TWENTY COACHWORK

The 27 bodies on the Twenty chassis were spread fairly evenly through the years in which Rolls-Royce offered the type. There were two in 1923, five in 1924, four in 1925 and six in 1926. After a poor year in 1927 when only two bodies were delivered, 1928 became the best year with a total of seven, and the figure dropped back to just one in 1929.

Like many coachbuilders in this period, James Young built multiple different body types, even though the strongest demand was for Saloons (and, latterly, for Weymann Saloons). The different types were as follows:

All-weather

Only one All-weather body came from James Young for a Twenty chassis, and that one was delivered in 1925 on chassis GSK1.

Cabriolets

Both Cabriolet bodies on the Twenty chassis were built in 1924. They were on chassis numbers GRK17 and GDK42.

Coupés

There were also two Coupé bodies. The first was on chassis GA74 in 1923, and the second on GPK12 in 1925.

Drophead Coupé

James Young built just one Drophead Coupé (strictly a "three-quarter" type with a quarter-light). This was for chassis GWL32 in 1928. Worth noting is that the company also built a Drophead Coupé in 1933 to rebody a 1928 chassis, GTM28.

Landaulettes

Between 1923 and 1926, there were four Landaulette bodies on the Twenty chassis, of which two were "three-quarter" types. The earliest was for chassis 86K5 in 1923. The bodies for GRK61 in 1924 and GYK45 in 1926 were the "three-quarter" types, and the remaining body was for GOK60 in 1926.

Saloons

As was the case with many other coachbuilders, Saloons were the most numerous of the body types that James Young built on the Twenty chassis. The first one was built in 1924. During 1927, the company changed over completely to Weymann construction for its Saloons, which sold well until the end of Twenty production in 1929. The list of Saloons, together with their delivery dates, is shown below in tabular form. Note that GXL38 and all those that followed it had Weymann types, which therefore accounted for more than half of the total of 15 Saloon bodies by James Young. The body on GEN45 was built to a design by the dealer Paddon Bros.

This six-light Saloon body on Twenty chassis GZK51 dates from 1926. It shows none of the originality that would later characterise James Young coachwork.

GDK8	1924	GMJ12	1926	GBM48	1928
GDK31	1924	GAJ49	1927	GBM50	1928
GPK22	1925	GXL38	1927	GKM70	1928
GZK51	1926	GYL79	1928	GFN21	1928
GMJ5	1926	GBM3	1928	GEN45	1929

Tourers

There were just two Tourer bodies in the middle of the decade. These were for GNK1 in 1925 and GZK23 in 1926.

20/25 COACHWORK

James Young built 88 bodies for the 20/25 chassis between 1929 and 1936. There was just one body in each of the first two years, and then the effects of the Depression were very obvious in 1931, when none were built. Numbers rose to eight in 1932, and then bounced back to 18 in 1933, 23 in 1934, and 30 in 1935. There were seven more in 1936, the year of transition to the 25/30 chassis.

All-weathers

The description "All-weather" can cover many different types of body, and the two that James Young built on the 20/25 chassis could hardly have been more different. The one for GWX68 in 1933 is described as an "All-weather de Ville" (which requires some imagination). The other has been described as both a four-light All-weather Tourer and as a four-light Cabriolet; it was built for chassis GLJ8 in 1935.

Coupés

Four bodies on the 20/25 chassis qualified as Coupés, if the Fixed-head Sedanca Coupé for GPG38 in 1935 is included. The earliest was built in 1932 for GHW11 and was notable for its adventurous treatment of running-boards and front wings. The other two bodies were for GYH15 and GLJ35, both in 1935.

Drophead Coupés

There was a typical variety of styles among the nine Drophead Coupé bodies for the 20/25. Five were described simply as Drophead Coupés, and these were for GEX37, GTZ47 and GYZ34 in 1933, and for GNC37 in 1934 and GYH67 in 1965. There was a single body described as a Three-position type for GHA28 in 1933, and in 1935 there was a single Bromley Drophead Coupé with James Young's patented parallel-opening doors for chassis GRF5. Finally, there was a pair of two-seater Drophead Coupés with dickey seats, for GZU9 in 1932 and GYH73 in 1935. See also GLR49 in the section for Tourer bodies, below.

Landaulettes

Just two Landaulette bodies were built, for chassis GHW28 in 1932 and GMD3 in 1934.

Limousines

There were three Limousines proper, plus one Limousine de Ville. The latter was for 1933 chassis GSY62. Quite special was the Bromley Limousine on GTK50 in 1936, with notably rounded front wings and rear-wheel spats as well. The other two were for chassis GED52 in 1934 and GOH49 in 1935.

Saloons

Unsurprisingly, the most numerous body type on the 20/25 chassis was the Saloon, although that description embraced several different varieties. The 65 bodies listed below include one two-door type, for

GKT40, and one Saloon Coupé, for GTK59. There was a single six-light Saloon for GTK32, and again just one six-light Streamline Saloon, responding to the latest fashion in 1934 on chassis GMD68. GHA15 was described as a Continental Saloon.

Many of these bodies were equipped with Divisions, as indicated by an asterisk (*) in the table below; note that it is not certain that the bodies for GWE65 and GBJ48 had one. The Bromley Saloon was introduced in 1934, and most Saloon bodies built from GAF50 onwards had elements of this specification. The 65 Saloon bodies are shown in the table below.

GGP34	1929	GKC11	1934	GYH49*	1936
GBT35	1932	GMD33	1934	GYH75	1936
GKT40	1932	GMD53	1934	GYH31	1936
GMU70	1932	GMD59	1934	GOH2*	1936
GHW12	1932	GMD68	1934	GOH5	1936
GRW36*	1932	GAE62	1934	GOH47	1936
GEX35	1933	GWE38	1934	GOH60	1936
GDX6	1933	GWE65*	1934	GOH63	1936
GDX29*	1933	GWE72	1934	GBJ48*	1936
GSY31	1933	GAF50*	1934	GBJ62	1936
GSY46	1933	GAF58	1934	GLJ16*	1936
GLZ66	1933	GAF68*	1934	GLJ33*	1936
GTZ20	1933	GNC66*	1934	GLJ65*	1936
GBA32	1933	GRC4*	1934	GCJ10*	1936
GBA67	1933	GSF35*	1934	GLJ80*	1936
GGA39	1933	GSF71	1935	GXK68*	1936
GHA3	1933	GRF35*	1935	GBK6*	1936
GHA15	1933	GLG2	1935	GBK37*	1936
GUB24	1934	GLG66*	1935	GBK57*	1936
GUB40	1934	GPG10*	1935	GTK32	1936
GUB47*	1934	GPG79*	1935	GTK59	1936
GUB77	1934	GHG23*	1935		

Sedanca de Ville

A single Sedanca de Ville was built, for GRC31 in 1934.

Tourer

There is some dispute about whether the body for GLR49 in 1930 was a Tourer or a Drophead Coupé.

25/30 COACHWORK

James Young built 45 bodies for the 25/30 chassis between 1936 and 1938, of which there were 27 in 1936, 16 in 1937 and two in 1938. The predominant demand was for Saloon bodies, of which many had Divisions, and Limousines came a close second numerically. Two Coupés and a single All-weather body completed the list.

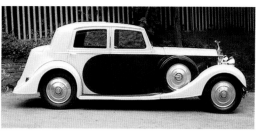

One of eight Sports Saloon bodies built for the 25/30 chassis, this one on GHL21 dates from 1936. (Real Car Company)

This car seems to have been the original Honeymoon Express – a name much better known in association with a 1957 Freestone & Webb body for a Rolls-Royce Silver Cloud. It was ordered through Jack Barclay by its first owner as a wedding gift for his bride and was a unique two-passenger coupé design for 25/30 chassis GXM54. (Real Car Company)

All-weather

James Young fielded only one order for an All-weather body, which was completed for chassis GUL66 in 1936. The body has folding centre pillars but only two doors and has sometimes been described as a Drophead Coupé.

Coupés

The two Coupé bodies were built, for GXM54 and GAN10, in both cases during 1936. They were quite different, GXM54 having just two seats and a long rear deck, while GAN10 was a five-seater with fabric-covered roof.

Limousines

Fitting a full-size Limousine body with occasional seats onto the 25/30 chassis was always a challenge, and some of the James Young efforts made that fairly clear. Nevertheless, this was the second most requested style of body for the 25/30 from this coachbuilder, and 15 examples were built. They were on the following chassis:

GTL33	1936	GAN58	1936	GRP15	1937
GHL9	1936	GWN61	1936	GRP34	1937
GRM44	1936	GRO69	1937	GRP79	1937
GRM68	1936	GHO61	1937	GMP67	1937
GXM23	1936	GMO15	1937	GGR5	1938

Saloons

James Young built 19 Saloon bodies for the 25/30 chassis, plus a further eight Sports Saloons. (For ease of reference, the Sports Saloon bodies are shown a separate table, below.) Of those 19 Saloon bodies, all except four were built with Divisions; the four without

Divisions were for chassis GUL73, GWN45, GRP81, and GLP14. The bodies with Divisions typically had smaller boots, so allowing the rear seats to be moved further rearwards to prevent loss of legroom to the division itself. The full list of 19 bodies, with dates, is below.

GUL49	1936	GXM72	1936	GUN6	1937
GUL72	1936	GGM24	1936	GRO46	1937
GUL73	1936	GGM34	1936	GHO80	1937
GTL6	1936	GWN20	1936	GMO6	1937
GRM4	1936	GWN45	1936	GRP81	1937
GRM77	1936	GUN1	1937	GLP14	1937
GXM14	1936				

Sports Saloons

The Sports Saloon bodies were all four-light types, but there was some variation in detail; some had fashionable razor-edge styling and others had more rounded contours. Just one of the eight was built with a two-door configuration; this was for GAN46, a 1936 body with the James Young patented Parallel Action Doors, as introduced at Olympia in 1935 on a Bentley Drophead Coupé. The eight Sports Saloon bodies were on the following chassis:

GHL21	1936	GAN34	1936	GRP66	1937
GXM38	1936	GAN46	1936	GAR81	1938
GAN33	1936	GHO49	1937		

WRAITH COACHWORK

The works at Bromley turned out a total of 30 bodies for the Wraith chassis, building nine of them in 1938 and the remaining 21 in 1939. There was a noticeable change in demand for body types on the new chassis, as the Limousine de Ville and the Saloon Coupé secured orders; Saloon Coupés would become a James Young staple after 1945.

Drophead Coupé

Just one order was placed for a Drophead Coupé body, and the one that James Young constructed in 1939 for Wraith WHC31 was very much in the style of the time, with a three-position folding head.

James Young used fashionable razor-edge lines for the four-light Saloon body on Wraith WHC80 in 1938.
(Frank Dale & Stepsons)

Limousines

Two new descriptions of Limousines entered the James Young vocabulary during the Wraith years. One was the Touring Limousine, which denoted a body with more luggage space than the traditional Limousine, and the other was the Limousine de Ville, which was more self-explanatory. Two Touring Limousine bodies were built in 1938, for chassis WRB22 and WMB21. The remaining five Limousine bodies were de Ville types, and three of them (on WXA20, WMB81 and WEC8) shared the same body style. WXA20 was displayed at the Earls Court Motor Show in 1938.

The seven Limousine bodies for Wraith chassis were as follows:

WXA20 1938	WRB70 1938	WMB81 1939
WXA49 1938	WMB21 1938	WEC8 1939
WRB22 1938		

There were three James Young Saloon Coupés to this design, number 4564, for the Wraith chassis. This one is on WEC2, and was new in 1939.

Saloon Coupés

The Saloon Coupé design developed for 1939 understandably shared several elements of its shape with the contemporary James Young four-door Sports Saloon. There were three of these two-door bodies to

the same design, all delivered in 1939 and on chassis WMB38, WHC47 and WEC2.

Saloons

The 15 Saloon bodies that James Young built on Wraith chassis are often described as Sports Saloons because of their four-light configuration. Nevertheless, either seven or eight of them incorporated a Division (as indicated by an asterisk (*) in the table below); it is not clear whether WEC27 did or did not have a Division. The lines, particularly at the rear, followed the contemporary vogue for razor-edges; some had partial rear-wheel spats, such as WHC6. The body on WMB46 incorporated a "High Vision" transparent roof panel in the HJ Mulliner idiom, and James Young clearly expected Divisions to remain popular in the coming season because the two cars intended for display at the cancelled 1939 Earls Court Motor Show, WEC49 and WEC50, both had one. The full list, with dates, is as follows:

WXA57* 1938	WHC64 1939	WEC27* 1939
WRB59 1938	WHC80 1939	WEC49* 1939
WMB46* 1939	WEC7 1939	WEC50* 1939
WMB53 1939	WEC18* 1939	WEC72* 1939
WHC6* 1939	WEC19 1939	WKC2 1939

Sedanca Coupés

It was no surprise that James Young should begin to offer Sedanca Coupé coachwork after the arrival of AF McNeil from Gurney Nutting, where he had made a speciality of such designs. Nevertheless, only two were built for the Wraith chassis, both in 1939. The body on WMB23 had a three-position folding head, but that for WMB70 had a fixed-head style.

Sedancas de Ville

Two of the 1938 bodies were Sedanca de Ville types, again no doubt drawing on AF McNeil's success with such styles for Gurney Nutting. These were for chassis WXA69 and WXA82.

JARVIS
London – Twenty

Jarvis & Sons Ltd was a coachbuilder based at Wimbledon in south-west London and was mainly known for its sporting and competition bodies. It made just one contribution to the story of the small-horsepower Rolls-Royce, and that was a Tourer body built in 1923 for Twenty chassis GF4. By 1930, Jarvis had effectively ceased coachbuilding and was sub-contracting orders to other coachbuilders. It eventually focused wholly on its dealership activities.

JOHN CHARLES
London – 20/25

The John Charles name consisted of the first names of its two founders, who were former employees of the Weybridge coachbuilder Hoyal (earlier Chalmer & Hoyer). They set up in business at Kew Gardens in south-west London in February 1932 and soon found work from several chassis manufacturers, for whom they built both open and closed bodies. The business expanded rapidly and in January 1934 they moved to larger premises in nearby Brentford. In this period, they began to use the Ranalah brand name on some of their bodies. However, the company's expansion seems to have been too rapid for its finances, and in early 1935 it failed and was reorganised as Ranalah Coachworks (qv). Some of the original John Charles designs were carried over to the new company.

John Charles & Co built seven bodies on new Rolls-Royce 20/25 chassis between 1933 and 1935; the John Charles Saloon body originally on an Alfa Romeo chassis was also transferred to a 1931 20/25 chassis, GFT40, during 1933. Of the new bodies, three were delivered in 1933, two in 1934, and two in 1935.

Three of these bodies were Saloons, the earliest being on GWX18 in March 1933. This may have been a four-light design; the later two certainly were, on GLZ2 in June 1933 and GSF81 in January 1935. Two bodies were Limousines, on GLZ21 in June 1933 and GSF76 in January 1935; the design of the latter was re-used by Ranalah Coachworks a year later under their own name. The remaining bodies were a solid-looking three-position Drophead Coupé on GUB59 in February 1934, and a three-position Sedanca Coupé that was delivered a month later on chassis GLB15. This latter body carried Ranalah coachplates.

KILBURN
Location unknown – Twenty

The Landaulette body built in 1928 for Rolls-Royce Twenty chassis GBM6 is listed as by Kilburn. There are no further identifying details of this coachbuilder, although the name suggests that it may have been located in the Kilburn district of north-west London.

KNIBBS (KNIBBS & PARKYN)
Manchester – Twenty, 20/25, 25/30

WH Knibbs & Son was a coachbuilder based in the Ardwick area of Manchester. The company could trace its origins back to 1840 and probably found most of its clientele in the Manchester area. There is not much information about its activities in the 1920s, but it seems likely that the company largely produced bodies for the trade and for motor manufacturers; there were also some

bus or coach bodies. During that decade, it claimed to specialise in Weymann coachwork and is known to have worked on Bentley and Daimler chassis as well as Rolls-Royce. Among the Rolls-Royce bodies were six for the Twenty chassis between 1925 and 1928.

In the early 1930s, and certainly by the end of 1932, the company was renamed as Knibbs & Parkyn, presumably having taken on an additional partner. In this decade, the company worked on a wider variety of chassis makes. Its output for Rolls-Royce chassis was more limited, and there were only two bodies on the 20/25 chassis in 1932-1933 and one on the 25/30 in 1938. Knibbs & Parkyn resumed coachbuilding after the war, notably for Alvis chassis, but soon changed its focus and became a motor dealer.

TWENTY COACHWORK

Of the six bodies on Rolls-Royce Twenty chassis, two were delivered in 1925, one in 1926, and three more in 1928. All were closed bodies except for a Tourer delivered in 1925 on GSK73. There was one Saloon in 1925, on GPK65. The following year saw delivery of an interesting Coupé on GUK65, with sliding windows in the doors and an oval rear quarter-light. A single Sedanca delivered in 1928, on GBM10, was a quite grand design that really needed a longer chassis to match its own pretensions; it is not clear why it

This was the only Drophead Coupé that John Charles built for a 20/25 chassis, and was on GUB59 in 1934.

The coachbuilder was called Knibbs at the time when it built this Saloon body for a Twenty chassis. The panels are clearly made of fabric, and the chassis must have been GPK65.

As Knibbs & Parkyn, the same company completed this four-door Tourer in 1938. It was their only coachwork on the 25/30 chassis, in this case number GZR3.

carried a London registration mark. There were then two Limousines in 1928, on GYL66 and GFN11, but it is not clear if they shared a common design.

20/25 COACHWORK

As Knibbs & Parkyn, the company built a single Saloon body on 20/25 chassis number GTZ64 that was delivered in August 1933. In December of the previous year, it had delivered its only other body on a 20/25 chassis, which was Landaulette on GRW56. Interestingly, Knibbs & Parkyn also built a Saloon Landaulette body on the 20/25 chassis on behalf of Cockshoot, also a Manchester coachbuilder. This was on chassis GBK60, delivered in February 1936, and it actually carried Knibbs & Parkyn coachplates. Whether the design was wholly by Cockshoot and only the construction was sub-contracted to Knibbs & Parkyn is not clear.

25/30 COACHWORK

So-called streamlined bodies were popular in 1935, and Lancefield built just one Saloon to this design. It was on 20/25 chassis GXK52.

There was just one body on the 25/30 chassis, and that was a four-door Tourer on GZR3 that was delivered in April 1938. This was a quite heavy-looking body that featured twin side-mounted spare wheels and an additional aero screen for the rear seat passengers.

LANCEFIELD
London – 20/25, 25/30, WRAITH

Lancefield Coachworks was a London coachbuilder that grew out of the earlier Gaisford & Worboys business (qv). The company was established in West Kilburn in 1927, and by 1929 had the confidence for a stand at the Olympia Show. In that year it also bodied its first new Rolls-Royce chassis, a late 40/50 Phantom I.

The company bodied a number of "WO" Bentley chassis and became particularly associated with the Stutz chassis imported from the USA. In the mid-1930s it was noted for its streamlined designs, and a notable characteristic of later bodies of all types was a falling waistline, which tended to give a very distinctive rear side window shape. The company rebodied a number of earlier Rolls-Royce chassis as hearses in this period, and was associated up to 1934 with Brainsby Woollard, which was primarily a coachwork broker but also put its name on some of the bodies it handled.

Lancefield is not known to have bodied any Rolls-Royce Twenty chassis. It delivered its first coachwork on a 20/25 in 1930, and would build a grand total of 25 bodies for these models into 1936, plus one rebody. However, its work on the small-horsepower Rolls-Royce then tailed off somewhat, with just three bodies for the 25/30 in 1936-1937, and only two for the Wraith in 1939. Bodies carried no identifying numbers, and although some designs were used more than once, the majority appear to have been bespoke.

20/25 COACHWORK

Demand for Lancefield coachwork on the 20/25 chassis seems to have varied over the years. Just one body was delivered in 1930, but there were four in 1931, two in 1932 (plus one rebody), five in 1933, six in 1934, six in 1935 and one in 1936. By far the majority of bodies were Saloons and Limousines, and in fact there was only one open body.

Of the dozen four-door Saloons by Lancefield, possibly all were four-light designs, and the known bodies have very neat shapes; the single streamlined or Airline Saloon (on GXK52 and delivered in December 1935) was also a four-light design. Four were delivered in 1931, on chassis GOS14, GOS39, GOS56 and GBT7. There were then no more until 1933, when bodies were completed for GEX7, GLZ42 and GYZ18. There was just one in 1934 (on GWE10), and then the four 1935 deliveries included two straightforward Saloons (GOH65 and GBJ26), one Saloon with a Division (GOH9) and the Airline Saloon already mentioned.

The company's eleven Limousine bodies were

probably all six-light types and included one rebody of an earlier 20/25 chassis, which was GFT24; the new body was delivered in 1932. Also delivered in 1932 was a Limousine on GBT1; two more followed in 1933, on GTZ34 and GYZ14, and there were four in 1934, on GUB72, GED14, GFE29 and GSF7. These were not all to the same design: the body on GED14, for example, was a very upright design but with the characteristic falling waistline, while that on GFE29 had a certain awkwardness, probably caused by the need to add a roomy boot and fit a side-mounted spare wheel. There was one more Limousine in 1936 on GTK9, but in the mean time two had been delivered in February 1935 to Daimler Hire Ltd in London (which did not, of course, use only Daimlers). These were on chassis GLG8 and GLG9, and probably had a few special features to suit the customer's requirements. They must have proved satisfactory, as a repeat order on the 25/30 chassis followed a year later, and then another on the Wraith chassis in 1939.

Then of course there were the one-off bodies, and in fact Lancefield's earliest body on the 20/25 chassis in 1930 was a six-light Landaulette with a rather upright and formal design on chassis GDP54. Interesting was the only open body, a high-sided four-door All-weather Tourer on GKT17 that was delivered in 1932. This was later given a fixed roof, but there is no evidence that Lancefield were responsible for the conversion. Lastly, another interesting body was the two-door Saloon in 1934 on GXB26, where the falling waistline created a most attractive design.

25/30 COACHWORK

Lancefield clearly had a good reputation for Limousine coachwork, and two of the three bodies the company built for the 25/30 chassis were Limousines. The earlier, delivered on GUL69 in May 1936, was for Daimler Hire Ltd and probably had special features to suit the customer. The later one was on GMO32 and was delivered as Lancefield's last 20/25 in June 1937. The third body was a well-proportioned six-light Saloon design which must have looked very modern when new in February 1937 on GRO3, and which retained the Lancefield characteristic falling waistline.

WRAITH COACHWORK

Both of the Lancefield bodies for the Rolls-Royce Wraith chassis were Limousines, and both were completed in 1939. The earlier one, delivered in March, was another order for Daimler Hire, and was on chassis WMB78. The later one, completed in June, was not actually delivered until 1941 and was on chassis number GMO32.

LAWRIE
Probably Paisley – Twenty

The names of R Laurie and R Lawrie are listed as responsible for one body each on Rolls-Royce Twenty chassis. Neither is further identified, but it is likely that both were actually R Lawrie of Sneddon Street in Paisley, a company that also built at least one ambulance body in the Edwardian period. No other information about this company's activities has come to light.

The two bodies for Twenty chassis were a Tourer, built in 1923 on 72A3, and a Landaulette, built in late 1928 or early 1929 on GFN77.

LAWTON-GOODMAN
London – Twenty, 20/25

By the time Lawton-Goodman came to body its first small-horsepower Rolls-Royce chassis in 1923, the company had existed for around ten years at Cricklewood in north-west London. It produced its own cars, mainly under the Whitlock name, and built several bodies for Rolls-Royce chassis before the First World War.

Between 1923 and 1930, the company put its name

Lancefield's Saloon body for 20/25 GOH9 in 1935 had a Division and neat if unspectacular lines. (Real Car Company)

Lawton-Goodman described this 1925 body for Twenty GNK59 as a Brougham. It had an open-drive design, and there appears to have been no De Ville roof to give the chauffeur protection from inclement weather.

to ten bodies for the small-horsepower Rolls-Royce, eight being for Twenty chassis and the last two for the 20/25. All of them were of the grander styles. William Lawton-Goodman died in 1932 but his sons continued the business, focusing on commercial bodies. Lawton-Goodman turned to repair work in the early 1980s and finally closed in 1991.

TWENTY COACHWORK

Four of the eight bodies for Twenty chassis were Landaulettes, beginning with one for 56S8 in 1923. The next one was for GXL44 in 1927, and there were then two in 1929, for GLN74 and GEN54. Two more bodies were Limousines, for GMK29 in 1924 and GSK65 in 1925. There was a single Brougham for GNK59 in 1925, and Lawton-Goodman also built a single Coupé de Ville, which was for GUJ50 in 1927.

20/25 COACHWORK

Lawton-Goodman built just two bodies on the 20/25 chassis, and both of them were Landaulettes. Both were also completed in 1930; they were on chassis GGP14 and GNS27.

LEWIS
Location unknown – Twenty

W Lewis was another one of the many coachbuilders who worked on early Rolls-Royce Twenty chassis but whose details are now lost. From the registration number (TX 1450) of the only known chassis bodied by this company, it is likely to have been based in Glamorgan. The body itself was a Tourer and was completed in 1926 on chassis number GZK56.

MACKAY
Location unknown – Twenty

Two otherwise unidentified companies with this name constructed coachwork for the Rolls-Royce Twenty,

and it is possible – but by no means proven – that they were in fact the same company. The earlier body was a Landaulette on chassis GPK43 in 1923 and was built by Mackay & Sons. The later one was a Saloon for chassis GUK80 in 1926 and is attributed simply to Mackay.

MADDOX
Huntingdon – Twenty, 20/25

During the 1920s, George Maddox & Sons was a successful and versatile coachbuilder in Huntingdon. In 1931, it converted to limited company status, and by 1933 seems to have been reconstituted as Archie Maddox at the same address. From the start of the 1930s, it tried to attract contract work from several manufacturers but without great success, and it appears to have ceased coachbuilding activities in 1935. Rolls-Royce was just one of the many makes for which Maddox built coachwork, and between 1923 and 1929 the company built 20 known bodies on Twenty chassis, following up in the 1930s with just three more on the 20/25 chassis.

TWENTY COACHWORK

Maddox provided bodies for Twenty chassis at a fairly steady rate, although there were none in 1925 – probably because of a major fire at the works in 1924. Of the 20 known bodies, there were four in 1923, three each in 1924 and 1926, five in 1927, three in 1928 and two in 1929. Maddox provided a range of body types over the years, but well over half all those it built were Saloons.

All-weather

There was a single All-weather body from Maddox for the Twenty, which was delivered in 1923 on chassis GH67. The customer was Australian Prime Minister Stanley Bruce.

Aiming for the top… Maddox built this All-weather body on Twenty chassis GH67 for the Australian Prime Minister in 1923.

Pictured some time around 1960, this is Twenty GAJ27 with Maddox Drophead Coupé body dating from 1927.

Coupé

Maddox built just one fixed-head Coupé body for the Twenty chassis. This was for GYL39 in 1928, and it featured a long rear deck that presumably incorporated a dickey seat.

Drophead Coupés

There were also two Drophead Coupés, each different from the other. The earlier one had a four-light design and was for chassis GAJ27 in 1927. The later one was a two-light body with a dickey seat, and was for chassis GVO16 in 1929.

Landaulette

Maddox built just one Landaulette body, which was for chassis 54S0 in 1923.

Limousines

There were two Limousines in the middle of the decade, the earlier on GOK81 in 1926 and the other on GRJ28 in 1927.

Saloons

There was a fairly consistent demand for Saloon coachwork on the Twenty from Maddox, the earliest being the only one built in 1923, on chassis GH53. Three more Saloon bodies followed in 1924, for GRK22, GDK28 and GDK39. There were then two in 1926 (for GOK43 and GOK77), and three in 1927 (for GAJ29, GRJ58 and GUJ46.

The first of the two 1928 Saloons is recorded as a Weymann type, on chassis GYL51, although that year's second example for GFN43 is not. The last of the dozen Maddox saloons on Twenty chassis was then for GXO4 in 1929.

Tourer

There was a single Maddox Tourer, which was built in 1923 for chassis number GH71.

20/25 COACHWORK

The three bodies from Maddox for 20/25 chassis were all different. The earliest was a Limousine, which was delivered in 1931 on chassis GOS49. Later the same year came a four-light Saloon on GOS76. The last Maddox body for a new 20/25 chassis was a Saloon with division, which was built for chassis GSY27 in 1933.

Tom Clarke records two 20/25s that were fitted with Maddox Tourer bodies in later life. The source of these bodies is unclear, but it seems probable that neither was originally built for a 20/25 chassis and that neither was fitted by the coachbuilder. One of these

Maddox built this imposing six-light Saloon body for a late Twenty chassis, GXO4, in 1929.
(Real Car Company)

bodies had been fitted to chassis GOS20 (which was originally a Mayfair Saloon Coupé) by 1938, and the other was fitted in 1999 to chassis GRW54 (originally a Freestone & Webb Saloon).

MANN EGERTON
Norwich – Twenty, 20/25, 25/30, Wraith

The two partners in Mann Egerton & Co Ltd were electrical engineer Gerald Mann and pioneer motorist Hubert Egerton, and they first worked together just before the close of the nineteenth century. They founded their company in 1905 in Prince of Wales Road, Norwich, to sell cars and carry out electrical installation work. Car bodywork manufacture was added to the portfolio in 1909, and in that year Mann Egerton was also appointed a Rolls-Royce agent and bodied its first example of the marque. It also set up a London sales office.

The sales agency side of the business expanded enormously, and as a result coachbuilding became something of a sideline in the Mann Egerton empire. Nevertheless, the company continued in the business, focusing on prestigious marques during the interwar years. Quality was unquestioned but, as Nick Walker put it, "the designs… had above all to be acceptable to the local clientele, which tended to mean safe and boring, not adventurous."

Mann Egerton ended its coachbuilding activities for cars in 1939, although during the war it made military ambulance bodies, among other items. In the late 1940s and early 1950s the company also built a number of bus bodies, but subsequently confined its activities to car sales and eventually sold out to the Inchcape Group in 1973.

Mann Egerton Limousine bodies were in demand for the 20/25 chassis, and this one for GAE10 in 1934 was fairly typical of the breed.
(Real Car Company)

TWENTY COACHWORK

There was a fairly steady demand for Mann Egerton coachwork on the Twenty chassis between 1922 and 1929, and 28 bodies are known to have been built. There were two in 1922, three in 1923, five in 1924, and three in 1925. In the second half of the decade, the figures were four in 1926, six in 1927 (the best year), one in 1928, and four in 1929.

Cabriolet

Just one Cabriolet body was built, for chassis GHJ11 in 1927.

Coupé

There was also only one Coupé body on the Twenty chassis, which was for GHJ33 in 1927.

Drophead Coupés

Two Drophead Coupé bodies were constructed, one for GUJ29 in 1927 and the other for GXL53 in 1928.

Landaulettes

Early demand for Landaulette coachwork tailed off, and Mann Egerton built just four bodies of that type. These were for chassis 43G2 in 1922, 60H3 and 60H6 in 1923, and GRK83 in 1924.

Limousines

Limousine coachwork would become a Mann Egerton strength, and there were seven examples on Twenty chassis. These were as follows:

GAK66	1924	GMJ36	1926	GXL8	1927
GRK84	1924	GRJ37	1927	GEN41	1929
GYK50	1926				

Saloon

The most numerous style of Mann Egerton coachwork on the Twenty chassis was the Saloon. Of the nine bodies, only one (GLN51) is described as a Weymann type. The nine were on the following chassis:

GRK79	1924	GSK49	1925	GLN51	1929
GNK29	1925	GYK51	1926	GLN56	1929
GSK11	1925	GRJ50	1927	GXO4	1929

Tourer

Three Tourer bodies were built, all of them early in the production life of the Twenty. They were for chassis 44G1 (in 1922), GH63 (1923) and GMK59 (1924).

Two-seater

Mann Egerton built just one Two-seater body for the Twenty chassis, and that was for GOK5 in 1926.

20/25 COACHWORK

Mann Egerton built 60 bodies for the 20/25 chassis between 1929 and 1935. Annual quantities gradually increased, from just one in 1929 to five in 1930 and 1931; there were just four in 1932 but numbers then rose again. Fourteen bodies were built in 1933, 16 in 1934, and 15 in 1935.

All of these were closed bodies, although there were some Landaulettes among the total. The largest quantities were of Limousines and Saloons, of which equal numbers were built.

Coupé

Just one of these bodies was for a Coupé, which was completed for chassis GRC45 in 1934.

Landaulettes

Five Landaulettes were built between 1929 and 1933. These were for chassis GXO14 (1929), GSR25 (1930), and for GSY82, GLZ40 and GHA22 (all 1933).

Limousines

The 27 Limousines on 20/25 chassis included just one Weymann type, for GTR32 in 1930. GNC21 was ordered by Daimler Hire, which probably speaks volumes about the reputation for durability that Mann Egerton bodies had acquired. The Limousine on GLG12 was displayed at Olympia in 1935. The full list, with dates, is as follows:

GLR55	1930	GTZ49	1933	GSF27	1934
GTR32	1930	GYZ27	1933	GRF17	1935
GTR38	1930	GXB3	1933	GLG12	1935
GNS64	1931	GNC21	1934	GLG64	1935
GOS71	1931	GED5	1934	GYH7	1935
GOS78	1931	GMD52	1934	GYH74	1935
GFT30	1931	GAE10	1934	GBJ32	1935
GRW51	1932	GWE32	1934	GCJ14	1935
GLZ19	1933	GWE77	1934	GXK47	1935

Saloons

The 27 Saloons on 20/25 chassis included both four-light and six-light types, the last of the latter probably being for GLB39 in 1934. In particular, the four-light Continental Saloon was clearly a success, with no fewer than 12 sold: these are marked with an asterisk (*) in the table below, but note that the identification of GLZ77 as one of the type is not confirmed. Also worthy of note is the single swept-tail Saloon for GPG17 in 1935. This also had a Division, and the body on GPG54 is thought to have had a Division as well. The full list is as follows:

GSR31	1930	GSY35*	1933	GFE19*	1934
GNS56	1931	GLZ77*	1933	GAF52*	1934
GAU31	1932	GGA60*	1933	GSF42	1935
GMU20	1932	GLB39	1934	GPG17	1935
GHW55	1932	GRC81*	1934	GPG54	1935
GEX66	1933	GED46*	1934	GYH41*	1935
GEX80	1933	GAE38*	1934	GOH34	1935
GDX8	1933	GAE55*	1934	GOH76*	1935
GSY34	1933	GWE64*	1934	GEH20	1935

25/30 COACHWORK

Mann Egerton constructed a total of 19 bodies for the 25/30 chassis, ten of them in 1936 and the other nine in 1937. The company's reputation as a builder of Limousines stood it in good stead, and no fewer than 14 of the 19 bodies were of that type.

Limousines

Eight of the 14 Limousine bodies were built in 1936, and the remaining six in 1937. They were on the following chassis:

GUL78	1936	GRM73	1936	GRO12	1937
GTL22	1936	GXM57	1936	GHO36	1937
GTL58	1936	GGM12	1936	GMP53	1937
GHL23	1936	GWN37	1937	GAR80	1937
GRM8	1936	GUN8	1937		

Saloons

Two of the Saloon bodies (for GRM35 and GUN28) were built with Divisions, and one (GHO20) was a Sports Saloon. The full list was:

GRM35	1936	GUN28	1937	GMP23	1937
GXM26	1936	GHO20	1937		

WRAITH COACHWORK

Of the six bodies that Mann Egerton built for Wraith chassis, there were three in 1938 and three in 1939, although one of these was not delivered to its owner until 1941. Limousines again predominated.

Saloons

There were just two Saloon bodies. The one for chassis WMB24 in 1939 had a Division, and the one for WHC32 was built in 1939 but not delivered until 1941.

Limousines

There were four Limousine bodies, of which three were built in 1938 and one in 1939. They were for chassis WXA24, WXA56 and WXA74 in 1938, and for WEC51 in 1939.

On 25/30 chassis GXM26, Mann Egerton built this solid-looking Saloon body in 1936.
(Real Car Company)

MALTBY
Folkestone – 20, 25/30, Wraith

The Maltby brothers, John and Hugh, entered the motor trade in 1902 and before the First World War had built both cars and buses. They also set up a coachbuilding division, which was well established by the time of their first body for a Rolls-Royce, which was a Cabriolet for Twenty GMK44 in 1924.

Under new ownership from 1926, Maltby's Motor Works stopped building chassis and focused instead on their dealership and coachbuilding operations. The company exploited its links with chassis makers to gain contracts for catalogued bodies, but continued with bespoke designs, some of which were clearly derived from their volume-built types. Drophead coachwork became a speciality, and Maltby developed the first power-operated hood design in Britain, branding it the Redfern.

The power-operated hood was used for Tourer coachwork, and one example of such a body was built for a 25/30 chassis, number GRP7, in 1937. A second with very similar lines was built for Wraith chassis WMB37 in 1939.

MARSHALSEA
Taunton – Twenty, 20/25

Marshalsea Brothers Ltd was a Taunton coachbuilder predominantly active in the 1920s, when it exhibited regularly at Olympia. Although there were no more Olympia stands after 1930, the company remained active as a coachbuilder until at least 1934.

The four bodies it built for small-horsepower Rolls-Royce chassis reveal only the sort of versatility required of a provincial coachbuilder, the three on Twenty chassis being a Tourer, a Saloon and a Coupé, and the single example on a 20/25 being a Limousine.

The first two bodies on Twenty chassis were built in 1923, the earlier being a Tourer on 57S4 and the second a Saloon on GH46. The third body was not built until 1926, and was a Coupé on GZK28. The Bristol registration number allocated to this car suggests that Marshalsea's business was not entirely local to Taunton.

The single body for a 20/25 was delivered in May 1934, and was a Limousine on chassis GKC23.

MARTIN WALTER
Folkestone – Twenty, 20/25, 25/30

Martin Walter Ltd began coachbuilding in 1914 after buying out a local coachbuilder to supplement its motor vehicle repairs business. This in turn had grown out of a business established in around 1773 as a saddle-maker, which had moved to Folkestone approximately a century later. The company built on a variety of chassis in the interwar years, and during the 1930s was perhaps best known for its convertible designs that were often catalogued by major manufacturers. Particularly successful was a four-door Cabriolet known as the Wingham type.

In 1937, the Martin Walter company was sold to Abbey Coachworks, who renamed it Wingham Martin Walter Ltd. In post-war years, it reverted to the plain Martin Walter name, building bus bodies and then, most successfully, motor caravan conversions under the Dormobile brand name. It closed its doors in 1994, although the Dormobile brand name has since been revived.

Martin Walter built a total of 16 bodies for the small-horsepower Rolls-Royce chassis. There were four for the Twenty, nine for the 20/25, and three for the 25/30. There were none for the Wraith.

TWENTY COACHWORK

The earliest Martin Walter body for a Twenty chassis was a Fixed-head Coupé, built on chassis GCK33 in 1925. There was then a gap of three years before the company was again commissioned to build on the small Rolls-Royce chassis.

All the three bodies that followed in 1928-1929 were Saloon types, the earliest being for chassis GFN61 in 1928. The next one, for GLN4 in 1929, appears to have been the only one that embodied the Weymann patents for which Martin Walter held a

licence. The last of the three Saloon bodies was for GEN55 in 1929.

20/25 COACHWORK

There were nine bodies for the 20/25 chassis between 1930 and 1936. Martin Walter built just one body for a 20/25 in 1930, three in 1931, one each in 1932 and 1933, two in 1934 and one in 1936.

Cabriolets

Four examples of the Wingham Cabriolet were built for 20/25 chassis. The Wingham was a four-door body with a special hood mechanism that made the convertible top easy to erect or to stow. This mechanism was licensed from the German coachbuilder Gläser of Dresden. The tight-fitting top of the Wingham Cabriolet had a beautifully smooth profile when erect, but was very bulky and Germanic-looking when folded down. The four examples on 20/25 chassis were for numbers GFT54 in 1931, GED67 and GSF14 in 1934, and GBK5 in 1936. There would be more on the 25/30 chassis.

De Ville designs

There were two De Ville bodies on the 20/25 chassis. The earlier one was a Sedanca de Ville for GSR70 in 1930, and the later a Coupé de Ville for GNS70 in 1931.

Limousine

There was a single Martin Walter Limousine body for the 20/25 chassis, and this was built for GPS37 in 1931. The chassis was rebodied many years later as a Shooting Brake, again by Martin Walter.

Saloons

There were two Saloon bodies for 20/25 chassis, each quite different from the other. The body for GZU32 in 1932 was a Sports Saloon, while that for GYZ30 the following year was a more sober six-light type.

25/30 COACHWORK

Martin Walter built just three bodies for the 25/30 chassis, and at least two of them were Wingham Cabriolets. These were for GRM48 in 1936 and GLP10 in 1937. The third body was another four-door Cabriolet, built in 1936 for chassis GRM67; it may also have been a Wingham type.

MASCOT

Mascot Motor Body Works was the parent concern of Glassbrook (qv), and that company's coachwork is sometimes described under this name.

With its hood erected, the Martin Walter Wingham Cabriolet body for 20/25 GED67 in 1934 looked very neat. The folding-top design was licensed from the German coachbuilder Gläser. (Real Car Company)

MAULE
Stockton-on-Tees – Twenty

E Maule & Son was established as a carriage builder in Stockton in 1825 and was building bodies for cars by at least 1911, and also bus bodywork by 1919. The company held a Weymann licence during the 1920s, and in that decade worked on Bentley, Crossley, Minerva and Vauxhall chassis as well as on Rolls-Royce.

The company built two Saloon bodies for Rolls-Royce Twenty chassis. The earlier one was for chassis GH51 in 1923, and the later one was a Weymann type for GYK62 in 1926.

MAY & JACOBS
Guildford – Twenty

May & Jacobs was a provincial coachbuilder at Guildford in Surrey and was active until the 1930s. It could trace its origins back as far as 1847, and was building coachwork on Rolls-Royce chassis as early as 1910. It also worked on Bentley, Bugatti and Invicta chassis over the years, and in the 1920s rebodied some Edwardian Rolls-Royce chassis.

The company was responsible for just two bodies on small-horsepower Rolls-Royce chassis, in the early 1920s. These were a Tourer on Twenty chassis 59S0 in 1923, and a Landaulete on chassis GAK26 in 1924.

MAYFAIR
London – 20/25, 25/30

When the partners in Motor Car Industries decided to go their separate ways in 1925, one formed the Carlton Carriage Company and the other remained at the firm's old premises in Kilburn, north-west London, taking on the name of Progressive Coach & Motor Body Company. From 1929, this became the Mayfair Carriage Company Ltd, and in 1934 it moved to new premises in nearby Hendon, ceding its old premises to the coachbuilder Corinthian.

In its early days as Progressive, Mayfair tended to focus on coachwork for imported chassis, but after 1930 most of its work was for British marques. The company formed a special link with Alvis and later with Armstrong-Siddeley, but also produced bespoke coachwork for Rolls-Royce and Bentley chassis, typically with a lightness of touch that some other coachbuilders failed to achieve. The interruption of the Second World War brought a change of direction, and when the company started up again in the 1940s its primary focus was on commercial bodywork.

Mayfair built coachwork for 33 of the 20/25 chassis and then for 17 of the 25/30s, making a total of 50 bodies. There were none for the Wraith.

20/25 COACHWORK

There was a gradual increase in the number of bodies Mayfair built each year during the production life of the 20/25, perhaps as the company became better known and its work better appreciated. So although there was only one body in 1931, there were three in 1931, five each in 1932 and 1933, seven in 1934, and nine in 1935. The lower total of three in 1936 doubtless came about because this was a "short" year for the 20/25, but the company's upward trajectory continued with a dozen bodies on the new 25/30 chassis (see below), making a total of 15 for the year. The largest number of orders was for Saloons, but Mayfair turned its hand to a variety of other types.

Drophead Coupés

There were three Drophead Coupés on the 20/25 chassis. These were for GPS5 (1931, a four-light design), GAU33 (1932), and GXK74 (1936).

Landaulette

Mayfair dealt with just one order for a Landaulette body, which was for chassis GWX77 in 1933.

Limousines

Five Limousine bodies were built between 1933 and 1936. These were for chassis GSY18 (1933), GED56 (1934), GLJ27 and GLJ59 (1935), and GTK2 (1936).

Limousines de Ville

There were also four Limousine de Ville bodies. These were for GTZ41 (1933), GAF27 and GAF28 (1934), and GYH70 (1935).

Saloons

The 17 Saloon bodies included a variety of different types, with both four-light and six-light designs. Notable among them were a Weymann metal-panelled Saloon for GFT76 in 1931 and a four-light Streamline Saloon in the then-current fashion for GTK1 in 1936. The full list, with dates, is overleaf:

Mayfair built four Limousine de Ville bodies on 20/25 chassis, of which GYH70 was the last in 1935. The lines work very well in this view. (Real Car Company)

Although the lines of this Mayfair body were a little out of fashion by 1936, the incorporation of a Tickford winding head was an attractive feature. This is chassis GUL76, a 25/30 model.
(Real Car Company)

GTR24	1930	GSY38	1933	GHG37	1935
GFT76	1931	GGA31	1933	GEH35	1935
GMU38	1932	GXB56	1934	GXK30	1935
GRW10	1932	GED75	1934	GXK51	1935
GRW40	1932	GAE68	1934	GTK1	1936
GRW64	1932	GWE58	1934		

Saloon Coupé

Mayfair constructed a single Saloon Coupé body, for chassis GOS20 in 1931.

Sedancas

The two Sedanca bodies on the 20/25 chassis were both built in 1935. The one for GLG6 was a Sedanca de Ville, and that for GBJ56 was a two-light fixed-head Sedanca Coupé.

25/30 COACHWORK

Mayfair built on their growing reputation in the mid-1930s and secured orders for a clutch of 25/30 bodies as the new chassis became available in 1936. Of the

17 bodies the company constructed, 13 appeared that year and the remainder in 1937. Saloon bodies were once again most in demand, and closely behind them came Limousine types.

All-weather

The body for GMP4 in 1937 was built as an All-weather Tourer, the only one of its type by Mayfair on the small-horsepower Rolls-Royce chassis.

Limousines

The seven Limousine bodies for 25/30 chassis were as follows:

GUL14	1936	GUL25	1936	GWN69	1936
GUL16	1936	GTL70	1936	GUN10	1937
GUL22	1936				

Saloons

The eight Saloon bodies included one described as a Sports Saloon (GWN28 in 1936) and one six-light body with a Tickford folding head. This latter car, GUL76 from 1936, has sometimes been inaccurately described as a Landaulette. Two of the bodies were built with Divisions, and these are marked with an asterisk (*) in the table below.

GUL28	1936	GXM28	1936	GRO30*	1937
GUL30*	1936	GWN6	1936	GAR10	1937
GUL76	1936	GWN28	1936		

Sedanca de Ville

Mayfair built a single Sedanca de Ville body on a 25/30 chassis, and this was for GAN18 in 1936.

MAYTHORN
Biggleswade – Twenty, 20/25

The Maythorn coachworks was established at Biggleswade in Bedfordshire in 1842, and the son of the founder expanded into car body building at the start of the 20th century. By then known as Maythorn & Son Ltd, the company became a subsidiary of Hooper in 1920, although the two companies retained their individual identities. In 1923, it lost a large part of its factory to a major fire, but by 1925 was operating from new and larger premises.

Much of the Maythorn work was on Daimler chassis, but the company also bodied many other types of expensive chassis, including Rolls-Royce and Bentley. However, as business declined in the recession and Hooper found itself with surplus capacity, Maythorn & Son Ltd was liquidated in 1931.

The company built a total of 68 bodies on the small-

The 1937 Mayfair Saloon body for 25/30 GAR10 looks well-built and heavy, with a suitable air of solemnity.

horsepower Rolls-Royce chassis. There were 30 bodies for the Rolls-Royce Twenty between 1923 and 1929, and 38 more for the 20/25 between 1929 and 1931.

TWENTY COACHWORK

There was no sign of Maythorn's later specialisation in Limousine bodies in its work for the Twenty chassis. Instead, there was a typically mixed variety of types, mostly unadventurous designs but well executed. Saloons predominated.

Cabriolets

There was just one Cabriolet body, which was built in 1923 for chassis GA58.

Coupés

Maythorn built five Coupé bodies for the Twenty chassis, of which the first was for 63H6 in 1923. There were then no more until 1926, when GMJ44 was bodied with a three-quarter Coupé style. Two more three-quarter Coupés were built in 1927, for GMJ81 and GRJ57, and the final Coupé body was also built in 1927, for GXL30.

Drophead Coupé

Only one Drophead Coupé body was built, which was on chassis GOK62 in 1926.

Landaulettes

At a time when Landaulette bodies were popular, it was no surprise to find Maythorn building five of them on Twenty chassis. The five chassis were GAK71 and GRK12 in 1924, GZK72 in 1926, GAJ40 in 1927, and GFN67 in 1929.

Limousines

Just three Limousine bodies came from the Maythorn works on Rolls-Royce Twenty chassis. The chassis were GSK7 from 1925, GAJ22 from 1927, and GYL59 from 1928.

Saloons

Nine Saloon bodies made that the predominant body type on the Twenty from Maythorn. The first one was on 7-G-II, the last of the original six Goshawk II prototype chassis, and the choice of Maythorn to build its body was perhaps an early indication of the esteem in which the company was held by Rolls-Royce. The full list of nine chassis was as follows:

7-G-II	1922	GZK38	1926	GXL64	1928
GRK38	1924	GHJ48	1927	GYL50	1928
GSK58	1925	GAJ20	1927	GLN42	1929

Biggleswade coachbuilder Maythorn constructed this attractive three-quarter Drophead Coupé with Dickey for Twenty chassis GRJ57 in 1927. (Real Car Company)

This 1931 Limousine design from Maythorn on 20/25 GOS 79 was distinctly conservative in outline. The treatment of the driver's signalling flap is of some interest. (Real Car Company)

Tourers

The popularity of the Tourer body during the 1920s brought Maythorn orders for five on the Rolls-Royce Twenty chassis. These were for 89 K6 in 1923, for GPK80 and GOK25 in 1925, for GZK15 in 1926, and for GRJ5 in 1927.

Two-seater

There was just one Two-seater body for the Twenty, and this was built in 1925 on chassis GSK18.

20/25 COACHWORK

All except one of the Maythorn bodies on 20/25 chassis were closed types, and by far the majority were Limousines.

Drophead Coupé

Maythorn built a single Drophead Coupé on the 20/25 chassis, which was for GXO77 in 1929. The body was equipped with a Dickey Seat.

Landaulette

All three Landaulette bodies for the 20/25 were built in 1931. They were for chassis GOS67, GPS1 and GPS9.

Limousines

The most popular Maythorn body style on the 20/25 chassis was the Limousine, of which 31 examples were built in 1930-1931. In March 1931, the Rolls-Royce design staff worked with Maythorn to produce an early example of standardised coachwork, which was an attractive D-back Limousine. The standardised design was intended to keep costs and therefore prices down without compromising on quality, but unfortunately few examples were built because Maythorn went into liquidation later the same year. The full list of Limousines is as follows:

GSR11	1930	GOS31	1931	GOS79	1931
GNS5	1930	GOS32	1931	GPS23	1931
GNS6	1930	GOS40	1931	GPS26	1931
GNS10	1930	GOS45	1931	GPS34	1931
GNS14	1931	GOS52	1931	GPS40	1931
GNS15	1930	GOS53	1931	GFT32	1931
GNS18	1930	GOS61	1931	GFT41	1931
GNS73	1931	GOS63	1931	GFT45	1931
GNS79	1931	GOS65	1931	GFT52	1931
GOS15	1931	GOS74	1931	GFT59	1931
GOS29	1931				

Saloons

Maythorn built just three Saloon bodies for the 20/25 chassis. There was a six-light type for GDP26 in 1930; later the same year GNS2 was given a Saloon body with Division; and the third body was built in 1931 for GOS24.

MCNAUGHT
Worcester – Twenty

A company called HA McNaught is recorded as building the Saloon body for Rolls-Royce Twenty GZK18 in 1926. This was probably McNaught & Co of Worcester, which also had premises in London's Knightbridge and in 1908 claimed to have been established for over 60 years. Unfortunately, nothing further is known about the company's activities in the 1920s.

MELHUISH
London – Twenty

John Melhuish & Company was a coachbuilder with premises in the Camden Town district of London. The company was most active in the 1920s, working on a variety of different chassis and mostly building Limousine, Landaulette and Coupé coachwork. Nick Walker notes, in *A-Z British Coachbuilders*, that the company was still in business in 1934, but its subsequent fate is not known.

Melhuish built four bodies for the Rolls-Royce Twenty chassis. Two were Tourers, for chassis GMK23 in 1924 and GTM28 in 1928. There was a Limousine for GRK23 in 1924, and the fourth body was a three-quarter Drophead Coupé for GXL61 in 1927.

MIDLAND MOTOR BODIES
Coventry – Twenty

The origins of Midland Motor Bodies are obscure, but the company seems to have been formed as an in-house coachbuilding division for the Riley company in 1918. Midland certainly did most of its work for Riley, and was absorbed into the main Riley company in 1931. In the mean time, it built a number of bodies on other makes of chassis, among which is known a single Rolls-Royce Twenty. This was a Tourer for chassis 72A4 in 1923.

MILLS, W
Cheltenham – Twenty, 20/25

W Mills & Sons was a small Cheltenham coachbuilder that built a single known body for a Rolls-Royce Twenty chassis in 1924. The company later changed its name to Williams & Bayliss, and under that name seems to have specialised in coachwork for imported American chassis. It also built just one body for a Twenty chassis. It then changed its name again to FJ Williams (Cheltenham) Ltd, and under that name built one more body of interest here, which was for a 20/25 chassis. The company took out a licence for the Weymann patents during the 1920s.

TWENTY COACHWORK

All three bodies for Twenty chassis by these companies were Saloons, but it is not clear which, if any, of them used the Weymann patents. The earliest, by W Mills & Son, was on chassis GAK20 in 1924. Next came a body by Williams & Bayliss in 1925, for chassis GPK57. The third one was by FJ Williams, and was for GXL22 in 1927.

20/25 COACHWORK

The company responsible for the only body on 20/25 chassis was FJ Williams. This certainly was of Weymann construction and was delivered in 1930 on chassis GLR76. It was a notably large-looking six-light Saloon, where the coachbuilder had made maximum use of the space available by placing the rear seats directly over the axle – which may not have provided the most comfortable ride for the occupants.

MITCHELL
Probably Radford – Twenty

A company called Mitchell built the Coupé body on a 1923 Rolls-Royce Twenty chassis, 86K2. This was delivered to the businessman and philanthropist Julien (later Sir Julien) Cahn, who lived in Nottingham. It is possible, but certainly not proven, that the coachbuilder was F Mitchell, a garage business in

Radford, which later became a major car dealership in the Nottingham area.

MORGAN
Leighton Buzzard – Twenty

Originally a London carriage maker, Morgan & Co moved to Leighton Buzzard when it bought out another company based there in 1886. By 1907 it held an agency for Adler cars. In liquidation by 1919, it was bought by RE Jones Ltd of Swansea. In this period, it began to use a patented all-metal system of construction called Zephyr that featured aluminium panels over high-tensile tubing, notably in bodies for Crossley and Alvis. The later history of the company is unclear, but it disappeared from the scene around 1928, perhaps after being bought out.

Morgan built six bodies on Rolls-Royce Twenty chassis. The first three all dated from 1923, and were Saloons for 67H0 and GF44, and a Tourer for 85K2. There was then a Limousine for GNK51 in 1925, and the last two bodies were built in 1927. These were a Saloon for GHJ18 and a Coupé for GAJ12.

MOSS
Location unknown – Twenty

Moss & Sons is another one of the many coachbuilders who briefly entered the story of the small-horsepower Rolls-Royce models but left no lasting trace. This company, presumably a small one, built a single Tourer body in 1923 on Twenty chassis number 53S9.

MOTOR BODIES
London – Twenty

The Motor Bodies & Engineering Co Ltd was based in the north London district of Holloway and appears to have been founded in 1919. Not much is known about its work in the 1920s except for the three bodies it built for Rolls-Royce Twenty chassis. In the first half of the 1930s, it built bodies for imported Chrysler and Hudson models and for the related Railton and Terraplane brands. There were also two bodies for the Rolls-Royce 20/25, but the company seems to have disappeared in the middle of the decade.

TWENTY COACHWORK

The three bodies for the Twenty began in 1923 with a Landaulette for chassis GA28. There were then two Saloon bodies, for GUK21 in 1926 and GUJ70 in 1927.

20/25 COACHWORK

Both the bodies for 20/25 chassis were Limousines. They were built on chassis GTZ22 in 1933 and GMD76 in 1934.

MULLINERS
Birmingham – Twenty, 20/25, 25/30, Wraith

In the distant past, Mulliners Ltd of Birmingham had family links with the other Mulliner coachbuilders – Arthur Mulliner and HJ Mulliner – but by the early 20th century it was a fully independent company. A major customer in the 1900s was Calthorpe, and from 1913 Mulliners were fully committed to building bodies for that company. When Calthorpe went under in 1924, its Managing Director, Louis Antweiler, bought the Mulliners coachbuilding business.

Antweiler pursued a policy of contract bodybuilding, following the success of that business with Calthorpe. From 1927, Mulliners gained a major contract with Austin for bodywork on the Seven, and then from 1931 there were further contracts with the Rootes Group (Hillman and Humber) and with the Daimler and Lanchester marques. In the 1930s, Mulliners in effect became the house coachbuilder for these last two, and from 1937 picked up work for Alvis as well. After the 1939-1945 war, the company worked for both large and small chassis makers but in 1958 was bought by Standard-Triumph, who closed it in 1960.

Alongside the contract work, Mulliners did a certain amount of bespoke coachbuilding, especially after 1926 when it first exhibited at the Olympia Show. It was an early user of the Weymann patents in the 1920s, and later moved on to the "semi-Weymann" system of mixed fabric and steel panels, becoming perhaps the largest user of that system in Britain.

Mulliners built either 18 or 19 bodies on the Rolls-Royce Twenty chassis, 26 for the 20/25, six for the 25/30, and two for the Wraith.

TWENTY COACHWORK

Mulliners built the coachwork for 18 Rolls-Royce Twenty chassis between 1927 and 1929, and the company may also have been responsible for a nineteenth body that was built in 1922. Every one of the bodies for the Twenty from 1927 was a Weymann type, and they were either Limousines or Saloons. Just one was built in 1927; there were seven in 1928, and ten in 1929.

Limousines

There were three Weymann Limousines on the Twenty chassis, for GBM11 and GFN19 in 1928 and for GLN86 in 1929. The disputed body in 1922 on chassis 45G8 was also a Limousine but is not specifically recorded as a Weymann type.

COACHWORK ON THE ROLLS-ROYCE TWENTY, 20/25, 25/30 AND WRAITH

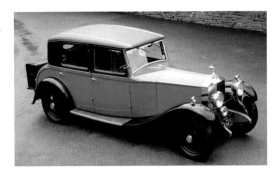

The Mulliners Saloon body for 20/25 GNS16 illustrates the "semi-Weymann" style that was briefly popular around the time it was built in 1931. (Real Car Company)

Notably slim windscreen pillars on this Mulliners Saloon body for Wraith WLB3 in 1939 give the whole car a lighter air. (Real Car Company)

Saloons

Fifteen Weymann Saloons were built between 1927 and 1929. They were on the following chassis:

GUJ71	1927	GFN6	1928	GEN29	1929
GYL6	1928	GLN30	1929	GEN34	1929
GYL34	1928	GLN73	1929	GEN36	1929
GYL72	1928	GEN12	1929	GEN38	1929
GBM41	1928	GEN20	1929	GEN57	1929

20/25 COACHWORK

Mulliners continued to build Weymann bodies into 1932, although from 1930 the fabric-panelled types were joined by metal-panelled and mixed metal and fabric types, and by the end of that year the Weymann patents seem to have been abandoned in favour of more orthodox construction with metal panels. Of the 26 bodies on 20/25 chassis, there were three each in 1929 and 1931, six in 1930, eight in 1932, two in 1933 and four in 1934. All were Limousine or Saloon types.

Limousines

None of the four Limousine bodies on 20/25 chassis appears to have had Weymann construction. The four were mounted on chassis GSR2 (1930), GMU56 (1932), GLB5 and GMD27 (both 1934).

Saloons

Both four-light and six-light Saloons for the 20/25 came from Mulliners, but only two are known to have had a Division; these were on chassis GWP12 in 1930 and GMU47 in 1932. The four-light body on GNS16 was a metal-panelled Weymann type, and on GKT28 Mulliners used the Silent Travel (Silentbloc) system of body mounting. For GBT12, the body was panelled in a mixture of fabric and metal. The full list of 22 Saloons was as follows:

GXO60	1929	GNS68	1931	GMU47	1932
GXO106	1930	GOS7	1931	GMU55	1932
GGP1	1929	GPS11	1931	GZU7	1932
GGP2	1929	GBT12	1932	GWX72	1933
GDP68	1930	GKT28	1932	GXB28	1933
GWP12	1930	GAU27	1932	GXB81	1934
GLR65	1930	GAU65	1932	GLB32	1934
GNS16	1930				

Bodies were tending to look heavier again by the time this Saloon was built for 25/30 GWN75 in 1937, despite advances in lightweight construction. The style is nevertheless pleasant enough. (Real Car Company)

25/30 COACHWORK

Mulliners' output for the later small-horsepower Rolls-Royce models was much reduced, and the company built only six bodies for the 25/30 chassis. Of these, five were Sports Saloons and there was a solitary Sedanca de Ville. There were two in 1936 and the remainder were built in 1937.

Sedanca de Ville

The Sedanca de Ville body was for chassis GAR34 in 1937 and has sometimes been described as an Arthur Mulliner product.

Sports Saloons

The Mulliners Sports Saloon for the 25/30 was a neat but unspectacular design. The five bodies were on chassis GRM12 and GGM37 in 1936, and in 1937 on GWN75, GRO76 and GLP33.

Wraith coachwork

Mulliners built just two bodies for the Wraith chassis, and both were Saloons. The earlier was for chassis WRB66 in 1938, and the other, which had a Division, was for WMB67 in 1939.

MULLION
London – Twenty

Almost nothing is known about the coachbuilder Mullion, although Nick Walker reports that it was a London carriage-maker that only just survived into the era of the automobile. The company is known for two car bodies, one a two-seater on Daimler chassis and the other a Drophead Coupé on Rolls-Royce Twenty chassis GYK36 in 1926.

MYERS & BURNELL
York – Twenty

Myers & Burnell was a garage business in York that held agencies for Napier, Siddeley-Deasy and Standard cars. The company also had a coachbuilding department, and as early as 1909 bodied a Rolls-Royce Silver Ghost chassis. Myers & Burnell also built coachwork for five Rolls-Royce Twenty models.

The five bodies consisted of two Landaulettes (for 42G8 in 1922 and GCK58 in 1925), two Saloons (for GMK4 in 1924 and GPK4 in 1925), and a single Tourer (for 73A8 in 1923).

NEWNS
Surbiton – Twenty

Coachbuilder EJ Newns was originally based at Long Ditton near Surbiton in Surrey, and from 1926 at nearby Thames Ditton. During the 1920s the company worked on locally-manufactured AC chassis and is said to have built fabric Saloon bodies. In the 1930s, it built bodies for a variety of makes, often using the Eagle brand name, and the company survived into the 1970s as a maker of plastic components.

Newns is known to have built just two bodies for the Rolls-Royce Twenty. These were a Limousine for 49G0 in 1923 and a Tourer for GUJ76 in 1927.

NORRIS
Location unknown – Twenty

A company called F Norris is recorded as building the Coupé body for Rolls-Royce Twenty GBM78 in 1928.

The Gloucestershire registration issued to the car (DF 5781) may provide a clue to the location of the coachbuilder, which has not otherwise been identified.

NORTHERN COACHBUILDERS
Newcastle-on-Tyne – 20/25

Northern Coachbuilders Ltd, often known by its acronym of NCB, was primarily a builder of commercial coachwork, and after the Second World War as a builder of bus bodies. The Smith family that founded it in 1931 also established a separate company that specialised in electric milk floats.

The company built a single six-light Saloon body, perhaps with a Division, for its founder Samuel Smith. This was on 20/25 chassis GBA24 in 1933.

NORTH OF ENGLAND
Newcastle-on-Tyne – Twenty

In the 1920s, the North of England Motor Trading Co Ltd of Newcastle-on-Tyne claimed to supply any make of car and that "high-class coachwork" was "a speciality." The company was an agent for several makes of car and for Vulcan lorries as well, and is known to have built a Doctor's Coupé body for a Daimler in 1922. In 1923, it built the Saloon body that was mounted on Rolls-Royce Twenty chassis number 79A4.

OFFORD
London – Twenty, 20/25

Offord & Sons was a west London coachbuilder that had been founded in 1791 as a carriage-maker. It was owned by members of one family for its entire existence, and for much of that time it had a responsibility for maintaining the carriages in the Royal Mews. An attempt to market ultra-light all-weather bodies in the early 1920s failed and left the company nearly bankrupt by 1923.

It was then re-organised with a different outlook. Offord became largely a broker, sub-contracting work to other London coachbuilders and putting its plates on the finished product. There was nothing remotely dishonest about this; such incestuous behaviour has always been common among small coachbuilders. Among the companies it certainly used were Harrison and Carlton, and Gill and Lancefield may also have carried out sub-contract work for Offord.

Offord also built a few racing bodies in its own workshops, notably for Eddie Hall on Bentley chassis in the mid-1930s. The company mostly worked with more expensive makes of chassis. During the 1930s, the company moved towards standardised designs. It closed as a coachbuilder in 1939.

Offord-bodied 20/25 GYZ8 is a rare survivor. Dating from 1933, it carries a nicely-proportioned Sedanca de Ville body. (Simon Clay)

The company built at least six bodies for the small-horsepower Rolls-Royce models.

TWENTY COACHWORK

Only one of those six bodies by Offord is known to have been for a Rolls-Royce Twenty chassis. This was a Coupé de Ville, delivered in 1924 on chassis GDK67. Whether it was really built by Offord or came from one of the company's sub-contractors is not known.

20/25 COACHWORK

The question of when Offord delivered its first coachwork on a 20/25 chassis is complicated by the question of sub-contracting. The earliest may well have been on GHW61 in November 1932, but that Saloon body is generally thought to have been built by Carlton and is usually described as a product of that company. Less contentious was the first 1933 delivery, a Coupé de Ville on chassis GYZ8 that was delivered in August that year. This was followed in September by another Saloon on GBA23, wearing Offord coachbuilder's plates but again generally thought to have been actually built by Carlton.

In September 1934, there followed a Landaulette body for chassis GWE49, and then the fifth Offord body for a 20/25 was not delivered until January 1936 and was an All-weather Tourer for chassis GBK56. In the mean time, Offord is thought to have been responsible for mounting a Park Ward Saloon body, originally built for the first of the experimental Rolls-Royce Peregrine chassis, to GYH40 in May 1935.

The De Ville roof was simply fabric, with dot fasteners on the cantrails and windscreen header rail. Though slightly crude by comparison with work by the leading coachbuilders, it did the job well enough. (Simon Clay)

The Art Deco scallop on the body sides is effective, but perhaps not quite as stylish as the efforts from the best coachbuilders. The top-opening boot was typical of the period. (Simon Clay)

The proportions looked well from the rear, too. The red fine lining on the wheel discs matches the fine lining on the body, helping to tie the whole together visually. (Simon Clay)

The chauffeur was provided with a good deal of comfort; perhaps the owner enjoyed driving himself on occasion, too. (Simon Clay)

Lounging room… the footwells visible in the floor added to the space available in the rear of the Offord Sedanca de Ville. (Simon Clay)

The Osborne Saloon body on 20/25 chassis GSF74 is another rare survivor, and is in fact the only Rolls-Royce coachwork known to have come from that builder of commercial bodies. Built in 1935, the six-light design has a fashionable falling waistline at the rear. (Real Car Company)

OSBORNE
Saffron Walden – 20/25

RW Osborne & Son was an Essex builder of commercial bodies founded in 1920. The company built just one body for a Rolls-Royce 20/25 chassis, which was a six-light Saloon for GSF74 in 1935.

Tom Clarke points out that this Osborne was not the same company that converted the Park Ward Sedanca de Ville body on GSF43 into a Saloon some time around 1945.

PAGE & HUNT
Wrecclesham – Twenty

Page & Hunt operated from premises at Wrecclesham, near Farnham in Surrey. Arthur Page was a coachpainter and former partner in another coachbuilding business, and Oliver Hunt put up the money for their joint venture in 1920. The company was active as a builder of car bodies during the 1920s, and in 1927 claimed to specialise in coupé coachwork. They also included bus and coach bodies in their repertoire.

However, in September 1929 the company went into voluntary liquidation. Its London sales manager, ED Abbott, took over the Page & Hunt premises and equipment, and set up a new company in his own name. Abbott's (qv) continued with the construction of both car and bus bodies.

Page & Hunt built some bodies on the larger Rolls-Royce chassis and provided the coachwork for three Twenties. There is little information about the earliest of these, which was a Coupé for chassis GH41 in 1923. However, the three-quarter Drophead Coupé on GFN44 in 1928 featured a fashionable raked windscreen with triangular side panels to improve

Page & Hunt were responsible for this three-quarter Cabriolet body built on Twenty chassis GFN44 in 1928. Note the triangular windows beside the windscreen. (Real Car Company)

Paid for by penny subscriptions from Scouts all around the world, this Twenty (GVO40) was bodied by Page & Hunt and presented to Lord Baden-Powell, founder of the movement, in 1929. (RREC)

vision at junctions, together with a dickey seat. The last Page & Hunt body on a Twenty was a six-light Saloon in 1929 on chassis GVO40, delivered just before the name change to Abbott. This was built for Lord Baden-Powell and was paid for by penny subscription from Scouts all round the world.

PALMERS
Dover – 20/25

Palmers (Dover) Ltd had been founded in 1875 and turned to motor car bodywork early in the new century. The company is thought to have had links with the London firm of Connaught (qv) from before the First World War and in later years Palmers certainly built bodies for Connaught; in fact, when a second works was built in Dover in the early 1930s, it was named Connaught Coach Works and Palmers Ltd.

Palmers are thought to have built six bodies for the 20/25 chassis between 1932 and 1934. There were two Limousines in 1933, for GEX74 and GBA66; the first one may have carried Connaught plates and GBA66

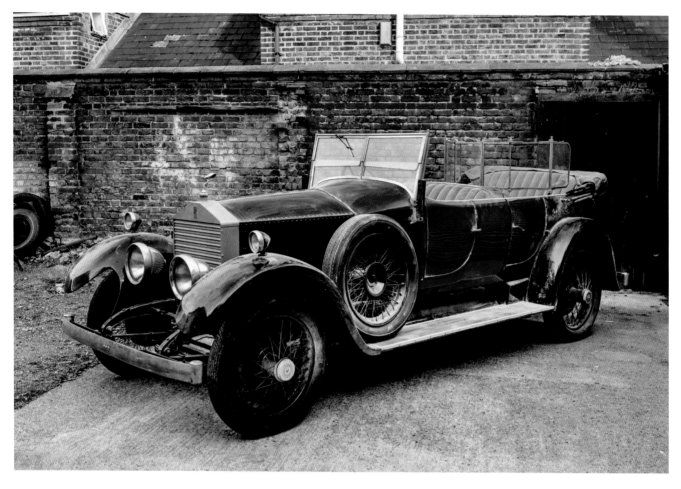

As found, albeit after a wash and polish! This "barn find" Twenty, GUK74 from 1926, originally carried Barker Tourer coachwork. In later years, its original body was swapped with the body from another Twenty – which was a Tourer built by Park Ward in the style of Barker! (Simon Clay)

definitely did. Two bodies are recorded as four-light Saloons, and these were for GHW59 in 1932 and GEX75 the following year. There was a single four-door Tourer, for GMD31 in 1934.

Palmers also built an estate body that was known as the Connaught type. One was for chassis GBA19 in 1933, and one was used to rebody GBK11 at an unknown date. There is some suggestion that the estate body currently on GHW59 is not a conversion of the original Saloon body or a replacement, but may have been fitted from new.

PARK WARD
London – Twenty, 20/25, 25/30, Wraith

Park Ward was the second most prolific coachbuilder on the small-horsepower Rolls-Royce chassis. The company was founded at Willesden in north-west London in 1919, and by 1920 was exhibiting its work at Olympia. That year it also built its first body on a Rolls-Royce chassis, and soon afterwards was invited by Rolls-Royce to participate in a scheme to construct standard-pattern bodies for the Twenty; for such a young coachbuilder to be among the select few

chosen for that honour indicates the quality and flair that the company was already showing. In practice, that scheme did not come to fruition, but it is clear that Rolls-Royce had its eye on Park Ward from early on.

So did customers who bought the grander chassis such as those made by Rolls-Royce and Bentley. Their preference for this coachbuilder meant that Park Ward was able to focus largely on chassis by those two makers during the 1920s. However, when the Recession began to bite and orders for top-quality coachbuilt bodywork dropped off alarmingly, Park Ward approached Rolls-Royce for help. The approach was timely; Rolls-Royce had been thinking again about standardised or batch-built bodies to ease an increasingly difficult market and the idea was soon formalised. In 1933, Rolls-Royce therefore took a stake in Park Ward, becoming a part-owner of the business.

This move also gave the chassis maker what it had always lacked, which was an in-house body building facility. As Ian Rimmer explains it in *Rolls-Royce and Bentley Experimental Cars*, "Rolls-Royce and Park

The windscreen for rear-seat passengers depended on simple mountings to the body sides. (Simon Clay)

The barrel sides of the body are very apparent in this close-up picture showing the front compartment. (Simon Clay)

Very assured lines distinguish this Park Ward Cabriolet for a 1926 Twenty chassis, GMJ61. (Real Car Company)

deteriorate from vibration; and they did not suffer from rot in the framework, which was another major cause of deterioration. More than a year after their appearance on Bentley chassis, the first was fitted to a Rolls-Royce 25-30.

Park Ward was also among those coachbuilders who were shown the Vanvooren pillarless body that Rolls-Royce had commissioned for a Bentley 3½-litre in 1934, and by the spring of 1937 had their own pillarless saloon design ready for production.

It was no surprise that Rolls-Royce took complete ownership of Park Ward in 1939. However, the outbreak of war soon afterwards and the very different conditions that existed in the market for luxury cars in the mid-1940s have obscured what its original plans for the coachbuilder may have been.

Park Ward built nearly 1300 bodies for the small-horsepower Rolls-Royce chassis. The individual figures were 332 for the Twenty, 620 for the 20/25, 162 for the 25/30, and 170 for the Wraith.

TWENTY COACHWORK

There were 332 known Park Ward bodies for the Twenty chassis. Although only six are recorded for 1922, the annual numbers quickly built up and the Twenty accounted for a sizeable proportion of Park Ward's business for the rest of the decade.

There were 46 bodies in 1923, 34 in 1924, 27 in 1925, 43 in 1926, 56 in 1927, 74 in 1928 (the record year), and 36 in 1929.

Cabriolets

In 1923-1924, by far the largest number of customers ordering Park Ward coachwork were asking for Cabriolet bodies, but that demand then thinned out quite rapidly as fashions changed. There were 34 such bodies in all, of which one was ordered for GNK84, the last Twenty with two-wheel brakes and three-speed gearbox in 1925. The full list, with dates, is as follows:

Ward had built up an association in the 'thirties over the building of bodies for experimental cars. Park Ward were happy to carry out any ideas on coachwork put forward by Rolls-Royce, through [Chief Projects Engineer Ivan Evernden], and these could be carefully monitored during the testing of the car. In return Park Ward could try out their own ideas on coachwork on Rolls-Royce experimental cars with an arrangement for sharing the cost."

The demand for batch-built "standard" bodies undoubtedly helped keep the Park Ward business afloat at a time when coachbuilding was entering a period of decline. Nevertheless, Park Ward never lost its ability to come up with bespoke designs for customers who wanted them, or to make minor variations on the "standardised" designs to meet individual tastes. In the later 1920s, the company took out a Weymann licence, but it is very noticeable that this was used sparingly on bodies for the Rolls-Royce Twenty; this was probably one result of that infamous 1926 memo from the Sales Department (see Chapter 2) that discouraged the use of Weymann bodies.

The special relationship between chassis maker and coachbuilder led to some valuable innovations that many other coachbuilders were reluctant to try. Park Ward were among the first to experiment with streamlining – although that proved a short-lived fashion. They started using steel centre pillars in their saloon bodies, which reduced weight and increased rigidity. During 1935 they began working on all-steel construction, patented a design, and introduced it on Bentley chassis in 1936. These all-steel bodies solved many long-standing problems with traditional coachwork: they were more rigid, which made them less likely to squeak and rattle, and less prone to

40G4	1922	79A3	1923	GLK58	1924
46G4	1922	84K1	1923	GLK81	1924
47G0	1922	87K7	1923	GNK84	1925
47G3	1922	GA30	1923	GPK59	1925
48G8	1923	GA75	1923	GUK62	1926
49G2	1923	GAK9	1924	GYK39	1926
51S9	1923	GAK10	1924	GMJ39	1926
59S5	1923	GAK46	1924	GMJ61	1926
59S6	1923	GDK23	1924	GRJ2	1927
62H2	1923	GLK7	1924	GUJ37	1927
65H3	1923	GLK16	1924	GYL11	1928
76A9	1923				

Coupés

There was quite a strong demand for Coupé coachwork on the Twenty, and of the 23 examples that Park Ward built there were nine with three-quarter (four-light) styles. These are marked with an asterisk (*) in the tables below. Even though Park Ward held a Weymann licence, the company built only one Weymann Coupé, which was for GWL25 in 1928. The 23 bodies were on the following chassis:

53S8	1923	GCK 27*	1925	GYL16	1928
71A0*	1923	GCK38*	1925	GWL25	1928
73A2*	1923	GCK57*	1925	GFN63	1928
86K7	1923	GOK70	1926	GEN35	1929
89K4	1923	GZK54*	1926	GEN68	1929
GRK77*	1924	GYK9	1926	GVO29	1929
GPK74*	1925	GMJ64	1926	GVO62	1929
GSK55*	1925	GRJ4	1927		

Coupé de Ville

Park Ward rarely built De Ville styles in this period, and the only one for a Twenty chassis was a Coupé de Ville for GMK8 in 1924.

Drophead Coupés

There was a steady but unspectacular demand for Drophead Coupé coachwork on the Twenty, and Park Ward eventually delivered a total of 20 such bodies. Five of them had a "three-quarter" configuration, and these are indicated with an asterisk (*) in the table below.

45G3	1922	GA42	1923	GYK75	1926
58S0	1923	GH66	1923	GMJ33*	1926
74A2	1923	GAK70*	1924	GRJ35*	1927
74A3	1923	GMK15	1924	GXL29	1927
75A5*	1923	GDK41	1924	GXL76	1927
84K5	1923	GLK45	1924	GEN78	1929
88K4	1923	GNK70*	1925		

Landaulettes

Demand for Landaulette coachwork was both strong and steady, and Park Ward delivered a total of 49 such bodies. Five were built using the Weymann patents in 1927-1928, and these are indicated with an asterisk in the list below.

43G9	1922	GMK12	1924	GUK60	1926
53S1	1923	GLK73	1924	GUK71	1926
GA1	1923	GPK46	1925	GUK81	1926
GF19	1923	GSK14	1925	GYK73	1926
GF27	1923	GSK66	1925	GYK84	1926
GF39	1923	GCK75	1925	GMJ2	1926
GAK6	1924	GUK10	1926	GMJ6	1926

GMJ24	1926	GUJ77	1927	GKM21	1928
GMJ32	1926	GXL27*	1927	GKM43	1928
GHJ49	1927	GXL58*	1927	GTM34	1928
GHJ60	1927	GYL54	1928	GLN35	1929
GHJ76	1927	GYL62*	1928	GEN31	1929
GRJ30	1927	GWL14	1928	GEN46	1929
GRJ31	1927	GBM4	1928	GEN59	1929
GRJ48	1927	GBM30	1928	GVO4	1929
GUJ17*	1927	GBM46	1928		
GUJ30*	1927	GKM19	1928		

Limousines

Orders for Limousine coachwork increased noticeably after 1926, and by the end of Twenty production Park Ward had met 55 of them. Interestingly, not one of these bodies appears to have been built using the Weymann patents. The full list, with dates, was as follows:

GA35	1923	GYL76	1928	GFN82	1928
GH9	1923	GWL7	1928	GLN46	1929
GAK72	1924	GWL36	1928	GLN59	1929
GMK62	1924	GWL39	1928	GLN68	1929
GRK48	1924	GWL40	1928	GLN71	1929
GLK78	1924	GBM2	1928	GLN82	1929
GPK67	1925	GBM70	1928	GLN84	1929
GCK9	1925	GBM72	1928	GEN21	1929
GCK12	1925	GKM4	1928	GEN27	1929
GUK30	1926	GKM15	1928	GEN32	1929
GYK15	1926	GKM42	1928	GEN44	1929
GYK47	1926	GKM47	1928	GEN76	1929
GMJ41	1926	GKM55	1928	GVO8	1929
GRJ10	1927	GKM57	1928	GVO14	1929
GUJ23	1927	GFN7	1928	GVO44	1929
GUJ27	1927	GFN31	1928	GVO50	1929
GXL15	1927	GFN69	1928	GVO61	1929
GXL47	1927	GFN76	1928	GXO3	1929
GXL60	1927				

Saloons

Park Ward built more Saloon bodies for the Twenty than any other type, after a fairly slow start to orders. There were 118 in all, including a single example of a two-door Saloon on chassis 79A6 in 1923. On current evidence, the company delivered 10 Weymann Saloon bodies between 1927 and 1929, but these represented only about 8% of all its Saloon bodies for the Twenty in that period. The Weymann bodies are marked with an asterisk (*) in the table below.

51S6	1923	GA36	1923	GH61	1923
77A4	1923	GH27	1923	GMK7	1924
79A6	1923	GH32	1923	GMK27	1924

GRK25	1924	GAJ69	1927	GBM56	1928
GRK26	1924	GAJ71	1927	GBM58	1928
GRK34	1924	GAJ73	1927	GBM61	1928
GRK59	1924	GAJ78	1927	GBM76	1928
GDK27	1924	GAJ80	1927	GBM81	1928
GDK32	1924	GRJ27	1927	GKM1*	1928
GLK8	1924	GRJ54	1927	GKM9	1928
GLK33	1924	GRJ70 (*)	1927	GKM39	1928
GNK50	1925	GRJ74	1927	GKM48*	1928
GPK19	1925	GRJ79	1927	GKM50	1928
GPK50	1925	GUJ16	1927	GKM67	1928
GPK60	1925	GUJ18	1927	GKM71	1928
GPK64	1925	GUJ33	1927	GTM4	1928
GPK75	1925	GUJ36	1927	GTM20	1928
GCK43	1925	GUJ40	1927	GTM22*	1928
GOK4	1926	GUJ42	1927	GTM26	1928
GOK16	1926	GUJ63	1927	GTM33	1928
GZK6	1926	GUJ78	1927	GTM39*	1928
GZK21	1926	GXL5	1927	GFN16	1928
GUK5	1926	GXL23	1927	GFN17*	1928
GUK18	1926	GXL37	1927	GFN27	1928
GUK70	1926	GXL48	1927	GFN45	1928
GYK60	1926	GXL49	1927	GFN55	1928
GMJ8	1926	GYL3	1928	GFN64	1928
GMJ11	1926	GYL9*	1928	GFN66	1928
GMJ45	1926	GYL36	1928	GFN80	1928
GMJ53	1926	GYL38	1928	GLN20	1929
GMJ63	1926	GYL45	1928	GLN25	1929
GMJ66	1926	GYL69	1928	GLN60	1929
GHJ17	1927	GWL3	1928	GLN80*	1929
GHJ26	1927	GWL16	1928	GEN8	1929
GHJ70	1927	GWL21	1928	GEN11	1929
GHJ77	1927	GWL24	1928	GEN17	1929
GAJ33	1927	GWL28	1928	GEN26	1929
GAJ35	1927	GWL33	1928	GVO25*	1929
GAJ36*	1927	GBM21	1928		
GAJ57	1927	GBM38	1928		

Tourers

Orders for Tourer coachwork started off quite strongly but gradually declined as enclosed bodies became more popular after the middle of the decade. The table below contains the chassis numbers associated with all

This Special Tourer coachwork by Park Ward on Twenty GPK29 from 1925 has a most interesting configuration at the rear. (Real Car Company)

18 Park Ward Tourer bodies for the Twenty.

48G6	1923	GLK17	1924	GOK46	1926
75A2	1923	GPK29	1925	GZK43	1926
GA17	1923	GSK48	1925	GYK48	1926
GH39	1923	GCK28	1925	GMJ20	1926
GAK8	1924	GCK36	1925	GRJ36	1927
GRK50	1924	GOK8	1926	GKM77	1928

Two-seaters

The Two-seater body was perhaps not really Park Ward's style, but the company did respond to three quite widely-spaced requests for examples. These were for chassis 49G1 in 1923, GNK54 in 1925, and GAJ11 in 1927.

Unknown

Finally, one Twenty chassis is known to have had a Park Ward body, but the type has not been recorded. This was chassis 57S2 from 1923.

20/25 COACHWORK

There were 622 Rolls-Royce 20/25 chassis that were fitted with Park Ward coachwork from new. From this total can be subtracted three for which the bodies were not new: GFT102 was renumbered from prototype 20-G-IV, the body from GEX71 was transferred to GXB38, and GYH40 was given a second-hand body from experimental car 1-PER-III. This then agrees with the total of 620 bodies that Tom Clarke gives in The Rolls-Royce 20/25hp.

Build volumes gradually built up from a slow start with 37 bodies in 1929 and 61 in 1930. There were only 48 in 1931, but the numbers rose again to 81 in 1932, to 138 in 1933 and to a peak of 150 in 1934. There were then 87 in 1935 and just 20 in 1936 as the 25/30 chassis took over from the 20/25.

All-weathers

All-weather Tourers for the 20/25 chassis were few and far between from Park Ward, and just six were built. These were for chassis GGP69 (1929), GLR56 (1930), GKT12 (1932), GTZ31 (1933), GAE27 (1934), and GLG51 (1935).

Cabriolet

Park Ward built two Cabriolet bodies on early chassis, which were GGP52 in 1929 and GBT73 in 1932, the latter described as a Saloon Cabriolet.

Coupés

For convenience, this group of 14 bodies includes Saloon Coupé types, of which there were just two;

these were for chassis GFT24 in 1931 and GDX35 in 1933. Generally speaking, Park Ward seem to have preferred the description of Fixed-head Coupé in this period for both two-light and four-light types. Most were two-light designs, but in 1933, GSY15 and GHA29 were both built with four-light designs. The full list is as follows:

GDP49	1930	GFT24	1931	GYZ23	1933
GLR27	1930	GKT38	1932	GGA15	1933
GLR61	1930	GDX35	1933	GHA29	1933
GNS29	1930	GSY15	1933	GBK54	1936
GOS47	1931	GSY40	1933		

De Ville types

Park Ward built 25 De Ville bodies for the 20/25, of which there were four basic types. There was just one Sedancalette body, a four-light design built in 1932 for chassis GMU41. Only two Brougham de Ville bodies were built, for GMD36 in 1934 and GLG50 in 1935. There were five Limousines de Ville, for chassis GOS59 and GOS75 in 1931, GXB67 and GNC1 in 1934, and GTK52 in 1936. The remaining 17 were Sedancas de Ville, as follows:

GFT72	1931	GGA68	1933	GBJ25	1935
GMU41	1932	GRC18	1934	GXK4	1935
GRW23	1932	GMD21	1934	GXK11	1935
GEX59	1933	GMD37	1934	GXK49	1935
GWX38	1933	GSF43	1935	GBK21	1936
GGA43	1933	GLG15	1935	GBK49	1936

Drophead Coupés

Fourteen Drophead Coupé bodies were built between 1930 and 1934, and two of these were equipped with Dickey seats; these were on chassis GNS65 in 1931 and GRC52 in 1934. The full list, with dates, was:

GWP1	1930	GAU11	1932	GHA1	1933
GSR3	1930	GAU28	1932	GXB9	1933
GTR5	1930	GLZ10	1933	GRC52	1934
GNS65	1931	GTZ46	1933	GED47	1934
GKT23	1932	GYZ32	1933		

Landaulettes

Even though Landaulette bodies were gradually going out of fashion in the early 1930s, Park Ward supplied a total of 23 examples for Rolls-Royce 20/25 chassis. These were:

GXO55	1929	GDP64	1930	GLR74	1930
GXO63	1929	GWP14	1930	GSR48	1930
GGP25	1929	GLR66	1930	GSR49	1930

GNS9	1930	GEX67	1933	GMD22	1934
GNS19	1930	GBA79	1933	GSF72	1935
GOS42	1931	GGA32	1933	GPG29	1935
GHW15	1932	GGA77	1933	GOH67	1935
GEX1	1933	GUB67	1934		

Limousines

Park Ward Limousine bodies were very popular on the 20/25 chassis, and the total of 228 built came second only to the company's Saloon types for this Rolls-Royce model. The list includes 18-G-IV, an experimental chassis that was given a Park Ward Limousine body in 1930. Just one of these bodies seems to have been made using the Weymann patents, but with metal panels, and this was for chassis GTR21 in 1930. In 1934, GED65 was described as a Standard Pullman Limousine, and GMD9 as a Special Limousine. The full list of the Limousine bodies is as follows:

GXO24	1929	GXO59	1929	GXO98	1930
GXO28	1929	GXO70	1929	GXO100	1930
GXO32	1929	GXO72	1929	GXO109	1930
GXO47	1929	GXO88	1929	GGP12	1929
GXO54	1929	18-G-IV	1930	GGP15	1929

Pictured in the early 1960s, at a time when many early Rolls-Royce cars had fallen on hard times, 1931 20/25 GFT72 still carried its Park Ward Saloon body with some pride.

Sleek lines characterised this Drophead Coupé by Park Ward for an early 1930s 20/25 chassis. (Rolls-Royce)

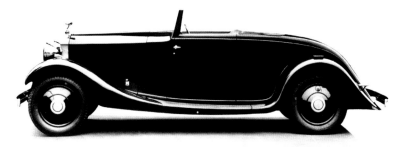

Novelist Sax Rohmer, originator of the Dr Fu Manchu stories, was pictured with his 1935 20/25 GLG15 that carried a Sedanca de Ville body. The fashionable falling waistline is clearly in evidence here.

GGP22	1929	GTR17	1930	GRW28	1932	GGA33	1933	GMD69	1934	GPG69	1934

GGP22	1929	GTR17	1930	GRW28	1932
GGP23	1929	GTR21	1930	GRW37	1932
GGP30	1929	GNS12	1930	GRW71	1932
GGP33	1929	GNS40	1931	GRW76	1932
GGP43	1929	GNS49	1930	GAW24	1933
GGP50	1929	GOS21	1931	GAW27	1933
GGP51	1929	GOS35	1931	GAW37	1933
GGP54	1929	GOS72	1931	GEX19	1933
GGP55	1930	GOS80	1931	GEX31	1933
GGP56	1929	GOS81	1931	GEX36	1933
GGP60	1929	GPS7	1931	GEX55	1933
GGP76	1930	GPS15	1931	GWX9	1933
GDP9T	1929	GPS16	1931	GWX33	1933
GDP17	1930	GPS30	1931	GWX49	1933
GDP18	1930	GPS31	1931	GWX69	1933
GDP24	1930	GPS35	1931	GDX10	1933
GDP67	1930	GPS36	1931	GDX28	1933
GWP16	1930	GFT11	1931	GSY7	1933
GWP19	1930	GFT19	1931	GSY23	1933
GWP24	1930	GFT48	1931	GSY25	1933
GWP32	1930	GBT45	1932	GSY41	1933
GWP39	1930	GAU48	1932	GSY71	1933
GLR23	1930	GAU51	1932	GSY81	1933
GLR38	1930	GAU56	1932	GSY91	1933
GLR39	1930	GMU16	1932	GLZ24	1933
GLR68	1930	GMU53	1932	GLZ36	1933
GLR71	1930	GMU69	1932	GTZ15	1933
GSR18	1930	GZU3	1932	GTZ25	1933
GSR21	1930	GZU27	1932	GTZ58	1933
GSR30	1930	GZU40	1932	GTZ73	1933
GSR68	1930	GHW10	1932	GYZ1	1933
GSR71	1930	GHW31	1932	GYZ33	1933
GTR7	1930	GRW2	1932	GBA33	1933
GTR10	1930	GRW17	1932	GBA57	1933
GTR16	1930	GRW21	1932	GBA69	1933

GGA33	1933	GMD69	1934	GPG69	1934
GGA35	1933	GYD2	1934	GHG6	1934
GGA36	1933	GYD34	1934	GHG9	1934
GGA41	1933	GYD43	1934	GHG21	1934
GGA46	1933	GYD49	1934	GYH10	1934
GGA50	1933	GAE16	1934	GYH37	1934
GGA62	1933	GAE39	1934	GYH39	1934
GHA10	1933	GAE57	1934	GYH43	1934
GHA14	1933	GAE74	1934	GYH63	1934
GXB34	1933	GWE3	1934	GYH65	1934
GXB37	1934	GWE17	1934	GOH25	1934
GXB46	1934	GWE30	1934	GOH55	1934
GXB72	1934	GWE43	1934	GOH78	1934
GUB4	1934	GWE54	1934	GEH28	1934
GUB18	1934	GWE76	1934	GEH38	1934
GUB25	1934	GWE78	1934	GBJ27	1934
GUB65	1934	GFE20	1934	GBJ36	1934
GLB25	1934	GFE33	1934	GBJ47	1934
GNC15	1934	GAF5	1934	GBJ59	1934
GNC17	1934	GAF9	1934	GLJ23	1934
GNC29	1934	GAF24	1934	GLJ37	1934
GRC3	1934	GAF45	1934	GLJ61	1934
GRC71	1934	GAF54	1934	GLJ66	1935
GKC3	1934	GAF69	1934	GCJ1	1935
GKC19	1934	GSF17	1934	GCJ5	1935
GKC24	1934	GSF25	1934	GCJ11	1935
GKC33	1934	GSF26	1934	GXK54	1935
GED8	1934	GRF3	1935	GXK73	1936
GED24	1934	GRF31	1934	GXK76	1936
GED51	1934	GLG3	1934	GXK80	1936
GED65	1934	GLG7	1934	GBK25	1936
GED70	1934	GLG45	1934	GBK74	1936
GED73	1934	GLG72	1934	GTK7	1936
GMD2	1934	GLG76	1934	GTK12	1936
GMD9	1934	GLG77	1934	GTK28	1936
GMD34	1934	GPG50	1934	GTK34	1936

Saloons

Park Ward built 305 Saloon bodies for the 20/25 chassis, and of course in the seven seasons of production there was a variety of types. Both four-light and six-light types came from the Willesden works, the four-lights being very much in the ascendant after 1931. There were also two Two-door Saloons; these were for chassis GXO80 in 1929 and GSY96 in 1933. Two Saloons were built in 1931 using the Weymann patents with metal panels; these were for GOS37 and GPS10. Several Saloons were of course fitted with Divisions, and these are identified by an asterisk (*) in the tables below.

Early four-light Saloons usually had large blind rear quarters, but from 1931 there was a remarkably neat four-light Sports Saloon style with an integral boot that initially went by the name of Continental Saloon. The first example was built for the Rolls-Royce Sales Division on experimental chassis 20-G-IV, and was later renumbered as GFT102.

The name of Continental may have come from the Phantom II Continental, for which a larger version of the style was available; it may simply have reflected the fact that the boot provided enough space for the luggage needed during a holiday on the European continent; or it may have been a happy combination of both. The style evolved over the next few years, and later versions gained larger but less attractive boots, and tended to be called Special Saloons rather than Continental Saloons. The original Continental Saloon concept inspired other coachbuilders to produce their own versions of the design, and to use the Continental Saloon name for them as well.

There were two swept-tail Saloons, on GRF37 in 1935 and GTK37 in 1936, but the style obviously did not prove popular. Another low-volume type was the D-back Saloon, of which there were again two: GAW9 in 1933 and GKC1 in 1934. GRW43 in 1932 was bodied as a Special Touring Saloon, and the body fitted to chassis GYH40 in 1935 was a four-light Saloon that had been built in 1932 for an experimental Peregrine prototype numbered 1-Per-II (the Peregrine was a smaller-engined model that did not reach production). The body was actually fitted to the 20/25 chassis by the London coachbuilder Offord.

The Saloon body on chassis GYH19 in 1935 was of Park Ward manufacture but was fitted by Cooper, perhaps because it had been removed from another chassis. The body originally built for GEX71 in 1933 was transferred to chassis GXB38 in 1934; GXB38 is not included in the tables below.

For ease of reference, the tables of Saloon bodies have been divided up into two-yearly tranches.

1929-1930

GXO41*	1929	GGP75	1929	GLR3	1930
GXO68	1929	GGP81*	1929	GLR60	1930
GXO80	1929	GDP61*	1930	GSR12	1930
GXO97	1930	GDP71*	1930	GSR19	1930
GGP6*	1929	GWP15	1930	GTR30	1930
GGP7	1930	GWP21	1930	GNS7	1930
GGP16	1929	GWP41	1930	GNS42*	1930
GGP70	1929	GLR1*	1930		

1931-1932

GNS77	1931	GOS36	1931	GPS22	1931
GOS5	1931	GOS37*	1931	GPS24	1931
GOS8	1931	GOS73	1931	GPS29	1931
GOS17	1931	GPS10	1931	GFT14	1931
GFT20	1931	GBT53*	1932	GMU60	1932
GFT22	1931	GBT76	1932	GMU61	1932
GFT46	1931	GKT3	1932	GMU73	1932
GFT47	1931	GKT5	1932	GMU76	1932
GFT51	1931	GKT6*	1932	GZU1	1932
GFT53	1931	GKT11	1932	GZU17	1932
GFT60	1931	GKT19	1932	GZU35*	1932
GFT61	1931	GKT21	1932	GHW30	1932
GFT64	1931	GKT36*	1932	GHW41	1932
GFT69*	1931	GAU2*	1932	GHW53	1932
GFT81	1931	GAU14	1932	GHW58	1932
GFT102	1931	GAU23	1932	GHW60	1932
GBT3*	1931	GAU29	1932	GHW73	1932
GBT8	1932	GAU30	1932	GHW78*	1932
GBT9	1932	GAU35*	1932	GRW5	1932
GBT25	1932	GAU45	1932	GRW8	1932
GBT27	1932	GAU74	1932	GRW15*	1932
GBT32	1932	GAU77*	1932	GRW43	1932
GBT44	1932	GMU27	1932	GRW50*	1932
GBT47	1932	GMU36	1932	GRW79*	1932
GBT51	1932	GMU40	1932	GAW3	1932
GBT52	1932	GMU46*	1932	GAW5*	1932

1933-1934

GAW7	1933	GSY63	1933	GBA42	1933
GAW9	1933	GSY80*	1933	GBA44	1933
GAW28	1933	GSY85*	1933	GGA1	1933
GEX16*	1933	GSY92	1933	GGA14*	1933
GEX23	1933	GSY95*	1933	GGA26	1933
GEX39*	1933	GSY96	1933	GGA47	1933
GEX50	1933	GSY100	1933	GGA58	1933
GEX58	1933	GSY101	1933	GGA80	1933
GEX61	1933	GLZ23*	1933	GHA6*	1933
GEX71	1933	GLZ28	1933	GHA7	1933
GEX76	1933	GLZ50*	1933	GHA12	1933
GWX7	1933	GLZ79*	1933	GHA34	1933
GWX14*	1933	GTZ3*	1933	GHA36*	1933
GWX30(*)	1933	GTZ6	1933	GHA38*	1933
GWX37	1933	GTZ19	1933	GXB10*	1933
GWX41	1933	GTZ30*	1933	GXB19	1933
GWX43*	1933	GTZ33*	1933	GXB49	1934
GWX58	1933	GTZ44	1933	GXB55	1934
GWX61	1933	GTZ52	1933	GXB57	1934
GWX67	1933	GTZ65*	1933	GXB60	1934
GWX79	1933	GTZ68*	1933	GXB68	1934
GDX14	1933	GTZ79*T	1933	GXB76	1934
GDX15	1933	GYZ6	1933	GUB5	1934
GDX22*	1933	GYZ10	1933	GUB23	1934
GDX30	1933	GYZ20	1933	GUB26*	1934
GDX32	1933	GYZ40	1933	GUB34	1934
GSY4	1933	GBA8	1933	GUB55	1934
GSY22	1933	GBA38*	1933	GUB56*	1934
GSY55	1933	GBA39	1933	GUB58	1934

Park Ward was first into the market with a Continental Saloon, and this example was built for late 1933 chassis GXB19, being delivered early in 1934. By comparison with many other Saloon designs of the time, this was a very modern-looking design. (Real Car Company)

1935-1936

GSF47*	1935	GHG11*	1935	GBJ58*	1935
GSF58	1935	GHG20	1935	GLJ81*	1935
GRF21	1935	GHG29*	1935	GCJ27*	1935
GRF37	1935	GHG40	1935	GXK26	1935
GRF40*	1935	GYH5	1935	GXK28*	1935
GLG23*	1935	GYH6	1935	GXK37*	1935
GLG28	1935	GYH19	1935	GXK39*	1935
GLG35	1935	GYH21	1935	GXK48*	1935
GLG44*	1935	GYH40	1935	GXK69*	1936
GLG58	1935	GYH48*	1935	GBK2	1936
GLG60	1935	GYH77*	1935	GBK33	1936
GLG80	1935	GOH21	1935	GBK80	1936
GPG6*	1935	GOH38	1935	GTK25	1936
GPG15*	1935	GEH12	1935	GTK37	1936
GPG32*	1935	GBJ6	1935	GTK48*	1936
GPG77*	1935				

Tourers

Tourer bodies were not a particular Park Ward speciality, and the company met orders for only four on the 20/25 chassis. These were for GEX17 and GSY36 in 1933, for GNC23 in 1934, and for GLG22 in 1935.

25/30 COACHWORK

Of the 162 bodies that Park Ward built for new 25/30 chassis, no fewer than 112 were Limousines of various types. The next most numerous were Saloons, again of various types, with the much lower total of 39. By comparison, other types of coachwork were made in penny numbers.

All-weathers

Park Ward built only two All-weather bodies for the 25/30 chassis, and the identification of one of those is in some doubt. The earlier of the two was built in 1937 for chassis GHO27, and the Park Ward records actually describe it as a Coupé de Ville. The second body was for GGR54 in 1938, and incorporated rear-wheel spats that perhaps added a little modernity to its appearance.

This Special Saloon of 1934 for 20/25 GRC28 was a further evolution of the earlier Continental Saloon, with a slightly heavier appearance.

GLB7	1934	GED38	1934	GAE19	1934
GLB10	1934	GED40	1934	GAE28	1934
GLB19	1934	GED41	1934	GAE44*	1934
GNC24*	1934	GED43	1934	GAE53*	1934
GNC38	1934	GED58	1934	GWE60	1934
GNC47	1934	GED63	1934	GWE66*?	1934
GNC57	1934	GED68	1934	GWE74	1934
GNC68	1934	GED78	1934	GFE17	1934
GNC78*	1934	GMD29	1934	GFE39*	1934
GRC9	1934	GMD40*	1934	GFE41*	1934
GRC24	1934	GMD45*	1934	GAF6	1934
GRC28	1934	GMD46	1934	GAF15	1934
GRC39	1934	GMD60	1934	GAF34	1934
GRC43*	1934	GMD65*	1934	GAF57	1934
GRC49	1934	GMD78	1934	GAF60	1934
GRC56	1934	GMD79	1934	GAF64	1934
GRC59	1934	GYD21	1934	GAF72	1934
GKC1	1934	GYD28*	1934	GAF74*	1934
GKC6*	1934	GYD30*	1934	GAF79*	1934
GKC21	1934	GYD45	1934	GSF8	1934
GKC39	1934	GYD47	1934	GSF21	1934
GED19*?	1934	GYD51	1934	GSF33	1934
GED30*	1934	GAE4	1934	GSF44*	1934
GED31	1934	GAE6	1934		

De Ville types

De Ville types were becoming rare by the later 1930s, and there were just two examples for the 25/30 chassis, both Sedanca de Ville bodies. The first was for GUL2 in 1936 and the second for GRO31 in 1937.

Drophead Coupés

Park Ward built just three Drophead Coupé bodies for the 25/30. These were for chassis GUL45 and GXM61 in 1936, and for GRO40 in 1937. The last of these three had a dickey seat.

Landaulettes

Even though Landaulette bodies were no longer fashionable, Park Ward supplied four of them on the 25/30 chassis, all during 1937. The four were on chassis GUN2, GUN41, GLP12 and GZR36.

Limousines

Limousines were the best sellers for Park Ward on the 25/30 chassis, and the company constructed no fewer than 112 bodies of this type. Many had an elegant swept-tail design. Six of them were described as four-light Touring Limousines: GRM26 and GWN38 in 1936, GWN63, GRP4 and GAR54 in 1937, and GGR71 in 1938. The full list of Limousine bodies was as follows:

GUL36	1936	GXM34	1936	GWN63	1937
GUL37	1936	GXM55	1936	GWN64	1936
GUL59	1936	GXM64	1936	GWN68	1936
GUL64	1936	GXM73	1936	GWN71	1937
GUL71	1936	GXM81	1936	GWN77	1937
GTL2	1936	GGM5	1936	GWN81	1937
GTL10	1936	GGM23	1936	GUN3	1937
GTL17	1936	GGM27	1936	GUN23	1937
GTL19	1936	GAN11	1936	GUN32	1937
GTL25	1936	GAN23	1936	GRO11	1937
GTL28	1936	GAN26	1936	GRO25	1937
GTL61	1936	GAN32	1936	GRO34	1937
GTL73	1936	GAN35	1936	GRO39	1937
GHL28	1936	GAN49	1936	GRO45	1937
GRM9	1936	GAN61	1936	GRO49	1937
GRM17	1936	GAN62	1936	GRO68	1937
GRM19	1936	GAN66	1936	GHO8	1937
GRM21	1936	GWN3	1936	GHO15	1937
GRM23	1936	GWN19	1936	GHO22	1937
GRM26	1936	GWN23	1936	GHO42	1937
GRM34	1936	GWN31	1936	GHO60	1937
GRM40	1936	GWN38	1936	GHO66	1937
GRM49	1936	GWN40	1936	GHO75	1937
GRM55	1936	GWN49	1937	GMO7	1937
GXM19	1936	GWN60	1936	GMO9	1937

GMO23	1937	GMP27	1937	GGR23	1938
GRP2	1937	GMP35	1937	GGR24	1938
GRP4	1937	GMP49	1937	GGR29	1938
GRP6	1937	GMP66	1937	GGR30	1938
GRP16	1937	GMP72	1937	GGR33	1938
GRP26	1937	GAR6	1937	GGR34	1938
GRP39	1937	GAR20	1937	GGR61	1938
GRP41	1937	GAR42	1937	GGR71	1938
GRP49	1937	GAR52	1937	GGR80	1938
GRP50	1937	GAR54	1937	GZR12	1938
GRP58	1937	GAR64	1937	GZR23	1938
GMP3	1937	GGR11	1938		
GMP6	1937	GGR15	1938		

The wheel spats on this 1938 All-weather body by Park Ward were a fashion of the time. It was built on chassis GGR54.

Saloons

The 39 Saloon bodies included both four-light and six-light types, and three were specifically described as Touring Saloons: these were for chassis GUL60 in 1936, GMP61 in 1937, and GGR38 in 1938. There was one swept-tail Saloon, for GRP73 in 1937, and two bodies had razor-edge lines: these were for GMP12 in 1937 and GZR22 in 1938. As always, several bodies were ordered with Divisions, and these are indicated in the table below by an asterisk (*).

GUL24*	1936	GHL3*	1936	GXM44	1936
GUL55	1936	GHL17	1936	GXM76*	1936
GUL60*	1936	GHL39	1936	GGM41	1936
GTL35	1936	GHL40	1936	GRO9*	1937
GTL41*	1936	GRM22	1936	GRO50	1937
GTL50*	1936	GRM27*	1936	GRO78*	1937
GTL69	1936	GRM69*	1936	GHO2*	1937

This Park Ward body for 1937 25/30 chassis GHO27 has been variously described as a Coupé de Ville and an All-weather. The heavy centre pillars detract from the overall appearance.

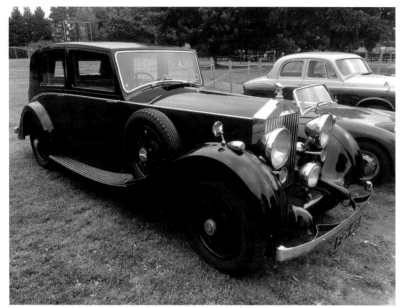

De Ville types

There was just one example of Brougham de Ville coachwork for the Wraith, which was for chassis WXA107 in 1938. This was both unique and stylish, and the swept-forward lines of its rear doors were emphasised by contrasting paintwork. There were also two Sedanca bodies on the Wraith chassis. The earlier of these was a Sedanca Drophead Coupé with three-position hood on chassis WXA79 in 1938. The later one was a Sedanca de Ville for WHC3 in 1939.

Limousines

Limousine bodies were the most numerous type from Park Ward on the Wraith chassis, and the overall total of 92 includes 14 Touring Limousines, which are listed in a separate table for convenience.

Three of the early Limousines were built in 1937 and were mounted onto prototype chassis that were subsequently renumbered with production numbers: WXA3 had started life as 24-G-VI, WXA5 had been 26-G-VI, and WXA8 had been 29-G-VI. All three of them had the same early Limousine style (to design 13031), and WXA3 promoted the type in the Wraith sales brochure. In practice, just one other example would be built, for chassis WXA9, and later Limousines were almost universally to the broadly similar design 13317.

Two late Limousines (WEC35 and WEC38) went to British Embassies overseas in 1939, and a further eight followed, but not until 1946; these were on chassis WKC7, WKC9, WKC11, WKC15, WKC18, WKC19, WKC22, WKC23 and WKC24. The list of Park Ward Limousine bodies on Wraith chassis was as follows:

WXA3	1938	WXA104	1938	WMB41	1939
WXA5	1938	WXA109	1938	WMB79	1939
WXA8	1938	WRB3	1938	WLB5	1939
WXA9	1938	WRB6	1938	WLB25	1939
WXA18	1938	WRB10	1938	WLB29	1939
WXA26	1938	WRB12	1938	WLB30	1939
WXA36	1938	WRB24	1938	WLB31	1939
WXA43	1938	WRB35	1938	WLB39	1939
WXA54	1938	WRB49	1938	WHC7	1939
WXA60	1938	WRB50	1938	WHC8	1939
WXA62	1938	WRB55	1938	WHC11	1939
WXA64	1938	WRB64	1938	WHC16	1939
WXA81	1938	WRB65	1938	WHC24	1939
WXA83	1938	WRB68	1938	WHC25	1939
WXA84	1938	WRB74	1938	WHC30	1939
WXA85	1938	WMB9	1938	WHC35	1939
WXA88	1938	WMB36	1939	WHC44	1939
WXA94	1938	WMB40	1939	WHC60	1939

Park Ward used fashionable razor-edge lines for this 1938 four-light Saloon with Division on 25/30 GZR22.

GHO41	1937	GMP61	1937	GGR70*	1938
GRP24*	1937	GLP30	1937	GGR74	1938
GRP73	1937	GAR25*	1937	GGR76	1938
GMP12	1937	GAR48*	1937	GGR77*	1938
GMP17	1937	GAR72*	1937	GZR17	1938
GMP58	1937	GGR38	1938	GZR22*	1938

Wraith coachwork

Park Ward built 170 bodies for the Rolls-Royce 25/30 chassis, and the overwhelming majority were Limousine and Saloon types; there were just three others. Five of these bodies were built in 1937, 74 in 1938, and 91 in 1939, although some of the 1939 bodies were not delivered until several years later.

WHC62	1939	WEC35	1939	WKC9	'39/46
WHC66	1939	WEC38	1939	WKC11	'39/46
WHC67	1939	WEC40	1939	WKC15	'39/46
WHC69	1939	WEC56	1939	WKC18	'39/46
WHC71	1939	WEC62	1939	WKC19	'39/46
WEC20	1939	WEC66	1939	WKC22	'39/46
WEC24	1939	WEC74	1939	WKC23	'39/46
WEC25	1939	WKC7	'39/46	WKC24	'39/46

Most of the Touring Limousines had design 13344 or 13345, although the body for WXA10 in 1938 was different, to design 13296. Three of these Touring Limousines were delivered to British Embassies overseas in 1946; these were on chassis WKC14, WKC17 and WKC20.

WXA10	1938	WRB16	1938	WEC68	1939
WXA28	1938	WMB8	1938	WKC14	'39/46
WXA61	1938	WMB10	1938	WKC17	'39/46
WXA70	1938	WMB12	1938	WKC20	'39/46
WXA103	1938	WLB17	1939		

Saloons

There were 75 Park Ward Saloon bodies for the Wraith chassis, mainly with four-light design numbers 13199 and 13293. A few earlier ones had design 13020, known as a Special Saloon, and among these were three former development cars built in 1937 that were renumbered as production types; these were WXA4 (formerly 25-G-VI), WXA6 (27-G-VI) and WXA7 (28-G-VI). Three bodies were described as Touring Saloons, and these were for chassis WXA99, WRB7 and WRB32. Several bodies had Divisions, and those are indicated with an asterisk (*) in the table below. One Saloon, on chassis WKC21, was delivered to a British Embassy overseas for official use; this was one of three cars not delivered until 1946 (the other two were on chassis WKC10 and WKC12).

WXA1*	1938	WXA89	1938	WRB76*	1938
WXA2*	1938	WXA91*	1938	WRB77*	1938
WXA4	1937	WXA96	1938	WRB78	1938
WXA6	1937	WXA99*	1938	WRB81	1938
WXA7	1937	WRB7	1938	WMB3	1938
WXA37	1938	WRB8*	1938	WMB11*	1938
WXA40*	1938	WRB19	1938	WMB33	1939
WXA41	1938	WRB32*	1938	WMB43	1939
WXA52	1938	WRB34*	1938	WMB50	1939
WXA55	1938	WRB44*	1938	WMB54*	1939
WXA58*	1938	WRB47	1938	WMB59*	1939
WXA59*	1938	WRB51*	1938	WLB9	1939
WXA67	1938	WRB62*	1938	WLB19	1939
WXA73	1938	WRB63	1938	WLB20	1939

WLB35*	1939	WHC61	1939	WEC34*	1939
WLB36	1939	WHC65*	1939	WEC36*	1939
WHC5	1939	WHC68	1939	WEC37	1939
WHC9*	1939	WHC73*	1939	WEC39	1939
WHC10	1939	WHC77*	1939	WEC45*	1939
WHC18*	1939	WHC78*	1939	WEC58	1939
WHC37	1939	WEC1	1939	WEC75	1939
WHC39	1939	WEC15*	1939	WEC81	1939
WHC42*	1939	WEC16	1939	WKC10	'39/46
WHC46*	1939	WEC30*	1939	WKC12	'39/46
WHC48	1939	WEC31	1939	WKC21	'39/46

Park Ward's only Brougham de Ville body for the Wraith was on WXA107 in 1938. The use of a contrasting colour for the rear door emphasises its Brougham shape and helps to create a very distinctive design.

PENMAN

Dumfries – Twenty, 20/25, 25/30, Wraith

AC Penman established his coachbuilding business in Dumfries after taking over another business in 1887. By 1906, the company was building bodies exclusively for motor vehicles, and in the 1920s it took a stand every year at Olympia as well as at the Scottish Motor Show, so ensuring that its sales were not confined to Scotland. It remained in business after 1930 mainly as a commercial body builder and motor dealer, and still exists as Penman Engineering, having changed its name in 1983.

The company built one body on a Rolls-Royce Silver Ghost chassis before 1917 and subsequently three on the New Phantom chassis. In the 1920s and 1930s it constructed a dozen bodies for the small-horsepower Rolls-Royce. There were seven on Twenty chassis, three for the 20/25, two for the 25/30, and just one on the Wraith.

TWENTY COACHWORK

The first two bodies on the Twenty chassis were both Cabriolets built in 1923, although it is not possible to say whether they shared a common design. These were for chassis 75A1 and GH77. There was then a

This well-known sales brochure shot shows the Limousine body on WXA3, which had started life as an experimental development car but was re-numbered in the production series. The chassis is a 1938 Wraith.

Limousine for GMK45 in 1924. Penman then made no more bodies for this chassis until 1926, when the company built a Limousine on GZK32 (John Fasal describes this as a Landaulette). In 1927 came a Tourer on GMJ73 and a Saloon on GUJ22, and the last Penman-bodied Twenty was a Saloon for GVO28 in 1929.

20/25 COACHWORK

The three bodies for 20/25 chassis were all six-light types with divisions, and were built between 1929 and 1931. The first was for GGP28 in December 1929, and is variously described as a Limousine and a Saloon with Division. The second was delivered as a Saloon with Division on GDP78 in March 1930. The last was a Limousine on GNS81, delivered in February 1931.

25/30 AND WRAITH COACHWORK

AC Penman built a single Limousine for 25/30 chassis GWN73 in January 1937, and followed this in June with the first of two bodies for the same customer, Colonel Charles Spencer. The first Spencer body was a Saloon on 25/30 chassis GMO41, and the second was on Wraith chassis WLB40 in March 1939. This later body was another six-light Saloon, but either when new or later was fitted with a tailgate that has earned it the description of a "shooting car".

PICKFORD
Probably Sheffield – Twenty

One 1927 Rolls-Royce Twenty chassis, number GHJ27, is recorded with Landaulette coachwork by EH Pickford. This is most likely to be EH Pickford & Co Ltd of Eccleshall Road in Sheffield, who were toolmakers and motor traders. The company continued in business as a car dealer for many years

afterwards, but there is no known picture of its coachwork on the Twenty.

PROGRESSIVE
London – Twenty

The Progressive Coach & Motor Body Company was formed out of the ashes of Motor Car Industries in 1925 when that company's partners split up. One went on to found the Carlton Carriage Company and the other remained at the original premises in Kilburn, north-west London and ran Progressive from there. A further re-organisation in 1929 saw Progressive renamed as Mayfair (qv).

Progressive built just one known body on the Rolls-Royce Twenty, which was a Limousine for GUJ81 in 1927.

RANALAH
London – 20/25

The Ranalah Coachworks arose in early 1935 out of the ashes of John Charles & Co, who had used the Ranalah brand name for some of their bodies. Operating from new premises in Merton, south-west London, Ranalah continued to use some John Charles designs. The company built bodies on several makes of chassis and in the later 1930s was one of the London coachbuilders that built replacement bodies for older Rolls-Royce chassis on behalf of both the Southern Motor Company of Clapham and Jack Compton in Kensington.

There were four Ranalah bodies on the 20/25 chassis, but none on the later small-horsepower models. The earliest was a two-door "Alpine" Saloon Coupé delivered on chassis GRF16 in January 1935. Later that year, the company produced two four-light Saloon bodies to a common design, which were delivered on GLG65 and GPG80 in March and May respectively. The last of the four was delivered in January 1936 and was a Limousine that used the John Charles design seen on 20/25 GSF76 in January 1935.

REGENT CARRIAGE
London – Twenty

The Regent Carriage Company had been established in the Fulham district of London by 1902, when they were "designers, manufacturers and finishers of motor-car bodies" according to their own advertisement. The company worked on some Rolls-Royce Silver Ghost chassis and in 1912 bought out the British branch of coachbuilder Rothschild. It tended to work on the more prestigious chassis, including several imported types. The company was active in the early 1920s, when it built the coachwork on two Rolls-Royce Twenty chassis, but appears to have closed around 1926.

The two Twenty chassis with Regent coachwork were GAK21, which was bodied as a Tourer in 1924, and GPK61, which received Saloon coachwork in 1925.

RIPPON

Huddersfield – Twenty, 20/25, 25/30, Wraith

Rippon Bros was one of Britain's major provincial coachbuilders, its main clientele being the gentry and leading industrialists in Yorkshire, where it was based. William Rippon had set up his coachbuilding business in Huddersfield in 1870, and from 1882 it was run by his two sons. Around 1904 the company described itself as "motor body builders and designers," and by this time it was selling cars – Renault and Darracq – as well.

Rippon Bros' first body for a Rolls-Royce was built in 1905, and the company constructed a total of 35 bodies for the marque before the First World War. In the 1920s, the company encouraged the story that its origins could be traced back to the Walter Rippon who constructed carriages for royalty in the 16th century, but this story has recently been proved unfounded. Building on many makes besides Rolls-Royce, the company won several awards for coachwork at the annual London Motor Show. Its styling was typically conservative, and Rippon bodies tended to be slightly heavy, very durable, and to be both comfortable and luxurious. Rippon continued as a coachbuilder until 1952, but then focused on its car dealerships, and eventually became Appleyard Rippon; the Rippon part of the name was subsequently dropped.

Rippon Bros played a large part in the story of the small-horsepower Rolls-Royce models. The company provided coachwork for 254 chassis in all, not counting later transfers. This total is made up by 67 Twenty chassis between 1922 and 1929; 130 20/25 chassis between 1929 and 1936; 42 25/30 chassis between 1936 and 1938; and 15 Wraith chassis in 1938-1939.

TWENTY COACHWORK

The numbers of bodies for the Twenty chassis built up quickly after the model was introduced in 1922. There was only one body in that year, but Rippon provided 12 more in 1923; nine in 1924; 10 in 1925; 13 in 1926; 10 in 1927; six in 1928; and a final six in 1929. The overwhelming preference of Rippon customers was clearly for Saloons, which accounted for 49 of the 67 bodies. The remainder were a smattering of different types.

Twenty GMJ31 represents Rippon's three Tourer bodies for that chassis. Like all Rippon bodies, this 1926 example appears robust and dependable.

Cabriolets

Both the Cabriolet bodies that Rippon built for the Twenty were on early chassis. The first was also Rippon's first coachwork for a Twenty, on chassis 41G7 in 1922, and the second was on chassis GH72 in 1923.

Coupés

Four Coupé bodies were spread across the years from 1923 to 1929. The earliest was on chassis GH74 in 1923. There were then no more until 1927, when GXL21 received Coupé coachwork. This was followed in 1928 by GKM34, and in 1929 by GVO33. At an unknown date, a Rippon Coupé body replaced the original Hooper Tourer on a 1924 Twenty chassis, GAK37.

Drophead Coupés

Drophead Coupé coachwork was not especially favoured by Rippon's customers, and there were just two examples for the Twenty, both built in 1923. These were on chassis 60H8 and GH54. At an unknown date, a Rippon Drophead Coupé body with dickey seat replaced the original Barker Tourer on a 1924 Twenty chassis, GAK40.

Landaulettes

There were just four Landaulette bodies between 1923 and 1929. The first two were both delivered in 1923, and were on chassis numbers 68H8 and GH7. The second two were both 1929 bodies, on chassis numbers GVO35 and GVO70.

Limousines

Orders for Limousine coachwork on the Twenty were few and far between, and the company constructed just three such bodies. The earliest was in 1923, for chassis GH36. The second was in 1926 on GCK53, and the last one was completed in 1928 for chassis GKM5.

Saloons

Perhaps a combination of the archetypal Yorkshire common sense and Yorkshire weather explains why so many customers called for Saloon bodies. All of Rippon's output for 1924 and 1925 on Twenty chassis was Saloon coachwork, and so were 11 of the 13 bodies in 1926 and nine of the 10 bodies in 1927. Yet there was plenty of room for variation in design. Some were six-light and some were four-light designs, and GKM40 from 1928 was a six-light with a fashionable vee-windscreen. In 1938, Rippon also rebodied a 1927 Twenty chassis, GRJ21, as a Saloon; it had originally carried a Weymann Saloon body by HJ Mulliner. The full list of 49 bodies, with dates, is below.

85K8	1923	GSK78	1925	GHJ23	1927
89K5	1923	GCK5	1925	GHK32	1927
GH78	1923	GCK6	1925	GHJ44	1927
GAK22	1924	GCK7	1925	GHJ57	1927
GAK35	1924	GCK19	1925	GHJ61	1927
GMK58	1924	GCK64	1926	GHJ67	1927
GMK78	1924	GCK67	1926	GAJ14	1927
GRK63	1924	GOK26	1926	GAJ51	1927
GRK67	1924	GOK38	1926	GYL1	1928
GDK25	1924	GOK45	1926	GYL14	1928
GDK37	1924	GUK73	1926	GKM12	1928
GDK74	1924	GYK5	1926	GKM40	1928
GNK20	1925	GYK26	1926	GLN81	1929
GNK40	1925	GYK31	1926	GLN85	1929
GSK30	1925	GYK42	1926	GVO15	1929
GSK36	1925	GMJ23	1926		
GSK42	1925	GMJ50	1927		

Tourer

There were just three Tourer bodies for the Twenty chassis, all in the earlier years of production. These were for 81K7 and GH48 in 1923, and for GMJ31 in 1926.

20/25 COACHWORK

Rippon built 130 bodies for the 20/25 chassis, which made the company one of the more prolific builders on that chassis. The company's best year was 1934, when it bodied no fewer than 40 chassis. Totals in the other years were seven in 1929, eight in 1930, 12 in 1931, 15 in 1932, 26 in 1933 , 20 in 1935, and two in 1936.

It was in this period that Rippon came to the fore as a specialist in Limousines. From an also-ran in the company's output for the Twenty, Limousines became the most numerous of all body types on the 20/25, with a total of 66 built. That represented 50% of all Rippon bodies for the 20/25. Saloons accounted for a large proportion of the other bodies, with a total of 52, and the remainder of the total was made up by a variety of small-volume types.

The company also rebodied some 20/25 chassis in later years, among others building shooting brake (estate) bodies in the late 1940s on GPS21, GAU19 and probably also GBA56. Rippon also supposedly built the ambulance body that was mounted to GLR69 in 1939.

Coupés

For convenience, the two Coupé bodies that Rippon built are listed together here, although they were very different from one another. The earlier one was a most unusual four-light Fixed-head Coupé for chassis GEX24 in 1933, and the later one was a four-light Saloon Coupé in 1935 for GLG36. Again, most unlike typical Rippon designs, this one contained hints of Gurney Nutting practice and was also fitted with rear-wheel spats.

Drophead Coupé

Only one Drophead Coupé came from Rippon on a 20/25 chassis, and that was in 1929 when GDP5 was bodied as a three-quarters type with a Dickey seat.

Landaulettes

Rippon built seven Landaulette bodies of various types on 20/25 chassis between 1931 and 1934. The body for GNS71 in 1931 was described as a Saloon Landaulette. The full list was as follows:

GNS69	1931	GBT48	1932	GUB66	1934
GNS71	1931	GHW16	1932	GWE51	1934
GOS77	1931				

Limousines

Limousines were a popular choice all the way through the period of 20/25 production from 1929 to 1935, although there were none in 1936. The Rippon designs conveyed an appropriate air of gravitas and dignity, and always looked solidly built, although their designs were rather conservative. The difference between a six-light Saloon with Division and a Limousine was sometimes not readily discernible, and in cases of doubt a body with occasional seats has been included in the Limousine list below. By this reckoning, Rippon built 66 Limousine bodies for 20/25 chassis.

GXO52	1929	GWP2	1930	GBT36	1932
GXO57	1929	GLR42	1930	GAU12	1932
GXO96	1930	GOS55	1931	GAU19	1932
GDP32	1930	GOS62	1931	GMU3	1932

GMU18	1932	GBA26	1933	GWE28	1934
GMU43	1932	GGA9	1933	GWE40	1934
GMU51	1932	GGA25	1933	GWE75	1934
GMU58	1932	GGA64	1933	GFE12	1934
GRW29	1932	GUB35	1934	GFE38	1934
GRW46	1932	GLB16	1934	GAF2	1934
GRW78	1932	GLB34	1934	GAF47	1934
GAW16	1933	GNC28	1934	GSF39	1935
GAW38	1933	GNC58	1934	GSF66	1935
GEX51	1933	GRC8	1934	GLG49	1935
GEX68	1933	GED66	1934	GPG9	1935
GDX40	1933	GMD19	1934	GPG56	1935
GSY11	1933	GMD54	1934	GYH54	1935
GSY37	1933	GYD5	1934	GOH22	1935
GSY59	1933	GYD61	1934	GBJ60	1935
GLZ76	1933	GYD65	1934	GBJ81	1935
GTZ12	1933	GAE11	1934	GLJ30	1935
GTZ54	1933	GAE49	1934	GLJ76	1935

Saloons

The 52 Saloon bodies included both four-light and six-light designs, although the latter were more numerous. A number of both types were built with a Division, and those are marked with an asterisk (*) in the table below. The body for GSY73 in 1933 had an interesting Brougham-like styling line ahead of each front door, and the body on GBJ30 was another four-light type, this time with the unusual (for Rippon) addition of rear-wheel spats; it was shown at Olympia in 1935.

GXO104	1930	GSY73	1933	GAE64	1934
GGP29	1929	GTZ29	1933	GWE14	1934
GGP32	1929	GTZ45	1933	GAF38	1934
GGP45	1929	GBA11	1933	GSF28	1934
GLR69	1930	GGA52	1933	GSF51	1934
GSR4	1930	GXB5	1933	GYH32	1935
GTR26	1930	GXB35	1933	GOH14	1935
GNS55	1931	GXB50	1934	GOH50	1935
GNS62	1931	GXB80	1934	GOH51	1935
GOS66	1931	GUB52	1934	GBJ11	1935
GOS70*	1931	GLB4	1934	GBJ30	1935
GPS20	1931	GNC52	1934	GCJ9	1935
GPS21	1931	GRC29	1934	GCJ28	1935
GFT62	1931	GRC48	1934	GXK25	1935
GBT39*	1932	GRC67	1934	GXK65	1936
GHW5	1932	GYD60*	1934	GXK79	1936
GEX6*	1933	GYD66*	1934		
GWX10	1933	GAE34	1934		

Sedancas de Ville

There were just two Sedanca de Ville bodies for the 20/25, and these were for chassis GGP78 in 1929 and GHA18 in 1933.

25/30 COACHWORK

Rippon built 42 bodies for the 25/30 chassis, of which 18 were completed in 1936, 19 in 1937, and the final five in 1938. Well over half were Limousines, about 30% were Saloons of one type or another, and there was a single Landaulette. The characteristic Rippon haughtiness was evident in most of these designs.

Landaulette

An unusual commission for Rippon was a Landaulette, the only one the company built for a 25/30 chassis. This was for GZR16 in 1938.

Limousines

The most numerous type of body from Rippon on 25/30 chassis was the Limousine. There were 28 examples in all, only one (for GWN55 in 1936) having the description of a Touring Limousine. Most were quite stiff and formal designs. The list was as follows:

GTL5	1936	GWN36	1936	GRP78	1937
GTL29	1936	GWN55	1936	GMP10	1937
GTL78	1936	GRO73	1937	GMP34	1937
GHL18	1936	GHO9	1937	GLP22	1937
GRM46	1936	GHO53	1937	GAR1	1937
GXM8	1936	GHO62	1937	GAR28	1937
GXM59	1936	GMO20	1937	GGR72	1938
GXM79	1936	GRP21	1937	GGR75	1938
GGM25	1936	GRP48	1937	GZR6	1938
GAN69	1936				

Rippon showed this four-light Saloon at Olympia in 1935, on 20/25 chassis GBJ30. The full rear wheel spats seem somehow out of place, even though they were becoming fashionable.

This Sedanca de Ville body on 1929 20/25 chassis GGP78 was a rarity from Rippon. Once again, it exudes that coachbuilder's air of solid dependability.

Saloons

There were often distinct similarities between Rippon's Saloons and their Limousines, and the formal air was common to both. Of the seven Saloon bodies on 25/30 chassis, four were built with Divisions; these are marked with an asterisk (*) in the table below.

GRM5	1936	GMO12*	1937	GAR15	1937
GWN15	1936	GLP9	1937	GZR19*	1938
GHO24*	1937				

Sports Saloons

The deep windows and high roof leave no doubt about the nature of this Rippon body on Wraith WMB1 in 1939. It became the official Limousine of the Lord Mayor of Leeds.

There was a somehow business-like air about the Rippon Sports Saloons, which may have had four-light designs but were certainly not overtly sporting. There were six of these rather elegant bodies in 1936-1937, as follows:

GRM28	1936	GAN29	1936	GUN37	1937
GXM42	1936	GAN52	1936	GMP22	1937

WRAITH COACHWORK

Rippon built 15 bodies for the Rolls-Royce Wraith, five of them in 1938 and the other ten in 1939. These were all Saloons or Limousines.

Limousines

Rippon was clearly strongly favoured as a builder of Limousine coachwork in this period, and 11 of its bodies for the Wraith were of this type. The formal Limousines were tall bodies, with deep side glass, supposedly to allow occupants to wear a hat. Characteristic of the Rippon designs was a pillarless division of the rear side glass, giving both the impression of a very long window and an unrestricted view out of the car.

Two were described as Touring Limousines (and are marked with an asterisk (*) in the table below), and one of these, WEC59, had a fashionable razor-edge design. WEC54 and WEC59 were intended for the Rippon stand at the cancelled 1939 Earls Court Show, and WEC54 went to the Ministry of War Transport in 1944, being used by the RAF during the Allied entry to Berlin a year later.

The 11 Limousine bodies on Wraith chassis were as follows:

WXA33	1938	WLB21	1939	WEC11	1939
WRB15*	1938	WLB27	1939	WEC54	1939
WMB1	1939	WHC51	1939	WEC59*	1939
WMB57	1939	WHC81	1939		

Saloons

Some of the four Rippon Saloon bodies for the Wraith made use of the long side window design characteristic of the Limousines. Two made in 1938 were described as "Observation Saloons", and these were for chassis WXA25 and WXA97. WXA25 probably had a Division, and the third 1938 body, a six-light Saloon for WXA53, certainly did. The fourth Rippon Saloon on the Wraith was for WMB42 in 1939.

RIST
Location unknown – Twenty

F Rist & Co is shown in Rolls-Royce records as the builder of a single body on a Twenty chassis. Unfortunately, no information is available about the company itself. The body was a Tourer, built in 1924 on chassis GAK79.

RITCHIES
Location unknown – Twenty

Nothing is known about the coachbuilder called

Ritchies that built a Landaulette body on Rolls-Royce Twenty chassis GVO9 in 1929. Ritchies is not known to have bodied any other small-horsepower Rolls-Royce models.

ROBERTSON

It is likely that the Glasgow coachbuilder John Robertson built all the bodies on Rolls-Royce Twenty chassis that are attributed to the Clyde Automobile Company (qv).

ROCK, THORPE & WATSON
Tunbridge Wells – 20/25, 25/30

Coachbuilder Rock, Thorpe & Watson Ltd came into being some time after 1922, but before this it had traded under several names as partners in the business had changed. It had been founded at Hastings in 1822 as a carriage maker, and had moved to Tunbridge Wells in 1893. Car bodywork followed early in the new century, and before the First World War it was building bodies for Rolls-Royce Silver Ghost chassis (as Rock, Thorpe & Chatfield). A Phantom I body followed in the 1920s.

The company also held agencies for several different makes of car, and built coachwork for some of them, notably Armstrong-Siddeley and Renault. Its clientele seems to have been largely local, in the Kent area. It remained in business until 1946, when it was bought by Caffyns (qv) for its dealership activities.

20/25 COACHWORK

Rock, Thorpe & Watson built four bodies on Rolls-Royce 20/25 chassis. Two were Limousines, for GWP7 and GLR67, and both were built in 1930. Also in 1930, there was an All-weather Tourer for GTR31. The fourth body was a four-light Saloon de Ville for GTK54 in 1936.

25/30 COACHWORK

There was just one body from this company for a 25/30 chassis, and that was a six-light Saloon that was built in 1938 for GGR22.

ROLLS-ROYCE
Derby – Twenty

It is perhaps a little unfair to suggest that the body that Rolls-Royce built at Derby in 1920 for the first experimental Goshawk chassis, 1-G-I, qualified as coachwork. As Ian Rimmer explains it in Rolls-Royce and Bentley Experimental Cars, it was "a very simple tulip style plywood test body… to enable testing to get under way." For the sake of completeness, it is included here.

ROSS
Location unknown – Twenty

The Ross Engineering Co constructed coachwork on two Rolls-Royce Twenty chassis for the same customer in 1923. Nothing is known about the company itself, but it may have been located in Herefordshire, where the two cars were registered. They were on chassis 56S3, which was bodied as a Saloon, and on GA72, which was given a Tourer body.

SALMONS
Newport Pagnell – Twenty, 20/25, 25/30

Founded in 1820 at Newport Pagnell, Buckinghamshire, Salmons & Sons remained in family ownership until 1939. It built its first car bodies in 1898, and from early on specialised in a variety of fabric-roof types, which it generally described as all-weather bodies (although the variety of types went way beyond the standard meaning of an All-weather).

Its major success came with the introduction of the Tickford patented winding-head design, named after the street where the coachbuilder's works was located. Announced in 1925 and available during 1926, this allowed the fabric top hamper to be raised or lowered by winding a handle, so simplifying an otherwise tedious operation. These evolved from 1928 into the Sunshine Saloon.

From 1932, the Tickford winding head was largely

The distinction between Saloon and Limousine was certainly tested by this body from Rippon, which was for Wraith chassis WXA53 in 1938. The coachbuilder called it a Saloon with Division.

Ritchies, a virtually unknown coachbuilder, produced this Landaulette body for Twenty GVO9 in 1929. (Real Car Company)

This Tourer body for Twenty GF12 in 1923 was an early Salmons production.

superseded by a three-position Drophead Coupé design, still with winding handle; and then from 1936 the supremely elegant Tickford Drophead Coupés depended on a spring mechanism to assist with raising and lowering the hood. After the Second World War, Salmons adopted the name of Tickford and focused on contract work for the likes of Alvis, Daimler, and Humber. Bought in 1955 by David Brown, they then worked exclusively for Aston Martin and Lagonda.

More recently, their focus has been on engineering services rather than coachbuilding.

Salmons & Sons built a total of 55 bodies for small Rolls-Royce chassis between 1923 and 1937, but there were none for the later Wraith models. There were 25 for the Twenty, a further 25 for the 25/30, and just five for the 25/30.

TWENTY COACHWORK
Salmons & Sons delivered the first of their 25 bodies for the Rolls-Royce Twenty in 1923, and the last in 1929. The annual totals suggest that demand fluctuated considerably: there were six bodies in 1923, just two in 1924, four in 1925, seven in 1926, one in 1927, three in 1928 and two in 1929. Despite the company's acknowledged expertise with folding-head bodies, these did not dominate its output for the Twenty. There were a few early Tourers and a couple of Landaulettes, but

Fairly typical of Saloon bodies for the early Twenty is this one by Salmons for GNK69 in 1925.

there were also several Coupés, Limousines and Saloons. After the winding-head Tickford body became available in 1925, it attracted a healthy number of orders.

The company also rebodied at least three Twenty chassis after production of the model had ended. The known ones are GPK70 (a 1925 chassis rebodied as a Sedanca Coupé in 1934); GCK65 (a 1926 chassis rebodied as a Tickford Cabriolet); and GOK64 (a 1926 chassis rebodied as a Drophead Coupé in the 1930s).

Coupés
There were five Coupés of various types between 1923 and 1926. The earliest, on GA38 in 1923, was strictly a "three-quarters" type with additional side windows. The 1924 and 1925 deliveries were simple Coupés, and were on chassis GDK71 and GSK53 respectively. There was then another "three-quarters" type in 1926 on GOK58, and the last one was a neat Golfer's Coupé on GMJ18, delivered the same year.

Drophead Coupés
As is so often the case, descriptions of bodies can vary. However, it looks as if there were three bodies on the Twenty chassis that could reasonably be described as Drophead Coupé types. The earliest was delivered in 1924 on chassis GAK4 and has also been described as a Cabriolet. The other two were both "three-quarters" types, and were for GMJ15 in 1926 and GTM14 in 1928.

Landaulettes
Two Salmons Landaulette bodies are recorded on the Twenty chassis. These were on 59S9 in 1923 and GOK21 in 1926.

Limousines
There were no fewer than five Limousine bodies from Salmons for the Twenty between 1925 and 1929. The first three (on GNK27, GNK28 and GNK69) were all built in 1925. There was then one in 1926, on GMJ14, and the last one was delivered in 1929 on GLN5.

Saloons
The Salmons mixture was leavened with a pair of orders for Saloon bodies on the Twenty. These were delivered on chassis GF74 in 1923 and on GLN64 in 1929.

Tickford Cabriolets
The winding-head Tickford Cabriolet entered production in 1926 and it appears that Salmons & Sons built five of them for the Twenty chassis. These

are sometimes described as Saloon Cabriolets, but it seems most sensible to use the Tickford brand name to describe them here. There were two of them in 1926, for chassis GUK40 and GUK56. Just one was delivered in 1927, on GUJ4, and the last two were 1928 deliveries, on GYL26 and GBM71.

Tourers
The three Tourer bodies were all ordered early in the Twenty's production run, and were delivered in 1923. They were on chassis 73A1, 88K1 and GF12.

20/25 COACHWORK
Salmons & Sons built a total of 25 bodies for new 20/25 chassis between 1929 and 1936. There were two in each of the years 1929, 1931 and 1934; three in 1930 and 1933; four in 1932; eight in 1935; and just one in 1936. The majority were versions of their Tickford winding-head design (now generally described as a Tickford Saloon), but there was a smattering of other types as well. One body, a Saloon on chassis GAU24, was built under contract to the London coachbuilder Whittingham & Mitchel.

Drophead Coupé
The body for GBA60 in 1933 has been rather grandly described as a three-position Drophead Sedanca Coupé, but was simply an early iteration of the three-position drophead style that would later become a staple Salmons product.

Limousine de Ville
Salmons & Sons built a single six-light Limousine de Ville body in 1930, for chassis number GNS43. The body was later converted to a Tickford (ie winding-head) configuration.

Saloon
There was just one Saloon, a four-door type that was built for Whittingham & Mitchel in 1932 on chassis GAU24.

Tickford styles
The remaining 22 bodies on 20/25 chassis were all variants of the Tickford winding-head style. All had four doors, but some were four-light types and others had a six-light design (such as GSR10, GSY47, GOH16, GEH26 and GBK46). Some were built with a Division (such as GFT74, GEH26 and GLJ20).

Most were Tickford Saloons, but at least two were examples of the "Jubilee" four-light design introduced for 1935 where the folded hood sat more nearly flush with the rear of the body. This was a more

This Salmons Landaulette is noticeably more rigid and upright than the contemporary Saloon illustrated above. It was built for Twenty chassis GOK21 in 1926.

rakish design than the standard Tickford Saloon, but of course featured fixed cantrails and the winding head. The two were GPG37 and GBJ21. The Jubilee name celebrated 25 years of building "open-closed" bodies according to a Salmons advertisement, and of course 1935 was also the Jubilee year of King George V.

The full list, with dates of their construction, is as follows:

GXO46	1929	GRW52	1932	GOH16	1935
GGP62	1929	GSY47	1933	GOH66	1935
GGP26	1930	GGA74	1933	GEH26	1935
GSR10	1930	GED21	1934	GBJ21	1935
GFT70	1931	GED35	1934	GLJ20	1935
GFT74	1931	GRF11	1935	GBK46	1936
GAU55	1932	GPG11	1935		
GAU57	1932	GPG37	1935		

25/30 COACHWORK
Salmons & Sons constructed five bodies for the 25/30 chassis in 1936-1937. Despite differing descriptions, the "Sedanca Coupé" on GXM5 in 1936 and the "three-position Drophead Coupé" on GHO48 in 1937 had essentially the same design. There were two four-light Tickford bodies with only detail differences for GHO56 and GRP32 in 1937, and the fifth body was a Limousine for GHO65, also in 1937.

The famous Tickford winding head is seen here in mid-deployment on a 1932 20/25 chassis, GAU55 by Salmons. (Real Car Company)

Built in 1933 for 20/25 chassis GBA60, this Salmons carefully-named "three-position Drophead Sedanca Coupé" was pictured with a proud owner at one of the concours d'élégance events common in the 1930s. (Copyright unknown)

SANDERSON & HOLMES
Derby – Twenty

Sanderson & Holmes was established in Derby in the late 1880s from an earlier carriage builder called Holmes. The company developed as motor engineers and coachbuilders, and later held a number of car dealer franchises. By 1927, the company's press advertisements aimed to catch the eye of Rolls-Royce owners bringing their cars to the factory at Derby for mechanical work; the idea was that coachwork maladies could be dealt with on the same visit.

The company built six bodies for the Rolls-Royce Twenty chassis between 1923 and 1927. Four of these were Coupé types, for 80A0 in 1923, GNK12 and GSK32 in 1925 (GNK12 was a three-quarter Coupé), and GRJ42 in 1927. The other two bodies were a Tourer for GF15 in 1923, and a Landaulette for GF49 in the same year.

SEWELL
Location unknown – Twenty

A company called Sewell is recorded as the builder of a Coupé body for Twenty chassis GF10 in 1923. Unfortunately, no further details of the company or its likely location have been found.

SHINNIE
Aberdeen – Twenty

R&J Shinnie was an Aberdeen coachbuilder formed by two brothers in the middle of the 19th century as a carriage maker. It built horse trams during the 1870s and its first car body in 1898. From 1919 it was also constructing charabancs and single-deck buses, including many for the Aberdeen Corporation fleet. Robert Shinnie died in 1924 and the company was voluntarily wound up the following year. Shinnie built a single body for the

Rolls-Royce Twenty chassis, which was a Coupé for GRK70 in 1924.

SHORT
Winchester – 20/25

Not to be confused with Shorts (see below), a Winchester company called Will Short Ltd was responsible for a single body on an early Rolls-Royce 20/25 chassis.

This was a Limousine delivered in November 1929 on chassis GXO83. The chassis was early enough to have been built as a Twenty (GVO59) but was modified appropriately by Rolls-Royce and renumbered before delivery.

SHORTS
Rochester – Twenty

The company shown in the record for Twenty chassis GYK23 as the builder of its Three-quarter Coupé body is Shorts. The completed car was registered in 1926 with a Kent registration number to an owner recorded as L Short, and it seems most likely that the body was built by the aviation company Short Brothers for a member of the owning family.

Short Brothers were well established at Rochester in Kent but the aircraft business went through a difficult period in the early 1920s. In order to keep the company afloat, Shorts diversified into coachbuilding, building a few car bodies but focussing mainly on lightweight bus and coach bodies that employed some aircraft construction principles.

SIMPSON
Location unknown – Twenty

A coachbuilder named Simpson created the Landaulette coachwork on a Rolls-Royce Twenty for the Raja of Bobbili (in modern Andhra Pradesh, India) in 1923. The recipient chassis was numbered GH26, but there is no further information about the identity of the coachbuilder.

SIMPSON & SLATER
Nottingham – Twenty, 20/25

Simpson & Slater was an old-established company in Nottingham that bodied a few high-quality chassis in the 1920s but would become best known for its hearse and shooting brake bodies. It was responsible for one body on a Rolls-Royce Twenty chassis, and one other on a 20/25.

The body for a Twenty chassis was a Tourer that was built in 1923 for chassis 56S6. The one for a 20/25 was a Saloon for GWE24 in 1934, and had the Continental style that was popular at the time.

SINCLAIR
St Annes – Twenty

Sinclair & Co was a coachbuilder at St Annes-on-Sea in Lancashire that was active during the 1920s. The company provided coachwork on at least two Bentley chassis and also on a single Rolls-Royce Twenty. This car had chassis number GAK81 and was bodied as a Saloon in 1924.

SMITH, GW
Stockport – Twenty

The coachbuilder GW Smith 1925 Ltd was a Stockport company that was active in the 1920s and bodied a large Sunbeam in addition to the two Rolls-Royce Twenty chassis for which it is known.

These were both Saloons, the earlier one being delivered in 1926 on chassis GYK80, and the later on GRJ39 in 1927.

STARTIN
Birmingham – Twenty, 20/25

The Birmingham coachbuilder Thomas Startin was founded in 1840 and was owned by the same family until 1987. Later trading as Thomas Startin Jr Ltd, its primary business was in commercial vehicle bodies and hearses, and the company still exists today as part of the Startin Group. It built two bodies on the small-horsepower Rolls-Royce chassis.

The first one was a Saloon, built in 1926 on Twenty chassis GOK35. The later one was a six-light D-back Limousine that was delivered in March 1931 on 20/25 chassis number GOS27.

STEANE
Location unknown – Twenty

A company recorded as J Steane built a single body on the Rolls-Royce Twenty chassis in 1925. Nothing is known about the company, but the car originally carried a Bournemouth registration number and it is possible that the company was locally based. The body was a rather elegant six-light Limousine, and the chassis was GLK72.

STEVENSON
Glasgow

JB Stevenson was a Scottish coachbuilder based in Glasgow that was active in the 1920s and 1930s. It displayed a Tourer body on an Austin 20 chassis at the 1921 Scottish Motor Show and in 1939 was supplying catalogued two-seater bodies for Lea-Francis.

The company built a single body for the small-horsepower Rolls-Royce chassis. This was a Tourer on Twenty GFN20 in 1929.

SW COACHWORKS
Location unknown – Twenty

No information is available about the SW Coachworks recorded as builder of a Tourer body for Twenty chassis GNK34 in 1925. John Fasal shows the car with a Paisley registration number, which may give a clue to the coachbuilder's location.

TAYLORS
Probably Wolverhampton – Twenty

Some bodies on the Rolls-Royce Twenty chassis are listed as by Taylor, and others as by Taylors. They were probably all by L & LT Taylor Ltd, a Wolverhampton company which in that form traded from 1922. The company built both commercial bodywork and car coachwork, and there are records of seven bodies on Rolls-Royce Twenty chassis. After 1930, the company changed hands and its name changed to Holbrook & Taylors.

Five of those bodies on the Twenty chassis date from 1925, and there was one each in 1923 and 1924. Taylors constructed both open and closed coachwork, displaying the versatility that was needed by provincial coachbuilders if they were to remain in business.

Three of the Twenty bodies were Saloons; these were for chassis GF52 (1923), GLK3 and GLK30 (both 1925). There was one Three-quarter Coupé (GMK3, 1924) and one Coupé (GRK68, 1925). The other two were both open bodies delivered in 1925. They were a Tourer for GNK3 and a Cabriolet for GNK61.

It is worth noting that GMK3 was registered as FY 7023 in Southport, Lancashire. This would suggest either that Taylors had an unusually wide catchment area for a provincial coachbuilder or that the body was built by another company with the same name. The registration numbers of the other six cars listed here are not known.

One of just two bodies that Startin built for the 20/25 chassis was this six-light D-back Limousine for GOS27 in 1931. It certainly fulfilled the requirement to look imposing.

THRUPP & MABERLY

London – Twenty, 20/25, 25/30, Wraith

Thrupp & Maberly was established in London's West End in 1858, when two older coachbuilders merged. It soon became a leading practitioner, and George Thrupp gained additional fame after 1877 when he wrote *The History of the Art of Coachbuilding*, still seen today as the definitive work on its subject. By 1896 the company was building motor car bodies.

In 1924, Thrupp & Maberly moved to new premises in Cricklewood, next door to the Rolls-Royce London Repair Depot. Whether their purchase by the Rootes Brothers the following year was related to this move is not clear, but the new owners made no attempt to move the company down-market. Thrupp & Maberly continued to build grand and well-respected coachwork on a variety of larger chassis, including Bentley and Rolls-Royce (for whom they bodied many New Phantoms and their successors in the 1930s). Overseen from 1928 by the Humber division of the Rootes empire, they also built coachwork for the grander chassis of that marque. In 1929, they constructed the body for Sir Henry Segrave's Golden Arrow land speed record car.

The company bodied at least 83 Rolls-Royce Twenty chassis from new, a huge total of 474 20/25 chassis, 206 of its 25/30 successor, and 42 of the Wraith chassis. During the 1939-1945 war, it was best known for its saloon and open tourer bodies on Humber staff cars, but subsequently ceased traditional coachbuilding and focused on special bodies only for the Rootes Group. In the 1960s, that work gradually dried up, and after Chrysler took control of the Rootes Group in 1967, Thrupp & Maberly ceased operations. It was wound up in 1968.

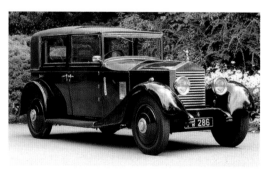

Thrupp & Maberly began building Sedanca bodies for the Twenty quite late on. This one was for chassis GBM42 in 1928. With the front section of the roof removed, it offers the right amount of pomp and circumstance for a De Ville design, and with the roof section in place it makes a solid-looking four-light Saloon. (Real Car Company)

TWENTY COACHWORK

Of the 83 known bodies for the Rolls-Royce Twenty that came from Thrupp & Maberly, the largest number were Limousines. There were 26 of those, and the next most numerous type was the Landaulette, of which there were 16.

Cabriolets

Six Twenty chassis received Cabriolet coachwork from Thrupp & Maberly between 1923 and 1928. The first two were for chassis GF30 and GF33 in 1923, but there was then a gap of four years until the next one was built for GAJ43 in 1927. The final three were all built in 1928, and were for chassis GXL66, GYL46 and GYL64.

Coupés

Four of the ten Coupé bodies for the Twenty were three-quarter types, and these are marked with an asterisk (*) in the table below. Once again, there was a four-year gap between the earliest cars and the later examples.

62H3	1923	GAJ75	1927	GKM68	1928
GA21	1923	GUJ48*	1927	GTM31*	1928
GA59	1923	GYL68	1928	GTM37*	1928
GHJ4*	1927				

Drophead Coupé

Thrupp & Maberly built just one Drophead Coupé body for the Rolls-Royce Twenty, and this was for chassis GUK8 in 1926. It was a three-quarter type.

Landaulettes

There was a fairly consistent demand for Landaulette bodies on the Twenty, and Thrupp & Maberly built a total of 16, as follows:

61H1	1923	GUK41	1926	GYL81	1928
GDK63	1924	GMJ76	1927	GBM5	1928
GSK22	1925	GHJ29	1927	GBM57	1928
GCK20	1925	GUJ66	1927	GFN75	1929
GZK5	1926	GYL35	1928	GLN75	1929
GZK9	1926				

Limousines
There was a steady demand for Limousine bodies from Thrupp & Maberly, although none were built for the Twenty chassis in 1924. The full list of 26, with dates, is as follows:

GA77	1923	GAJ5	1927	GBM54	1928
GLK55	1925	GAJ9	1927	GBM64	1928
GSK37	1925	GAJ17	1927	GKM32	1928
GOK39	1926	GAJ50	1927	GKM78	1928
GUK3	1926	GRJ56	1927	GFN18	1928
GYK4	1926	GRJ71	1927	GLN57	1929
GYK12	1926	GXL4	1927	GVO18	1929
GYK37	1926	GXL43	1927	GVO63	1929
GMJ19	1926	GYL12	1928		

Saloons
Nine Saloon bodies were delivered between 1925 and 1929, and were on the following chassis:

GNK6	1925	GUK38	1926	GYL27	1928
GOK52	1926	GUK42	1926	GTM27	1928
GOK64	1926	GMJ1	1926	GLN19	1929

Sedancas
There were also nine Sedanca bodies, the first of which was not built until 1927. The full list, with dates, is below.

GRJ81	1927	GKM52	1928	GLN83	1929
GBM26	1928	GKM61	1928	GEN51	1929
GBM42	1928	GLN24	1929	GEN70	1929

Tourers
Six Tourer bodies were built for the Twenty between 1924 and 1929. The last one, for chassis GLN39, became a Rolls-Royce trials car (ie a demonstrator)

before eventually finding a new owner in India. The six chassis, with dates, were:

GDK80	1924	GOK65	1926	GRJ80	1927
GCK59	1925	GZK81	1926	GLN39	1929

20/25 COACHWORK
There were 474 Thrupp & Maberly bodies on new Rolls-Royce 20/25 chassis, of which by far the largest number were Limousines. There were 255 of these, and Saloons came next with a total of 131 examples.

Thrupp & Maberly made wide use of standard designs during the 20/25 era, introducing new ones from time to time in order to keep their products looking fresh. However, orders for an older design were often completed alongside the first examples of a new one, and the company remained ready to produce bespoke designs as well.

When RI Musselwhite left Thrupp & Maberly in 1930 to revive the old Cunard company (qv) with VE Freestone from Freestone & Webb, he sub-contracted some coachwork orders to Thrupp & Maberly. One was a Landaulette on chassis GSR63 in 1930. Also likely to have been built by Thrupp & Maberly was the Sedanca de Ville body for Cunard's GNS25 later the same year.

Thrupp & Maberly also rebodied several 20/25s. Tom Clarke lists these as GXO92, GSO23, GGP21, GEX71, GTZ41, GMD44, GPG18, GLJ22, GCJ8, and possibly GBK7.

All-weathers
All-weather bodies were not a regular part of the Thrupp & Maberly repertoire for the Rolls-Royce 20/25, but three examples were built as one-offs. The earliest of these was described as an All-weather Kellner Cabriolet and was for chassis GAU76 in 1932; this

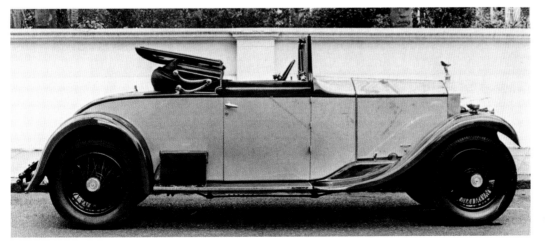

Twenty GXO92 was new in 1929 and initially carried a Saloon body by TH Gill & Sons, but as early as March 1930 it was rebodied by Thrupp & Maberly as a Drophead Coupé. (Frank Dale & Stepsons)

presumably incorporated design elements patented by the Parisian coachbuilder Kellner.

For the body on GRW30 in 1932, the company once again used another company's design under licence. In this case, the six-light coachwork incorporated the Tickford folding-head patents held by Salmons & Sons, although it was recorded by Rolls-Royce as an All-weather type. The last of the three was an All-weather Saloon for chassis GUB41 in 1934. Tom Clarke describes this body as a four-door Faux Cabriolet type with a pillarless upper B-post.

Coupés

Coupé bodies were not numerous in the Thrupp & Maberly output for the 20/25 chassis, and there were just seven in all – including one body that was actually a Saloon Coupé. This was for chassis GLR12. At least three shared a design known as R170/A, and these were for chassis GXO62, GDP43 and GLR8. The body for GXO12 had design number R164, and that for GDP34 was a "three-quarter" type (that is, a four-light design). The full list is below.

GXO12	1929	GDP43	1930	GLR8	1930
GXO62	1929	GWP3	1930	GLR12	1930
GDP34	1930				

De Ville types

There were 42 De Ville bodies of various types.

Four of these were Cabriolet de Ville types, which were for chassis GGP5 in 1929, GWP6 in 1930, GFT34 in 1931, and GEX81 in 1933.

Five bodies were Limousine de Ville types. These were for chassis GDP33 in 1929, GDP11 and GNS44 in 1930, GBT14 in 1932, and GSF24 in 1934.

The largest number of these De Ville body types were Sedancas de Ville, of which there were 19 examples. (Note that the body on GNS3 is described in records as a "Fixed cabriolet de ville".) These were on the following chassis:

GXO31	1929	GWX59	1933	GMD8	1934
GXO67	1929	GLZ47	1933	GWE70	1934
GTR19	1930	GTZ7	1933	GFE8	1934
GNS3	1930	GTZ35	1933	GAF35	1934
GAU69	1932	GNC74	1934	GSF59	1935
GRW27	1932	GRC34	1934	GRF19	1935
GAW10	1933				

In 1933, Thrupp & Maberly introduced a three-position Sedanca Coupé style that proved popular.

It is not clear how many different designs were used among the 14 examples built, but from late 1934 the leading design was numbered TF961/C. Included here for convenience are the bodies for GAE58 (described uniquely as a Drophead Sedanca Coupé) and GSF68 (a "Fixed-head Sedanca Coupé").

These bodies were on the following chassis:

GTZ74	1933	GAE58	1934	GPG18	1935
GXB36	1933	GAE80	1934	GYH62	1935
GXB69	1934	GAF81	1934	GEH30	1935
GUB30	1934	GSF36	1934	GCJ8	1935
GKC38	1934	GSF68	1935		

Drophead Coupés

Drophead Coupés were not one of the more numerous body types from Thrupp & Maberly on the 20/25 chassis, but became more popular from 1933. In all, 11 examples were built between 1930 and 1935, but note that the body on GYZ25 in 1933 is not confirmed as a Drophead Coupé. The body for GXO94 in 1930 had a dickey seat, and the one for GGA54 in 1933 was a three-position type. The 11 bodies were on the following chassis:

GXO94	1930	GYZ25	1933	GED10	1934
GFT67	1931	GGA54	1933	GMD39	1934
GBT62	1932	GUB 73	1934	GBJ79	1935
GLZ9	1933	GNC31	1934		

Landaulettes

There were 23 Landaulette bodies, with some different designs. The earliest example, for GGP48 in 1930, had design number V114/B, and the standard design for 1935 and 1935 was TC1015/F. The body on GLR78 in 1930 was described as a Saloon Landaulette. The list is as follows:

GGP48	1930	GDX1	1933	GLB2	1934
GDP66	1930	GLZ35	1933	GED69	1934
GLR78	1930	GLZ62	1933	GFE28	1934
GSR81	1930	GLZ64	1933	GEH41	1935
GNS24	1931	GTZ5	1933	GBJ71	1935
GBT38	1932	GTZ27	1933	GLJ51	1935
GWX71	1933	GGA79	1933	GTK51	1936
GWX78	1933	GUB36	1934		

Limousines

Limousines accounted for by far the largest number of bodies on the 20/25 by Thrupp & Maberly, and there were no fewer than 255 of them. Various designs were used over the years: the earliest example, on GXO75 in 1929, had number R213/B; a design 108 followed, of which there were A and B variants, and then in 1931 design TC447A appeared. By mid-1933 there was a TC761, which continued into 1934, and during that year the primary design became TC878/C. New during 1935 was TC1015/D, and by the end of the year this had become TC1015/G. The last "volume" design was TC1138, which appeared in 1936.

Many of these Limousines were described in records simply as "standard" types. This probably means that they had the design that was standard at the time they were built. However, it would be unwise to assume that all those not designated as "standard" were necessarily bespoke designs.

Three Thrupp & Maberly Limousines became trials (demonstration) cars. GRW70 in 1932 later passed to the Rolls-Royce School of Instruction; GYZ3, a "standard" Limousine from 1933, did its duty in India; and GAE20X from 1934 carried a D-back Limousine body. This last named had spent some time as an experimental car at Rolls-Royce, attracting the X in its chassis number.

The Thrupp & Maberly Limousines on Rolls-Royce 20/25 chassis are listed in the table below.

On both the 20/25 and 25/30 chassis, Thrupp & Maberly were best known as builders of Limousines. This one was for 20/25 GMU29 in 1932. *(Real Car Company)*

GAU6	1932	GRW3	1932	GSY2	1933
GAU8	1932	GRW6	1932	GSY61	1933
GAU46	1932	GRW14	1932	GSY67	1933
GAU50	1932	GRW55	1932	GSY70	1933
GAU58	1932	GRW65	1932	GSY93	1933
GAU78	1932	GRW70	1932	GSY98	1933
GMU19	1932	GAW36	1933	GLZ3	1933
GMU29	1932	GEX9	1933	GLZ6	1933
GMU32	1932	GEX10	1933	GLZ11	1933
GMU50	1932	GEX26	1933	GLZ33	1933
GZU18	1932	GEX43	1933	GLZ45	1933
GZU19	1932	GEX46	1933	GLZ51	1933
GZU20	1932	GEX73	1933	GLZ69	1933
GZU34	1932	GWX5	1933	GLZ70	1933
GHW2	1932	GWX6	1933	GTZ4	1933
GHW33	1932	GDX5	1933	GTZ14	1933
GHW34	1932	GDX9	1933	GTZ21	1933
GHW54	1932	GDX24	1933	GTZ23	1933
GHW68	1932	GDX25	1933	GTZ42	1933
GHW69	1932	GDX37	1933	GTZ53	1933
GRW1	1932	GDX39	1933	GTZ60	1933

GXO75	1929	GSR80	1930	GBT24	1932
GGP53	1929	GOS51	1931	GBT33	1932
GGP57	1929	GFT10	1931	GBT59	1932
GLR4	1930	GFT65	1931	GBT63	1932
GLR21	1930	GBT16	1931	GBT77	1932
GLR54	1930	GBT19	1932	GKT37	1932

Drophead Coupés looked very different by the time this one was built for 20/25 chassis GNC31 in 1934. It was, of course, a three-position type, which gave the choice of fully open, fully closed, or De Ville mode with the front of the roof remaining open. *(Magic Car Pics)*

The interior of the Drophead Coupé for GNC31 was well-appointed but quite workmanlike, with no deliberately ornate touches. *(Magic Car Pics)*

By 1935, swept tails were becoming fashionable, and this is Thrupp & Maberly's design TC878/G, by this time the "standard" Limousine, on 20/25 chassis GSF50. (Real Car Company)

GLG32	1935	GOH57	1935	GCJ33	1935
GLG42	1935	GOH59	1935	GXK10	1935
GLG46	1935	GOH62	1935	GXK17	1935
GLG47	1935	GOH70	1935	GXK18	1935
GLG70	1935	GOH80	1935	GXK22	1935
GLG74	1935	GEH11	1935	GXK35	1935
GPG27	1935	GEH15	1935	GXK41	1935
GPG33	1935	GEH22	1935	GXK53	1935
GPG39	1935	GEH23	1935	GXK59	1935
GPG48	1935	GEH34	1935	GXK81	1935
GPG52	1935	GBJ18	1935	GBK7	1936
GPG64	1935	GBJ19	1935	GBK20	1936
GHG7	1935	GBJ24	1935	GBK29	1936
GHG34	1935	GBJ40	1935	GBK43	1936
GHG35	1935	GBJ45	1935	GTK18	1936
GYH2	1935	GBJ49	1935	GTK22	1936
GYH24	1935	GBJ69	1935	GTK23	1936
GYH33	1935	GLJ36	1935	GTK27	1936
GYH50	1935	GLJ40	1935	GTK31	1936
GYH61	1935	GLJ49	1935	GTK43	1936
GYH78	1935	GLJ77	1935	GTK45	1936
GYH81	1935	GCJ3	1935	GTK47	1936
GOH4	1935	GCJ20	1935	GTK53	1936
GOH12	1935	GCJ21	1935	GTK56	1936
GOH19	1935	GCJ24	1935	GTK61	1936
GOH33	1935	GCJ29	1935	GTK62	1936
GOH56	1935	GCJ32	1935	GTK63	1936

GTZ61	1933	GUB15	1934	GYD41	1934
GTZ69	1933	GUB39	1934	GYD50	1934
GYZ3	1933	GUB 42	1934	GYD54	1934
GYZ17	1933	GUB57	1934	GYD59	1934
GYZ21	1933	GLB1	1934	GAE7	1934
GYZ31	1933	GLB6	1934	GAE20X	1934
GBA4	1933	GNC32	1934	GAE23	1934
GBA7	1933	GNC43	1934	GAE24	1934
GBA14	1933	GNC67	1934	GAE42	1934
GBA17	1933	GNC73	1934	GAE63	1934
GBA25	1933	GNC80	1934	GWE26	1934
GBA50	1933	GRC5	1934	GWE62	1934
GBA68	1933	GRC11	1934	GWE71	1934
GGA5	1933	GRC74	1934	GWE79	1934
GGA23	1933	GRC75	1934	GAF10	1934
GGA24	1933	GRC76	1934	GAF17	1934
GGA42	1933	GRC79	1934	GAF26	1934
GGA57	1933	GKC10	1934	GAF31	1934
GGA65	1933	GKC22	1934	GAF48	1934
GGA69	1933	GKC27	1934	GAF55	1934
GGA73	1933	GED1	1934	GAF56	1934
GHA4	1933	GED36	1934	GAF61	1934
GHA8	1933	GED76	1934	GAF77	1934
GHA19	1933	GED77	1934	GSF2	1934
GHA23	1933	GMD7	1934	GSF18	1934
GXB2	1933	GMD11	1934	GSF40	1934
GXB12	1933	GMD15	1934	GSF49	1935
GXB14	1933	GMD57	1934	GSF50	1935
GXB42	1934	GYD8	1934	GSF63	1935
GXB61	1934	GYD17	1934	GRF33	1935
GUB9	1934	GYD23	1934	GRF39	1935

Dating from two years later, the body for GXB42 was a "standard" Limousine, and is very similar to its 1932 predecessor; note, though, that the door hinges are concealed on this later body. (Real Car Company)

Saloons

The 131 Thrupp & Maberly Saloons on the 20/25 chassis came as four- and six-light types. An early design was TE484; TF988 was a four-light Sports Saloon introduced in 1935, and TF1012 followed in 1936. Several were built with a Division, which is indicated by an asterisk (*). GSR23, a TE484 design, was displayed at the Paris Salon in 1930. The full list is as follows:

GGP21	1929	GBT50	1932	GHW74	1932
GGP37*	1930	GBT54	1932	GRW18	1932
GGP41*	1929	GAU25	1932	GRW57	1933
GDP27	1930	GAU67	1932	GRW74	1933
GDP36*	1930	GAU73	1932	GRW75	1933
GDP62	1930	GMU63	1932	GAW22*	1933
GSR23	1930	GZU14	1932	GAW29*	1933
GTR20	1930	GZU25	1932	GAW39	1933
GNS74	1931	GZU30	1932	GEX2	1933
GOS60	1931	GZU39	1932	GEX15	1933
GPS28*?	1931	GHW7	1932	GEX60	1933
GFT6	1931	GHW18	1932	GWX20	1933
GFT33	1931	GHW42	1932	GWX22	1933
GFT63	1931	GHW48	1932	GWX27	1933
GFT80	1931	GHW49	1932	GWX31	1933
GBT11	1931	GHW64	1932	GWX35	1933

GWX45	1933	GXB79	1934	GAF20	1934
GWX60	1933	GUB22*	1934	GAF32	1934
GWX70	1933	GUB62	1934	GAF70	1934
GWX74	1933	GUB70	1934	GSF48	1935
GDX33	1933	GNC9*?	1934	GSF69*	1935
GSY28	1933	GNC25	1934	GLG4	1935
GSY49	1933	GNC33	1934	GLG5*	1935
GSY52	1933	GNC55	1934	GLG41	1935
GSY83	1933	GNC61	1934	GLG59	1935
GLZ1	1933	GNC72	1934	GPG7	1935
GLZ49	1933	GRC23	1934	GPG14	1935
GLZ80	1933	GRC50	1934	GPG46	1935
GYZ4	1933	GKC5	1934	GHG31*	1935
GYZ37	1933	GKC15	1934	GYH42	1935
GBA31	1933	GED9	1934	GOH18	1935
GBA46	1933	GED33	1934	GOH41	1935
GBA52	1933	GED57	1934	GBJ5	1935
GBA73	1933	GMD18*	1934	GBJ39	1935
GBA77	1933	GMD44	1934	GBJ54	1935
GGA8	1933	GMD64	1934	GBJ66	1935
GGA19	1933	GMD80	1934	GBJ67	1935
GGA67	1933	GYD29	1934	GBJ78	1935
GHA39	1933	GYD36	1934	GLJ10	1935
GXB31	1934	GAE32	1934	GLJ64	1935
GXB41	1934	GWE27	1934	GLJ72	1935
GXB44	1934	GWE61	1934	GBK64	1936
GXB47	1934	GFE30*	1934	GTK30	1936
GXB51	1934	GAF11*	1934		

Tourers

Tourer bodies went out of fashion in the early 1930s, and Thrupp & Maberly built only two for the Rolls-Royce 20/25 chassis. These were for GXO15 and GXO71, both in 1929.

25/30 COACHWORK

Thrupp & Maberly built a total of 206 bodies on new Rolls-Royce 25/30 chassis, including one on the prototype of the chassis. The company's most successful designs on the 25/30 chassis were Limousines, of which there were 76 in three main types. Next most numerous were Saloons and Sports Saloons (65). There were also a few Landaulettes, all derived from Limousine designs, a handful of Six-light Saloons, and a smattering of other individual types.

Landaulettes

There were three Landaulettes in 1936-1937, all of them based on six-light Limousine designs and retaining the design numbers of the parent Limousines. The first two were TC1138/D types, derived from the Standard Limousine TC1138.

The third one was derived from design TC1254 and seems to have retained that design designation without any distinguishing suffix. The three bodies were built for chassis GRM80 in 1936, and for GHO57 and GAR55 in 1937.

Limousines

Thrupp & Maberly built 124 Limousine bodies for the 20/25 chassis, using three major design families. These three were TC1015/G, TC1254, and TC1138.

Design TC1015/G was a D-back Limousine that had first appeared on the late 20/25 chassis and was used on the prototype 25/30. A total of 27 examples were built on 25/30 chassis. Note that the body on GRM2 in 1936 is recorded as a TC1015/G type but has a swept tail rather than a D-back; it may have been some kind of prototype for the later bodies with this feature.

22-G-V	1936	GUL74	1936	GHL4	1936
GUL3	1936	GTL3	1936	GHL30	1936
GUL8	1936	GTL34	1936	GRM2	1936
GUL10	1936	GTL40	1936	GRM61	1936
GUL31	1936	GTL44	1936	GXM2	1936
GUL42	1936	GTL45	1936	GXM9	1936
GUL53	1936	GTL54	1936	GXM17	1936
GUL63	1936	GTL57	1936	GXM27	1936
GUL65	1936	GTL62	1936	GAN31	1936

Design TC1254 then appeared in early spring 1937 as the successor to TC1015/G, and 49 examples (including variants) were built on the 25/30 chassis between then and the middle of 1938. The first one, on chassis GHO43, was used for the Coronation of King George VI before finding a permanent home in India. There were four variants of the design with minor differences, and these were TC1254, TC1254/B, TC1254/C and TC1254/J. All had the same basic design with six windows, occasional seats, and a boot lid that curved inwards to match the swept lines of the lower tail.

There were six examples of variant TC1254/B, all built in 1937. They were GMO39, GRP5, GRP23, GRP62, GRP67 and GMP19. GRP23 spent its first year or so as a demonstrator for Rootes. There was one example each of TC1254/C (GRP74) and TC1254/J (GGR56).

GHO43	1937	GMO39	1937	GRP42	1937
GHO67	1937	GRP5	1937	GRP47	1937
GMO17	1937	GRP23	1937	GRP53	1937
GMO18	1937	GRP28	1937	GRP62	1937

GRP67	1937	GLP7	1937	GGR21	1938
GRP74	1937	GAR4	1937	GGR27	1938
GMP1	1937	GAR9	1937	GGR35	1938
GMP7	1937	GAR11	1937	GGR39	1938
GMP11	1937	GAR16	1937	GGR52	1938
GMP19	1937	GAR35	1937	GGR55	1938
GMP29	1937	GAR38	1937	GGR56	1938
GMP32	1937	GAR49	1937	GGR60	1938
GMP41	1937	GAR58	1937	GGR64	1938
GMP45	1937	GAR63	1937	GGR67	1938
GMP48	1937	GAR68	1938	GZR14	1938
GMP52	1937	GAR71	1938		
GLP2	1937	GGR4	1938		

Between 1936 and 1938 there was an alternative design that was known as the Standard Limousine. This was numbered TC1138, and 48 examples were built on new chassis. This was a very upright and formal body, and the description of "standard" presumably meant that only minimal variation from a standard specification was possible, thus reducing costs a little. The example on chassis GAN54 of 1936 spent some time as a trials and promotional car. Note that the identification of the body on GGR9 from 1938 as a Standard Limousine is tentative; it could possibly have been an example of the TC1254 design.

GRM52	1936	GWN4	1936	GRO24	1937
GXM20	1936	GWN12	1936	GRO32	1937
GXM45	1936	GWN16	1936	GRO35	1937
GXM49	1936	GWN18	1936	GRO47	1937
GXM71	1936	GWN59	1936	GRO52	1937
GGM16	1936	GWN72	1936	GHO10	1937
GGM29	1936	GUN5	1937	GHO23	1937
GAN1	1936	GUN15	1937	GHO30	1937
GAN5	1936	GUN19	1937	GHO40	1937
GAN12	1936	GUN21	1937	GHO76	1937
GAN14	1936	GUN22	1937	GHO78	1937
GAN38	1936	GUN34	1937	GHO79	1937
GAN53	1936	GUN38	1937	GMO22	1937
GAN54	1936	GRO15	1937	GMO29	1937
GAN76	1936	GRO17	1937	GLP11	1937
GAN77	1936	GRO23	1937	GGR9	1938

Saloons (four-light) and Sports Saloons

There were 65 Four-light Saloons or Sports Saloons, that description probably being used interchangeably to suit the customer. The earliest of these designs was number TF988/E; TF1100 followed during 1936 and TE1247 briefly in 1937. The last major design was TE1262 that lasted from 1937 to 1938, but there were also two one-off designs in 1938, numbered TE1234/D and TE1339.

Design TF988/E was a rather curvaceous Sports Saloon style with a falling waistline moulding. Five examples were built, four in 1936 and the last in 1937. The 1936 examples were for chassis GTL11, GHL19, GHL29 and GGM1, and the single 1937 body was for GHO25.

Design TF1100, again regularly described as a Sports Saloon, had much squarer lines, perhaps influenced by the vogue for razor-edge styling, although it was not itself a razor-edge design. The waistline was straight and was highlighted by a slim bright metal strip. There were 37 examples of this built between summer 1936 and early 1938. The earliest variant bodies had design TF1100/C, of which nine examples were built in 1936-1937 on chassis GHL27, GRM70, GXM35, GXM52, GGM14, GGM32, GAN6, GAN24 and GWN56. The main design then changed to TF1100/K, although there were also single examples of TF1100/F (on GRM39), TF1100/M (GAN68) and TF1100/S (GUN24). One example of TF1100/K (GAN51) was built with a Division. The full list is as follows:

GHL27	1936	GWN51	1936	GMO4	1937
GRM39	1936	GWN56	1937	GMO8	1937
GRM70	1936	GUN4	1937	GMO25	1937
GXM35	1936	GUN11	1937	GRP14	1937
GXM52	1936	GUN24	1937	GRP37	1937
GGM14	1936	GRO14	1937	GRP60	1937
GGM32	1936	GRO44	1937	GMP37	1937
GAN6	1936	GRO66	1937	GGR17	1937
GAN24	1936	GRO72	1937	GGR26	1938
GAN51	1936	GRO77	1937	GGR28	1938
GAN68	1936	GHO4	1937	GGR40	1938
GWN11	1936	GHO45	1937		
GWN32	1936	GHO63	1937		

The next Sports Saloon design was number TE1247/A, of which just four examples were built in 1937-1938. There was some evidence of the razor-edge influence on this one, but it was not itself a full razor-edge design. The four were on chassis GHO16, GRP68 and GRP76 in 1937, and on GZR35 in 1938.

Saloon design TE1262 was initially simply a four-light type, not specifically a Sports Saloon, and it was built in three variants. The earliest was TE1262/C, which was first seen in summer 1937. There were 10 of these, the last in early 1938, plus a solitary TE1262/F (on chassis GLP21). From early 1938 there was then a third variant, TE 1262/H, which is sometimes described as a Sports Saloon. There were six of these, on chassis GGR14, GGR43, GZR31, GZR37, GZR39 and GZR40, and all were built in 1938. The full list of chassis with TE1262 variants is below.

GRP29	1937	GAR30	1937	GGR58	1938
GRP71	1937	GGR14	1938	GZR31	1938
GLP1	1937	GGR25	1938	GZR37	1938
GLP21	1937	GGR43	1938	GZR39	1938
GLP34	1937	GGR45	1938	GZR40	1938
GLP37	1937	GGR57	1938		

There were also two late designs of which only a single example was built. These were Saloon design TE1234/D (for chassis GZR29) and Sports Saloon TE1339 (for GZR2), both dating from 1938.

Saloons with Division

Five Thrupp & Maberly bodies on the 25/30 chassis were described as Saloon with Division types, and each one was different. All of them had some resemblance to contemporary Saloon designs but were given separate design numbers and were therefore presumably considered as individual designs.

Design number TF983/B was used for chassis GUL83 in 1937 – interestingly, a 20/25 chassis that had been modified to 25/30 standard and was used for testing and development by Rolls-Royce. This body had a swept tail design with a relatively small boot. During 1936, design TF1128/A appeared on chassis GUL54, and TE1136 on GTL20. The fourth design was TE1235/B, which was built for GGR65 in 1938, and the fifth was TE1312, for GAR47 in late 1937.

Saloons (six-light)

There were five six-light Saloon bodies, of which four were to design TC1012. The two built in 1936 were TC1012/B types (GTL65 and GWN21), during 1937 there was a single swept-tail TE1012/D (GHO58), and the last was a TE1012/G in 1938 (GGR81). The fifth body with a Six-light Saloon design was built in 1936 to design TE1156/A for chassis GRM81 and remained unique.

Other types

Thrupp & Maberly built four other bodies on the 25/30 chassis as individual types to order. There was one All-weather to design TE1196/A, on late-1936 chassis GAN4. This was mainly notable for its rear wheel spats, which were not normally a Thrupp & Maberly feature. A single Drophead Coupé was built to design TF961/C on 1936 chassis GRM42; it was later modified to a Fixed-head Coupé. There was a rather sporty-looking Faux Phaeton (with an unknown design number) on chassis GHL41 in 1936. Lastly, the company also built just one Sedanca de Ville, to design TC1291/A for chassis GLP27 in 1937.

Characteristically Thrupp & Maberly in its solid appearance, the Sports Saloon on 1938 25/30 chassis GGR43 is nevertheless elegant and relatively light in appearance. (Klaus-Josef Rossfeld)

WRAITH COACHWORK

Just 42 bodies were built on the Rolls-Royce Wraith chassis in 1938 and 1939 and, as with the 25/30 chassis, the dominant style was the Limousine. There were 20 of these, 18 Saloons of various types, and four bodies of other types.

Limousines

There was a single "volume" design for Limousines on the Wraith chassis, and 19 examples of it were built. There was then a twentieth Limousine body, to a special design in 1939.

The primary Limousine design was numbered TE1394, and it had the typical swept tail of such designs, with a flush-mounted boot lid. Three examples delivered in 1939 had a variant design numbered TE1394/F, and these were on chassis numbered WMB80, WEC61 and WEC65. The 19 examples of TE1394 variants were:

WXA27	1938	WMB55	1939	WHC76	1939
WXA51	1938	WMB80	1939	WEC3	1939
WXA71	1938	WLB18	1939	WEC9	1939
WXA77	1938	WLB32	1939	WEC21	1939
WRB14	1938	WHC20	1939	WEC61	1939
WMB44	1939	WHC75	1939	WEC65	1939
WMB45	1939				

The single bespoke Limousine design was delivered in 1939 to the Duke of Gloucester and had design number TE1485. This was on chassis WMB62.

Saloons

The basic Saloon design for the 25/30 chassis was number TE1417; of the 14 examples built, at least 12 were the TE1417/A variant; one (on WRB36) was built with a division as a TE1417/C; and one was an undisclosed variant on chassis WEC41. This body had not been completed when coachbuilding ceased for the duration of the war, and was completed in 1946 by coachbuilder James Young. The body on WEC22 has been described as a Touring Saloon but has the standard TE1417/A design designation. The

This six-light Saloon to design TE1417/A looks robust and imposing in the Thrupp & Maberly fashion. It is on Wraith chassis WXA92 and was new in late 1938. (Real Car Company)

TE1417 bodies were on the following chassis:

WXA92	1938	WMB63	1939	WHC59	1939
WRB17	1938	WHC15	1939	WEC22	1939
WRB36	1938	WHC21	1939	WEC41	1939
WRB57	1938	WHC28	1939	WKC3	1939
WRB67	1938	WHC41	1939		

There were four other Thrupp & Maberly Saloon designs for the 25/30, each one individual and therefore presumably bespoke. In numerical order, these were TE1467 for WRB28 in 1938, TE1468 on chassis WMB27 in 1939, TE1479 for WMB68 in 1938, and TE1506/A for WHC27 in 1939. Design TE1468 has been described as a Touring Saloon, and TE1479 was an unusual four-light type with large blind rear quarters and a division.

Other types

As had been their practice during the currency of the 25/30 chassis, Thrupp & Maberly adapted a Limousine design to produce a Landaulette for the Rolls-Royce Wraith and numbered it as a variant of the basic closed design. Just one example of design TE1394/F was built, for chassis WEC79, and this was intended for the company's stand at the cancelled 1939 Earls Court Show in 1939.

Two Limousine de Ville bodies were built. The basic design was numbered TE1418 and was built for chassis WLB11 in 1939, but the later body for WEC73 that year had a variant of this numbered TE1418/A.

There was also an All-weather design, number TE1444. This style of body was rather outmoded by the late 1930s but Thrupp & Maberly made a typically elegant job of the single example that was built, for chassis WRB9 in late 1938.

TILBURY
London – Twenty

The Tilbury Motor Company was based in the Hammersmith area of west London and was active in the first half of the 1920s. Bizarrely, it exhibited its wares at the Scottish Motor Show rather than the more local one at Olympia. The company built two known bodies for the Rolls-Royce Twenty. One was a Landaulette for chassis GH62 in 1923, and the other a Limousine for GPK9 in 1925.

UNION MOTOR CO
London – Twenty

The Union Motor Co had its headquarters in the Victoria district of London, and among other activities built coachwork using a Weymann licence. The company built three bodies for Rolls-Royce Twenty chassis, of which two were Weymann Saloons. These were for chassis GSK74 in 1925 and GMJ43 in 1926. The third body was a Landaulette for GYK63 in 1926.

Design TE1506/A for the Wraith chassis was another four-light Saloon with the robust look for which Thrupp & Maberly were well known. This example on chassis WHC27 broke no new ground but was nonetheless very much in fashion when delivered in summer 1939. (Frank Dale & Stepsons)

VANDEN PLAS
London – Twenty, 20/25, 25/30

The Vanden Plas company that was operating in Britain during the later 1920s and the 1930s was only distantly related to the original Belgian coachbuilder. Re-established in 1923 after a financially troubled period, the British branch had formed a strong alliance with Bentley, with which it was a neighbour at Kingsbury on the northern outskirts of London. After Bentley's collapse in 1931, Vanden Plas survived by offering designs that were adaptable to several of the major quality chassis of the day. So similar bodies were built on Alvis, Armstrong-Siddeley, Bentley, Daimler, Lagonda, Rolls-Royce and Talbot chassis.

Vanden Plas would always be more closely associated with Bentley than with Rolls-Royce, and the old-established link with that marque remained alive after it was re-established under Rolls-Royce ownership. In the 1920s, the company built only one body for a Rolls-Royce Twenty chassis. On the 20/25 chassis, there were then 16 Vanden Plas bodies, and these were followed by four for the 25/30.

TWENTY COACHWORK

The sole Vanden Plas body for a Rolls-Royce Twenty was a Tourer, built in 1928 for chassis GYL43. It is recorded as being finished in Blue and Black and as having Barker dipping and swivelling lights.

20/25 COACHWORK

The earliest body that Vanden Plas built for a 20/25 chassis was completed in 1932, although the Belgian Van den Plas (see Chapter 4) had already built several for this chassis. Thereafter, commissions for the 20/25 chassis picked up, quite likely on the back of increased interest in the new Bentley chassis. Vanden Plas used the London dealer Oxborrow & Fuller to display their products, and also made a special "Continental Tourer" design exclusively for them. The most numerous bodies were nevertheless Saloons of various types.

Drophead Coupé

The two Drophead Coupé bodies for 20/25 chassis were both completed in 1934 but were completely different designs. They were for chassis GRC22 and GSF6.

Limousines

The single Limousine body was for chassis GTZ38 in 1933 and was a most attractive D-back six-light design.

Saloons

Eight Saloon bodies were built, all of them except GRW48 in 1932 having four-light designs. Two (GRW48 and GSY69) embodied the Silent Travel mounting principles that Vanden Plas had developed and used on several bodies for other chassis. GAE30 and GAE56 shared the Continental Saloon style (number 1123 in the Vanden Plas canon) that was popular at the time, and GAE56 had a Division. There was a fashionable swept-tail design, too, built on the 20/25 chassis only for GAF16 in 1934. The eight Vanden Plas Saloons were:

GRW48	1932	GKC30	1934	GWE33	1934
GSY69	1933	GAE30	1934	GAF16	1934
GHA33	1933	GAE56	1934		

Sedanca Coupé

There was a single three-position Sedanca Coupé for chassis GRW44 in 1932.

Tourers

Vanden Plas constructed a single All-weather Tourer for chassis GTK55 in 1936, a four-door design which in open form had the sleek lines more usually associated with a Drophead Coupé. Before that there were three Continental Tourers in 1934, using the patented Oxborrow & Fuller design that was used on several other makes of chassis at the time. In Rolls-

This Saloon body for 20/25 GSY69 in 1933 was one of two that incorporated the Vanden Plas Silent Travel mounting principles. It also showed the company's skills at their best in its neat and well-proportioned design.

The Drophead Coupé body for 20/25 GRC22 in 1934 was one of only two by Vanden Plas on that type of chassis, but was a typically well-resolved design.

The Oxborrow & Fuller Continental Tourer was a quite sporting body that almost seemed too sporting for the 20/25 chassis. This was one of three that Vanden Plas built in 1934, in this case on chassis GFE9.

Royce form, it was Vanden Plas design number 1135, and the three cars that had it were on chassis GWE6, GFE9, and GFE14.

25/30 COACHWORK

The four bodies from Vanden Plas for 25/30 chassis were all different. In 1936 came a four-light Saloon for chassis GXM68, to the same design as the owner's existing Saloon on 20/25 number GWE33. In 1937 there was a Drophead Coupé for GMO40, and later in the year a Sports Saloon for GAR41, derived from a Show design on Daimler chassis. The last of the four was a four-seat Sports Tourer for chassis GZR30 in 1938.

VICKERS
Crayford – Twenty

Vickers (Crayford) Ltd was a branch of the major British industrial combine founded in 1888 to manufacture Maxim machine guns for the armed forces. In 1923, the Crayford factory announced its intention of building car bodywork, but it was a project that did not last long. The company soon turned to bus and coach bodies instead, and ceased

Vanden Plas built only four bodies on the 25/30 chassis, and this Sports Saloon was based on an earlier design for a Daimler chassis. The chassis was number GAR41.

this activity as well some time in the early 1930s.

The foray into car bodywork lasted long enough for Vickers to put its name to a single Limousine body for a Rolls-Royce Twenty. This was on chassis number GMK28 and was completed in 1924.

VICTOR BROOM
London – Twenty, 20/25

Victor Broom was a small London coachbuilder with headquarters at Rochester Road in Camden Town, London NW1. The company was founded in 1921 but was never a financial success. It was restructured in 1928 to become Victor Broom (1928) Ltd, but built its last known coachwork in 1930 and had closed by 1931.

Victor Broom focussed on high-quality enclosed bodies for expensive chassis, and its clientele were the wealthy upper classes in London, many of whom placed their orders through the Henlys dealership in Camden Town. It was known for discreetly grand bodies that were designed to impress, and that had lavish woodwork. Victor Broom coachwork on Rolls-Royce chassis included at least one 40/50 Silver Ghost and one Phantom II. As for the small-horsepower models, the company is known to have built bodies on nine Twenty chassis between 1924 and 1929, and on three 20/25 chassis in 1929-1930. The bodies were not individually numbered and were probably all to bespoke designs. Survivors are not numerous.

TWENTY COACHWORK

Victor Broom built one body for the Twenty chassis in each of the years from 1924 to 1926, and then two in each year between 1927 and 1929. By far the most numerous were Saloons, of which there were six. There was one Coupé, one Landaulette, and one Limousine.

The six Saloons were on chassis GDK6 (in

This 1929 Saloon by Victor Broom for Twenty chassis GLN45 has an interesting trace of Brougham influence in the shape of the contrast panel's leading edge.

1924), GOK6 (1926), GHJ52 (1927), GYL56 and GFN10 (both 1928), and GLN45 (1929). The sole Landaulette was on GNK21 and was delivered in 1925. The Coupé was delivered in 1927 on chassis GHJ78 and was a typically imposing design, with a long rear end that contained a dickey seat. The Limousine was on GEN24 and was a 1929 delivery.

20/25 COACHWORK

All three Victor Broom bodies on the Rolls-Royce 20/25 chassis were Saloons, and all three were completed within a three-month period from December 1929 to February 1930. The earliest was a four-light Saloon with Division on GDP21 that was delivered in 1929. There was a second Saloon with Division on GDP58, and the third body was a six-light Saloon on GDP69. Both were delivered in February 1930, the last one actually being on GDP58 on the last day of that month.

VINCENTS

Reading – Twenty, 20/25, 25/30

William Vincent Ltd was founded in 1805 as a wheelwright and wagon maker. The company built its first car body in 1899 and had become an important provincial coachbuilder by the 1920s. Its first body for a Rolls-Royce chassis was built in 1906, and the company built several bodies for Silver Ghost chassis before the First World War, but it became far better known for its horse box bodies, a field in which it was a pioneer from 1912.

Vincents were also agents for several makes of car, including Rolls-Royce, and constructed bodies on some of the more prestigious chassis. They were never particularly innovative, and some bodies were curiously conservative, but that seemed to be what their customers wanted. Vincents bodies were designed to convey the wealth and status of the owner, and were often lavishly fitted inside; many were deliberately formal limousines.

The company resumed coachbuilding activities on a small scale after the Second World War and even enjoyed a brief career as a builder of bus bodies in the 1940s and 1950s, when demand was high. From 1952, Vincents nevertheless abandoned the car body market to focus on its commercial bodywork and on its car dealerships. It built its last horse-box around 1981 and survives today as a chain of car dealerships.

Vincents built 32 bodies for new small-horsepower Rolls-Royce chassis, the totals being 15 for the Twenty, 15 for the 20/25, and two for the 25/30. There were also several rebodies, but there were no known bodies for the Wraith.

TWENTY COACHWORK

The 15 bodies for the Twenty chassis were built between 1923 and 1927. There were five in 1923, four each in 1925 and 1926, and one each in 1924 and 1927. By far the most popular type was the Saloon, of which Vincents built nine examples.

Coupé

Vincents built a single Coupé – strictly a Three-quarter type – and this was for chassis GCK2 in 1925.

Saloons

The nine Saloon bodies were built between 1923 and 1926, and were for the following chassis:

76A3	1923	GDK77	1924	GZK68	1926
80K1	1923	GNK15	1925	GYK19	1926
GF78	1923	GSK52	1925	GYK81	1926

Landaulettes

There were three Landaulette bodies, and these were for chassis 78A3 and GA46 in 1923, and for GMJ38 in 1926.

Limousine

Vincents built a single Limousine body on the Twenty chassis, and this was for GSK60 in 1925.

Tourer

There was just one Tourer body, which was for chassis GRJ12 in 1927.

20/25 COACHWORK

Vincents built its first coachwork for the 20/25 chassis in 1930, and there were 15 bodies in all between then and 1936. There were three bodies in each of the years 1931, 1933 and 1935, two each in 1930 and 1932, and one each in 1934 and 1936. By this stage, it was clear that customers favoured Vincents primarily for their Limousine coachwork, and nine of the 15 bodies were of this type.

One body, a Tickford Saloon with Division, was built for Vincents by Salmons & Sons and carried

Vincents of Reading were known as makers of Limousine coachwork, and this example was for 20/25 chassis GHW1 in 1932. The design was not adventurous, but in typical Vincent style it looked robust. (Real Car Company)

Vincents coachplates. This was on chassis GEH26 in 1935. Vincents also rebodied five 20/25 chassis in later years. GGP64 became a horse box (a Vincents speciality!) in 1939, and GDX15 became a van. There were shooting brake bodies for GSY80 (in 1948) and for GLB25. Lastly, GNC49 was rebodied as a Tourer – a most unusual body to come from this coachbuilder.

Limousines

The nine Limousine bodies were built between 1931 and 1935. The body on GBT49 is described as a "Tall Limousine". The nine bodies and their dates were on the following chassis:

GOS50	1931	GHW1	1932	GPG1	1935
GFT68	1931	GBX4	1933	GLJ25	1935
GBT49	1932	GMD74	1934	GLJ62	1935

Saloons

The second most numerous coachwork type from Vincents on the 20/25 chassis was the Saloon. Of the five bodies, one (for GBA59 in 1933) had a Division, and one (for GBK27 in 1936) was a four-light type with a rather awkward appearance. The five bodies were for the following chassis:

GWP26	1930	GBA59	1933	GBK27	1936
GOS64	1931	GGA16	1933		

Tourer

Tourer bodies were not really Vincents' style, but the body they had built for Twenty GRJ12 in 1927 was transferred onto new 20/25 chassis GXO95 in 1930.

25/30 COACHWORK

There were just two Vincents bodies for the 25/30 chassis, and both were Limousines. The one for GXM62 was built in 1936 and was rather old-fashioned and very upright in typical Vincents fashion. The second was built for chassis GMP56 in 1937.

WADHAM BROS
Waterlooville – Twenty

The Wadham Bros who provided coachwork for two Rolls-Royce Twenty models was most probably Wadham Bros (Coachbuilders) Ltd, who were based at Waterlooville, Hampshire. This company was the ancestor of the later Wadham Stringer (Coachbuilders) Ltd that was known for its commercial bodywork. Wadham Bros was best known in the inter-war years for its ambulance bodies.

The two bodies for Twenty chassis were a Tourer on GRK76 in 1924 and a Saloon on GLK50 in 1925.

WATSON
Liverpool – Twenty

Liverpool-born champion cyclist and motoring pioneer William Watson founded W Watson & Co in 1901, and the company grew to become the largest chain of car dealers in the north-west of England. The company also opened a coachbuilding department, and in the 1920s and 1930s was particularly associated with coachwork for Rolls-Royce and Morris chassis, for both of which it held a franchise. In the 1930s, there were also some bus and coach bodies for local independent operators. Watson built bodies for at least 25 Rolls-Royce chassis, of which seven were Phantom I chassis and no fewer than 18 were Twenties.

All 18 bodies for the Twenty were built on early chassis between 1923 and 1925. There were nine in 1923, seven in 1924, and two in 1925. Most were Tourers; next most popular were Landaulettes; and there was a handful of other types.

Landaulettes

The earliest of the five Landaulette bodies was for 75A9 in 1923. There were then three more in 1924, for GAK75, GAK78 and GRK35. The last one was built in 1925 for GNK9.

Saloons

Just two Saloon bodies for the Twenty came from the Watson works, both in 1923. They were for chassis 83K2 and GA49.

Tourers

The eight Tourer bodies were all built in 1923 and 1924. In 1923, they were for chassis 50S5, 62H8, 76A1, GF23, and GH80. These were followed in 1924 by bodies for GAK38, GAK47 and GRK65.

Other types

The remaining three bodies were all one-offs. The 1923 body on 50S6 (which survives) was a solid-looking and quite attractive Drophead Coupé, although it has been variously described as a Two-seater and even as a Doctor's Coupé. There was then a Cabriolet for GMK6 in 1924, and Watson's last body for a Twenty was a Coupé de Ville for GNK18 in 1925.

WATSON
Lowestoft – Twenty, 20/25

The Lowestoft company of PW Watson & Sons Ltd was best known as a builder of commercial bodies, but also turned its hand to car coachwork and held several car sales franchises as well. Founded in 1830, it was building car bodies by 1902 and in the early 1920s also

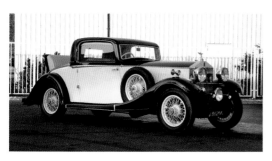

began building coach bodies, initially for a fleet that the company operated itself and later for other operators over quite a wide area. On the car side of the business, Watson became associated with upmarket marques such as Armstrong-Siddeley, Daimler and Minerva. Nick Walker, in *A-Z British Coachbuilders,* says that the company was noted for the quality of its interior woodwork. The Watson company built 17 bodies for Rolls-Royce Twenty chassis, and five for the 20/25.

TWENTY COACHWORK

The Watson company built small numbers of bodies for the Rolls-Royce Twenty chassis each year between 1922 and 1927, and the total of 17 bodies was made up of four in each of the years 1923-1925, two in each of 1922 and 1927, and one in 1926. Most bodies (eight) were Tourers, and there were four Landaulettes.

Cabriolet

There was just one Cabriolet body, which was for chassis 55S1 in 1923.

Landaulettes

The four Landaulettes were for GA19 in 1923, GDK51 in 1924, GUK17 in 1926, and GAJ6 in 1927.

Limousines

There were two Limousine bodies, which were for 44G0 in 1922 and GLK39 in 1924.

Saloons

Watson also met orders for two Saloon bodies, which were delivered on chassis GSK44 in 1925 and GRJ16 in 1927.

Tourers

The major demand was for Tourer bodies, all of which were built between 1922 and 1925. There were eight of these, as follows:

41G0	1922	GRK30	1924	GSK57	1925
50S3	1923	GDK53	1924	GCK62	1925
61H5	1923	GPK16	1925		

20/25 COACHWORK

Watson built just five bodies for the 20/25 chassis and its products were clearly in less demand than they had been for the Twenty. Two bodies were built on 1930 chassis; two on 1934 chassis; and a single example on a 1936 chassis.

Each body was different from the last. They were a single Coupé with Dickey seat for GLB18 in 1934, a single Landaulette for GSR52 in 1930, a single Sedanca de Ville for GTK41 in 1936, and a pair of different Saloon bodies. The earlier of these was a Saloon with Division for GSR56 in 1930, but the later one had a somewhat confusing description. While described as a Saloon, the body for GMD56 in 1934 was also described as an Enclosed Cabriolet, which seems contradictory.

The Watson business also rebodied 1932 chassis GAU73 as a Shooting Brake at an unknown date. Its original body was a Thrupp & Maberly Saloon.

WEYMANN
Putney, London – Twenty, 20/25

Not only did Charles Weymann license his method of coachwork construction to multiple coachbuilders in Britain, but from 1925 he actually set up his own company to build such bodies himself. It was called the Weymann Motor Body Co, and was able to hit the ground running by taking over the old Cunard works at Putney in London. The popularity of Weymann bodies in the mid-1920s was immense, and the Weymann company itself was certainly not

Dreams and reality: Geoffrey Smith, Editor of The Autocar *magazine, requested a unique fabric-panelled Coupé from Weymann on a Twenty chassis in 1929. The sketch appears to be some preliminary thoughts for the design, and makes the car look rather longer than it actually was. The triangular windows at the edges of the screen were dropped, too. The close-up of the real thing gives a good idea of the space within the body.*

then 12 during 1927, and the rapid success of the Weymann business was reflected in a total of 24 during 1928 – which was, of course, only a fraction of the company's total output for that year. There were just nine in 1929, but that was of course a short "year" for the Twenty because its production had ended by the autumn.

Coupé
Weymann built just two Coupé bodies for the Twenty chassis. The earlier was a special design for Geoffrey Smith of *The Autocar* on GYL2 in 1928, and the later a quite different design of Doctor's Coupé on GEN81 in 1929.

Limousines
There were three Limousine bodies for the Twenty chassis. These were on GXL6 in 1927, and on GYL33 and GTM11 in 1928.

Saloons
No fewer than 40 of the 47 Weymann bodies on the Twenty chassis were described as Saloons, although they were by no means all to the same design. Many were four-light designs, and of these some had dummy landau irons on the rear quarters and some did not. Some were six-light designs, an example being the body for GYL60 in 1928. There were at least two two-door bodies, on GEN40 and GEN62 in 1929. The full list, with dates, is below.

GYK71	1926	GYL44	1928	GKM72	1928
GMJ74	1927	GYL47	1928	GTM12	1928
GAJ1	1927	GYL49	1928	GTM17	1928
GAJ63	1927	GYL60	1928	GFN37	1928
GAJ68	1927	GYL63	1928	GFN62	1929
GAJ77	1927	GYL67	1928	GLN1	1929
GRJ38	1927	GYL78	1928	GLN34	1929
GUJ24	1927	GWL1	1928	GEN9	1929
GUJ38	1927	GWL6	1928	GEN40	1929
GUJ79	1927	GWL38	1928	GEN58	1929
GXL34	1927	GBM63	1928	GEN62	1929
GXL68	1928	GKM14	1928	GEN67	1929
GYL21	1928	GKM37	1928		
GYL25	1928	GKM65	1928		

short of custom; in fact, expansion was so rapid that it had to move into new and larger premises at Addlestone in Surrey during 1928.

Nevertheless, 1928 was also the peak year for popularity of Weymann body construction. It was already becoming clear that Weymann-patent bodies had poor durability, and by the time of the 1929 Paris Salon, Weymann was looking at alternative construction methods. The company dealt with the durability problem by announcing a "semi-Weymann" design where the lower panels were of metal and fabric was used only for the roof. This was only a temporary solution, however, and by 1931 Weymann had already refocused its business on bus bodywork.

The Weymann company put its name to no fewer than 47 bodies for the Rolls-Royce Twenty chassis between 1926 and 1929, but there were only seven for the 20/25 chassis in 1929-1930.

TWENTY COACHWORK
The 47 bodies that Weymann built for the Rolls-Royce Twenty were predominantly fabric-panelled Saloons. There was also a smattering of Limousines and Coupés, and single examples of a Two-seater and a Tourer. The earliest body was delivered in 1926 but was the only one that year. There were

Tourer
There was just one example of a Tourer body, which was for chassis GHJ50 in 1927.

Two-seater
There was also a single Two-seater body in 1927, which was for chassis number GUJ31.

20/25 COACHWORK

Weymann did not continue building coachwork for long into the 20/25 era, and probably closed their order book around the end of 1929, leaving the last two bodies on 20/25 chassis to be completed and delivered in the early months of 1930.

Of the seven bodies by Weymann, six were Saloons and just one was a Drophead Coupé, which had fairly austere lines and was delivered on GXO49 in late 1929. Of the six Saloons, five had traditional Weymann fabric-panelled bodies with a four-light design; less detail is known about the last one, GDP65. Two of them (GXO50 and GGP42) had divisions as well. GDP63 was another car for Geoffrey Smith of *The Autocar* and incorporated several special features. It is likely that Weymann also built the fabric Saloon body for GGP77 in late 1929 under contract to Cockshoot. The six Saloons on 20/25 chassis were:

| GXO50 | 1929 | GGP42 | 1929 | GDP63 | 1930 |
| GXO69 | 1929 | GGP58 | 1929 | GDP65 | 1930 |

WILLIAM ARNOLD
Manchester – Twenty, 20/25, 25/30

William Arnold vied with Joseph Cockshoot as the leading Manchester coachbuilder in the inter-war years, although within their rivalry there is also evidence of mutual support. Arnold's had been building car bodies since 1910, and the company was highly respected for the quality of its coachwork, which tended to be conservative in design. Nevertheless, the 1930s brought a more adventurous tail design with curves that incorporated a built-in luggage compartment, and the company was not afraid to experiment with streamline designs or with pillarless construction. It also developed its own individual style of Landaulette, which it branded the Arnaulet. There were some bus bodies between 1928 and 1931, too. After the Second World War, the company continued in business as motor dealers and built commercial and taxi bodywork.

TWENTY COACHWORK

The company provided a total of 26 known bodies for the Rolls-Royce Twenty chassis, its best years being 1926 to 1928, when there were six, seven, and six bodies delivered respectively. There were smaller quantities in other years: two in 1922, one in 1923, two in 1925 and two in 1929. The most numerous body type was the Saloon, of which 11 were built; there were four Landaulettes and four Limousines, other styles being built in only penny numbers. The figures for the Twenty are shown below.

Cabriolet
The single William Arnold Cabriolet for a Twenty chassis was built on 46G7 in 1922.

Coupés
The three Coupé bodies were on chassis 46G5 in 1922, GHJ69 in 1927, and GFN22 in 1928.

Drophead coupé
Only one customer ordered a Drophead Coupé from William Arnold for a Rolls-Royce Twenty chassis. This was mounted on chassis GCK79 in 1926.

Landaulettes
The four Landaulette bodies were for GCK56 in 1925, GUK29 in 1926, GHJ54 in 1927 and GEN7 in 1929.

Limousines
The first William Arnold Limousine body for a Twenty chassis was built in 1926, for GZK8. A second followed for GHJ47 the following year; and the last two were built in 1928 for GKM74 and GFN47.

Saloons
Saloons were the most numerous of the William Arnold types for the Twenty, and there were 11 of

William Arnold called this body design an Airline Saloon. The fashion for "aerodynamic" shapes in 1935 led to some dreadful creations, but this was not one of them. Even so, the coachbuilder did not make any more like it, and 20/25 GEH4 remained unique. (Real Car Company)

them between 1923 and 1929. The full list, with dates, is below.

55S0	1923	GHJ16	1927	GBM45	1928
GUK39	1926	GAJ45	1927	GFN34	1928
GMJ17	1926	GAJ54	1927	GLN55	1929
GMJ37	1926	GYL65	1928		

Tourer

Just one customer ordered a Tourer body from this coachbuilder for the Twenty chassis, and the body was supplied in 1925 on GCK34.

Two-seater

There was also only one two-seater body from William Arnold. This was built for chassis GHJ2 in 1927.

20/25 COACHWORK

The 27 bodies that William Arnold built for the 20/25 chassis followed much the same pattern as those for the Twenty: most (17) were Saloons of one sort or another; there were then nine Limousines; and there was a single Coupé. Nevertheless, there was considerable variation of design among the Saloons, and even the Limousine designs had their own interest. There was just one body in each of the three years 1930, 1932 and 1936. There were two in 1933 and three in 1931, and the two outstanding years were 1934 and 1935, when eight and 11 bodies were provided respectively.

As evidence of the relationship between Arnold's and fellow Manchester coachbuilder Cockshoot, Arnold's are thought to have built the bodies for Cockshoot on GWP23 and GLR11, while Cockshoot may have built the body on GXB11 for Arnold's. All three bodies are listed under Cockshoot here. In addition, William Arnold may have built the body on GPG44 for the Birmingham coachbuilder Flewitt, under whose name it is listed here.

Coupé

The single Coupé body was a four-light design for chassis GFT68 in 1931, and was almost self-consciously modern for its time, with cycle-type wings supplemented by shaped fairings behind the front wheels.

Limousines

Of the nine Limousines between 1931 and 1936, perhaps the most interesting was the Sports Limousine for GBJ29 in 1935, which featured rear wheel spats and was displayed on the William Arnold stand at Olympia. GAE12 was also an Olympia exhibit, in 1934. The nine bodies were on the following chassis:

GOS1	1931	GAE12	1934	GPG59	1935
GFT18	1931	GLG10	1935	GBJ29	1935
GTZ50	1933	GLG61	1935	GXK61	1936

Saloons

Among the 17 Saloon bodies there were both four-light and six-light types, and at least one (GED55) had a division. Most interesting were the bodies on GSR45, which was the only Arnaulet Saloon (strictly a Landaulette) on a small-horsepower Rolls-Royce; on GMU24, which was pillarless (although an ugly boot spoiled it); and a pair of streamlined examples on GRF6 and GEH4. These latter were quite different from one another, the earlier one meeting the fashion without flamboyance, while the later one (which Arnold's called an Airline) was more self-consciously styled. The bodies were as follows:

GSR45	1930	GED55	1934	GPG31	1935
GMU24	1932	GWE2	1934	GYH8	1935
GGA6	1933	GFE6	1934	GOH6	1935
GUB6	1934	GFE25	1934	GEH4	1935
GNC56	1934	GRF4	1935	GCJ38	1935
GED26	1934	GRF6	1935		

25/30 COACHWORK

Arnold's constructed seven bodies for the 25/30 in each of the 1936 and 1937 calendar years. There were no unusual bodies this time, and all were either Saloons (8) or Limousines (6).

Saloons

Several of the Saloons have been described as Sports Saloons, perhaps because such descriptions were becoming more fashionable in the mid-1930s. The full list is as follows:

GTL36	1936	GGM2	1936	GRO63	1937
GTL75	1936	GGM7	1936	GRP9	1937
GTL 77	1936	GWN30	1937		

Limousines

The six Limousines were as follows:

GHL7	1936	GWN65	1937	GHO19	1937
GRM29	1936	GRO16	1937	GMP20	1937

WILLIAMS & BAYLISS
Cheltenham – Twenty

This Cheltenham company was responsible for one body on a Rolls-Royce Twenty chassis. It traded under various other names over the years; see the entry for W Mills & Sons.

WILLIAMS, FJ
Cheltenham – Twenty, 20/25

This company built one body on Rolls-Royce Twenty chassis, and a second on a 20/25 chassis. See the entry for W Mills & Sons.

WILTON
Croydon – Twenty

The Wilton Carriage Company was based in Croydon, Surrey. In the early 1920s it specialised in Ford Saloon bodies and in various bodies for Alvis. The company also built PSV bodies in the 1920s, and was still active into the 1930s. It probably built its first body for a Rolls-Royce in 1921, and is known to have met two orders for coachwork on the early Twenty chassis. These were for a Saloon on 55S8 and a Cabriolet on 85K1, both in 1923.

WINDOVERS
Huntingdon – Twenty, 20/25, 25/30, Wraith

Windovers began life in the 1600s as a saddlery business, and began building carriages in 1796. Although the family name was Windover, the business was usually known as Windovers in the 20th century – but both names appeared in its advertisements. Windovers built their first body for a Rolls-Royce chassis in 1910, and by 1920 were firmly established as a major coachbuilder for the marque. The company always worked on quality chassis, particularly Daimler and Rolls-Royce, and in the 1930s built on marques such as Alvis, Armstrong-Siddeley, Bentley Lagonda, Lanchester and Mercedes-Benz.

Windovers became one of the most prolific coachbuilders on Rolls-Royce chassis in the interwar years. Best known for their formal limousines, and always ready to add an air of formality to their body designs of all kinds, Windovers were nevertheless innovative coachbuilders who aimed to reduce weight wherever they could. From 1924, the company opened a second workshop at Colindale, in north-west London, and it was probably from here that it forged links in the 1930s with Vanden Plas, a near neighbour in Cricklewood, whose designs it used for some coachwork in the mid-1930s. Some bodies were built for stock and some to individual order, but standardised bodies were not a Windovers speciality.

After the Second World War, the focus of the Windovers business changed as the market for hand-built car bodies shrank. There were bodies for Beardmore taxis and hearses, and in the 1950s for some of the Green Goddess fire engines built for Civil Defence. However, the main focus of Windovers' activities from 1947 was on passenger coach types. In 1956, the company sold out to the London car dealer Henly's, and coachbuilding work ceased that year.

Windovers built many bodies for the larger Rolls-Royce chassis of the interwar years. On the small-horsepower types, there were around 160 for the Twenty, 240 for the 20/25, 70 for the 25/30, and 25 for the Wraith.

TWENTY COACHWORK

Windovers built the coachwork for the first production Twenty in 1922 (a Landaulette for 40G1) and were asked to provide Tourer coachwork for two of the development (experimental) Goshawk chassis. These were indications that their coachwork met with Rolls-Royce approval. Over the eight calendar years of the Twenty's production, and including these three, they built at least 160 bodies for new chassis; the total has been variously quoted and obviously depends on whether rebodies are counted or not (in this case, they are not).

Cabriolets (18 bodies), Coupés (19 bodies) and Landaulettes (23 bodies) were popular, but the two most numerous types from Windovers were Tourers (39 bodies) and Limousines (48 bodies). As open coachwork became less popular in later years, Windovers would go on to become an acknowledged leader in the Limousine field.

All-weather

Just one All-weather body was built, for 1924 chassis GAK69.

Brougham

Three Brougham bodies were built, and could perhaps be added to the total of Limousine types as a variant of that design. They were for 1925 chassis GPK2 and GSK40, and for 1928 chassis GBM60.

Cabriolet

Windovers were asked to build Cabriolets throughout the production life of the Twenty, and the list below shows a total of 18. Of these, the body for GA6 has sometimes been described as an All-weather, and the body for GVO3 was a Cabriolet de Ville. Another

The coachwork for Twenty GSK15 in 1925 qualified for the description of Cabriolet – but this was no ordinary Cabriolet. It was ordered from Windovers by the Maharajah Bharatpur in India with a multiplicity of special features. (Klaus-Josef Rossfeldt)

The customer for this Coupé by Windovers presumably wanted to combine the style of a Coupé with the space of a Saloon, and this unusual body for Twenty GZK34 in 1926 was the result. (Real Car Company)

Built on 1927 Twenty chassis GRJ47, this well-preserved Windovers Landaulette was fairly typical of such designs at the time. (Real Car Company)

Cabriolet de Ville type was built to rebody GEN18.

46G0	1922	GMK39	1924	GUK1	1926
78A1	1923	GLK57	1924	GHJ51	1927
78A9	1923	GLK61	1924	GXL55	1927
GA6	1923	GSK15	1925	GKM2	1928
GF62	1923	GSK70	1925	GEN53	1929
GAK32	1924	GZK60	1926	GVO3	1929

Coupés

Windovers generally constructed three-quarters (four-light) Coupés unless otherwise asked, and only the first and last of the 19 Coupés they built for the Twenty chassis are not recorded as three-quarters types. The list of 19 is below.

47G9	1922	GNK7	1925	GHJ40	1927
83K3	1923	GNK56	1925	GRJ3	1927
87K3	1923	GPK66	1925	GBM31	1928
GAK53	1924	GSK25	1925	GBM73	1928
GRK24	1924	GZK34	1926	GKM25	1928
GDK17	1924	GZK70	1926	GVO55	1929
GLK19	1924				

Drophead Coupés

Drophead Coupé coachwork made a late appearance among the Windover offerings for the Twenty chassis, and just four examples were built between 1927 and 1929. Three were on 1927 chassis, and these were GAJ32, GRJ55 and GXL79; the last of these was a three-quarters type. The fourth body was on a 1929

chassis, GVO23, and the car was exhibited at Olympia that year.

Landaulette

Windovers' Landaulette coachwork remained in demand for most of the Twenty's production life, and 23 examples were built in all. One, for GCK54, was described as a three-quarters type, and one, for 61H9, was built for a member of the Windover family. The full list is below:

40G1	1922	GH3	1923	GRJ49	1927
40G6	1922	GH22	1923	GUJ34	1927
46G8	1922	GAK3	1924	GUJ55	1927
61H9	1923	GAK19	1924	GYL48	1928
69H4	1923	GRK20	1924	GWL18	1928
89K0	1923	GPK25	1925	GKM69	1928
GF24	1923	GCK54	1925	GFN29	1928
GF66	1923	GHJ19	1927		

Limousines

In the later years of the 1920s, Limousine coachwork was Windovers' predominant type for the Twenty chassis. There were 48 bodies of this type in all, that on 43G0 having an open-drive design. The chassis that carried these bodies from new were as follows:

43G0	1922	GZK19	1926	GXL42	1927
58S8	1923	GZK77	1926	GYL22	1928
73A4	1923	GUK58	1926	GWL4	1928
77A3	1923	GMJ46	1926	GWL22	1928
GH37	1923	GHJ41	1927	GBM52	1928
GAK56	1924	GAJ76	1927	GBM66	1928
GMK50	1924	GRJ8	1927	GKM31	1928
GRK43	1924	GRJ11	1927	GKM45	1928
GLK47	1924	GRJ15	1927	GFN14	1928
GLK62	1924	GRJ20	1927	GFN51	1928
GNK65	1925	GRJ24	1927	GLN33	1929
GPK26	1925	GRJ46	1927	GLN70	1929
GPK48	1925	GUJ47	1927	GLN78	1929
GPK52	1925	GUJ49	1927	GEN19	1929
GOK9	1926	GXL7	1927	GVO39	1929
GOK32	1926	GXL20	1927	GVO45	1929

Saloons

The 10 Saloon bodies for the Twenty chassis were spread out over the decade, the popularity peak being on 1927 chassis. The full list is below.

45G0	1922	GYK91	1926	GUJ68	1927
53S5	1923	GHJ5	1927	GKM7	1928
GF57	1923	GRJ34	1927	GVO42	1929
GNK20	1925				

Sedancas de Ville

Just two Sedanca de Ville bodies came from Windovers for the Twenty chassis, and both were for late production chassis. They were for GFN1 in 1928 and for GLN62 the following year.

Tourers

Windovers built 39 Tourer bodies for the Twenty between 1924 and 1927. Two of them were for experimental chassis (8-G-III and 9-G-III) in 1924-1925. Among the 39 were also 14 Tourer bodies for Russia between 1924 and 1926. The full list is in the table below.

41G5	1922	GMK72	1924	GCK55	1925
43G5	1922	GMK77	1924	GCK73	1925
71A4	1923	GLK6	1924	GOK1	1926
74A0	1923	8-G-III	1924	GUK4	1926
79A0	1923	9-G-III	1925	GUK15	1926
79A1	1923	GNK64	1925	GUK23	1926
GF11	1923	GNK94	1925	GUK25	1926
GF17	1923	GPK42	1925	GUK27	1926
GH45	1923	GCK3	1925	GUK32	1926
GH49	1923	GCK15	1925	GUK52	1926
GH65	1923	GCK25	1925	GYK14	1926
GAK63	1924	GCK31	1925	GMJ3	1926
GMK42	1924	GCK48	1925	GXL82	1927

Two-seaters

Windovers probably preferred to build something more grand than Two-seater coachwork whenever possible, but did deliver three bodies of this type on 1923 Twenty chassis. These were numbers 57S9, 58S3 and 86K6. The coachwork on 58S3 incorporated a dickey seat.

20/25 COACHWORK

Windovers built 240 bodies for new 20/25 chassis, giving an average of 30 bodies for each calendar year the model was produced. The actual annual figures were: 1929 (10); 1930 (19); 1931 (18); 1932 (44); 1933 (43); 1934 (51); 1935 (42); and 1936 (13). In 1935 and 1936, the company built a number of bodies to Vanden Plas designs.

All-weather

All-weather coachwork remained a minority type during 20/25 production, and the sole All-weather Tourer body was built in 1932 for chassis GMU67.

Brougham

Brougham coachwork remained rare, and Windovers built two Brougham de Ville types and one enclosed Brougham. The latter was for chassis GLR43 in 1930, and the two De Ville types were for GOH81 and GXK50 in 1935. The body from GOH81 was later transferred to a 25/30 chassis (GUL48) and the one for GXK50 was built to a Vanden Plas design.

Cabriolet

Windovers built just one Cabriolet body for a 20/25 chassis. This was in 1934 for chassis GWE29, and the body incorporated a Kellner patent head (Kellner being the Parisian coachbuilder; see Chapter 4).

Cabriolet de Ville

There was a single Cabriolet de Ville body, which was built in 1929 for chassis GGP24.

Coupé

Windovers built a single Coupé body for the 20/25 chassis. This was a three-seat type for chassis GWP40 in 1930.

Drophead Coupés

Drophead Coupé bodies from Windovers remained quite rare, and there were just seven examples – one each year from 1930 to 1936. Three (GDP56, GOS10 and GAW12) had dickey seats, and one (GTK19) was built to a Vanden Plas design. The seven bodies were on the following chassis:

GDP56	1930	GAW12	1933	GLG11	1935
GOS10	1931	GKC36	1934	GTK19	1936
GBT74	1932				

Landaulettes

Landaulette bodies proved popular for the 20/25 chassis, as they had for the Twenty. There were 19 of them, and they are listed below:

GXO34	1929	GBT5	1931	GWX63	1933
GXO48	1929	GBT69	1932	GNC18	1934
GXO65	1929	GAU1	1932	GNC48	1934
GGP27	1929	GHW20	1932	GLG29	1935
GLR19	1930	GEX27	1933	GEH29	1935
GLR51	1930	GWX50	1933	GBK47	1936
GNS58	1930				

Limousines and Limousines de Ville

As they had for the Twenty, Windovers specialised in Limousine coachwork for the 20/25 chassis. There were 111 examples of this type, many of them with the supremely elegant D-back design associated with this coachbuilder that gave both character and shape to the rear of the body.

Windovers were a leading maker of Limousine bodies for the 20/25 chassis, and this magnificent example shows why. It was built in 1933 for chassis GHA16 and remained in one family ownership for more than 70 years.
(Real Car Company)

Built just a year later than GHA16, the Limousine body for GLB8 shows how a two-colour paint scheme could alter the appearance of the typical Windovers product.
(Real Car Company)

GAU53	1932	GGA61	1933	GLG17	1935
GAU60	1932	GGA78	1933	GLG43*	1935
GMU25	1932	GHA16	1933	GLG56	1935
GZU5T	1932	GHA25	1933	GPG62	1935
GZU12	1932	GHA26	1933	GHG25	1935
GZU26	1932	GHA40	1933	GYH1	1935
GZU38	1932	GXB30	1933	GYH23	1935
GHW25	1932	GXB33*	1933	GYH68	1935
GRW7	1932	GXB48	1934	GEH6	1935
GRW31	1932	GUB1	1934	GEH39	1935
GRW35	1932	GLB8	1934	GBJ37	1935
GRW68	1932	GNC3	1934	GBJ52	1935
GRW77	1932	GRC2	1934	GBJ63	1935
GEX38	1933	GRC47	1934	GLJ3	1935
GEX69	1933	GRC63	1934	GLJ38	1935
GWX64	1933	GED20*	1934	GXK1	1935
GWX75	1933	GYD22	1934	GXK2	1935
GSY1	1933	GAE8	1934	GXK12	1935
GSY26	1933	GWE42	1934	GXK64	1935
GSY33	1933	GWE50	1934	GBK24	1936
GSY39	1933	GAF1	1934	GBK35	1936
GLZ73	1933	GAF36	1934	GBK38	1936
GTZ55	1933	GAF71	1934	GTK3	1936
GBA9	1933	GSF30	1934	GTK49	1936
GBA10	1933	GSF37*	1934		
GGA34	1933	GSF62	1934		

Saloons

After Limousines, Saloons were the next most numerous Windovers body type on the 20/25 chassis. There were 61 of them: three each in 1930 and 1931, 10 in 1932, 13 in 1933, 18 in 1934, 12 in 1935 and two in 1936. There were both four-light and six-light designs. Chassis GAW4 in 1933 had a Saloon version of Windovers' elegant D-back design, and the body for GYD62 was a solitary four-light Saloon Coupé. Bodies with a Division are marked with an asterisk (*) in the table below, which shows that their popularity increased markedly from 1934. Two of these bodies, for GCJ23 in 1935 and GBK9 in 1936, were six-light types built to Vanden Plas designs.

Of this grand total of 111, eight examples were Limousines de Ville:

GXO107	1930	GFT37	1931	GXK24	1935
GSR16	1930	GUB16	1934	GXK33	1935
GPS33	1931	GUB63	1934		

Of the other 103 bodies, three or four were "Opera" types with a four-light design, and these are marked in the table with an asterisk (*). The identification of GED20 as an Opera type is in question. One body (for GLJ38 in 1935) was built to a Vanden Plas design.

GXO33	1929	GPS39	1931	GKT8	1932
GGP4	1929	GPS41	1931	GKT10	1932
GDP29	1930	GFT5	1931	GKT14	1932
GLR28	1930	GFT55	1931	GKT22	1932
GLR40	1930	GFT79	1931	GKT31	1932
GSR28	1930	GBT4	1931	GAU3	1932
GTR36	1930	GBT21	1931	GAU4	1932
GPS27	1931	GBT28	1932	GAU20	1932
GPS38	1931	GBT79	1932	GAU36	1932

GDP1	1930	GHW9*?	1932	GWX1	1933
GLR6	1930	GHW51*?	1932	GWX34	1933
GTR35	1930	GHW67	1932	GDX21	1933
GNS76	1931	GRW49	1932	GSY17	1933
GFT15	1931	GRW58	1932	GLZ31	1933
GFT21	1931	GAW4	1933	GGA18	1933
GMU15	1932	GAW14	1933	GXB18*	1933
GMU31	1932	GAW31	1933	GXB66	1934
GMU57	1932	GEX11	1933	GUB37	1934
GMU77	1932	GEX45	1933	GUB76	1934
GZU8	1932	GEX52	1933	GLB37*	1934

GNC34*	1934	GFE11*	1934	GOH61*	1935
GNC60	1934	GFE32*	1934	GEH10*	1935
GRC17*	1934	GAF59	1934	GBJ72*	1935
GRC30	1934	GAF76*	1934	GLJ14*	1935
GRC35*	1934	GSF46	1935	GCJ7*	1935
GYD62	1934	GLG68*	1935	GCJ23*	1935
GED64	1934	GPG35*	1935	GBK9*	1936
GMD5*	1934	GPG72*	1935	GBK78	1936
GYD40*	1934	GHG5*	1935		
GWE52	1934	GOH44	1935		

Sedancalettes

Windovers built four Sedancalette bodies on the 20/25 chassis. These were for GXO17 in 1929, GNS54 in 1930, GLB23 and GED37, the latter two both in 1934.

Sedancas de Ville

Windovers built 28 Sedanca bodies for the 20/25 chassis. All were Sedanca de Ville types except for the one on GHA30 in 1933, which was a three-position Sedanca Coupé. Vanden Plas designs were used for the bodies on GBJ20 (which was shown at the 1935 Paris Salon) and GBK42 in 1936. The popularity of these Sedanca de Ville types increased after a slow start in 1929-1930, and some were built with the D-back design favoured on Windovers Limousines of the period.

GXO81	1929	GWX51	1933	GOH3	1935
GSR51	1930	GLZ44	1933	GBJ20	1935
GNS75	1931	GLZ58	1933	GLJ63	1935
GOS28	1931	GHA30	1933	GCJ36	1935
GFT4	1931	GUB31	1934	GXK16	1935
GKT35	1932	GUB44	1934	GXK75	1936
GMU11	1932	GED6	1934	GBK32	1936
GMU48	1932	GYD9	1934	GBK42	1936
GHW23	1932	GWE11	1934	GBK50	1936
GWX36	1933				

Tourers

Tourer bodies had fallen out of fashion generally by the early 1930s, and Windovers built only three on the 20/25 chassis. These were for GGP8 in 1929, GLR9 in 1930, and GMD73 in 1934.

25/30 COACHWORK

Strong demand for Windovers bodies was evident again during the period of 25/30 production, and the company bodied a total of 70 chassis of the type between 1936 and 1938; of these, one (a Brougham de Ville for GUL48) was not new but was transferred from an earlier 20/25 chassis. Including that one,

there were 30 in 1936, 35 in 1937, and five in the "short" 1938 season before the Wraith took over. In 1936-1937, Windovers continued to use Vanden Plas designs for some bodies.

Broughams de Ville

The Brougham de Ville body fitted to chassis GUL48 when it was new in June 1936 was not a new one but was transferred from 20/25 chassis GOH 81. Both cars were resident in France. The body had faux cane side panels.

Cabriolet

Windovers built just one Cabriolet body for a 25/30 chassis, and that was a four-door, four-light type for GMP77 in 1937.

Drophead Coupés

As usual, few customers came to Windovers for Drophead Coupé coachwork, but the company did build three such bodies for the 25/30 chassis. The first, on GXM51 in 1936, had a dickey seat. The second, on GWN41 the same year, incorporated rear-wheel spats but still managed to look sturdy and upright in the Windovers fashion. The last of the three was for chassis GGR10 in 1938.

Landaulettes

The popularity of Landaulette bodies was low at this period, and Windovers built only two for the 25/30 chassis. These were for GHL33 and GAN55, both in 1936.

Limousines

Windovers remained a major builder of Limousine bodies while the 25/30 chassis was in production, and built a total of 33 examples for it. There were 15 in 1936, 16 in 1937, and two in 1938. Just one, for GXM77 in 1936, depended on a Vanden Plas design. GRM50 was displayed at Olympia in 1936.

GUL33	1936	GTL21	1936	GRM66	1936
GUL61	1936	GTL30	1936	GXM22	1936
GTL4	1936	GRM50	1936	GXM36	1936

The four-light Saloon body for 20/25 chassis GAF59 was quite adventurous for 1934, and incorporated a Division. It is hard not to get the impression that Windovers were a little uneasy with this design. (Real Car Company)

Not surprisingly, Windovers' Limousine de Ville coachwork had a good deal in common with their plain Limousine styles. This one was on 25/30 chassis GWN17 in 1936. (Real Car Company)

GXM77	1936	GUN12	1937	GMP65	1937
GGM35	1936	GUN40	1937	GLP15	1937
GAN20	1936	GRO51	1937	GAR12	1937
GAN28	1936	GRO64	1937	GAR19	1937
GAN44	1936	GHO29	1937	GAR29	1937
GWN22	1937	GMO16	1937	GAR36	1937
GWN43	1937	GRP8	1937	GAR57	1938
GWN57	1936	GMP24	1937	GAR74	1938

Limousines de Ville

Limousine de Ville coachwork was still in demand, and Windovers built nine examples on the 25/30 chassis. Three of these were built to Vanden Plas designs: GRM1 and GRM32 in 1936, and GMP51 in 1937. GRM32 was displayed at the 1936 Paris Salon. The full list was as follows:

GRM1	1936	GRO62	1937	GMP51	1937
GRM32	1936	GHO64	1937	GMP54	1937
GWN17	1936	GRP43	1937	GGR6	1938

Saloons

Several of the dozen Saloon bodies for the 25/30 chassis had Divisions, and these bodies are marked with an asterisk (*) in the table below. There were also four Sports Saloons, which are listed separately. The Saloons were for the following chassis:

GAN7	1937	GHO50	1937	GLP28	1937
GAN67*	1937	GRP65	1937	GLP40	1937
GRO21*	1937	GMP18	1937	GLP41*	1937
GRO58*	1937	GMP44*	1937	GGR50	1938

Sedanca de Ville

Like other De Ville designs, the Sedanca de Ville

Although the body on Wraith WHC63 is recorded as a Limousine, the neat boot suggests it was really a Touring Limousine, and the treatment of the rear side windows is very similar to that on other Windovers Touring Limousines for the Wraith. This was the only body built to design 5299 and was completed in 1939. (Real Car Company)

was becoming less popular by the mid-1930s, and Windovers built only five such bodies for the 25/30 chassis. One of those, on chassis GGM19, is described as a copy of the 1936 Paris Salon car (GRM32), which is also described as a Limousine de Ville and is listed as such here (see above). The five Sedanca de Ville bodies were on the following chassis:

GTL55	1936	GHO39	1937	GAR62	1937
GGM19	1936	GHO52	1937		

Sports Saloons

Four Sports Saloon bodies on the 25/30 chassis attested to the increasing popularity of such designs. They were for chassis GUL46, GHL5 and GHL20 in 1936, and for GHO11 in 1937.

WRAITH COACHWORK

Windovers put their name to just 25 bodies for the Wraith chassis, of which one (on 1939 chassis WEC60) was only partially completed before the outbreak of war and was not actually competed until 1946. Of the other 24, nine were on 1938 chassis and 15 on 1939 chassis. As usual for Windovers, the majority of bodies were Limousine types, of which some were the newly fashionable Touring Limousines.

All-weather Tourer

There was a single All-weather Tourer for the Wraith, which was built on chassis WMB32 in 1939.

De Ville types

There were just four De Ville bodies on the Wraith chassis. One was a Sedanca de Ville and was on chassis WXA19; it was displayed at the Earls Court Show in 1938. The other three were all Limousines de Ville built in 1939, and were for chassis WHC22, WHC58 and WEC4.

Landaulettes

The Landaulette style was no longer fashionable by the late 1930s, and Windovers' only example for the 25/30 chassis was on WMB66 in 1939.

Limousines and Touring Limousines

There were nine traditional Limousine bodies and four Touring Limousines. The latter are marked in the table below by an asterisk (*) and all shared the same design, number 5412/B. (Nevertheless, the body on WHC63 also appears to be a Touring Limousine, albeit to a unique design, number 5299.) Three of the Windovers Limousines were delivered to the Ministry of War Transport in 1939: those on WHC43 and WEC12 had been commissioned for Indian Maharajas but could not be shipped, and the third was on WEC55 and had been intended as a Windovers exhibit at the cancelled 1939 Earls Court Motor Show.

WXA29*	1938	WRB73	1938	WHC43	1939
WXA39*	1938	WMB28	1939	WHC63	1939
WRB23*	1938	WMB47	1939	WEC12	1939
WRB33	1938	WMB77	1939	WEC55	1939
WRB52*	38/46				

Saloons
Every one of the six Saloon bodies by Windovers on the Wraith chassis had a Division. The last two, for WHC57 and WEC60, had a swept-tail design. WEC60 was intended for the 1939 Earls Court Show but the construction of its body was interrupted by the war and was not completed until 1946. The six bodies were on the following chassis:

WXA90	1938	WMB25	1939	WHC57	1939
WXA108	1938	WMB58	1939	WEC60	39/46

WOODALL NICHOLSON
Halifax – Twenty
Woodall Nicholson is best known today for the hearse bodies in which it has specialised since the early 1930s. Founded in Halifax in 1873, the company bodied several makes of British chassis during the 1920s before running into financial difficulties in 1929. Reconstructed, the company then continued as a coachbuilder, with a decreasing focus on passenger cars. It was eventually bought out in 1982 by its main competitor in the hearse business, Coleman Milne.

The company produced just one body for a Rolls-Royce Twenty chassis, which was a Tourer for GCK65 in 1925.

WOOD, REEVES
London – 20/25
A Wood, Reeves & Co were the successors of R Harrison & Sons, who had built a number of bodies on early Bentley chassis but closed in 1931. The company built just one body for a small-horsepower Rolls-Royce, and this was a Saloon with Division for chassis GNC11 in 1934.

WOOLLEY
Nottingham – Twenty, 20/25, 25/30
Woolley was a Nottingham coachbuilder, car dealer and repairer that was established in 1909 or 1910 when John Woolley joined forces with an old-

established company called Story, Starrey or Starey. It built 11 bodies in all on Rolls-Royce chassis, including two on the Phantom II and two on the Phantom III. Customers were mostly local and included serial buyers Sir Thomas Shipstone (of Shipstone's Brewery, two bodies) and Sir Julien Cahn (of the furniture business, three bodies). One was for a local cricketer who played for the team that Sir Julien ran and was also his Private Secretary.

Woolley's were known for the high quality of their work and built seven bodies on the small-horsepower Rolls-Royce chassis. The first was on a Twenty in 1923; there were then four on the 20/25 chassis between 1930 and 1935, and two on the 25/30 in 1936-1937.

TWENTY COACHWORK
The only Woolley body known on the Twenty chassis is a Landaulette that was built for Sir Thomas Shipstone in 1923. It was on chassis number 60H2.

20/25 COACHWORK
Three of the bodies for 20/25 chassis were Limousines, the earliest being for Sir Thomas Shipstone on GSR58 in December 1930. There was then one on GRC32 that was delivered in May 1934, and the third (a six-light design) was delivered in December 1935 on GLG20.

The fourth body was a Saloon that was delivered in November 1933 on GGA66.

25/30 COACHWORK
Both bodies for the 25/30 chassis were Saloons. The earlier one, on chassis GRM58 in September 1936, may have been ordered as a speculative venture by a Nottingham dealer. It did not sell (or perhaps the original order was cancelled) and was eventually passed on to Henlys in London who found a customer for it in 1938. The design was competent but unexceptional, with a falling waistline.

The second body had broadly similar lines but only two doors. This was on chassis GWN76 and was delivered in January 1937 to the local cricketer, Frederick Newman.

The Windovers Limousine body for Wraith WMB47 in 1939 still has many of the traits seen in earlier designs, but in this case the longer bonnet of the Wraith chassis makes the car look larger and the choice of a single paintwork colour gives the whole thing a restrained and refined air. (Real Car Company)

WRIGHTS
Location unknown – Twenty
A coachbuilder called Wrights is recorded as making the Cabriolet body on Twenty chassis 80K3 in 1923, but there are no further identifying details of the company.

WYLDER
Kew, Surrey – Twenty, 20/25
G Wylder & Co was established as a coachbuilder at Kew in Surrey in 1923. It was initially known for sporting coachwork, including some on Bentley chassis, but by 1926 also claimed to be "the largest builder of Laudaulettes for the hire trade." The company remained independent until 1937, when it was purchased by Alpe & Saunders and was turned over to that company's primary business of hearse manufacture. It built just two bodies on small-horsepower Rolls-Royce chassis, one for a Twenty and one for a 20/25. Both were unusual.

TWENTY COACHWORK
The single body for a Twenty was on chassis GPK33 and was supplied to an Indian Maharaja in April 1926. It was a four-door saloon with a vee windscreen that was specially equipped for hunting, and the outer panels were in polished aluminium.

Wylder also rebodied a 1929 chassis, GWL35, in a more modern-looking Drophead Coupé style during the 1930s.

20/25 COACHWORK
The four-door Saloon that Wylder built on 20/25 chassis GSY44 in 1933 was in some ways just as unusual as the company's earlier effort for the Maharaja. It had oddly angular lines and an unusual rear end design.

WYLIE & LOCHHEAD
Glasgow – 20/25
Wylie & Lochhead were cabinet makers and funeral directors with headquarters in Glasgow but many branches in other parts of Scotland, and also in Manchester. The company built just one body for the Rolls-Royce 20/25 chassis in 1931, which was a Limousine on GOS54.

Chapter Four

THE OVERSEAS COACHBUILDERS

M any overseas buyers of a small-horsepower Rolls-Royce chassis were content to take it with British-built coachwork as well, perhaps because it added to the "Britishness" of the whole vehicle. Nevertheless, a number of buyers – particularly in continental Europe and in Australia – chose to have coachwork built in their own countries.

There were several reasons for this. At this level of the market, lower costs can probably be discounted as a motive. Patriotism or the wish to support local trade must have been among the main reasons. Another might have been habit; and yet another would have been the wish simply to have something different or unusual. In the case of Australia, the country's notoriously harsh roads made short work of British-built coachwork, and buyers often preferred to deal with a local coachbuilder who was used to building bodies better suited to local conditions.

Not every overseas coachbuilder has been satisfactorily identified, and there are gaps in the records currently available. There were many chassis that went to France or to Switzerland that must have been bodied there, but the identity of the coachbuilder and the type of body remain unknown. Eventually, a combination of diligent research and sheer good luck will probably uncover most of the remaining secrets – but there are still plenty of them, nearly a century after the first Twenty chassis left British shores on its way to a coachbuilder overseas.

THE OVERSEAS COACHBUILDERS

Who and how many? Overseas coachwork on the small-hp Rolls-Royce

	Twenty	20/25	25/30	Wraith	Total
AUSTRALIA					
Agate	3				3
Clothier	1				1
Jackson, Jones & Collins		1			1
Kellow-Falkiner			1		1
Mackey				1	1
Martin & King		8	4	1	13
Melbourne Motor Body	1 (2?)				1
Richards	1				1
Ruskin			1		1
Smith & Waddington	14	1			15
Spencer	1				1
Standard	1				1
Waring Bros	3				3
AUSTRIA					
Stein	1				1
BELGIUM					
D'Ieteren		1			1
Van den Plas	3	4			7
Vesters & Neirinck			5		5
FRANCE					
Belvalette	1				1
Binder	21	22	3 (4?)	11	57
Chapron	1	1	1		3
Delage		1			1
De Villars				3	3
Felber	1				1
Fernandez & Darrin		8			8
Figoni		1			1
Franay	1	3			4
Gallé	2	1			3
Hibbard & Darrin		2			2
Janssen		4			4
Kellner	36	26	4	1	67
Kelsch	1				1
Letourneur & Marchand		2			2
Million-Guiet	8	1			9
Pingret & Breteau	1				1
Rothschild	1				1
Saoutchik	7			1	8
Unidentified	10	1	1		12
Vanvooren		4		7	11
Weymann	1				1

	Twenty	20/25	25/30	Wraith	Total
GERMANY					
Erdmann & Rossi		3	3	2	8
Kathe	1				1
Klein-Roche	2				2
Neuss		1			1
Seegers	1				1
INDIA					
Steuart	2				2
IRELAND					
Mawhinney	5				5
NETHERLANDS					
Schutter & van Bakel		1			1
Van Pipwyk	1				1
Veth & Zoon		1			1
NEW ZEALAND					
Johnson & Smith	1				1
Neilson	1				1
SPAIN					
Bettla	1				1
Fiol		1			1
Labourdette	3	1			4
SWITZERLAND					
Brichet	2				2
Gangloff	2	7			9
Gygax		1			1
USA					
Brewster	10	4	1		15
Inskip				7	7
Locke	3				3
Murphy	1				1
Wood		1			1

Most Agate bodies for the Twenty chassis were Tourers, but this one for GOK74 in 1926 seems to have been a fairly conventional Saloon, no doubt built robustly in typical Australian fashion.

AGATE

Australia – Twenty

English-born Ernest Edwin Agate was a qualified coachbuilder when he migrated to Sydney in 1886, and he set up on his own in the Summer Hill district in 1892. His company (usually known as EE Agate) had moved into motor body construction by 1920 and built several bodies on Rolls-Royce chassis during the 1920s. These included at least three on the Twenty chassis.

The three known Agate bodies were all Tourers, and all were built in 1926. They were for chassis GCK50, GOK36, and GOK63. However, it seems likely that Agate also built at least one six-light Saloon of fairly conventional profile on a Twenty chassis in the same year. This is thought to have been for GOK74, and may later have been transferred to an earlier chassis, GA79, to replace an unidentified Tourer body.

BELVALETTE
France – Twenty

Parisian coachbuilder Alfred Belvalette was among the earliest French coachbuilders to work on motor cars. In the 1920s, the company expanded as it bought out the Mühlbacher coachworks, and then took over the clientele of the Rothschild coachworks. Although other bodies on Rolls-Royce chassis are known, the only one on a small-horsepower model was a Brougham that was built on Twenty chassis GOK54 for a British resident in 1926.

BETTLA
Spain – Twenty

Very little is known about the Spanish coachbuilder Bettla Hermanos (Bettla Brothers), which was based in Barcelona. It was certainly active by 1914, when it built a torpedo body on Hispano-Suiza chassis.

The company built just one body on a Rolls-Royce Twenty chassis in 1923, and this was a Cabriolet for a Spanish lady. The chassis was number 75A0.

BINDER
France – Twenty, 20/25, 25/30, Wraith

Carrosserie Henry Binder was one of France's leading exponents of the coachbuilding art for nearly 40 years. Never avant-garde in its designs but always elegant, this Parisian company bodied only top-quality chassis from the beginning. Established around 1860, the company was active in the motor trade before the First World War and from 1920 Binder focused on coachwork for the leading car chassis of the day. Henry Binder himself had died in 1901, but the business was continued in the same traditions by Maurice Cottenet.

Many Binder bodies were grand and formal types, such as Limousines and Coupés de Ville, but there were elegant Saloons too. Perhaps more typical of Binder than the bodies it built for the small-horsepower Rolls-Royce models were those for the larger chassis, and there were many superb creations for the Silver Ghost, and for the Phantoms I, II and III that made clear why Binder was the real crème de la crème of French coachbuilders.

Binder's success continued through the 1930s but

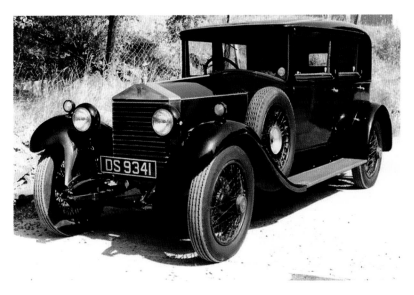

The Binder Saloon body for Twenty GKM30 in 1928 was built for an American customer, and its lines suggest the influence of contemporary American designs. (Real Car Company)

its workshops closed on the outbreak of the Second World War, and coachbuilding did not resume when peace came. Instead, Binder joined forces with coachbuilder Janssen (qv) in 1946 to become Binder-Janssen and sell GM cars, especially Cadillacs.

There were 21 bodies for Rolls-Royce Twenty chassis, 22 for the 20/25, either three or four for the 25/30, and 11 for the Wraith.

TWENTY COACHWORK

Binder became a more sought-after provider of coachwork for the Twenty as the years went by. The company built just one body for a Twenty in each of the years 1923 and 1924, and none in 1925. There were then three in each of 1926 and 1927, 11 in 1928, and two in 1929, making 21 in all. The destinations of these bodies were a clear demonstration of the spread of the Binder reputation, and although most were sold in France there were also customers in Argentina, Britain, Holland, Portugal and Spain.

Broughams

Formal coachwork was a Binder speciality, and the company built three Brougham designs for the Twenty in 1928-1929, with the open driving compartment, enclosed passenger compartment, and doors that curved forward at the toe that were all typical of the breed. The three were for chassis GBM18 and GKM29 in 1928, and for GLN43 the following year.

Cabriolets

Binder built six Cabriolet bodies for the Twenty, all between 1926 and 1928. However, the descriptions of some of these bodies vary: GKM10 has been called a Drophead Coupé and GFN73 has been called a

This was the only Sedanca de Ville body that Binder built for the Twenty chassis, and was delivered to a French customer in 1929.

Binder built a total of nine Saloons for the 20/25 chassis, and this four-light type on GNS66 in 1931 incorporated a Division. (Real Car Company)

Sedanca de Ville. The six were as follows:

GUK72	1926	GXL69	1927	GFN32	1928
GUJ73	1927	GKM10	1928	GFN73	1928

Coupés

There appear to have been two Coupé bodies, which were for GMK17 in 1924 and GYK66 in 1926. Nevertheless, GMK17 has also been described as a Brougham!

Coupé de Ville

Binder built a single Coupé de Ville body, which was for GBM28 in 1928.

Drophead Coupé

There was just one Drophead Coupé, which was for chassis GF51 in 1923. However, note that GKM10 has also been called a Drophead Coupé; it is listed here as a Cabriolet.

Limousines

All three Binder Limousines for the Twenty chassis were built in 1928. They were on GYL8, GKM44, and GFN4.

Saloons

Binder probably built four Saloon bodies for the Twenty chassis between 1926 and 1928. These were for GUK2 (in 1926), GXL33 (in 1927), GKM30 and GKM46 (both in 1928). The body on GXL33 has nevertheless been reported as both a Coupé and a Drophead Coupé. Note, too, that Binder rebodied GPK15, originally a Million-Guiet Landaulette, as a Saloon, and that this car survives in the Schlumpf Museum.

Sedanca de Ville

Just one Sedanca de Ville body was created for the Twenty chassis, and this was on GVO19 in 1929.

20/25 COACHWORK

Binder provided coachwork for 22 new 20/25 chassis between 1929 and 1936. There was just one in 1929; there were then seven in 1930, four in 1931, three in 1932, and two in 1933. The annual figure for 1934 was just one, but 1935 saw an improvement to three, and there was one in the 20/25's final year of 1936.

Cabriolets

Two Cabriolet bodies were built, for GGP17 in 1929 and for GOS57 in 1931.

Coupé

The body for GSY32 in 1933 was built as a Coupé for a customer in Portugal. It survives with spats and chromed features that would have been very advanced for 1933, and these may have been added at a later date.

Drophead Coupés

Three Drophead Coupé bodies were built in 1930-1931. The first was for GXP56 and went to a customer in Argentina. The two 1931 bodies were for chassis GFT23 and GFT28.

Landaulette

There was a single Landaulette body, for GXO111 in 1930.

Limousines

Binder fielded three orders for Limousine bodies on the 20/25 chassis, and these were built for GXO101 in 1930, and for GAU38 and GRW22 in 1932.

Saloons

Nine Saloon bodies were built between 1930 and 1936. The one for GNS66 had a Division, and the one for

GTZ59 saw Binder experimenting with the fashion for pillarless construction. This body was exhibited at the Paris Salon in 1933, and GAE2 was at the 1934 Paris Salon. The descriptions of the bodies on GAE2 and GPG67 as Saloons have been questioned. The bodies and their dates were as follows:

GSR22	1930	GMU10	1932	GPG19	1935
GTR39	1930	GTZ59	1933	GPG67	1935
GNS66	1931	GAE2	1934	GXK77	1936

Sedancas de Ville

Three bodies with broadly similar characteristics are grouped together here for convenience. The earlier two, both dating from 1930, were a Cabriolet de Ville for GDP48 and, for GLR73, what appears to have been an open-drive body that has been described as a Faux Cabriolet. The true Sedanca de Ville was on chassis GBJ8 and was displayed at the 1935 Paris Salon.

25/30 COACHWORK

Binder built either three or four bodies for the 25/30 chassis. The Saloon with Division on 1937 chassis GHO38 is thought to be by Binder, but this identification has not been confirmed beyond doubt. The other three bodies were all different, one from another.

They were a Saloon for GUL4 in 1936, a Limousine for GHO81 in 1937, and a Cabriolet for GMP74, also in 1937.

WRAITH COACHWORK

There were 11 bodies for the Wraith chassis, all on 1938 models except for the last one. Sedanca de Ville types were particularly popular, and accounted for seven of these bodies. The other four were all Saloons.

Saloons

The first three Saloon bodies were built in 1938 and the fourth in 1939. They were for chassis WXA44, WRB20, WRB46, and WMB71. Just one, that on WRB46, was built with a Division.

Sedancas de Ville

Binder showed a Sedanca de Ville on the Wraith chassis at the Paris Salon in 1938, and it may be that this inspired some or all of the other six orders for such coachwork. The seven chassis that had these bodies were are follows:

WXA14	1938	WXA63	1938	WRB69	1938
WXA17	1938	WXA86	1938	WMB15	1938
WXA48	1938				

A Binder customer in Portugal commissioned this Coupé for 20/25 chassis GSY32 in 1933. Whether the spats and chrome were original to the body is questionable. (Klaus-Josef Rossfeldt)

BREWSTER
USA – Twenty, 20/25, 25/30

James Brewster founded his carriage works at New Haven, Connecticut in 1810, and rapidly gained a reputation for building the best carriages in the USA. Brewster & Co soon expanded, notably adding a branch in New York. The company built its first motor car body in 1896, and in 1914 was chosen as the primary American supplier of bodies for Rolls-Royce models sold in that country.

When Rolls-Royce established its own chassis plant at Springfield, Massachusetts, in 1921, Brewster remained its coachbuilder of choice. In 1925, Rolls-Royce America, Inc took ownership of the company, but after the Springfield branch was closed in 1931 Brewster was unable to survive the effects of the Depression. By 1935, the coachbuilder was bankrupt. Some elements of the body business, and the sales side, passed into the ownership of the company's former head of sales, JS Inskip, who operated for a time from the old Brewster premises in New York. (See Inskip, below.)

TWENTY COACHWORK

Of the 14 Rolls-Royce Twenty chassis that were bodied by US coachbuilders when new, 10 were

Brewster built this Sedancalette for 20/25 chassis GSR65, and these pictures show it with all roof sections in place (upper picture, Klaus-Joseph Rossfeldt) and then with the De Ville roof removed and the Landaulette hood open (lower picture, Real Car Company). The car's appearance has been freshened up with a contrasting colour for the side panels, but originally it was probably black all over.

bodied by Brewster. Most had elements of the ornate, sometimes flamboyant style that was favoured by Brewster's wealthy customers at the time. Two were bodied in 1924, six in 1925, one in 1927 and one in 1928.

The most popular of the Brewster coachwork types was the open-drive Brougham, of which there were six examples. These were on chassis GRK6 and GRK27 in 1924, GNK76 and GNK89 in 1925, GAJ15 in 1927 and GKM79 in 1928. The other four bodies were all different, and all were built in 1925. They were a Cabriolet (with division) for GNK81, a Limousine for GNK82, a Landaulette for GNK87, and a Town Car (ie a Sedanca de Ville) for GNK90.

20/25 COACHWORK

Brewster provided coachwork for just four Rolls-Royce 20/25 chassis between 1930 and 1934. In 1930, there was a Saloon for chassis GLR57, and this was followed later that year by a Sedancalette on GSR65 for Frederick F Brewster, a second cousin of William Brewster who was then running the coachbuilding business. The later bodies were both

Town Cars (Sedancas de Ville), and they were for chassis GKT20 in 1932 and GWE19 in 1934.

25/30 COACHWORK

When JS Inskip took over at Brewster, he began to produce special bodies in quantity and to a more or less standardised design for relatively inexpensive American chassis. Among those he used was the Ford V8, for which there was a curvaceous and flamboyant Town Car (Sedanca de Ville) style. In 1936, one of these bodies built for a Ford chassis was transferred to a new Rolls-Royce 25/30 chassis, number GXM69.

BRICHET
Switzerland – Twenty

Francois Brichet worked with a number of Parisian coachbuilders before setting up his own coachworks in Geneva in 1920. Although early bodies were for everyday marques, Brichet began to work on grander chassis from about 1924, including Rolls-Royce.

Two bodies are known on the Twenty chassis, and both were for Swiss customers. The earlier one was a Tourer on GLK4, built in 1924, and the second one was a Weymann saloon built in 1926 or 1927 on GMJ26.

CHAPRON
France – Twenty, 20/25, 25/30

Henri Chapron was one of the great French coachbuilders of the 20th century, but he built only three bodies on the small-horsepower Rolls-Royce chassis. He established his company at Neuilly-sur-Seine in late 1919, and four years later moved to nearby Levallois, the home of many Parisian coachbuilders. By the end of the 1920s he was working on the grand French chassis of the day, but it was in the later 1930s that his real reputation was established. Always tasteful and restrained despite the contemporary taste for flamboyance, Chapron was particularly associated with Delahaye chassis, and he regularly exhibited at the London Motor Show.

Chapron's first coachwork for a small-horsepower Rolls-Royce was a Saloon on Twenty chassis GUJ75 in 1927, built for a French resident. He then built a de Ville body for a British resident on 20/25 chassis GLZ57 in 1933; this one has been variously described as a Sedanca de Ville and a Coupé de Ville. His third and last body for these models (Chapron continued to work on Rolls-Royce chassis after the war) was another Saloon for a French resident. This was built on 25/30 chassis GAR14 in 1937.

CLOTHIER
Australia – Twenty

Coachbuilder HG Clothier had premises at Petersham, a suburb of Sydney. It was active by the mid-1920s, when it built a roadster body for a Bugatti T23, but very little else is known.

Clothier built just one body on Rolls-Royce chassis, and this was a Tourer completed in 1926 on Twenty chassis number GOK71. The body no longer exists.

DELAGE
France – 20/25

Delage was not strictly a coachbuilder, but one 20/25 chassis was fitted in France with the body from a Delage car. The body is thought to have been a Saloon and the customer was a French socialite who was also a member of the Rothschild family. The chassis was number GEG36.

DE VILLARS
France – Wraith

Carrosserie De Villars was founded at Courbevoie in 1925 by the American millionaire Frank Jay Gould, and took its name from his aristocratic son-in-law. Originally established to maintain the cars of Gould's high-society friends, the company soon began to provide them with top-quality coachwork to individual designs on the prestigious chassis of the day. De Villars coachwork was often rather haughty in appearance, and the large blind rear quarters requested by some customers tended to unbalance the otherwise elegant lines.

Just three De Villars bodies were built on small-horsepower Rolls-Royce chassis, all of them on the Wraith in 1938. One was a Coupé, on chassis WXA12, for the French actress Gaby Morlay; this car was displayed at the 1938 Paris Salon. There was a Saloon with division on WXA72 for the husband of cosmetics magnate Helena Rubinstein, and the third was a Sedanca de Ville, on WRB61, built for an American socialite living in France.

D'IETEREN
Belgium – 20/25

The D'Ieteren coachworks could trace its origins back to 1805 in Brussels, but it was the grandsons of the founder who first turned to coachwork for motor cars, in 1897. In 1919, the business became a limited company with the name of Anciens Etablissements D'Ietereren Frères, and during the 1920s was one of many coachbuilders to take on a Weymann licence. From 1931, they turned their attention to all-aluminium coachwork using patents from Million-Guiet.

The company bodied just one small-horsepower Rolls-Royce, although there were several D'Ieteren bodies on the larger models. The car was a 20/25, number GPS3, which was built as a Limousine for a Belgian customer in 1931.

ERDMANN & ROSSI
Germany – 20/25, 25/30, Wraith

Karosserie Erdmann & Rossi was one of the mostly highly respected coachbuilders in Germany by the

Erdmann & Rossi built this Drophead Coupé as their first effort on a 20/25 chassis in 1930. The design makes GSR61 appear more compact than it really was. The rear treatment is characteristically German, as is the bulk of the folded top.

Very square-rigged lines characterise this Limousine body from Erdmann & Rossi for 20/25 chassis GEX3 in 1933.

The Erdmann & Rossi stamp across this picture obscures the front of the car slightly, but it is still possible to admire the sleek lines of the Saloon Coupé body for 25/30 GZR33 that was built in 1938. The treatment of the bonnet sides is also quite unlike British practice of the time.

The rear-wheel spats and more forward radiator grille on this Wraith make the car look heavier than the earlier Saloon Coupé by Erdmann & Rosssi, but the basic lines of its Saloon Coupé coachwork are very similar. This one, on chassis WXA106, was pictured at the Berlin Show in 1938.

elaborate bodies on large chassis. The Erdmann & Rossi name was associated with glamour and style, and the company bodied several Rolls-Royce and Bentley chassis after becoming the German distributor for both marques. Alongside coachwork on the larger Rolls-Royce chassis, there were three bodies on the 20/25, three on the 25/30, and two on the Wraith.

20/25 COACHWORK

The earliest of the 20/25 bodies was a Drophead Coupé on GSR61 built for a Swiss customer in 1930. A Saloon (for GAW11) and a Limousine (for GEX3) followed in 1933, the latter looking distinctly heavy with a formal body supposedly sharing its lines with one mounted on the customer's Maybach Zeppelin chassis.

25/30 COACHWORK

Erdmann & Rossi were not commissioned to build any more bodies on the small-horsepower Rolls-Royce for another four years, and by the time they received their first commission for a 25/30 chassis their style had changed considerably. More curvaceous than earlier designs, the bodies on the 25/30 chassis all had a boot neatly integrated into the lines of the body. For chassis GHO31 in 1937 there was a Drophead Coupé that the coachbuilder described as a Sport-Cabriolet, a term often used by German coachbuilders in the 1930s but normally applied to rather smaller creations. There was a Saloon with Division for GRO20 the same year, and the third body was a sleek Saloon Coupé with a split rear window for GZR33 in 1938.

1930s. The company was founded in Berlin in 1898, but when Rossi died in an accident in 1909, Erdmann decided to sell the company to an employee, Friedrich Peters. As the name was already well established, Peters retained it.

In the inter-war years, Erdmann & Rossi focused on the luxury market, bodying most of the grand chassis of the period and becoming known for its

WRAITH COACHWORK

There were clear traces of the earlier Saloon Coupé on a 25/30 in the two bodies of the same type built for Wraith chassis. They shared a common design, slightly more haughty than the body for the 20/25 and incorporating rear-wheel spats. The earlier example, for WXA106, was displayed at the Berlin Show in 1938 and the second one was probably ordered as a copy of it. This was for chassis WHC45 in 1939.

FELBER

France – Twenty

Parisian carriage maker Charles Felber built his first motor car body in 1898, and rapidly gained commissions for more from foreign royalty. From 1919, Felber's two sons took over the reins, and the company moved to Puteaux with the new name of Felber Frères. The company was a quite prolific builder of bodies on several makes of chassis, including some of the grand marques, but never really developed a distinctive style of its own.

Felber built just one body for a Rolls-Royce Twenty chassis, a Brougham on GVO21 for a Briton living in France during 1929.

FERNANDEZ & DARRIN

France – 20/25

After Tom Hibbard of Hibbard & Darrin (see below) returned to his native USA, "Dutch" Darrin teamed up with the South American banker Fernandez, a Paris resident who was already running his own coachbuilding company. The Fernandez tradition was to work only on top-quality chassis; Darrin rose to the occasion and created fashionable, glamorous and luxurious coachwork that made imaginative use of colour and aerodynamic shapes. Some coachwork was built in London rather than Paris, and one 20/25 body is actually recorded as being built by Corinthian, who presumably sub-contracted to Fernandez & Darrin. The venture closed in autumn 1937 when Darrin returned to the USA.

Fernandez & Darrin built grand coachwork on several Rolls-Royce Phantom chassis but also bodied eight 20/25 chassis between 1933 and 1935. The 1933 output consisted of two Sedancas de Ville (both probably built in London, and on chassis GSY74 and GLZ43), one Fixed-head Coupé on GSY78, and what was probably a Saloon for GLZ38. All except one were for French customers, one of the Sedancas going to the USA. The two 1934 bodies were a Drophead Coupé on GNC40 for a Dutch Countess living in France and a three-position Sedanca Coupé on GRC26 for a UK resident. The last two bodies were built in 1935, one

being a Saloon with Division for GYH22 that was built in London by the coachbuilder Corinthian and went initially to the Rolls-Royce agent in Monaco, but soon found a home with a British MP. The second 1935 body was a striking Coupé de Ville on GBJ22 for a customer resident in Canada.

In 1936, the company also carried out some modifications to the Hibbard & Darrin body on chassis GXO110, a 1930 "Opera" Coupé that was normally resident in Denmark.

FIGONI

France – 20/25

Joseph Figoni established his works at Boulogne-sur-Seine in 1923, initially carrying out body repairs but soon progressing to building complete bodies. He became known for curvaceous and sporting designs, and for an interest in colour and aerodynamics. In 1935, he was joined by Ovidio Falaschi, and as Figoni & Falaschi the company produced some spectacular and flamboyant coachwork on the grand French chassis of the time.

The only known Figoni coachwork on a small-horsepower Rolls-Royce chassis is a Saloon with Division on 20/25 chassis GNC71 in 1934. This very neat and subtly curvaceous design was typical of the pleasing shapes associated with Figoni before his association with Falaschi.

FIOL

Spain – 20/25

Baltasar Fiol was born in Barcelona, where he established his coachworks probably some time in the 1920s. Early designs showed the influence of British coachbuilders such as Barker and Hooper, but by the 1930s the influence was largely French, and Fiol bodies were much more ornate. Many Fiol bodies were on grand chassis, especially from Hispano-Suiza, and there were some for the larger Rolls-Royce chassis as well, beginning with the Silver Ghost.

There was just one body on the small-horsepower Rolls-Royce chassis, and that was a Cabriolet built in 1935 on 20/25 chassis number GSF12 for a Spanish lady. It was displayed at the 1935 Motor Show in Barcelona.

FRANAY

France – Twenty, 20/25

Jean-Baptiste Franay set up his own business in 1903 after doing an apprenticeship with the coachbuilder Henri Binder. The company's early motor car bodies were solid but unexciting, but in 1922 Franay died and his son Marius took over, successfully refocusing the business on luxury coachwork for the top makers of the day. The Franay reputation was greatly enhanced, and by the 1930s the company's products were appearing on many of the grand chassis of the time and were regularly entered in concours d'élégance events.

The first Franay body on the small-horsepower chassis was a Saloon for a Twenty in 1928 that was built for a French customer. This was on chassis GTM1. However, the other three bodies were all examples of the elegant de Ville styles in which Franay continued to specialise even though they had become an anachronism in the economic circumstances of the 1930s. All three were built on 20/25 chassis in 1935 and all were for French residents, the first two being described as Cabriolet Sedanca de Ville types and the third as a simple Sedanca de Ville. The second body, on chassis GEH8, was displayed on Franay's stand at the 1935 Paris Salon. The other two bodies were on chassis GHG32 and GCJ19.

GALLÉ
France – Twenty, 20/25
Louis Gallé had begun building car bodies as early as 1909 and the company could trace its origins right back to 1840. Based at Boulogne-sur-Seine, the Gallé company built on many of the grand chassis of the 1920s, and towards the end of the decade was commissioned to design a complete range of bodies for the Belgian marque Minerva. The Gallé characteristics were conservative lines allied to a high quality of execution.

Gallé is known to have built two bodies on Twenty chassis and a third on a 20/25. The earliest of these was a Saloon that was built in 1925 for a US customer on GPK17, but the other two were both Limousine bodies. On the Twenty chassis there was one for a French customer in 1929 on GLN69, and the last of the three Gallé bodies, on 20/25 GDP47, was delivered to a customer in Switzerland during 1930.

GANGLOFF
Switzerland – Twenty, 20/25
Georges Gangloff established his coachworks in Geneva during 1903, and by 1928 had headquarters at Berne. A French branch of the company, established in 1919, was also closely associated with Bugatti. Gangloff held a Weymann licence and displayed a Weymann body on a Silver Ghost chassis at Geneva in 1923; from 1928 his company began to work on American chassis, and increasingly the Gangloff output focused on the most expensive chassis by the top makers. Gangloff was at his peak between 1928 and 1932, when he was probably Switzerland's most respected and fashionable coachbuilder, known for high-quality workmanship and beautiful designs.

The company built at least two bodies on the Twenty chassis, and seven more on the 20/25, but closed down in the mid-1930s.

TWENTY COACHWORK
Both the known bodies on the Twenty chassis were Tourers that were delivered to Swiss residents. They were on chassis GZK58 in 1926 and GAJ60 in 1927.

20/25 COACHWORK
Of the seven bodies on the 20/25 chassis, all except one were closed types. The exception was a Cabriolet on chassis GDP4, built in 1930 for a Swiss Countess. There was a single Coupé in 1932 on GKT18 for another Swiss resident, and the remaining bodies were Saloons or Limousines. Three of them were for the same owner, an architect and entrepreneur who took a Limousine on GFT31 in 1931, a Saloon or Limousine on GBT55 in 1932, and a Saloon on GRW59 in 1932. GBT55 was displayed at the 1932 Geneva Show. There was a six-light Limousine for a Swiss nobleman on GDP23 in 1930, and the remaining car was a Saloon on GRW33, delivered to a Swiss resident after being on the show stand at Geneva in 1933.

GYGAX
Switzerland – 20/25
Jean Gygax founded his coach works in 1896 in Biel. Although his first car bodies were built on Swiss-made chassis, by the 1920s he was building All-weather types on a variety of makes. He moved on to luxury car chassis, and like most Swiss coachbuilders created some notable Cabriolets. Gygax was joined in 1932 by Alexis Kellner, whose own coachbuilding company in Berlin had failed.

The sole body that Gygax built for a small-horsepower Rolls-Royce was a neat two-door Saloon on 20/25 chassis number GEX8. This was ordered by a customer in Switzerland and still survives today.

HIBBARD & DARRIN
France – 20/25
American Thomas Hibbard came to France with the intention of establishing a branch of his Le Baron coachbuilding company, but instead set up a new business in Paris in 1923 with a fellow American, the stylist Howard "Dutch" Darrin. Workshops were established at nearby Puteaux. The company was soon focussing on coachwork for the prestigious chassis of the day, and Darrin came up with some avant-garde designs and also a new method of coachwork construction (called Silent Lyte). Here, each panel was made from an individual aluminium casting and was supported

on a cast frame of the same material – an extremely expensive way of combining strength and lightness.

Hibbard & Darrin built just two bodies on Rolls-Royce 20/25 chassis, both during 1929. The earlier of the two was a Fixed-head "Opera" Coupé (with folding occasional seats in the rear) for GXO110, that was shown at the Paris Salon and then delivered in 1930 to a buyer in Denmark. It was characterised by large blind rear quarters that carried ornamental "opera lights". The later car was a "Transformable" five-seater for GGP73, with a removable lightweight roof section (it has also been inaccurately described as a Cabriolet de Ville). It was delivered to an owner in Egypt when new, and still survives today.

INSKIP
USA – Wraith
John S Inskip was the President of Brewster & Co (see above) when the company folded in 1934, and he did his best to keep the traditions of the old company going. Still employing Brewster craftsmen, he built a number of bodies in the old factory, including a special Town Car (Sedanca de Ville) for the Ford V8 chassis, which proved quite popular in the New York region. Inskip took on the US franchise for Rolls-Royce and Bentley cars in 1937, and continued building coachwork for them into the 1940s.

This coachwork included seven bodies on the Wraith chassis in 1938-1939, five of which were Town Car types. There was one Limousine, for WRB80 in 1939, and one Saloon with Division, for WEC44 in 1939. The first Inskip-bodied Wraith, for WXA98 in 1938, became a demonstrator. The seven chassis were:

WXA98	1938	WEC78	1939	WKC6	1939
WRB80	1939	WKC1	1939	WKC8	1939
WEC44	1939				

JACKSON, JONES & COLLINS
Australia – 20/25
Messrs Jackson, Jones and Collins were all employees of Surrey Motors in Parramatta, near Sydney in New South Wales, Australia. They worked as coachbuilders for that company, where they built three bodies on Rolls-Royce Silver Ghost chassis before deciding to branch out on their own. Still in the Parramatta district, they formed their company in 1921 and built for a number of prestigious chassis types, including Minerva and Rolls-Royce.

The company eventually constructed as many as 18 bodies for Rolls-Royce chassis. There were more for Silver Ghosts, for Phantoms and Phantom IIs, and just one for a 20/25. This was a four-light Saloon for

chassis GBA75 in 1933. The company also carried out some rebodies of earlier chassis.

JANSSEN
France – 20/25
The Parisian coachbuilder Janssen & Cie was established at the start of the 20th century, and later moved to the motor industry suburb of Levallois-Perret. The company was associated with luxury coachwork from its early days, and was able to survive the Great Depression thanks to a strong relationship with Panhard & Levassor. The company ceased coachbuilding at the end of the 1930s, and in 1946 joined forces with the coachbuilder Binder (qv) to sell General Motors products in France as Binder-Janssen.

In the mean time, Janssen had constructed four bodies for Rolls-Royce 20/25 chassis. All were completed in 1930, and each was different from the last. The earliest was a Saloon with Division for GWP25, which displayed Janssen's wares at the Prague Show in 1930 and subsequently became a demonstrator for the company. There followed a Faux Cabriolet for GSR46, a Sedanca de Ville for GSR50, and a Limousine de Ville for GTR25. However, this coachbuilder never returned to the smaller Rolls-Royce chassis.

JOHNSON & SMITH
New Zealand – Twenty
Johnson & Smith were established as coachbuilders in Christchurch by 1921, and built coachwork for the larger Rolls-Royce models as well as the Twenty. The company was responsible for just one body on this smaller-horsepower chassis, which was a Tourer for chassis 79A8 in 1923.

KATHE
Germany – Twenty
Ludwig Kathe had been in business as a wagon maker in Halle since 1833, and from the start of the new century his grandsons Ludwig and Alfred took over and began to build motor car bodies. In the first half of the 1920s, the business expanded to include a second workshop in Chemnitz, and this worked closely with Audi, DKW, Horch and Wanderer (who became Auto Union in 1932).

The Kathe business built just one body for the small Rolls-Royce chassis, and this was a Cabriolet for a Swiss customer in 1928. It was mounted on Twenty chassis GTM6, and was clearly very satisfactory because he had it transferred in 1932 to a new 20/25 chassis, GRW24. The transfer was carried out by Alexis Kellner in Berlin.

This is a rear view of the Kellner Salamanca body illustrated on p185. It is on Twenty chassis GSK81 and was new in 1925. (Simon Clay)

KELLNER
France – Twenty, 20/25, 25/30, Wraith

Kellner was one of France's most highly regarded coachbuilders before the Second World War. Founded in Paris in 1860 to build custom bodies for horse-drawn carriages, it was steered into the emergent motor car business by the founder's sons, and built its first car body in 1894. In the early years of the new century it traded as Kellner & ses Fils (Kellner & Sons) and from the early 1920s it was generally known as Kellner Frères (Kellner Brothers).

Kellner's focus was always on luxury coachwork, and its reputation during the 1920s was of a company that produced the best. Quality was unsurpassed, and Kellner counted both royalty and the French president among its clients. Best known for its work on Hispano-Suiza chassis, the company built on most of the top-quality chassis of the day, including Rolls-Royce. Nevertheless, the 1930s brought a downturn in demand, and Kellner's elegant, conservative designs were overshadowed by the more glamorous creations from other French coachbuilders.

All coachbuilding activity ceased when France was

occupied in 1940, and two years later the company's head, Jacques Kellner, was shot as a member of the French Resistance. The company did not reopen after the war.

Kellner of course built many bodies for the larger Rolls-Royce chassis, and these are generally better known than the 67 for the small-horsepower types. These consisted of 36 for the Twenty, 26 for the 20/25, four for the 25/30, and a single body for the Wraith, those dwindling numbers reflecting the inescapable fact that Kellner was gradually falling out of fashion during the 1930s.

TWENTY COACHWORK

Kellner built 36 bodies on new Twenty chassis, and also rebodied some others in later years. There were three bodies each for 1923 and 1929 chassis, four for 1926 chassis, five for 1927 chassis, six each for 1925 and 1928 chassis and nine for 1924 chassis. The destinations of several of these bodies bear witness to the widespread reputation of the Kellner company, and there were several for members of the aristocracy and others in Spain, while others were delivered to the

In this case, Kellner upholstered the rear seat in leather, and produced some impressive but discreet inlaid wood for the garnish rails and the companions on the Division. The Division itself has two separate winding glass sections, and contains two occasional seats as well.
(Simon Clay)

The chauffeur's compartment was neatly but quite basically finished. (Simon Clay)

Kellner was well enough established not to need to say much on its coachbuilder's plates. (Simon Clay)

USA, Argentina, Germany and the UK. By far the most popular body type was the Cabriolet.

Broughams

French customers favoured the Brougham style (which was of course British in origin) during the 1920s, and Kellner responded to orders for six such bodies between 1924 and 1929. One (for GFN 30) was an open-drive type. There was also a later rebody of chassis GAJ2, as a Brougham de Ville.

The six Brougham bodies for new chassis were:

GRK31	1924	GYK41	1926	GFN30	1928
GDK10	1924	GRJ43	1927	GVO69	1929

Cabriolets

No fewer than 17 Cabriolet bodies were built for the Twenty chassis between 1923 and 1929, and several were for customers outside France. The full list is as follows:

67H6	1923	GCK30	1925	GXL26	1927
GRK58	1924	GCK71	1925	GYL17	1928
GRK66	1924	GOK31	1926	GFN50	1928
GDK38	1924	GZK65	1926	GLN36	1929
GNK78	1925	GAJ67	1927	GLN38	1929
GSK41	1925	GRJ44	1927		

Coupés

Four Coupé bodies were built for the Twenty between 1923 and 1928. These were for 1923 chassis GA62 and GH30, for 1924 chassis GRK3, and for 1928 chassis GBM15.

Coupé de Ville

Just one Coupé de Ville was constructed, for a Spanish customer, on 1926 chassis GZK48.

Landaulette

The single Landaulette body was built for a British customer, on 1924 chassis GLK29.

Limousines

Of the three Limousine bodies built in 1927-1928, only the last was delivered to a French customer. There was a Spanish buyer for the one on 1927 chassis GHJ59, and the one on 1928 chassis GKM73 was for Argentina. The third Limousine was also on a 1928 chassis, GFN28.

Salamanca

Kellner built just one Salamanca body for the Twenty, which was delivered to a US customer on 1925 chassis GSK81.

Tourers

The first and last of the three Tourer bodies for the Twenty were for Spanish customers. The three were for 1924 chassis GMK56 and GMK66, and 1925 chassis GNK93.

20/25 COACHWORK

Kellner met orders for 26 bodies on new 20/25 chassis. The largest number (six) were on 1934 chassis; there were five on 1930 and 1935 chassis, four on 1933 chassis, and three each for chassis dating from 1931 and 1932. Changing fashions were reflected in the types of bodies that attracted the most orders, and there were 10 Saloons of various types and eight Sedanca de Ville bodies.

Cabriolet de Ville

There was a single Cabriolet de Ville body, which was for 1932 chassis GZU33.

Coupé

Kellner built two Coupé bodies for the 20/25 chassis, each quite different from the other. The earlier one was a Brougham Coupé with dickey seat for 1930 chassis GGP47. The later one, simply described as a Coupé, was for 1934 chassis GSF11 and was ordered by a Spanish customer.

Drophead Coupé

The single Drophead Coupé body that Kellner built for the 20/25 was on 1934 chassis GKC14.

Limousines

There were three Limousine bodies between 1930 and 1935. On 1930 chassis GLR46 was an open-drive type, which remained unique among Kellner's output for the 20/25. The second Limousine was for 1934 chassis GAE3, and the third was for 1935 chassis

Kellner built this open-drive body for Twenty chassis GFN30 in 1928. In French terms, it was a Brougham (a British coachbuilder might have called it a Brougham de Ville), and the toe-forward shape was incorporated into the body pillar just ahead of the door. (Real Car Company)

GYH71 and was exhibited at that year's Paris Salon.

Saloons

There were probably 10 Saloons of various types, although the identity of the bodies on GTZ78 and GAE26 as Saloon types has been questioned. GBT30 represented Kellner at the 1932 Geneva Show, and GTZ78 (whatever its body may have been) was at Paris in 1933. The body for GXB32 was built with a Division, and for GPG34 there was a full roll-back roof, making the type a Convertible Saloon. The 10 chassis, with their dates, were as follows:

GSR54	1930	GWX76	1933	GAE26	1934
GBT30	1932	GTZ78	1933	GSF5	1934
GHW76	1932	GXB32	1934	GPG34	1935
GEX5	1933				

Sedancas de Ville

There is a question mark over the identity of the body on GSF52 as a Sedanca de Ville. GTR18 was delivered to Argentina. The eight bodies were:

GTR18	1930	GFT71	1931	GSF52	1935
GTR37	1930	GFT77	1931	GYH38	1935
GFT1	1931	GTZ36	1933		

Sedanca Coupé

There was a single Sedanca Coupé body for the 20/25, which was built on 1935 chassis GHG1.

25/30 AND WRAITH COACHWORK

Despite the declining popularity of Kellner coachwork among buyers of the small-horsepower Rolls-Royce chassis, the company was clearly still favoured as a builder of De Ville types. There were three Sedanca de Ville bodies for these cars, two on 1936 25/30 chassis GTL80 and GRM25, and one on a 1938 Wraith chassis, WXA42. A Brougham de Ville was built for 1936 25/30 chassis GRM74.

A Kellner Coupé body was mounted on 1936 25/30 chassis GRM74, which went to the same customer who owned 20/25 Coupé GSF11 (see above). It seems likely that the body was not a new one but was actually transferred from the earlier chassis.

KELLOW-FALKINER
Australia – 25/30

Kellow-Falkiner Pty Ltd was a car sales agency in Melbourne, Australia that had been involved with coachwork since the 1920s, either building bodies itself or transferring them from one chassis to another. It seems to have chosen the latter option on behalf of a customer for Rolls-Royce 25/30 chassis GLP5, which was shipped to Australia in chassis-only form when new in 1937. The company fitted a sports Coupé body that appears to have come from an American-built General Motors chassis and to have been built by that company's Fisher Body Division. (Some sources suggest that it was built by Fisher & Ludlow in Britain, which seems less likely.) Kellow-Falkiner added their own plates to the completed car, which still survives.

KELSCH
France – Twenty

Clément Kelsch was apprenticed for a time to Kellner in Paris, and in 1893 set up his own business in the suburb of Levallois. Before the Great War, the company had become known for its sporting bodywork on cars. In the 1920s there was a close association with Chenard & Walcker, and the business expanded. Most Kelsch bodies were on French chassis.

Nevertheless, the sole Kelsch body on a small-horsepower Rolls-Royce was a Landaulette, which was built on Twenty chassis GZK1 for a Spanish nobleman in 1926.

KLEIN-ROCHE
Germany – Twenty

Two Twenty chassis from the mid-1920s are listed by John Fasal as having coachwork by Klein-Roche. It is not clear who this coachbuilder was, but it may well have been Bernhard Klein, whose address was in Altona, near Hamburg. Very little is known about this company except that it was active during the 1920s.

The two Klein-Roche Twenties were a limousine built in 1924 on GDK40 and a Coupé built in 1925 on GNK10. There are no known pictures of either. Both were built for German customers.

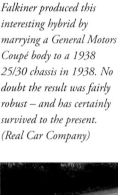

In Australia, Kellow-Falkiner produced this interesting hybrid by marrying a General Motors Coupé body to a 1938 25/30 chassis in 1938. No doubt the result was fairly robust – and has certainly survived to the present. (Real Car Company)

LABOURDETTE

Spain – Twenty, 20/25

Although there was a well-known Parisian coachbuilder called Labourdette, the one that built at least three bodies on the Twenty chassis and a fourth on the 20/25 was based in Madrid. Initially known as Hijos de Labourdette (Labourdette Sons) and, from 1928, as Luis Labourdette, the company was established by nephews of the Parisian coachbuilder. They set up their business in 1905, specialising in ultra-light coachwork, but by the 1920s were specialising in luxury coachwork and also owned some agencies for imported chassis.

The three Twenty bodies were all built in 1927, and were a Coupé de Ville on GMJ67 (for Spain), a Saloon on GAJ61 (for Brazil) and a Cabriolet on GRJ9 (for Portugal). The sole 20/25 body was a Sedanca de Ville on chassis GXO53 for a Spanish customer in 1929.

LETOURNEUR & MARCHAND

France – 20/25

Two former employees of the Binder coachworks set up on their own in Paris in 1905, focussing initially on contract work for other coachbuilders. By 1907 they were turning out their own designs. By the 1920s, they had become more ambitious, and Letourneur et Marchand bodies were found on several high-class French makes. The same was true of the 1930s when, despite a close association with Delage, the company worked on several other grand chassis of the time.

These grand chassis included Rolls-Royce, and alongside several Phantoms the company bodied two 20/25 chassis. Both bodies were grand, elegant and formal, in the established Letourneur et Marchand style. The first was a Saloon with Division for GWX32, and the second a Coupé de Ville for GWX73. Both were delivered to customers in France.

LOCKE

USA – Twenty

Justus Vinton Locke founded his coachworks in New York City in 1903, and gradually built it up. By 1919 he was building bodies on the most prestigious chassis then available, a particular speciality being faux canework. Over the next decade, there were many bodies for the Springfield-built Silver Ghost and New Phantom.

Locke himself died in 1925 but the company continued in business, attracting contracts for small-run custom bodies for Ford, Chrysler, and others,

and adding a second workshop in Detroit, Michigan. However, orders dried up during the recession of the early 1930s, and in 1932 Locke moved into the business of refurbishing older coachwork. The company eventually closed in 1937.

The Locke company built three bodies on Rolls-Royce Twenty chassis, each one different from the last. The first was a Salamanca for GNK14 in 1925. A Drophead Coupé for GNK66 followed the same year, and the final example was a Coupé for GYL53 in 1928.

MACKEY

Australia – Wraith

John Mackey Ltd was a coachworks business in Sydney, New South Wales that had developed out of a carriage-making business founded in 1877. The company built both car and commercial coachwork, and developed a speciality of taxis. In the 1920s and 1930s, the company rebodied several Rolls-Royce chassis, but it only ever built two bodies for brand-new chassis. One of these was for a 40/50 Silver Ghost in 1911, and the other was a Saloon for a 1938 Wraith, WRB38.

MARTIN & KING

Australia – 20/25, 25/30, Wraith

The two partners who had founded Martin & King Pty Ltd in Melbourne during 1888 went their separate ways after a year, when Martin left and A King continued with the business. Early work was for horse-drawn coaches and wagons, and the first motor body was for a Model T Ford in 1914. King was joined by his two sons and car body construction became the focus from 1922.

Martin & King built their first body for a Rolls-Royce chassis in 1924, and were soon known

When Martin & King built this Saloon body for 20/25 chassis GAE65 in 1934, swept-tail styles were fashionable in Britain, and the Australian coachbuilder followed the trend. (Real Car Company)

for bodying prestigious chassis of all types. They became Rolls-Royce's own favoured coachbuilder in Australia. Much of their early work focused on rebodies, and they were particularly known for such work on older Rolls-Royce chassis imported into Australia after the Depression – a common practice in those difficult economic times. Martin & King bodies were better suited to Australia's poor roads than were British bodies, but as a result of more rigid construction were also often heavier.

The company built eight bodies on new 20/25 chassis, four for the 25/30, and just one for the Wraith.

20/25 COACHWORK
The earliest of the eight bodies for 20/25 chassis was a Weymann Saloon – probably entirely unsuitable for Australian roads! This was for chassis GXO21 in 1929. Also dated 1929 were a Saloon for GXO42 (although this may have been transferred from or originally intended for a Twenty chassis, GEN66), and a two-door Saloon for GXO91.

The other five bodies consisted of two Saloon Coupés and three Saloons. The two-door types were for GLB27 in 1934 and GXK72 in 1936. The three Saloon bodies were all built in 1934 and were mounted on chassis GMD72, GYD15, and GAE65.

There were also several rebodies of earlier 20/25 chassis.

25/30 COACHWORK
The four Martin & King bodies for 25/30 chassis consisted of three Saloons and one Sports Saloon. The Saloons were for 1936 chassis GUL12 and GHL14, and for GMO27 in 1937. The Sports Saloon body was also built in 1937, for chassis GAR43.

WRAITH COACHWORK
The only Martin & King coachwork for the Wraith chassis was a Saloon for WRB40 in 1938.

MAWHINNEY
Ireland – Twenty
Surprisingly perhaps, no information seems to be available about the Irish coachbuilder Mawhinney. The fact that one Rolls-Royce Twenty chassis that carried its bodywork also carried a Belfast registration plate suggests but does not prove that it may have been based in the north rather than in the Republic of Ireland.

The company built five bodies for the Twenty in 1924-1925. Three were Saloons, on chassis GNK36, GNK37 and GPK62, and all were built in 1925. The

other two were a Cabriolet on 1924 chassis GAK31, and a Tourer for GDK57, another 1924 chassis.

MELBOURNE MOTOR BODY
Australia – Twenty
Tarrant Motors took over a Melbourne coachbuilder in 1905 to build the bodies for its cars. The Tarrant car was not a success, but Tarrant then took on a Ford franchise and the business expanded massively to cope with demand for coachwork. A new plant was opened in West Melbourne in 1923 and the company became the Melbourne Motor Body & Assembling Company. By 1926 it had 400 employees, was the largest body-making operation in the state of Victoria, and was building bodies for a great variety of chassis. The company did not weather the Depression and was re-formed in 1930 as Ruskin Motor Bodies Ltd (qv).

Among the chassis that passed through the MMB workshops was at least one Rolls-Royce Twenty, which was bodied as a four-door Tourer in 1927. This chassis was number GAJ26. The company also built a six-light Saloon body on a 1926 Twenty chassis, number GHJ64, although it is not clear whether this was the first body (which is described by Fasal as a Tourer) or a later replacement. Both bodies were clearly influenced by British styles of the time.

MILLION-GUIET
France – Twenty, 20/25
Former carriage-maker Million-Guiet began building car bodies in the Levallois district of Paris at the start of the 20th century and from 1908 even had a London branch. The company built several bodies on the Rolls-Royce Silver Ghost chassis both before and after the Great War, and in the 1920s specialised in impressive luxury bodies for prestige makes. It also held a licence to build Baehr transformable bodies.

An alliance with former aviator Jean de Vizcaya led to Million-Guiet taking out a patent for his all-aluminium "Toutalu" lightweight bodywork designs and from January 1930 acquiring exclusive rights. However, there were no known bodies on the small-horsepower Rolls-Royce after 1930. In addition to several bodies on 40/50 Silver Ghost chassis, the company built eight bodies on the Twenty chassis and just one on the 20/25.

TWENTY COACHWORK
The bodies on the Twenty chassis were all built in 1924-1925 and consisted of the usual spread of types. Most were for French residents, but the Cabriolet on GFN79 in 1928 seems to have gone

to Czechoslovakia. The eight Twenty chassis with Million-Guiet coachwork were as follows:

GMK67	1924	Cabriolet
GRK2	1924	Limousine
GDK65	1924	Cabriolet
GDK72	1924	Coupé
GPK15	1925	Landaulette
GZK4	1926	Limousine
GZK63	1926	Cabriolet
GFN79	1928	Cabriolet

20/25 COACHWORK

The single body on the 20/25 chassis was a closed type for a French resident, although it is not clear whether it was a Saloon or a Limousine. It was new in 1930 for chassis GDP52.

MURPHY
USA – Twenty

Walter M Murphy established his coachbuilding company at Pasadena in California in 1920, and was well placed to attract custom from the newly wealthy celebrities of the developing movie business in Hollywood, about 15 miles away. The company built a good number of bodies on the larger Rolls-Royce chassis of the period, and rebodied several as well, but the Twenty was not as popular among a clientele that could afford the biggest and the best.

Nevertheless, Murphy did build one saloon body on a Twenty chassis, GEN23, in 1929. The car returned to Britain in 1939 but was lost in a fire in 1953.

NEILSON
New Zealand – Twenty

CL Neilson appears to have been a New Zealand coachbuilder in the 1920s, although no further information is available about the company.

Rolls-Royce records show that the company built a single body on a Twenty chassis in 1923. This was 73A0, bodied as a Tourer.

NEUSS
Germany – 20/25

The Neuss coachworks in Berlin had become one of Germany's most highly regarded coachbuilders by the 1920s. Its focus was on luxury coachwork for the most expensive chassis of the day. However, in the more difficult economic times of the early 1930s, the company began to work on less glamorous chassis as well.

The only Neuss body known on a small-horsepower Rolls-Royce chassis is a Drophead Coupé that was built on 20/25 number GEX18 in 1933. Neuss was bought out by Erdmann & Rossi later that year, although the new owners retained the prestigious name for another couple of years.

PINGRET & BRETEAU
France – Twenty

This Parisian coachbuilder developed a reputation for high-quality coachwork on some of the grander chassis in the first decade of the 20th century, after building its first motor bodies in around 1904. Initially known as Pingret, Guion & Breteau, it reduced to two names in 1918 and by 1926 was moving into the bus and commercial bodywork business as Breteau Frères et Cie, operating from the original address.

The company built just one body on the small Rolls-Royce chassis, and that was a Brougham on a Twenty for a French customer in 1927, on chassis number GAJ24. This body may have been one of the last it built for a car.

RICHARDS
Australia – Twenty

TJ Richards & Sons was a prolific Adelaide coachbuilder that was second only to Holden Body Works. From 1922, it produced bodies for a wide range of imported car chassis, later becoming the first Australian body maker to introduce an all-steel saloon (in 1937).

Just one Richards body is known for certain on a Rolls-Royce Twenty chassis, and like most Australian-built bodies of the time, that was a Tourer. It was built in 1926 for chassis GOK7, but (as so often happened to the Twenty models) was replaced by a more modern Saloon seven years later.

ROTHSCHILD
France – Twenty

The Rothschild carriage works was established in Paris in 1838, and although it had no known links with the famous banking family, the association of the name probably proved beneficial. By 1896, the founder had sold out to two of his employees, but they retained the name. Early on, the company broke new ground in the use of sheet metal for coachwork, and in 1899 created the aluminium body for Camille Jenatzy's cigar-shaped 1899 La Jamais Contente record-breaker. Most Rothschild bodies, however, were elegant and formal, and appealed to a conservative clientele who mostly ordered them on quality chassis such as Delaunay-Belleville and

Rolls-Royce. In the early part of the 20th century, Rothschild became one of the most prestigious French coachbuilders, and in 1906 established a branch in Turin as well. However, a downturn in business towards the end of the 1920s proved fatal, and the company did not survive beyond 1930.

Rothschild built a single body for the Rolls-Royce Twenty, which was a Coupé on chassis GRK5 in 1924.

RUSKIN
Australia – Wraith

Melbourne Motor Bodies (qv) was re-organised during 1930 and emerged under a new name as Ruskin Motor Bodies Pty Ltd. Still based in Melbourne, the company was bought out in 1945 by Austin, and changed from a bespoke coachbuilder to a producer of series-manufactured bodies. Nevertheless, it found enough time and skilled men to build a Saloon body for its own Managing Director on a 1939 Wraith chassis, WEC23, that had remained unbodied during the Second World War.

SAOUTCHIK
Paris – Twenty

Jacques Saoutchik was a Russian (or possibly Ukrainian) expatriate, and founded his coachbuilding company in a suburb of Paris in 1906. By the early 1920s, Saoutchik was ranked as one of the top Parisian coachbuilders and was known for its high quality and above all for its flamboyant designs which made great but tasteful use of ornamentation.

Saoutchik always worked only with top-class chassis, and gained multiple commissions from

royal families outside France. At home, Saoutchik designs represented the essence of Parisian chic, with a distinctive modernistic style that depended on exterior brightwork, creative use of colour, and interiors that were exuberant and often exotic. The company retained its leading position among French coachbuilders in the 1930s, but despite some elegantly flamboyant designs that caught international attention after the Second World War, commissions were too few and the company closed in 1955.

Unusually, Saoutchik built only on the earliest and last of the small-horsepower chassis, and not on the 20/25 or the 25/30. There were seven bodies for the Twenty and just one for the Wraith.

TWENTY COACHWORK

Of Saoutchik's seven bodies for the Twenty, one remained in France, three were for Brazilian customers, one was for the Queen of Siam, and two were for customers in Britain.

Two of the bodies were Cabriolets, which were on chassis GOK34 and GUK78 in 1926. Two more were Tourers, for GNK4 in 1925 and GMJ49 in 1926. One was an All-weather, delivered to coachbuilder HW Allingham in Britain on chassis GZK40 in 1926. One was a Coupé, delivered to Brazil in 1928 on chassis GWL37. The last one was a Brougham on GVO77 in 1929 that went to Siam.

WRAITH COACHWORK

The only Saoutchik body for a Rolls-Royce Wraith was a Saloon with Division. This was built on chassis WMB51 for an Englishwoman resident in France.

SCHUTTER & VAN BAKEL
Netherlands – 20/25

The Amsterdam coachbuilder Schutter & van Bakel built its first car body in 1901, and during the 1920s gained a strong reputation for elegant luxury coachwork on a wide variety of chassis. Although the company's market was eroded by the recession of the early 1930s, bodies were still being built by the end of the decade and the company even survived the war, finally closing in 1953.

Just one Schutter & Van Bakel body was constructed on a small-horsepower Rolls-Royce chassis, and this was a quite remarkable Saloon on 20/25 number GSY58 for a Dutch customer in 1933. The customer had earlier been a devotee of Voisin cars, and he clearly wanted his new four-light Saloon to look like a Voisin design – which it did, even though the lines were quite dated for the time.

When French aviation pioneer Gabriel Voisin entered the car business, he and his collaborator André Noel developed what they called "rational" coachwork. Visually, it was distinguished by angular lines and large luggage boxes. The customer for 20/25 chassis GSY58 wanted its body to look like a Voisin type, and Dutch coachbuilder Schutter & van Bakel obliged. (Via Pinterest)

SEEGERS
Germany – Twenty

The Seegers company, formally F Seegers & Sohn of Leipzig, was building bodies for Horch chassis as early as 1904 or 1905. By the 1920s it was creating coachwork for several different German chassis, and in 1928 showed a formidably expensive Limousine body on a Rolls-Royce New Phantom chassis at the Berlin Motor Show.

In 1927, Seegers had also created a Drophead Coupé body on a Twenty chassis, GAJ37. This heavy-looking body is sometimes described as a Tourer (eg by John Fasal). It still survives.

SMITH & WADDINGTON
Australia – Twenty, 20/25, 25/30

Smith & Waddington Ltd was established as a coachbuilder in the Camperdown district of Sydney in September 1922. Two of the partners – Charles Fairs and Leslie Smith – were professional coachbuilders, and the money came from British-born Frank Waddington, a wealthy cinema owner. The company rapidly became Australia's leading coachbuilder, working on a variety of imported chassis that included Rolls-Royce. In 1923, they were claimed to be building coachwork for 85% of all Rolls-Royce chassis imported to Australia. From 1924, the company also began building bus bodywork, and in 1926 the company was appointed a sub-retailer for Rolls-Royce.

Despite this success, by 1928 Smith & Waddington was in trouble, and in 1931 the receiver was called in. Its assets were taken over by a new company called Amalgamated Motor Bodies, which absorbed coachbuilder Morley Motor Bodies at the same time. Smith & Waddington-re-emerged as the Waddington Body Co Ltd, and became primarily known for bus and railway bodywork, eventually being renamed Commonwealth Engineering in 1946 and remaining active (latterly as COMENG) until 1989.

Smith & Waddington built 14 bodies for the Rolls-Royce Twenty chassis, and one further new body for a 20/25. Nevertheless, it also had a hand in a second 20/25, to which one of its earlier bodies was transferred. Then as the Waddington Body Co, it transferred two more early bodies to 25/30 chassis.

TWENTY COACHWORK

Fourteen of the Twenty chassis shipped to Australia between 1922 and 1926 were bodied by Smith & Waddington, and there may have been a fifteenth. The bodies were mostly Tourers.

Coupés

There were two, and possibly three, Smith & Waddington Coupé bodies on new Rolls-Royce Twenty chassis. The two that are certain were for GLK66 in 1924 and for GNK8 in 1925; the latter body would eventually be fitted to four different small-horsepower Rolls-Royce chassis. The 1923 chassis GF36 also had a Smith & Waddington Coupé body by 1930, but it is not clear if this was original to the chassis.

Saloon

Only one Saloon body is known, and that was for the earliest of the Twenty chassis to pass through the Smith & Waddington workshops. It was for 42G1 from 1922.

Tourers

Eleven Twenties were bodied as Tourers between 1923 and 1926. It appears that GCK69 was originally bodied as a Tourer but remained unsold until 1928, when it was sold and fitted with the Coupé body from GNK8. That body would see service on to two more small-horsepower chassis during the 1930s....

The list of Twenty chassis originally bodied as Tourers is as follows:

64H5	1923	GA12	1923	GCK8	1925
83K5	1923	GLK49	1924	GCK69	1925
83K8	1923	GLK68	1924	GUK76	1926
87K9	1923	GSK10	1925		

20/25 COACHWORK

Smith & Waddington bodied two 20/25 chassis, but the earlier of these was transferred from an earlier chassis. When 1929 chassis GGP19 reached Australia, the Coupé body from GCK69 (originally built for GNK8) was transferred to it. This body would have a further lease of life on a 25/30 chassis, as explained below. The second body, for GEX49 in 1933, was a six-light Saloon.

25/30 COACHWORK

There were no new bodies from Smith & Waddington (by then trading as the Waddington Body Co), but the saga of bodies transferred from one chassis to another continued. GMO10 became the third chassis to carry the Coupé body originally built in 1925 for Twenty chassis GNK8, and it was transferred from GCK69 by Waddington's in 1937. Finally, in 1938 25/30 chassis number GGR79 received a six-light Smith & Waddington Saloon body that had once been on Twenty chassis GCK69 but was of indeterminate provenance (GCK69 had originally been bodied as a Tourer).

SPENCER
Australia – Twenty

The Tourer body for Twenty chassis 84K4 in 1923 is recorded as being by a company called Spencer, who were based in Adelaide. Unfortunately, no further details are available.

STANDARD
Australia – Twenty

Twenty chassis GZK42 was exported to Australia in 1926 and is recorded as having a Saloon body built by Standard. There is no confirmation that this coachbuilder was actually Australian, and nothing is known about the company.

STEIN
Austria – Twenty

One Rolls-Royce Twenty chassis went to Austria in 1922, where it was bodied locally and was delivered to an Austrian Count. As quoted by John Fasal, the record for 42G9 says it was bodied as a Tourer by Stein of Vienna. Unfortunately, it is not clear who this coachbuilder was, and there are no known pictures of the car, either.

STEUART
India – Twenty

Steuart & Co was a Calcutta coachbuilder that claimed to date back to 1775. It is known to have built coachwork on Napier and Thornycroft chassis, as well as several very solid-looking bodies for the Rolls-Royce Silver Ghost. The company built just one body for the Rolls-Royce Twenty, which was a Tourer on GLK53 and was delivered to an Indian ruler in 1924.

The same company was almost certainly responsible for the Two-seater body for a Maharajah that was built slightly earlier in 1924 on Twenty chassis GMK63. The coachbuilder is recorded in John Fasal's book as Stewart.

UNIDENTIFIED FRENCH COACHBUILDERS

Twelve small-horsepower Rolls-Royce chassis were delivered to France and were presumably bodied locally. In all cases, the body type is known but the identity of the coachbuilder is not. Ten of these unidentified bodies were on Twenty chassis; there was one 20/25, and one 25/30.

The ten Twenty chassis were all early examples. They were as follows:

Chassis no	Date	Type
56 S7	1923	Coupé
82 K8	1923	Coupé
61 H8	1923	Tourer
GA29	1923	Landaulette
66 H8	1923	Cabriolet
GA81	1923	Cabriolet
73 A7	1923	Landaulette
GH76	1923	Cabriolet
80 K2	1923	Cabriolet
GRK37	1924	Limousine

The 20/25 bodied by an unidentified coachbuilder was delivered to France but was also used in Egypt, and there is an implication in the chassis records that it may have had a British-built body. This was a Limousine, and the chassis was GYH53 from 1935. The 25/30 was GHO38 from 1937, and had an all-steel Saloon body with a Division; Bernard King suggests that the all-steel body on this car may be by the Parisian coachbuilder Henry Binder.

Van den Plas built two similar Saloon bodies on the 20/25, and this could be either GHW 75 from 1932 or GAE79 from 1934. Both had Divisions. The coachbuilder certainly achieved an air of gravitas with this body, which was probably not as physically heavy as it looks.

Van den Plas in Brussels built just one Coupé on the Rolls-Royce 20/25 chassis, which was this accomplished-looking body for GFT49 in 1931.

VAN DEN PLAS
Belgium – Twenty, 20/25

Van den Plas was one of the great Belgian coachbuilders of the early 20th century. It was founded in Brussels 1870 as a wheelwright's business, but in 1898 became the coachwork company Carrosserie Van den Plas. Later, there would be a British branch (which eventually became an independent company) and a less-successful branch in Paris as well. Stylist Alexis de Sakhnoffski was engaged in 1924, and he designed some superbly proportioned bodies for the expensive chassis of the day. Van den Plas went on to forge a close relationship with Belgian chassis maker Minerva, but could not survive its demise and closed in 1935.

There were three bodies on the Twenty chassis by Van den Plas (plus one from the British company, see Chapter 3) and four on the 20/25.

TWENTY COACHWORK

All three Twentys were sold in Portugal, which rather suggests that Van den Plas was making a sales push there at the time. The first of these was a Cabriolet de Ville (which Rolls-Royce chose to call a Salamanca) delivered in 1925 on chassis GCK14. Also delivered in 1925 was a Tourer on chassis GSK20, with a separate windscreen for the rear-seat passengers and an unusual assortment of stowage boxes that included a pair under each running-board and a tall container on the left-hand front wing (and possibly on the opposite side as well). The last of the Van den Plas Twenties was a Coupé de Ville, delivered probably in 1927 on chassis GMJ47.

20/25 COACHWORK

The four bodies on 20/25 chassis included two very similar four-light Saloons with divisions, on GHW 75 in 1932 and GAE79 in 1934. GHW75 was built for a Venezuelan government official in the Netherlands, and GAE79 was for a Belgian resident. There was a smart Fixed-head Coupé (a Faux-Cabriolet, but without the dummy landau irons) for a Belgian customer in 1931 on GFT49, and the other body was a Drophead Coupé on GRW81 in 1933. This was an undistinguished-looking body that was nevertheless built for that year's Amsterdam Show stand, and went to a first owner in the Netherlands.

VAN PIPWYK
Netherlands – Twenty

No information is available about a coachbuilder recorded as Van Pipwyk against 1922 Twenty chassis

41G4. The chassis was exported to the Netherlands and carried a Landaulette body, and it seems probable that this was built in the country of its destination.

VANVOOREN
France – 20/25, Wraith

Based in the Parisian suburb of Courbevoie, Carrosserie Vanvooren was known for its innovation in both design and manufacturing methods, and worked on grand chassis from both French and foreign car makers. It was particularly known for building bodies that combined good structural strength with low weight. Vanvooren also developed a flexible body mounting system that depended on rubber bushes and was patented under the Silentbloc name in 1930. Yet despite such advances, Vanvooren remained a fundamentally conservative coachbuilder, preferring restraint and elegance to the flamboyance embraced by many of its contemporaries in the 1930s.

That decade saw Vanvooren develop close ties with both Rolls-Royce and Bentley. The link was furthered by Walter Sleator, who ran the company's French importer Franco-Britannic in Paris and had been Vanvooren's sales director in the 1920s. A pillarless saloon on a Bentley 3½-litre chassis was examined at Derby and greatly impressed the Rolls-Royce staff. Vanvooren soon became the company's favoured French coachbuilder and subsequently bodied a large proportion of the Rolls-Royce and Bentley chassis sold in France. It was also chosen to build the lightweight bodies for the streamlined Corniche model that was abandoned when war broke out in 1939. The company started up again after the 1939-1945 war, but closed in 1950.

20/25 COACHWORK

There were four Vanvooren bodies on 20/25 chassis, all delivered in 1932-1933. Two were Saloons, one

Vanvooren produced this Sedanca Saloon for 20/25 chassis GAU47 in 1932. The Parisian coachbuilder made an excellent job of making the car look larger and grander than it really was.

was a rather upright Sedanca Saloon, and one was a Drophead Coupé. All were initially ordered by French residents, and it is likely that most of them had Silentbloc coachwork. GZU16 may have been at the 1932 Paris Salon, and was subsequently delivered to Brazil. GZU24 was supposedly intended for André Dubonnet, the French aviator and inventor. It was not delivered to him but went to the Rolls-Royce Sales division as an experimental coachwork car and found its first owner in June 1933. The four Vanvooren bodies on 20/25 chassis were as follows:

Chassis no	Date	Type
GAU47	1932	Sedanca Saloon
GZU24	1932	Saloon
GZU16	1932	DHC
GTZ39	1933	Saloon

WRAITH COACHWORK

Vanvooren coachwork was far more common on Bentley chassis than on the small Rolls-Royce types in the 1930s, and there was none at all on the 25/30 chassis. There were then seven bodies for Wraith chassis in 1938-1939, all of them closed types. The first three may have been bodied as a batch with broadly similar Saloon bodies; WXA11 and WXA16 were certainly very much alike and had quite angular four-light bodies that reeked of British influence. There were then two more Saloons for French owners, one with a division; and an Argentinian buyer took both a Limousine and a supremely elegant faux-cabriolet Fixed-head Coupé.

The first of the Vanvooren Wraiths, WXA11, was on the Rolls-Royce stand at the 1938 Paris Salon

This neat Saloon design was contemporary with the visually similar Continental Saloons that came from British coachbuilders in the early 1930s. Vanvooren built it for 20/25 chassis GZU24 in 1932.
(Real Car Company)

and later went to Spain as a demonstrator. Although WRB79 was a late-1938 chassis, the body was not completed until October 1939 and this car was not delivered to its new owner until 1940.

The seven Vanvooren bodies on Wraith chassis were as follows:

Chassis no	Date	Type
WXA11	1938	Saloon
WRB54	1938	Saloon w/ Division
WRB79	1938	Limousine
WXA15	1938	Saloon
WXA16	1938	Saloon
WLB15	1939	Saloon
WEC14	1939	FHC

VESTERS & NEIRINCK
Belgium – 25/30

The Brussels coachbuilder Vesters & Neirinck was established in 1923 when Mijnheer Neirinck joined the established Carrosserie Vesters. It exhibited regularly at the major European motor shows in the inter-war years.

The company built on several of the more expensive chassis during the 1930s, and is particularly remembered for some very attractive bodies on Bentley chassis towards the end of the decade. It also built on Rolls-Royce – notably on half-a-dozen Phantom III chassis – and created five bodies for the contemporary 25/30 in a flurry of activity during 1936-1937. All had different body types, and the most attractive was a Faux Cabriolet that was on the coachbuilder's stand at the Brussels Show in 1936. The five bodies were as follows:

Chassis no	Date	Type
GXM30	1936	Limousine
GXM46	1936	Faux Cabriolet
GHO17	1937	Saloon
GRO27	1937	Sports Saloon
GRO38	1937	All-weather

VETH & ZOON
Netherlands – 20/25

Carrosseriefabriek Veth & Zoon built its reputation in the horse-drawn carriage trade before turning to car bodies. This Arnhem company was never one of Holland's better-known coachbuilders, but it built coachwork for a number of prestigious chassis in the inter-war years.

There was a single Drophead Coupé on 1933 20/25 chassis GBA65 for a Dutch resident. The company went on to build a pair of drophead bodies for Bentley chassis in 1935 and 1936.

WARING BROS
Australia – Twenty

Waring Bros was a coachbuilder based in Melbourne that was active early in the 20th century and built the coachwork for several Rolls-Royce Silver Ghost chassis. The company bodied three Twenty chassis when they were new, but also rebodied several others in a variety of styles.

The bodies on new Twenty chassis were two Tourers, for 69H8 in 1923 and GLK48 in 1924, and a Limousine for GNK63 in 1925.

WEYMANN
France – Twenty

The Weymann body construction method that was used by so many British coachbuilders in the 1920s was French in origin, and its co-inventor Charles Terres Weymann had originally set up his business in Paris in 1922. This business remained active long after Weymann had made his fortune by licensing his construction system around the world, and constructed the body for a single Rolls-Royce Twenty chassis in 1927. This was a Saloon for a French officer, on chassis GRJ62.

WOOD
USA – 20/25

FR Wood & Sons were commercial body builders in the Brooklyn area of New York, but also turned their hand to car coachwork, including some for Rolls-Royce Silver Ghosts and Phantoms. The company built just one body for a new small-horsepower chassis, which was an All-weather Town Car for 20/25 GWP37 in 1930. A similar body was also constructed to replace the original Park Ward Saloon on GLR60 not long after it was new in 1930, and the Wood company later built a Station Wagon body to replace the Mann Egerton Limousine on 1932 chassis GRW51.